**BUILDING BRIDGES**

**The Selected Psychoanalytic Papers of**
**Helen K. Gediman, Ph.D., ABPP, FIPA**

# BUILDING BRIDGES

# The Selected Psychoanalytic Papers of Helen K. Gediman, Ph.D., ABPP, FIPA

IPBOOKS.net
International Psychoanalytic Books

International Psychoanalytic Books (IPBooks)
New York • http://www.IPBooks.net

International Psychoanalytic Books (IPBooks)
Astoria, NY 11102
Online at: www.IPBooks.net

Cover Design by Kathy Kovacic
Back Cover Photo by K. William Fried

ISBN: 978-0-9995965-1-7

I dedicate this book to the psychoanalytic journals that have published the papers that appear in this book and to their editors and staff who have helped on my work with their helpful critiques: *The Journal of the American Psychoanalytic Association*; *The International Journal of Psycho-analysis*; *The Psychoanalytic Quarterly*; *Psychoanalytic Dialogues; Psychoanalytic Psychology*; and *The Psychoanalytic Review, and of course, International Psychoanalytic Books.*

# TABLE OF CONTENTS

# ACKNOWLEDGEMENTS

In this day and age, most psychoanalytic publications do not publish or wish to publish a given author's "Selected Papers" that have been written over the major part of a lifetime. An exception is Dr. Arnold Richards, to whom I owe an unprecedented debt of thanks. As Editor of *International Psychoanalysis*, he has invited me to submit *Building Bridges,* my selected papers, under the joint imprint of International Psychoanalytic Books (IPBooks) and The Contemporary Freudian Society (CFS). I take great pride in contributing to this series that Arnie has so generously and imaginatively created, and to see my name along with those of the eminent psychoanalysts who have contributed to this unique series, so competently put together by Lawrence Schwartz and Tamar Schwartz. I thank Dr. Richards for his unflagging confidence in my contributions to psychoanalysis over the years. When he was editor of *The Journal of The American Psychoanalytic Association*, he confidently appointed me as a regular reader of submitted manuscripts, and suggested, several times, appointing me as an Editor of that journal, a position ultimately elected by the Editorial Board of that journal. Unfortunately, my self-promoting political activities to be an Editor were approximately nil then, as always, so I did not become one, but happily, there and then elsewhere continued, to this day, to pursue my interest in reading and critiquing manuscripts. Most recently, Arnie has been an indispensable member of the Plumsock Prize Committee that I have been chairing for many years at the CFS, and I wish to thank him for the opportunity to work with him continuously in an area we both love: psychoanalytic paper writing.

I also want to thank the late Leo Rangell for taking a keen and very friendly interest in my work, especially in ideas that thrilled him to discover we had in common. I refer, of course, to his additive or aggregate approach to theories and his wish to dispense with either/ or thinking about what made a theory valuable without discarding earlier precedents to later revisions. He was always fully supportive of my attempts to spare babies while throwing out excessive bathwaters.

I thank my friend, colleague and office-partner, Fred Pine, for his careful reading of the papers that comprise *Building Bridges*, and for writing an en pointe Introduction that tells me he understands and appreciates me and the way my mind works. I have known Fred since 1956 when we worked together for years at the New York University Research Center for Mental Health, under the directorships of Robert R. Holt and George S. Klein. More recently,

Fred's seminal ideas (1988, 2003) have been the linchpin of the multiperspectivism and the multiple models approach that underlie most everything I have ever created for my teachings and writings.

I should like next to acknowledge the many people who helped me to develop my ideas, most of whom were co-authors or discussants at formal presentations of early versions of the papers selected for publication in this book. Among them are: Sheldon Bach, Ph.D.; Leopold Bellak, M.D.; Professor Martin S. Bergmann; Harold P. Blum, M.D.; Charles Brenner, M.D.; Curtis S. Bristol M.D.; Nancy Chodorow, Ph.D.; Jodie Davies, Ph.D.; Carolyn Ellman, Ph.D.; Gerald Fogel, M.D.; Arnold Goldberg, M.D.; Adrienne Harris, Ph.D.; Marvin Hurvich, Ph.D.; Theodore Jacobs, M.D.; Selma Kramer, M.D.; Janice S. Lieberman, Ph.D.; Fred Pine, Ph.D.; Donald M. Kaplan, Ph.D.; Harvey A. Kaplan, Ed.D.: Paul Ornstein, M.D., Leo Rangell, M.D.: Joseph Reppen, Ph.D.; Roy Schafer, Ph.D.; Bruce Sklarew, M.D., Joyce Slochower, Ph.D., Ellen Handler Spitz, Ph.D.; Edward Weinshel, M.D.; and Fred Wolkenfeld, Ph.D.

Additionally, I would like to thank my dear friends and colleagues who have, in recent years, been constantly and unusually supportive of me in the substance and style my writings, particularly K. William Fried, Ph.D. and Phyllis L. Sloate, Ph.D.

# PREFACE

I have, in this collection, placed 20 of my articles that have been previously published separately in refereed psychoanalytic journals or as chapters in psychoanalytic books. The papers are ordered in six "Parts," not chronologically but according to subject matter that fits together by topic or area of interest. Each part involves a topic that had customarily been thought of in binary terms, but may now may now be thought of not as "either/or" theoretical and clinical issues, but more integratively. Of utmost importance to the nature of my thinking as I put this work together, is the fact that I had not always known that a paper developing and arguing issues on one subject would some day turn out to be intimately and significantly related to a paper developing and arguing issues on another subject. It was only after the fact that I discovered the connections. But is that not exactly how we expect our minds to preconsciously learn and then influence our consciously grasped ideas and outcomes? I am attempting, in my author's introduction to each of the six parts of this book, to elucidate retrospectively how some of my ideas that germinated at one time related to those that developed at another time, although those connections were certainly preconscious initially.

My introductory Chapter 1, that appeared in the book, edited by Joseph Reppen *Why I Became a Psychotherapist*, contains two misnomers: the first is in the book's title, and the second is in the title of my chapter that appears in it. The book's publisher, Jason Aronson insisted on the misnomer: he did not want the word, "Psychoanalysis" to be included in the book's title, and he persuaded Editor Reppen to remove it and replace it with the word, "Psychotherapist." The word, "Psychoanalysis" would, Aronson believed, no longer successfully market any books on psychoanalytically informed treatment. He had similarly persuaded me to use a misnomer to take the word "Psychoanalysis" out of the title of another book, the one I co-authored in 1996 with Janice S. Lieberman, *The Many Faces of Deceit: Omissions, Lies, and Disguise in Psychotherapy*. Aronson used the same reasoning with us that he did with Joe Reppen, which apparently made sense to him as he banned the word, "Psychoanalysis" from the titles of any of the books about that form of psychotherapy that he published around that time. The second misnomer, as Fred Pine points out, refers to the word, "Influences." But that is only in part a misnomer. The persons and events I refer to were indeed significant influences on me, but my eventual writing was the product of far more than their influence: they may have thrown the balls to me but I did catch them and run with them in my very own ways.

# INTRODUCTION: FRED PINE, PH.D.

## BUILDING BRIDGES: SELECTED
## PAPERS OF HELEN GEDIMAN

In the opening chapter of this selection of her papers, a chapter spelling out her route into the psychoanalytic world that she has inhabited well for many years, Helen Gediman again and again describes herself as having been "in the right place at the right time" with peers, colleagues, teachers, and even her particular parents, so that she was the recipient of all that these many (and many outstanding) individuals had to offer. What she modestly fails to say, however, is how much she was "the right person" in each of those several situations, able to take in the intellectual and attitudinal richness around her and, ultimately, to transform it into contributions that are distinctly her own. This book is the result of that (latter) history—not the history of her fortunate origins and development, but the history of her transformative work. It was not the luck of her early intellectual and professional development (though that is nice to have), but talent, capacity and an active mind that produced the work in this volume.

The writings selected and organized here cover four and a half decades of her productive work, and in it we see her engaged seriously, with both impressive range and impressive depth, with many of the major conceptual and clinical issues in psychoanalysis during that near half-century. In some sense the work also is, by illustration, a history of psychoanalysis during that period—moving from a grounding in Freud and the kinds of basic questioning once associated with David Rapaport; through the radical changes in our theories that have culminated in a vast pluralism; a developmental orientation; the flowering of object relations points of view and psychologies of the self, the import of Kleinian thinking across the ocean and into the United States; the relational turn, and postmodern thinking. Our author here shows herself to be not only conversant with it all, but impressively knowledgeable as well, and able to engage with it receptively though not passively, actively though without evident preformed biases, and ultimately creatively reflecting her own style of thinking.

And what is that style? From very early on she is a "both/and" thinker rather than an "either/or" one. The concept that is referred to again and again is Freud's "complemental series," but applied well beyond his original usage.

When there is more of this, there need be less of that; and when less of this, there is more of that — but room for both or more. The "this's and that's" vary from body to environment, from ruptures in stimulus barrier to the disruptions of fantasy, from conflict to deficit, from interpretation to holding — all of which becomes clear in the reading. And she is both an in-depth thinker in the world of theory and an experienced clinician throughout. She tackles her subjects with openness, yet confidence and force. There is no evasiveness in the space she gives to the "both this and that" that are to be taken into account.

Following her opening biographical chapter, Dr. Gediman divides the book into six parts, or sections: Trauma and Fantasy; Conflict and Deficit; Love and Death; Sex and Gender; Deceit and the Deceptions of Everyday Life; and Treatment and Supervision—all followed by a rich and substantive Epilogue, which serves, in fact, to highlight her full contribution. Even the titles of the first four of these reflect her interest in the tensions existing between each of the paired concepts named. The "this and that" of the last two section titles are simply additive, not implying a tension to be resolved, though deeply involved in controversy and clarification nonetheless. I shall comment briefly on each part.

Part I, consisting of three chapters on trauma and fantasy, examines in several ways the relative and related roles of traumatic inputs and fantasy creations in the evolution and structure of certain pathologies. Her view of the evolution of the stimulus barrier as an adaptive ego function, paired with her recognition of real ruptures to that barrier, and linked to Freud's early distinction between actual neurosis and psychoneurosis, all reflect her thorough familiarity with core issues of "classical" analytic theory and her capacity to work with them openly and with originality. But, then, outdoing herself, in her last chapter in this section —" Seduction Trauma: Complemental Intrapsychic and Interpersonal Perspectives on Fantasy and Reality" — she gives even the most sophisticated reader a close-up and informative look at the whole history and the inner workings of the trauma concept in psychoanalysis. Since we can ordinarily, she suggests, not be certain in what degree "real" trauma happened, was rewritten by fantasy imposed on traumatic events, or reflected distortions in the interpretation of events to start with, a complemental series approach to the work on trauma must be available to us in our thinking. Though this approach must never be applied rigidly, lest it lead to an analyst's grossly contradicting a patient's inner experience – it is a form of traumatic "gaslighting" in its own right as she points out. And her reference to "gaslighting" as a trauma to the sense of reality is itself a real eye opener.

Part II has two chapters under the overall heading of conflict and deficit.

She speaks here with the voice of an experienced clinician. In both chapters her approach is, again, unifying rather than exclusionary. "Unification" is in fact in the subtitle of one of these chapters, and the complemental series idea works easily here. Her view: deficits, defects, deficiencies, developmental failures — call them what you will, and they have been referred to under these headings and others — are not immune to becoming part of, endowed with, conflict. In fact, such failings may be magnets for conflict; they may accumulate meanings in the mind, serve as attractors of fantasy, and thus for a strong move into a conflict sphere. Since all intrapsychic conflict involves contradictory internal elements, such developmental deficiencies merely affect the nature of one of the elements in the conflict. Thus, for example, some conflict elements to be found among deficits would be not strong and organized defenses but primitive ones; not signal anxiety but overwhelmedness. But none of the elements that traditionally have signified deficit are immune to conflict, and each becomes a party to a particular compromise formation. And deficiencies need not be "caused" by conflict; they may certainly be a direct result of bodily anomalies, parental failures, or adventitious life events, but they can nonetheless be worsened by conflict. All things are possible in the mind, for good or ill. Dr. Gediman illustrates all of this with an in-depth exploration of "annihilation anxiety," a form of deficiency in the developmental line of anxiety towards more functional signal anxiety. This discussion is itself an education for the reader regarding this concept, its many varieties, and its setting within different levels of personality organization. Again, there is no single track thinking here.

Part III includes three chapters on love and death reflecting Dr. Gediman's long term work on these themes in early publications and in her 1995 book: *Fantasies of Love and Death in Life and Art*. This whole section is quite unique. We are taken on a fascinating and learned tour through the worlds of art, opera, literature, psychoanalytic theory, and psychoanalytic clinical work. Themes of sadomasochism, of separation and merger and longings for permanent union, of a pairing of erection and resurrection find central place. The writing here fully reveals the author's professional lifetime of engagement with these subjects in psychoanalysis and the arts.

The two chapters in Part IV on sex and gender again display the author's combination of openness and breadth, on the one hand, and capacity to take her own stand in controversial matters, on the other. Again we are treated to an excursion through the arts, this time in the form of the gender-bending play: "M. Butterfly", probably known to only a portion of the readers. She goes on to consider, as one chapter title indicates, premodern, modern, and postmodern thinking on the subjects of sex, gender, identity, and object choice. One can sense her own position — post-Freud radical change in his equation of the feminine with passivity and the masculine with activity — as she recognizes both the substance and the possible excesses of a fully postmodern deconstructionist view of sex and gender. As in every one of the book's sections, the writer is always illuminating, challenging, and deeply knowledgeable.

Part V, with two chapters on deceit, again brings us into an area that the author has a long involvement in and that is represented in her 1996 book (co-authored with Janice S. Lieberman), *The Many Faces of Deceit*: imposters and imposture — not something that most of us have thought about deeply. But as presented here it is utterly fascinating once again. It is a wonderful clinical and educational tour. It is a clinical tour because we hear case material in depth from an experienced clinician who is alert to issues of unconscious fantasy, transference and countertransference, and the full panoply of overdetermination and multiple function. And it is an educational tour both because, in the simplest sense, Dr. Gediman is very knowledgeable and educates us, but more particularly because she shows how issues of deceit and imposture enter readily into the psychoanalytic educational process. Candidates have to manage internal tendencies and even are required to identify with their patients, their analysts, and their supervisors, each in different ways, and yet to hold onto their own individual self, which ultimately is the self they will carry along into their subsequent clinical work.

And finally, in Part VI, with six chapters on treatment and supervision, Dr. Gediman brings the reader to a familiar yet often embattled set of subjects. The chapter titles convey the range: the transition from psychotherapy to psychoanalysis, criteria for termination, the therapeutic action, self-disclosure, and the parallelism phenomenon in supervision and therapy. In each, the author brings her flexible, integrative, depth-oriented, and strong thinking to bear on the subject at hand. It is a fitting finale to an already strong book.

In her Epilogue, which is a full, independent paper in itself, Dr. Gediman addresses what she describes as "cutting edge controversies". This is a truly sweeping review of much that is currently an embattled "playing field" for some in our field, while those same arenas present opportunities for major advances in psychoanalytic thinking for others. She is clearly in the latter group, and demonstrates that thinking issue by issue as she frames each in head-on and clear ways.

Helen Gediman has produced an impressive body of work. Her intellectual range is demonstrated throughout. While she engages deeply with a very specific subject in each of the several chapters and sections of this book, the collection as a whole takes us on a wide-ranging, clinically and theoretically grounded, tour of psychoanalysis and its development in a large part of the second half of the 20th century and right up to the present. And our tour, not by the author's design but simply by who she is and how she thinks, turns out to have, in that author, a most excellent tour guide.

## AUTHOR'S POSTSCRIPT TO FRED PINE'S INTRODUCTION

I am enormously appreciative of Fred Pine's emphasis on my being the right person to have produced what I've produced as opposed to my own emphasis on being in the right place at the right time. Perhaps that issue of what is more "right," luck or pluck, is the first of the binaries that my attempts at building these bridges has addressed. I was in the right place at the right time and luckily the beneficiary of many wonderful influences. Additionally, I knew how to push ahead and carve out my own reconciliations in a way that I am pleased and proud that Fred judges as creative and constructive.

I must take miniscule issue with Fred's comment that my final two sections, or Parts V and VI do not really deal with binary issues. His observations are entirely accurate in regard to the way those two sections were entitled and written at the time he got to see the draft. Then, the titles implied a position that seemed merely additive and did not suggest any binaries or false dichotomies that I might study in depth and then attempt to reconcile. His keen observations, however, prompted me to change the titles and some of the emphases from what they were when he read the draft to what they are now in the published book. Part V, entitled "Deceit and Deceptions of Everyday Life," when Fred read it, has been changed to "Pathological Self Deceptions and the Deceptions of Everyday Life." Part VI, entitled originally "Treatment and Supervision" has been changed to "Treatment and Supervision: Intrapsychic and Interpersonal Perspectives." With these changes there is now a symmetry to the underlying purposes of all six parts and not the two inconsistencies that were there when Dr. Pine read an earlier draft of my book proposal. My miniscule disagreement has morphed into munificent gratitude. I thank Fred for his help in my ever-changing efforts to move onward and upward toward integrating the body of my work. What all sections or Parts have in common is the idea of building bridges between theoretical and between clinical points of view often seen as conflicting and controversial with no resolution, by taking always a "both/ and" rather than an "either/or approach, as Dr. Pine has noted in his introduction to these works. Eliminating false binaries, in addition to being didactically sound, also encourages those who are so inclined to some grand, if not grandiose internal fantasies, such as having the best of every-thing, or having and being it all. All-inclusive aggregate thinking that builds bridges may not work when one is attempting to create a stand-by-itself to-tally self-consistent theory as theory. But when we deal with the clinical and corresponding theoretical realities of psychoanalysis, we are served best by multiples models that, together, allow us to apply multiple perspectives to all of the points of view that vary within our large, diverse, and pluralistic corpus. Perhaps, speaking intrapsychically, an unconscious fantasy behind the con-viction that building bridges to eliminate false dichotomies, goes something like: if one can have and think "everything," one can have and be "everyone."

# Chapter 1: Influences: Parents, Teachers, Colleagues

[Gediman, H.K. (1998). Influences: parents, teachers, colleagues.
In J. Reppen, Ed. *Why I Became a Psychotherapist.*
Northvale, NJ: Jason Aronson]

I dreamed and daydreamed of being a psychotherapist when I was in high school. At that time, the only kind of psychotherapist I had ever heard of was a psychoanalyst, so naturally my fantasies were of being a psychoanalyst, but at the age of 14 I do not think I believed that joining that august body would ever materialize into a real possibility. A beloved uncle was then studying to be an analyst. During summer vacations that our families spent together on Cape Cod, he "practiced" giving Rorschachs to me. He seemed very impressed that I saw ice-cream cones and sundaes on quite a few cards where nobody to his knowledge had ever seen them before. I was absolutely delighted when he interpreted my orality to my parents, cousins, aunts, and uncles as indicating that I had a creative and original turn of mind as well as a lust for life. Although nobody to whom he bragged about me could know for sure whether he was right or wrong, deep down I must have had an unflagging trust in his judgments about me. My favorite uncle also had Freud's *Collected Papers* on our communal shelves, and I dug into them in the wee hours as though I were surreptitiously sneaking into me all the ice cream I could possibly get, and that was the beginning of my addiction to and my burgeoning love affair with psychoanalysis. His Havelock Ellis books did nothing to retard the process.

As I write this mini-memoir, I am struck by how my adolescent enthusiasm, excitement, and idealization of my psychoanalytic heroes is reactivated, now in the present. It would be a while before the initial love affair and infatuation was gradually transformed, in the process of "becoming," into the more mature forms of passionate love, devotion, and respect, along with that quieter, more reserved love that I bring to my being a psychoanalyst, today.

A few years later, as a freshman at Harvard (we called it Radcliffe, then, and I still call it Radcliffe today as a testament to my strong feelings of support for top-quality education of women, and to my firm identity as a woman psychoanalyst) it still had not dawned on me that I, the little girl from Brooklyn, could actually become a psychoanalyst. There was also a similar feeling of disbelief that it was actually I who walked the streets of Cambridge, and had become a regular habitué to Harvard Yard. Despite those initial feelings of disbelief, of unreality, I can now look back and say I was at the right place at the right time, and blessed with very good fortune. I began my serious voyage by following my anxious parents' advice to seek out a major that would qualify me for a teaching license in the New York City public school system, which is where my parents and most of my aunts and uncles worked. Knowing how hard my parents worked to send me to what I believed to be the best college in the world in order to prepare me for teaching in the only world they knew well, I decided to major in English. However, that decision was very short-lived, because my final grade in English I was a B, and I hated the course, and my final grade in Social Relations Ia (Harvard's program for human psychology), taught by Gordon Allport, was an A, and I loved the course. Social relations became my major. In the years to follow, I became fairly well acquainted with the works and the persons of Robert White, Daniel Levinson, and most of all Henry Murray, who was a faculty affiliate of my dorm. Once a month he would have dinner at the table of all the social relations majors living in Cabot Hall, and once a month we would have dinner at his gracious home in the lovely Back Bay area of Boston. In those days, psychoanalysis was the only game in town for a psychology major at the undergraduate level, and Freudian thinking permeated every course I took. Even my forays into literature and art brought me into direct contact with the basics of psychoanalytic interpretation and ideas. I was so smitten then that when I analyzed Yeats' poem "Leda and the Swan" wildly, as though it were some unknown person's random dream, completely ignoring the poet's intent, my English instructor rewarded me with a D- grade. Perhaps that lapse in judgment signaled the beginnings of the lifelong process of reining in some tendency to unbridled excitement about psychoanalysis and psychoanalysts that had begun when I was a teenager.

My career path was direct and unambivalent from the beginning. Those were very peculiar times. Dean Mildred Sherman, Radcliffe's dean of women, was convinced that a liberal arts education for women should have the sole and simple goal of preparing them to be good wives to successful men, culminating in their being good conversationalists at formal dinner parties, and while pouring the demitasse that followed in their wake. I fought her all the way, however, and managed to graduate magna cum laude, having written an honors thesis on cognitive processes under the tutelage of Eugenia Hanffman. By that time, although I probably did not know it yet, I clearly was beginning to find my own voice (I think I thought I was simply a lucky overachiever), and I did not have to rely so much on the proximity to idealized successful people to bolster my self-esteem. I now enjoy the pleasures of connections to accomplished colleagues for myriad other reasons. Strange as it may seem, I was among the puny 5 percent of Radcliffe graduates in my class who went on to graduate school immediately upon graduating (it is now closer to 95 percent), and on that account was considered a rebel by the dean, who gave me no support whatsoever and did her best to discourage me from going on to graduate school in my chosen profession. Thank goodness my own parents, anxious as they might have been about the unknown-to-them career path I chose, gave me the loving support and encouragement that I sorely needed. Although I was not headed in a direction that would land me a license to teach in the New York City school system, it was unheard of to my parents that any child, boy or girl, be sent to away to an expensive Ivy League college (the cost for tuition, room, and board was then $1,000 per annum!), supported by both of their hard-earned incomes, and not go on to some profession or career. My choice was closer to my parents' aspirations than to Dean Sherman's. However, possibly as a concession to the latter, I did marry on the afternoon of my graduation. It took subsequent divorce, remarriage, and two analyses to understand the full meaning of that action.

One cannot write an account of how one became a psychoanalyst without reference to motivations that spring from personal history. So, in the brief digression that follows, I choose not to go into the details of either of my two analyses, but will supply the readers with some selected relevant background information, preferring that they use their own imagination in interpreting my particular motivational route to becoming a psychoanalyst to their being burdened with my explicit analyses.

To begin, I did not need the support of the feminist movement, which was to gain momentum a decade after my college graduation and would flourish two decades later, in order to maintain my resolve in pursuing life goals involving marriage, motherhood, and my profession. I had the support of my father, who had immigrated to the United States from the Ukraine at the turn of the century, and of my mother, whose parents arrived here from Vilna, Lithuania, during the blizzard of 1888, before she was born. My mother was the eldest of eight, and she remained single, working as an English teacher, and supporting all of her brothers and sisters until they had graduated from college, graduate school, or law school. Only then did she marry my father, continuing on in her profession. My mother, a feminist without knowing she was one, was my role model, cheering me on, completely uncomprehending of and baffled by the stifling antifeminist bias, like that held by Dean Sherman, of the 1950s. Her life was not an altogether easy one, and she suffered the tragedy, at the age of 39, of losing her first child, Marjorie, a 2-year-old girl who died from a strep throat complication of scarlet fever.

I was born two years later, to a mother who was still depressed. I was not expected to survive the first year of my life, being afflicted with a condition that was at that time diagnosed simply as diarrhea, so my mother, more depressed than ever, then became pregnant with my twenty-one month younger sister, Cecil. Thanks to my stalwart father's daily trips, after his workday as a school principal ended, to Manhattan from our home in Brooklyn to buy some kind of special milk to treat my condition, I survived. My parents, whose lives were not directly touched by the Holocaust because their families came to this country earlier to escape the pogroms, were thus blessed with two "replacement" children. I grew up with a mother who never stopped grieving for a lost daughter who, judging from the picture of Marjorie that never left her bureau top, looked exactly like me. And she was a mother who never stopped protecting and overprotecting me and my younger sister Cecil, in her determination that we survive well in every endeavor of our lives.

This brief historical capsule provides some background for understanding how I got in touch with my own vulnerabilities and those of others around me, and how I must have been driven to distinguish myself in unusual ways simply to survive and to be loved. That sense of vulnerability has been a major source of my love of learning, doing, and teaching psychoanalysis, and has always rung out as a critical counterpoint to what some others might easily (mis) understand simply as a very ambitious wish to achieve and to be admired.

After graduating from college and defying the dean of women, I went on without missing a beat to graduate schools, earning my doctorate in clinical psychology from New York University, which at that time was heavily focused on psychoanalytic thinking. I was invited by George Klein to join the staff of NYU's Research Center for Mental Health, which he codirected with Robert Holt, both of whom were schooled in the traditions set by David Rapaport at the Menninger Foundation, and who were determined to carry on his mission. My five years as a National Institute of Mental Health (NIMH) predoctoral research fellow in that heady environment kept me on track. Among those with whom I lunched, usually at the Cedar Street Tavern of Beat Generation fame, and with whom I schmoozed almost daily were Morris Eagle, Leo Goldberger, Paul Lippmann, Irving Paul, Fred Pine, and Donald Spence. This list of names and others that appear throughout this chapter, while subject to misconstrual as name-dropping, are intended solely to convey my extreme good fortune in having had the opportunity to connect all along with myriad colleagues who have become major contributors to psychoanalysis in all its facets.

Looking back, it is easy to see that once again I was fortunate to be in the right place at the right time, thriving on the benefits of shared passionate concerns with people of like minds. We were all doing some kind of psychoanalytically based empirical research. I was working on my dissertation, sponsored by George Klein, on the topic of ambivalence and stimulus ambiguity. We were all doing something on cognitive style and psychoanalysis, and most of us were very involved in tachistoscopic studies of subliminal stimuli, and with studying the effects of LSD on manifest dream content. To accomplish the latter, all of us staff members were soberly encouraged to take the drug, and then either look at subliminal stimuli or spend the night sleeping at the dream lab at Downstate Medical School, reporting our dreams each time we were awakened during a period of REM sleep. We were also expected to describe at staff meetings our personal experiences with our own altered states of consciousness. We didn't know then that we were "tripping"—I do not believe the term had yet been coined. Robert Langs was the medical consultant on that dicey project. In the end, we were all left with an unflappable conviction about the existence of the unconscious. And we all served as subjects for each other's studies, which were discussed in weekly conferences, along with some talmudic style seminars in such areas of interest to Rapaport and his disciples as Chapter 7 of Freud's "Dream Book."

During one of my graduate years, I was a school psychologist in training at the Bureau of Child Guidance of the New York City Board of Education. That work did indeed qualify me for a license that my parents had heard of, but I opted out and headed in other directions. Courses in the clinical psychology program, headed by Bernard Kalinkowitz, were all psychoanalytically oriented. I took the psychotherapy practicum and was supervised by Esther Menaker, one of the few nonmedical analysts in New York at that time who had been trained at the Vienna Institute. Since she had been analyzed by Anna Freud, I thought of Sigmund Freud as my great-grandfather, thus acquiring another relative as a psychoanalytic ego ideal in addition to my Rorschaching uncle. Although I am certain that by this time, my adolescent excitements and infatuations with highly idealized people of great accomplishment were on their way to being tamed, I am equally certain that in writing this chapter those older and much more raw feelings have surfaced once more, and I am reliving them, knowing they will have to be worked over again and again, with less and less time and effort, I hope, than in the past.

I knew by then that the next step would be formal psychoanalytic training, an idea that had moved out of the fantasy land of my adolescence into the more thoughtful world of viable and more sober reality, but I did not yet know where or how. Sad to leave the Research Center and my friends, I moved on to do a two-year NIMH postdoctoral fellowship in psychotherapy—and still the only kind of psychotherapy I was taught was psychoanalytic—in the Department of Psychiatry at Albert Einstein College of Medicine, headed then by Milton Rosenbaum. My mentors in the Psychology Division there, at Jacoby Hospital, were Walter Kass and Sybille Escalona, who had sprung from the same Menninger tradition as Holt and Klein, so there was considerable continuity and consistency in my training. I was fortunate enough to be at Einstein during the halcyon days when just about everyone on staff was an analyst, and nearly every resident in psychiatry and intern in psychology eventually became one. Once again, the right place at the right time with people of like minds. Among the psychiatry residents there at the time of my training were Sander Abend, Anna Burton, Robert Kabcenell, Theodore Jacobs, Arnold Richards, Elise Snyder, and Martin Willick. Among the psychology interns and fellows were Sheldon Bach, Doris Silverman, and Joyce Steingart. My first personal analysis was in full swing, and I was privileged to be in psychotherapy supervision with Robert Grayson, William Grossman, and Lester Schwartz. In addition, I took seminars with Jose Barchilon, Eleanor Galenson, Norman Margolis, and Andrew Peto. The exciting smorgasbord continued into weekly grand rounds when presentations by Robert Bak, Edith Jacobson, Margaret Mahler, Sandor Rado, John Rosen, and Harold Searles, to name but a few, contributed significantly to a broad range of exposure to psychoanalytic thinking, even before my formal training had begun. Space limitations force me to give just the menu, but the food was delicious and nourishing even though it took years to digest in the continuous process of finding my own preferences to be expressed in my very own voice. And it took years for my vociferous and gregarious hunger to be transformed into a passion for the richness of psychoanalytic work.

Following the Einstein years, I became chief psychologist at the Tappan Zee Mental Health Clinic at Phelps Memorial Hospital in Tarrytown, where Lawrence Friedman was also on staff. My work consisted exclusively of psychoanalytically oriented psychotherapy in a suburban community setting. My case load there was large and was added to in 1961 by cases in my private practice, which I had just started in Riverdale. It was definitely time to start psychoanalytic training.

My psychiatric colleagues at Einstein who were affiliated with the New York Psychoanalytic Institute encouraged me to apply there as a waiver candidate. My research background made it likely that I would have been accepted, but I was mostly interested, then, as now, in clinical psychoanalytic practice.

I did not want to get where I wanted to go through the backdoor, and had I gone that route I could not have gotten what I wanted to get: full recognition of my identity as a clinical psychologist-psychoanalyst. So I decided to study at the NYU Postdoctoral Program in Psychotherapy and Psychoanalysis, a decision I have never regretted, because it helped to consolidate my identity as a psychologist-psychoanalyst, and laid the foundation for understanding the balance between diversity and common ground that are so much at the forefront of psychoanalysis today, worldwide.

I matriculated in 1962, one year after the program had been founded, the very first psychoanalytic and psychotherapy training program for psychologists affiliated with an academic institution. Although I identified myself as Freudian, the program, which taught both Freudian and interpersonal psychoanalysis, did not then have separate tracks, as it has now. I took courses with such diverse faculty members as Avram Ben Avi, Leopold Bellak, Ruth Jean Eisenbud, Erich Fromm, Rosalind Gould, Robert Holt, William Menaker, Esther Menaker, and Edward Tauber. My supervisors were William Menaker, Ruth Jean Eisenbud, and Leopold Bellak. Among the candidates in my classes were Abby Adams Silvan, Sheldon Bach, Shirley Feltman, Mark Grunes, Marvin Hurvich, Edwin Levy, Martin Nass, Irving Steingart, and Mark Silvan. Yes, another list, but the privilege of being connected with people such as these, as well as their predecessors and successors, was yet one more instance of being at the right place at the right time, and my good fortune constituted a critical part of the process of becoming a psychoanalyst. Before my graduation in 1968, I was invited to join a research project funded by the NIMH and directed by Bellak on "Ego Functions in Schizophrenics, Neurotics, and Normals," eventually culminating in the book with the same title, coauthored by Leopold Bellak, Marvin Hurvich, and Helen K. Gediman. The project was based at the NYU postdoctoral program but located near Roosevelt Hospital where most of the research was conducted. Others participating in the project were Morris Eagle, Nancy Goldberger, Milton Kapit, and Mark Silvan. The work was exciting, and took us to Washington on trips to the NIMH, which was hanging fire during its last years of funding research in psychoanalysis. I also learned the ins and outs of writing a grant proposal. Although this was the last formal empirical research project in psychoanalysis that I had been involved in, the increasing focus on my practice of psychoanalysis and psychoanalytic psychotherapy have enabled me to continue my interests in research in the more general sense of arguing psychoanalytic issues with illustrative case material.

Since then, I have practiced primarily psychoanalysis, averaging during any given year four analytic cases, and psychoanalytic psychotherapy. However, there was a considerable period of time when I worked no more than half time. That began in 1964, when my son was born, and when I left the Tappan Zee Clinic. My office was in my home, and I had no daytime commutes to take me away from my child and my work, and was able to combine my analytic control work with active involvement in my son's school and social activities, an arrangement I will never regret. I eventually opened a second part-time office in Manhattan, and by the time I moved there in 1977, my practice was back to full time, and in Manhattan only. Presently, all of my psychotherapy, even my work in one-time-a-week individual and couples therapy, is guided by psychoanalytic principles and a psychoanalytic attitude. So, in the broad sense I would say that all of my time currently is devoted to psychoanalysis, although not strictly speaking, if we are going to take into account specifics such as frequency and so forth.

An important part of my development as a psychoanalyst came with the founding of Division 39 of the American Psychological Association. I was in on that from the very beginning, and was a founding member of Section I. I remember the now long gone pleasures of intimate groups holding meetings at small tropical resorts. The first was at Ixtapa, Mexico, in 1981, and several others followed at other lovely beaches before Division 39 grew to its present size of thousands. My identity as a psychologist-psychoanalyst has been fortified by becoming a Diplomate in Psychoanalysis through ABPsaP, the American Board of Psychoanalysis in Psychology. I am also a member of the New York Freudian Society and its training institute, and the International Psychoanalytic Association (IPA). The American Psychoanalytic Association accepted me this year, [1995] with no strings or waiver. While I had mixed feelings about joining an organization that had excluded nonmedical analysts for far too long, I could exact some personal satisfaction from entering through the front door with their belated acceptance of me, while at the same time maintaining my primary identity as a psychologist-psychoanalyst.

Becoming a psychoanalytic therapist is a process that never ends. Most of my continuing education is a by-product of my psychoanalytic practice, teaching, and supervision. I teach classes in clinical theory and technique, as well as continuous case seminars. Presently, I am Clinical Professor of Psychology at the New York University Postdoctoral Program in Psychotherapy and Psychoanalysis. I am also on the faculty, and a training and supervising analyst at the New York Freudian Society. I find that the best way to keep current is to read all the recent psychoanalytic journals, as well as to attend and present at regular meetings of local, national, and international psychoanalytic organizations. I have attended most Division 39 meetings, all but one IPA meeting since 1979, and this past winter participated as a presenter in a study group of the American Psychoanalytic Association, and one at the Federation of Latin American Psychoanalysts (FEPAL) with a group of clinicians from North and Latin America. I tend to publish my work and new ideas as soon as I am able to formulate them. I also participate in several peer groups in which senior and junior colleagues present their clinical work, and in which literature at the cutting edge of theory and technique is priority reading. In addition to teaching and peer groups, I am actively involved in psychoanalytic administrative activity, chairing committees, evaluating candidates' progression, and am on the board of directors of the New York Freudian Society. I publish and deliver papers regularly, and am presently preparing several articles for edited books. I have published two psychoanalytic books in the past year. The first, *Fantasies of Love and Death in Life Art* (1995) is a work on applied psychoanalysis and the culmination of many years of prior work. The second, coauthored with Janice Lieberman, *The Many Faces of Deceit* (1996) deals particularly with deception and gullibility in the analytic dyad. I am currently working on a new book on the subject of successful women.

I designate my professional framework as a contemporary Freudian psychoanalyst with a multiperspectival bent. Following Pine's schema, and others with multiperspectival underpinnings, I look at clinical material from the points of view of drive, object, ego, and self. I have never regarded object relations, ego psychology, and the psychology of the self as outside of a contemporary Freudian framework, which includes more than a technique involving the interpretation of conflict and compromise formation. Additionally, my work is influenced by Melanie Klein and the contemporary Kleinians of London. This multiperspectival view is not to be confused with an eclectic view. I am respectful of the basic Freudian technique as it has evolved over the years, particularly with respect to developments in the principles of neutrality (which does not mean indifference to the patient, but does mean respectfulness toward all sides in a conflict); anonymity (which does not mean being a blank screen, withholding of personal responsiveness and information, but does involve disclosure of all personal responses that are relevant to the patient's knowledge of how the process works toward development of his or her own self understanding); and abstinence (which does not mean nongratifying of the patient, as any good interpretation or empathic understanding is a gratification essential to the process). I believe that the therapeutic action of psychoanalysis involves more than the imparting of insight by interpretation, depending also on the establishment of a real and therapeutic object relationship, which is integrally related to the transference and countertransference. I believe that enactments, and relational and intersubjective components enter into the analytic process in a contemporary Freudian analysis, but, as opposed to certain other orientations, the patient is always at the center. In what I have just summarized, I have been influenced by the work of Freud, Glover, Strachey, Klein, Hartmann, Jacobson, Winnicott, Loewald, Kohut, Stone, Rangell, and, more contemporaneously, Boesky, Renik, Chused, Arlow and Brenner, Kernberg, Mahler, Stern, Busch, Jacobs, and Pine.

I have always managed to practice, teach, and write, and I am now reminded of another anecdote relating to my family. One day, having returned from my August vacation, my father called to ask if any of my patients had returned to me after my absence. I said, "Don't worry, Dad. If they don't come back, I can always write." To which the anxious, and obviously ambivalent man replied, "Does anybody read that stuff?"

Becoming a psychotherapist, especially a psychoanalytic psychotherapist, is a full-time process and a lifetime proposition, and certainly not a one-time goal to be achieved and maintained in any static manner. One does not simply arrive, but continues to learn and to develop, and if one is lucky, remains young at heart in the process. In what other field can an individual reaching an age that in other fields signifies retirement time still function at peak levels?

These can be regarded, in Dickensian terms, as the best of times and the worst of times. With the constant challenge of keeping up with evolving theories and techniques, and of balancing the virtues of diversity and common ground, my life as a psychoanalyst has never been more exciting and productive than it is right now. It has also never been as exasperating and frustrating, what with the encroachments of managed care on such indispensable conditions as autonomy and confidentiality for psychoanalytic therapists and patients alike. But the ills of the managed care system are so horrendous that I cannot believe it can do anything other than self-destruct, helped along, of course, by our own concerted outreach into the broader community to revive and revitalize psychoanalysis as we once knew it, and as it has the potential to evolve into being more of. I hope for everybody's sake, particularly that or the younger generations that I have been privileged to teach, that those misanthropes who share my father's ill-founded apprehensions will be outnumbered by those trusting souls who share his obvious pride in the work that his daughter chose for herself.

**REFERENCES**

Gediman, H.K. (1995). *Fantasies of Love and Death in Life and Art: A Psychoanalytic Study of the Normal and the Pathological.* New York: New York University Press.

——— & Lieberman, J. S. (1996). *The Many Faces of Deceit: Omissions, Lies, and Disguise in Psychotherapy.* Northvale, NJ: Jason Aronson.

# PART I. TRAUMA AND FANTASY

## AUTHOR'S INTRODUCTION

There is no doubt that the three chapters in this Part I, "Trauma and Fantasy" each and together deal with issues that I believe I've always thought consciously are related to each other. They are not as manifestly far apart in content as most of my other works are to them and to each other. I remember one fairly well known analyst who kidded me when he heard that I had submitted my paper on the "Actual Neuroses and Psychoneuroses" to the *International Journal of Psycho-analysis*. "Helen," he chided, "you know the idea of the actual neurosis was totally given up by Freud when he replaced it with the concept of the psychoneuroses." A paper with that title could never be published now." Just as he meant every word he said, so did Leo Rangell, who was in the audience discussing that paper when I presented it at the winter meetings of the American Psychoanalytic Association. Leo boastfully announced to the group at hand, "Helen, you know that you and I are the only two psychoanalysts in the world who still believe in Freud's truth." He was referring, of course to his own landmark paper, in which he argued that Freud never replaced his first theory of anxiety with the second. Rangell's support of my position was voiced in the heyday of his ideas about the value of accretion of the new and the old in revising and evaluating the value of psychoanalytic theories and ideas. Leo cautioned against totally replacing old paradigms with new ones and advocated saving the best from each and discarding the worst. As gallant and chivalrous as he was, Leo was not quite right that he and I were the only ones thinking additively about aggregates in old and new perspectives. My paper was in fact published, widely read, and used for teaching at several psychoanalytic institutes. Around that same time in the 1980's, Gerald Fogel asked me to write a piece for the *Newsletter of the American Psychoanalytic Association* (see Gediman, H.K., 1985). He wanted me to critique Janet Malcolm's book, *In The Freud Archives*, and add my ideas about Jeffrey Masson's position on Freud's supposed abandonment of his seduction theory. By then, there were at least three of us analysts who believed that Freud had never abandoned the seduction theory and believed that psychic trauma as well as unconscious fantasy figured in the etiology, psychogenesis, and psychopathology of the psychoneuroses. Isn't it good to know that today most analysts accept that broader, integrative view?

# Chapter 2: The Concept of Stimulus Barrier: Its Review and Reformulation as an Adaptive Ego Function

[Gediman, H.K., (1971). The concept of stimulus barrier: its review and reformulation as an adaptive ego function. *International Journal of Psycho-analysis* 52: 243–257. ]

"Stimulus barrier" as an important personality factor has received rather too little attention. Yet in the development of children it may play a crucial role. In some adults a particularly high or low stimulus barrier may be one of their outstanding characteristics. It may also be true that in the functioning of a large number of adults, stimulus barrier does not play a marked role. In distinction to its role in children, it may have something of an all-or-none quality in adults.

This paper is clearly divided into three main sections: (1) a general review of the concept; (2) a review of the literature implying that stimulus barrier may be usefully classified as an ego function; and (3) a specific reformulation of stimulus barrier as an ego function originally proposed by Bellak and which has emerged from our ongoing research on 11 other ego functions as well. The specific idea proposed here is that stimulus barrier is a complex ego function rather than a simple sensory or perceptual threshold, composed of a number of component factors, observable and measurable along a continuum of maladaptiveness–adaptiveness.

## GENERAL REVIEW OF THE CONCEPT

Although it was in "Beyond the Pleasure Principle" (1920) that Freud most fully elaborated his ideas on stimulus barrier, early harbingers of his interest are found in the Fliess Papers (1892–1899) and the Project (1895). In the latter, he introduced the notion that the *Reizschutz* (or stimulus barrier) was a necessity for the organism's survival in a stimulus-charged world. The most intensive presentation of his ideas occurred after World War I, when he had occasion to observe many men suffering from the trauma of shell-shock. So the concept of stimulus barrier arose in the context of the traumatic neurosis. It was a way of explaining how a person managed to survive in an environment bombarding him with too much stimulation or excitation (1920). The traumatic neuroses were assumed to result from a breach in the stimulus barrier.

Freud felt that any experience is traumatic when a stimulus is too powerful to be dealt with in the usual way; and a traumatic neurosis represents a breach or extensive rupture in the stimulus barrier, caused by powerful excitation exerted from the external world. The mental apparatus becomes flooded by large amounts of stimulation (1920, p. 29). Fenichel elaborates the relation of traumatic neurosis to *Reizschutz*:

> The excitation already at hand has to be mastered before new stimuli can be accepted. The organism develops different ways of protecting itself against too great a quantity of stimulation (*Reizschutz*). Refusing to accept new stimulation is a primitive means of re-establishing such protection after it has been broken down by the trauma ... (1945, p. 118).

Furst (1967a) has compiled a series of contributions expanding on the trauma concept. He himself feels there has been a blurring of the stimulus barrier concept recently, due to a broadening of the trauma concept. Trauma, as now conceived, does not always imply a one-shot manifest breakthrough of the stimulus barrier and an ensuing state of helplessness. It could also involve a rent or crack in the barrier instead of a breakthrough, or else a slow breaking through rather than a piercing trauma (M. Kris, 1964). Such phenomena have been variously called "strain trauma" (Kris, 1956a, 1956b) or "cumulative trauma" (Khan, 1963). Properly functioning, the stimulus barrier "scales down" the intensity of external stimuli to a level which the organism can manage. Although described by Freud mainly in the context of trauma, the stimulus barrier concept was clearly applied by him to all pathological states and to normalcy as well, and later (1940) was seen as a constitutional precursor of the ego, serving a primitive defence function which foretells the ego's more elaborate and highly developed protective mechanisms. Freud described the workings of the stimulus barrier in "Beyond the Pleasure Principle" (1920): the external covering of the apparatus to manage excess stimulation is directed against incoming stimuli, while the next layer is differentiated into an organ for the perception of stimuli. Even this second layer processes only minimum quantities, or samples, of incoming stimuli.

Now let us look further into what Freud said about this mechanism to which he attributed the dual function of *Protection* against and *reception* of stimuli:

> Let us picture a living organism in its most simplified possible form as

an undifferentiated vesicle of a substance that is susceptible to stimulation ... It would be easy to suppose, then, that as a result of the ceaseless impact of external stimuli on the surface of the vesicle, its substance to a certain depth may have become permanently modified, so that ... it would present the most favourable possible conditions for the reception of stimuli ... This little fragment of living substance is suspended in the middle of an *external* world charged with the most powerful energies; and it would be killed by the stimulation emanating from these if it were not provided with a protective shield against stimuli ... its outermost surface ... becomes to some degree inorganic and ... resistant to stimuli ... *Protection* against stimuli is an almost more important function for the living organism than reception of stimuli ... The main purpose of the reception of stimuli is to discover the direction and nature of the external stimuli; and for that it is enough to take small specimens of the external world. ... In highly developed organisms the receptive *cortical layer* ... has long been withdrawn into the depths of the interior of the body, though portions of it have been left behind on the surface immediately beneath the general shield against stimuli. These are the sense organs, which consist essentially of apparatus for the reception of certain specific effects of stimulation, but which also include special arrangements for further protection against excessive amounts of stimulation and for excluding unsuitable kinds of stimuli ... they deal only with very *small quantities* of external stimulation and only take in samples of the external world. They may perhaps be compared with feelers which are all the time making tentative advances towards the external world and then drawing back from it (1920, pp. 26–29).

Under the influence of the external world, a portion of the id has undergone special development—what was originally a cortical layer equipped with organs for receiving stimuli and with arrangements for acting as a protective shield against stimuli ... [from this] a special organization called the ego has arisen (1940, p. 145).[1]

These quotations present concisely a number of though-provoking issues: the subsequently much-questioned (even by Freud) notion that the stimulus barrier functions only to regulate the impact of external (as opposed to internal or drive) stimuli; the recently disputed neurological assumptions underlying

---

1   Certain key words and phrases are italicized, so as to alert the reader to the focal points of elaboration in this paper

Freud's conceptual model of stimulus barrier, in which levels of abstraction shift and in which the boundaries between a purely neurological model and a psychological one seem hazy; the relation of stimulus hunger to the protection against stimuli; elaborations of the relation of psychic trauma to stimulus barrier. The issues foreshadow current lines of thought and research, which treat stimulus barrier not only as a threshold mechanism, but also as the precursor of an ego function, and an ego function as such. Let us deal with each of these issues in turn.

## PROTECTION AGAINST INNER OR OUTER STIMULI?

A question, which we shall see is a moot one, is whether the stimulus barrier is erected against outer reality alone or against both inner and outer reality. What makes it a moot question is the now expanded notions of reality, both inner and outer. Repeatedly, Freud stated that there was no *Reizschutz* protecting the psychic apparatus from the *drives*, but only from external environmental reality, or from injurious effects from without. His early position was that "the organism cannot withdraw itself from endogenous stimuli] as it does from external stimuli" (1895, p. 297). Still later, he made the following distinction:

> Let us imagine ourselves in the situation of an almost entirely helpless living organism ... which is receiving stimuli in its nervous substance ... On the one hand, it will be aware of stimuli which can be avoided by muscular action (flight); these it ascribes to an external world. On the other hand, it will also be aware of stimuli against which such action is of no avail ... instinctual needs ... (Freud, 1915, p. 119).

In his latest writings, Freud somewhat obscures the functional differences between protection against outer and protection against inner stimuli: "an excessive strength of instinct can damage the ego in a similar way to an excessive stimulus from the external world" (1940, p. 199). Anna Freud (1967) speaks for those who interpret Freud's distinction as implying two stimulus barriers, one against inner and one against outer stimuli.

A number of writers have independently come to the conclusion, in later elaborations of Freud's stimulus barrier concept, that the inner–outer distinctions do not hold, either conceptually or experientially. Clinical data abound with evidence of the organism treating disturbing internal stimuli as though they were external, attempting to deploy the same protective measures against both. Experimental evidence points to the same conclusion, reversing the emphasis. Eagle (1962), summarizing the evidence on subliminal sensitivity, concludes that the residue of external input acts exactly like internal intuition or "hunch". When information was presented without any indication of where it came from, subjects reacted to it as if it were a drive derivative: the ways they tended to deal with drives predicted sensitivity to subliminal stimuli. In keeping with these findings, Benjamin (1965) broadens the concept of stimulus barrier, stating (1) that projection makes use of stimulus barrier; (2) that the infant often treats internal stimuli as external and does so also at a later stage; (3) that the assumption that the shield is effective only against external stimulation implies the development of an outside–inside differentiation, and that this differentiation is in fact difficult to determine.

Hartmann (1939) believed there was no barrier against instinctual drives, but later appears to have revised his view: "The ego ... serves as a protective barrier against excessive external, and, in a somewhat different sense, internal stimuli" (1950, pp. 114–15). More recently, we find Winnicott (1958) stating that impingements on the organism indicate a failure to dose and regulate stimuli, both internal and external. If inner stimuli can be conceived of as other than drive or instinct in the classical sense, then it becomes easier to view the stimulus barrier as protecting against both inner and outer stimuli. It is not difficult to see the pseudo nature of the inner–outer dispute. We can assuredly say that the stimulus barrier concept, when introduced, did not deal with drive states (in the psychoanalytic sense), but we would be too limited if we banned the concept from applying to many other inner states. I would summarize this issue, agreeing with Holt as he discussed Freud's comparison of stimulus barrier with cell membrane:

> It seems to me therefore useful to conceive of the ego membrane as protecting the conscious ego ... from inner emotional impressions as well as from outer ones ... (1948, p. 9).

## BIOLOGICAL AND NEUROLOGICAL ASSUMPTIONS

The chief biological assumption which Freud used to account for the workings of the stimulus barrier was that of the constancy, stability or Nirvana principle:

> The nervous system is an apparatus which has the function of getting rid of the stimuli that breach it, or of reducing them to the lowest possible

level; or which, if it were feasible, would maintain itself in an altogether unstimulated condition (1915, p. 120).

Thus, Freud said, the stimulus barrier, following the laws of the Nirvana principle, strives to keep stimulation at a minimum. Now, this tension-reduction theory has been the subject of much controversy. There is certainly some very convincing evidence to show that, at times, people indeed do whatever they can to keep themselves in a relatively tensionless state. But we also are confronted, at the other extreme, with unequivocal observational data of people whose life appears dedicated to the pursuit of stimuli as in the sensory-happy seekers of "psychedelic" experiences, or among the "hippies" of today. Do these data invalidate the Nirvana principle, or can that tenet be modified to include the seemingly contradictory clinical observations? We must also consider here the plethora of biological and neurological writings appearing these days, both as evidence for confirming or refuting Freud's biological assumptions and as analogues to illustrate them. Among the first to consider the issue of stimulus hunger in relation to tension-reduction theory was Fenichel, whose ideas were elaborations of the simple observation that the life of the infant alternates between states of hunger and other disturbing stimuli, and of sleep. He interpreted a basic contradiction in human life: the longing for complete relaxation (constancy or Nirvana principle) and a longing for objects (stimulus hunger). Wolff (1960), too, borrowing Piaget's concept of nutriment or aliment, feels that both increase and decrease of tension are essential for structure formation. The point being made has to do with "optimal" stimulation rather than with too much. Amacher (1965) feels there were flaws in Freud's neurological education that had great influence on psychoanalytic theory. Mainly, he feels that in the erroneous set of assumptions Freud inherited from his teachers was the view that there was no protective shield against drives; and that he saw reality as isolated, momentary stimuli, whereas he regarded drives as continuous. The nervous system was seen by Freud as passive, with the primary function of ridding itself of stimulation in such a way that external stimulus energies entering directly into the nervous system needed to be scaled down by the stimulus barrier.

Much criticism of the Nirvana principle is summarized in Greenfield & Lewis (1965). Their book contains contributions by people whose ideas have evolved from Freud's major concepts; and it attempts to update the biological assumptions in psychoanalytic theory in order to bring them in line with present-day knowledge, yet without at the same time discarding Freud's major concepts and clinical observations, especially those regarding the stimulus barrier. According to Benjamin (1965), Freud's attribution of major importance to the concept of protective shield was a logical consequence of his views of the essential noxiousness of stimulation. While the Nirvana or constancy principle played a major role in Freud's metapsychology, most of the findings of neuroanatomy speak against any general validity for this thesis of Freud's.

> ... there is spontaneous activity not only in the brain, but also in the sense organs themselves, the discovery of positive reinforcement as well as aversive centers in the limbic system ... and, following Hebb's original work, the results of many behavioral studies of the effects of partial afferent isolation are sufficient evidence ... that the concept that the organism strives to keep stimulation at a minimum, or if possible at a zero level, is without biological foundation (Benjamin, 1965, p. 61).

Pertinent here are Magoun's (1958) conclusions about the function of the ascending reticular system and also the work of others questioning Freud's biology in the light of more current knowledge (Bexton et al., 1954; Delgado et al., 1954; Lilly, 1956; Olds & Milner, 1954; Pribram, 1965; Solomon et al., 1961). All this discussion leads naturally into some more intensive consideration of stimulus hunger in general and its relation to stimulus barrier in particular.

**STIMULUS HUNGER**

Bellak, in his thinking of stimulus barrier, has also made frequent reference to the concept of stimulus hunger. An early reference to stimulus hunger following sensory deprivation is found in the work of Buerger-Prinz & Kaila (1930), who note that in some cases of brain pathology there are no satiation experiences with respect to various stimuli. They feel this is a most impressive example of a lack of stimulus barrier, and not that this hunger reflects a too high or strong stimulus barrier. More recently, (Rapaport, 1967; Wolff, 1960; Rubinfine, 1962; Wallerstein, 1967; Engel, 1962) have used the concept of stimulus aliment or nutriment (as coined by Piaget) to explain certain relationships between the seeking of sensory stimulation on the one hand, and stimulus barrier on the other. Wallerstein cites the conclusions of a panel who agree that the stimulus barrier itself guarantees an appropriate intake of *optimal* level of stimulation in addition to protecting against too much. Spitz (1945, 1946), in his work on hospitalism and anaclitic depression in infants, presents quite convincing evidence of the need for optimal stimulation to ensure survival in infants. Bellak (1963), offering some conceptual considerations of diffuse acting out, says such behaviour occurs from:

> a general overstimulation and sensitization for all stimuli ... An infant needs a certain amount of sensory input for development ... It also seems that a "system" may get a permanent overload; such a person then has a lifelong experience of excessive stimulus hunger, matched only by the inability for containment and the constant need for discharge ... (p. 381)

We often deal with the apparent paradox where a person attempts to reduce the impact of a stimulus upon himself through stimulus-seeking behaviour. Sometimes we have to recognize defensive raising and lowering of thresholds through such behaviour. Perhaps the quest for excitement serves to reduce the effectiveness of other potentially more threatening stimuli, such as those resulting from closeness in object relations. Attention is thus deflected from the relatively more conflictual to a less conflictual source of stimulation.

There are other ways as well to understand the apparent paradox of people seeking overstimulation, who by all other indications have a very *low* stimulus barrier. Many a frenetic searcher of stimuli suffered greatly as a child from being exposed to the frequent rantings and ravings of a psychotic mother who provided a maternal and household setting of chronic overexcitement. We might assume that such a person was left helpless and undefended, with no provision for effectively warding off massive stimulus assaults. The quest in adolescence and young adulthood for similar stimulation might represent an attempt to master the early trauma through repetition. It seems likely that this stimulus hunger results not from stimulus deprivation and/or a strong stimulus barrier, but from a chronic overstimulation in infancy and childhood and/or a weak stimulus barrier—despite their apparent ability to tolerate high levels of sensory input.

## CUMULATIVE TRAUMA, OBJECT RELATIONS AND MOTHERING

The term "cumulative trauma", introduced by Khan (1963), can replace "traumatic neurosis" to bring fresh perspective to the developmental and ego aspects of stimulus barrier. Khan contrasts the nature of cumulative trauma with what has been called traumatic neurosis:

> My argument is that cumulative trauma is the result of the breaches in

the mother's role as a protective shield over the whole course of the child's development, from infancy to adolescence—that is to say, in all those areas of experience where the child continues to need the mother as an auxiliary ego to support his immature and unstable ego functions. … Cumulative trauma thus derives from the strains … in the context of his ego dependence on the mother as his protective shield and auxiliary ego (p. 290 f.).

Singly, these breaches need not be traumatic, but may achieve the effect of trauma, affecting the stimulus barrier, as they accumulate silently over the course of time. Anna Freud also refers to cumulative trauma as successive failures of the mother to act as the child's protective shield, but she feels this trauma occurs only during infancy, when the child is most vulnerable to stresses and strain. Like Khan, Rangell (1967) sees that cumulative and retrospective trauma may result from events not traumatic at any one point in life, but which become traumatic when their magnitude has accumulated sufficiently so that they would have such effects on anyone when the sensitization or reaction point of the particular host had been reached.

Rubinfine (1962) notes how attempts at relative autonomy from thralldom to painful stimuli are originally directed to percepts threatening object loss, and thus have a special role in conserving object relations. Engel (1962) indicates that when there is loss of supplies needed to retain an object and thus to enhance self-esteem, and all solutions to regain the object fail, there may be a giving up of the object and a raising of the barrier against stimuli from outside. Infants experiencing unusual stress may have a reduced readiness to perceive external stimuli and to organize perception (Brody & Axelrad, 1966). We should then find an inverse relationship between cumulative physiological stress and the capacity for object perception which leads to object cathexis.

The relationship between stimulus barrier and mothering could hardly be called new, considering that Freud, in 1895, had this to say: When the helpful person has performed the work of the specific action in the external world for the helpless one (child), the latter is in a position … to carry out in the interior of his body the activity necessary for removing the endogenous stimulus (p. 318).

Khan elaborates on Freud's ideas:

If we replace in Freud's model "the undifferentiated vesicle of a substance that is susceptible to stimulation" by a live human infant, then we get what Winnicott (1962) has described as "an infant in care". The infant in care has for his protective shield the caretaking mother (p. 290).

He adds that the mother's role as a protective shield constitutes the average expectable environment for the anaclitic needs of the infant. By making herself available as a protective shield, she enables growth of autonomous ego functions and instinctual processes, and allows herself to become maximally receptive to the infant's needs. She also facilitates the synthetic functioning of the ego, and helps to build up primary narcissism by lending the infant her own ego functions through her role as a protective shield. Khan's reference to Winnicott's notion that 'an infant in care has for his protective shield the caretaking mother" is expanded here by quoting from Winnicott:

> The mother who is able to give herself over, for a limited spell, to ... her natural task, is able to protect her infant's going-on-being. ... If reacting to impingements is the pattern of an infant's life, then there is a serious interference with the natural tendency that exists in the infant to become an integrated unit, able to have a self with a past, present and future ... (1963, p. 86).

Parallel lines of thought have been expressed by Jacobson (1964), who says that maternal stimulation of motor, proprioceptive, kinaesthetic, touch, temperature, visual and acoustic pleasure experience promotes ego growth; by Rubinfine (1962), who says that maternal care can serve as an adequate buffer against too intense stimulation; and by Murphy (1962), who concludes that a child's thresholds for tension are dependent upon the total dynamic setting, especially the mother–child relation. Benjamin (1961), too, stresses that the mother-figure must intervene to help in tension-reduction or else the infant would be overwhelmed by stimuli and become prone to outbursts of undifferentiated negative affect expression. Elsewhere he states that the enhanced vulnerability of the infant during that time when the passive stimulus barrier is no longer effective and the active one has not developed makes greater demands on the mother or mother-substitute. During this critical period, the infant's protective function must "... be taken over by the mother, undoubtedly the best of all potential 'stimulus barriers' for the young infant, though by no means always a successful one in practice ..." (Benjamin, 1965, p. 62).

Winnicott goes so far as to define inadequate mothering as identical with her failure as a stimulus barrier, or when she allows too many impingements to reach the child during its infancy so that it cannot achieve a real ego or "true self". Because impingements are so disruptive to true ego integration, they lead to premature or disruptive defensive integration and functioning (Winnicott, 1958, 1960, 1963). Following Winnicott's observations, Guntrip (1964) defines bad mothering as the permitting of impingements on the infant, or forcing the infant to be aware of pressures of external and interfering reality when he is not feeling such needs. Impingement is thus an intrusion on the infant at times when he is not reaching out actively into the outer world for stimulation, and it results in forms of withdrawal from the unwanted impact. Khan (1963) sees three types of failure of the mother as a protective shield: (1) excessive intrusion of the mother's pathology; (2) loss of, or separation from, the mother; (3) constitutional sensitivity of the child imposing handicaps on the mother. The effects of strain and impingements in the mother's role as a protective shield may lead to any or all of the following conditions: premature ego development; special responsiveness to the mother's mood; precocious functioning without a "coherent ego"; excessive concern for the mother; and/ or precocious organization of inner and outer reality, and disruption of the synthetic function. Finally, we quote Rubinfine's statement of the mother's function as stimulus barrier:

> ... maternal care serves as an adequate buffer against too intense external or internal stimulation. However, if the maternal partner adds to the excessive external stimulation, or if internal stimuli are too intense or prolonged, the result is that aggression differentiates first ... it seems to me that such a failure of mothering is responsible for the reduction in the effectiveness of the stimulus barrier ... (1962, p. 269).

I believe that familiarity with the way the mother fails to assume the role of the stimulus barrier provides an empirical basis for gauging degrees of adaptiveness–maladaptiveness of the stimulus barrier as an ego function.

## SOME CRITICISMS OF THE STIMULUS BARRIER CONCEPT

One of the major difficulties in the early literature on stimulus barrier was the failure to differentiate clearly between a biological–neurological model of the psychic apparatus (and, in particular, stimulus barrier) and a psychological one. The notion which appears most questionable from a conceptual point of view is Freud's description of the perceptive apparatus as having two layers: an external protective barrier against stimuli whose task it is to diminish stimulation, and a surface behind it which receives the stimuli, namely the system Pcpt.–Cs. Thus Freud said, "stimulus barrier is one of two layers of a purely psychological structural concept 'the perceptive apparatus of the mind'" (1925). At another time, Freud thought of the *Reizschutz* in more neurophysiological terms, in which sources of excitation come up against nerve endings and are broken up into quotients by "contact barriers", summation and resistance in the paths of conduction in neurons (1895, p. 315). Bergman & Escalona (1949) feel these switches in conceptual level make stimulus barrier a baffling and provocative concept applied by Freud to a variety of related but not identical phenomena. Wallerstein (1967), summarizing a panel report, emphasized the conceptual problems in making the transition from biological to psychological consideration, yet concluded that, in the long run, neurophysiology and psychoanalysis complement each other. This way of putting the matter in a sense begs the question, or at least diverts us with a ready-made reconciliation without going into careful theory-building analysis. To my mind, the most thoughtful critical discussion of Freud's model-building with respect to stimulus barrier is offered by Holt. He notes that Freud sometimes thinks of the shield as anatomical (sense organs arranged for the reception of and protection against stimuli), while later he makes it one of two layers of a purely psychological structural concept. In a review of Freud's biological assumptions, Holt (1965a) elaborates this issue:

> The central concept of the protective shield is tantalizingly elusive … When he first introduces it, by his fanciful genetic hypothesis of a one-celled organism, the protective crust baked on by environmental energies is clearly physical in nature. Then … he switches to the realm of metaphor: the barrier is no longer physical, since "preparedness of anxiety and the hypercathexis of the receptive system constitute the last line of defense of the shield against stimuli" (Freud, 1920, p. 31). On the one hand, it sounds continually as if the protective shield is some sort of physical barrier, since it guards against the inflow of physical energies which have to be mastered lest they overwhelm the organism; yet the rupture of the barrier in traumatic neurosis does *not* mean that the skin is broken, for we are told that a "gross physical injury caused *simultaneously* by the trauma *diminishes* the chances that neurosis will develop" ( Freud, 1920p. 33).

> If Freud had kept to an anatomical-physiological model, he would never have been able to make his concept perform such gymnastics and would not have approached an explanation in this way at all (pp. 116–117).

Most recently, Holt has summarized this point by saying that Freud relied too much on metaphor instead of serious model-building.

> The basic trouble is that this metaphorical way of thinking makes too many equations and generalizations about matters that are determined by more or less independent structures (specific sensory thresholds, absolute and differential; thresholds of emotional arousal; empathy; capacity to concentrate and isolate, etc.) (Holt, personal communication, 1967).

Now that these internal inconsistencies have been noted, I would like to develop further the clinical usefulness of this concept. Perhaps our final model of stimulus barrier as an adaptive ego function will not depart too much from Freud's original concept, even if the latter stands only as an "analogue" to the phenomena we have been studying.

## REVIEW OF STIMULUS BARRIER CONCEPT AS EGO FUNCTION

The position taken here is that stimulus barrier can best be conceptualized as a complex ego function having multiple component factors rather than as a simple threshold measure of concretized "membrane". A review of pertinent literature will lead to a specific reformulation of stimulus barrier as used in our current work on ego functions generally.

In this connexion, Freud (1892–1899) described the first threshold, representing the stimulus barrier as that quantity of excitation from the outside, coming against nerve endings and broken up into quotients, below which no quotient at all comes into being. The effectiveness of stimuli is thus restricted more or less to medium quantities. Germane to the threshold discussions were Freud's considerations of "contact barriers" and "cortical layers", related to the receptive and protective functions of the stimulus barrier (1895, 1920). Recently, the threshold notion has been elaborated, for instance, by Bellak, who, in a clinical context, describes certain forms of acting out as resulting from: a general overstimulation and sensitization for all stimuli—in the sense of a much lowered threshold for both input and output (1963).

Engel (1962, p. 117) views stimulus barrier as a threshold apparatus of the autonomous ego which includes systems of perception. Shevrin & Toussieng (1965) define threshold functionally as a protective measure controlling cognition of cravings.

Hints that thresholds are not such a simple matter when considered in relation to *Reizschutz* come from a good deal of speculation and empirical data that they may be either raised or lowered when excitations increase. One consequence of a raised threshold representing a lowered stimulus barrier is the defence of withdrawal (Rubinfine, 1962). Allied to this is Anna Freud's observation (1967) that children react with either sensitization (lowering of thresholds) or adaptation (raising of thresholds) when there is a traumatic on-slaught of stimuli. Similarly, Bridger (1962) notes the apparent paradox that a strong stimulus produces sleep in the neonate, but when the stimulus intensity increases, a point is reached where the baby awakens. The same phenomena are described by Cameron (1963), who says that a low or weak stimulus barrier accounts for such behaviour as being engrossed in activity, or falling asleep. The issue of raising and lowering of thresholds is discussed most extensively by Shevrin & Toussieng (1962, 1965). In the context of tactile stimuli especially, they state : "... the main ways ... these children cope with tactile conflicts is either by a defensive raising of thresholds ... or through protective fluctuations in the physical distance between themselves and other people ..." (1965, p. 311).

Elaborating on defensive withdrawal as a means of coping with excessive stimulation, they state that when thresholds are excessively raised and the child is spending considerable time sleeping, impoverishment of inner stimulation then gets matched by withdrawal from external stimuli, as more and more potential satisfactions become a threat and require compensatory thresholds.

Engel (1962) also sees a defensive or paradoxical behavioural heightening of the stimulus barrier among people for whom it is constitutionally low, leading to defensive withdrawal following attempts to reduce incoming stimuli. Schizophrenic children, especially, would appear to show a hyposensitivity to strong sensory stimulation. Goldfarb summarizes these observations 'The term 'hypersensitivity' may be confusing since sometimes it signifies sensory threshold and at other times signifies manifestations of distress and defensive avoidance" (1961, p. 96). He goes on to say that hypersensitivity is not the consequence only of lowered sensory thresholds (acuity), but also of the *integration* of sensory experience.

Perhaps the best-known work on thresholds in the newborn is that of Bergman & Escalona (1949), who also refer to protection against stimuli by thresholds. Although they would probably see stimulus barrier purely as a threshold measure, they do state its relation to ego functioning by saying that when the stimulus barrier is too low or too high, ego development is interfered with. Escalona (personal communication, 1967) prefers to limit the term "stimulus barrier" to perceptual sensitivity, since it is descriptive and "has the advantage that one is not committed to a host of theoretical implications". Thus she opts to steer clear of conceptualizing stimulus barrier as a complex, adaptive ego function. My own preference is to lay bare the various theoretical positions, wade cautiously into the ambiguities, and see if the rich theoretical and clinical background for the concept permits us to treat stimulus barrier as a complex, adaptive ego function, having various components in addition to sensory thresholds.

Apparently all people are endowed congenitally with threshold potentials for stimuli in all sensory modalities, and thus bring to bear in their total response repertoire something called "state" of the organism. But the ego, in its totality of developmental vicissitudes and multiple functions, is responsible for the eventuation of congenitally determined sensory thresholds in each person's unique mode of responding to stimuli by *organizing and integrating* his sensory experience. So there are ego response measures other than absolute or differential thresholds for stimuli, which determine the status of stimulus barrier as an ego function. The literature has often focused on either the threshold aspect or the integrative aspect of sensory experience.

A focus on the congenital component alone might be inferred from Anna Freud, who stated (1967) that there is a constitutional tolerance underlying individual differences in the degree of stimuli with which one can cope without being endangered. A view which holds the stimulus barrier as congenitally determined, but which defines "congenital" in terms broader than the purely genetic, is presented by Greenacre. She feels that an overload of potential in the prenatal, neonatal and immediate postnatal experience leads to "a genuine physiological sensitivity, a kind of increased indelibility of reaction to experience ..." 1941, p. 50). Then there are numerous references which focus on environmental impact as most crucial for the stimulus barrier, and we come across such notions as Benjamin's "*overstimulation* during critical periods" (1965); Bellak's concern that "a 'system' may get a permanent *overload*" (1963); Winnicott's treatment of *impingements* (1963); Kris's discussion of "a specific kind of overstimulation which was bound to produce mounting tension in the child" (1962); Wallerstein's panel discussion of *surplus excitation* in the postnatal period (1967); and Furst's description of the mental apparatus being *flooded* (1967b). I have underlined certain key terms which, together with other such frequently found words as *overwhelming, bombarding, disorganizing*, could form a lexicon of terms found in the psychoanalytic literature alerting us to what happens when there is a breach in the stimulus barrier.

According to Freud, a breach in the stimulus barrier is a function of (1) the strength and intensity, and (2) the degree of preparedness of the barrier.

Brody & Axelrad (1966) review literature on interrelationships between congenital "states", i.e. and other activities of the organism (Brazelton, 1962; Brown, 1964; Escalona, 1962; Paine, 1965). They conclude that differences in state affect the neonate's freedom to distinguish and adapt to external stimuli. And, of course, when we speak of organism–environment interactions directed towards adaptation, we are considering the ego, or at least a potential ego. It should be noted that other ego functions, particularly the autonomous and synthetic, have traditionally been regarded as having both congenital and other elements.

Freud made an explicit statement of the stimulus barrier as a "potential ego", ego root or nucleus. I present here Benjamin's summary of Freud's position, which states that the stimulus barrier is a true *precursor* of various aspects of defensive and adaptive ego functioning:

> This concept of the *Reizschutz* as a prototypic homologue of some defensive and adaptive functions of the ego, or perhaps even a true precursor in the sense of a co-determinant of one important but limited ego function, seems entirely plausible. ... Specifically, individual variability in the degree of success with which the young infant masters external stimulation by this means may turn out ... to have some demonstrable predictive value as a co-determinant ... of defensive and adaptive ego functioning as a whole (Benjamin, 1965p. 63 f.)

Benjamin himself (1959, 1963), using a variety of behavioural indices, developed a scale of how infants protect themselves from excessive stimulation by actively exerting effort. These indices have, he claims, proved to be one of our more accurate predictors of later ego development. Freud's other followers also have emphasized that the mastery aspect may be regarded as a prototype or precursor of later ego functioning (Hartmann, 1933). Expanding on Hartmann's work about the conflict-free sphere of ego function, Rapaport comments, in a note to Bergman & Escalona's major paper (1949), that unusual endowments in children with special sensitivity to stimuli facilitate conflict-free solutions of problems, and are related to innate differences in stimulus barrier. There will be fragmentary development of ego functions, particularly those related to intellect. The need to erect a secondary protective barrier against external stimuli, say Bergman & Escalona, produces the capacity for certain ego functions that ordinarily would mature at a later date.

Integration of sensory experience is the focus of Goldfarb's (1961) work with schizophrenic children, which convinced him that hypersensitivity to stimuli is not a simple consequence of sensory acuity or lowered sensory thresholds, but also of the integration of sensory experience by an active, volitional effort of the ego. A most compelling presentation of the relation of mastery of stimuli to ego development is offered by Murphy:

> ... the average expectable amount of stimulation is more than some infants and children can handle, while it is insufficient for others. Thus, the area of management of stimulation, whether eliciting more of it or selecting and reducing it, is *not only a basic coping task related to sensory thresholds ... but is central for shaping coping style ...* 91962, p. 3390.

Holt (1948) states that sensitivity, receptivity and perceptivity are not related merely to threshold or a constitutional barrier against stimuli. He feels these observable events are involved with a whole set of ego functions which grow up to take over and extend the job originally performed by the neonatal stimulus barrier. The ego functions then operate in a unitary fashion, and could be generalized to a *higher level of abstraction as the ego equivalent of the functional stimulus barrier of infancy* (my italics). Holt's position seems consistent with my own, and more or less summarizes the major point of what this paper is attempting to say about stimulus barrier as an ego function.

## STIMULUS BARRIER: ACTIVE OR PASSIVE MECHANISM?

Any consideration of mastery must imply active, if not "volitional", efforts on the part of the ego, so Freud's (1920) original notes on mastery of excessive stimulation in the repetition compulsion might be regarded as a good foundation for conceptualizing an active stimulus barrier in addition to regarding it as merely a congenital threshold. The latter was the focus of considerations regarding *Reizschutz* as essentially passive and a developmental consequence of certain neonatal, neurological maturation. It would seem as though passive aspects of the stimulus barrier refer to a certain neurological state of affairs in the neonate. Spitz (1950a, 1950b) has dwelled at length on the neonatal stimulus barrier as a manifestation of neural immaturity which recedes after several months. Emphasis on the passive aspects even of so-called active mastery comes from Pumpian-Mindlin's review (1967) of some aspects of the repetition compulsion which are now questionable, e.g. the presentation of the repetition compulsion and death instinct as primitive, stereotyped, passive defensive behaviour, exemplified in traumatic dreams, traumatic neuroses and fate neuroses. For example, in considering stimulus barrier as arising not from the id, but as an autonomous ego function, Hartmann says: "It might be that the ways in which infants deal with stimuli ... are later used by the ego in an active way. We consider this active use for its own purposes of primordial forms of reaction a rather general characteristic of the developed ego ..." (1950, p. 125).

Holt (1965) feels it is difficult to account for ego autonomy as long as the assumption of a basically passive psychic apparatus is retained, and concludes that Freud's model of the protective shield in "Beyond the Pleasure Principle" pictures the organism as passive and helplessly at the mercy of dangerous energies penetrating the presumably passive screening effects of the *Reizschutz*. Holt invokes Murray's (1938) concept of "press" as one way of describing how active coping is involved in escaping from stimuli. He feels that input from the environment is relevant to behaviour not only as it provokes passive reactivity to stimuli, but also as it supplies information and tonic support. A major contribution to the active-integrative aspects of stimulus barrier comes from Brody & Axelrad:

> The essential nature of the protective shield with which we are dealing is not whether the shield can be pierced by stimuli of a certain intensity—that is a matter of neurophysiological responsiveness. We are concerned rather with the psychological organization of manifold stimuli which impinge upon the organism—an active, integrative process, rather than a mechanical registration: a process advanced by both the protective *and* the receptive functions of the protective shield ... (1966, p. 224).

So the concern here is with both the passive and the active elements of stimulus barrier, where the passive aspects relate to the receptive function (threshold) and the active aspects are modeled on the protective function (active accommodation to stimuli). Hartmann (1953), too, feels there is both an active and a passive stimulus barrier which can be broken through, an idea on which Holt elaborates by saying that autonomy from the environment may involve freedom from distracting stimuli by either of two strategies which cut down afferent inputs to the cortex: sensory deprivation or concentration on something else. The former is a passive function, the latter active.

We come now to the most recent, and to me the most original and persuasive, presentation of stimulus barrier as an active, adaptive ego function, and this is Benjamin's approach, which does not disregard the clinically valid observations of its passive aspects as well. His article is a major contribution to *Psychoanalysis and Current Biological Thought* (Greenfield & Lewis, 1965) and every contribution in that book is consistent with his own updating of some of Freud's general biological notions, as well as those which refer only to stimulus barrier. He bases his conclusions on the observation that infants display increased sensitivity to stimulation at age three to four weeks, and have EEGs which shift from being relatively flat and undifferentiated to being distinctly periodic. Benjamin assumes that this sudden appearance of behavioural change is a function of neuroanatomical and physiological maturation at this particular time, and he states his major position:

> We consider that our findings point rather strongly to the conclusion that the so-called stimulus barrier, or protective shield against stimulation, of the very young infant (which is, of course, only a relative and in no sense an absolute "barrier") is ... a purely passive mechanism, due to relative lack of functioning connections. In contrast, we see later how the older infant and young child (as well as the adult) often exerts active efforts to protect himself from excessive stimulation (1965, p. 60).

He believes that the capacity to shut out stimuli actively starts at approximately eight to ten weeks and matures rapidly. The stimulus barrier is important in that the mature organism has developed a variety of ways of receiving, processing and warding off stimulation. He thus postulates two barriers against external stimulation in infancy: the *passive* barrier, which is a function of a lack of neural maturation, and an *active* barrier, which might be a precursor or prototype of defence, yet is in itself a more advanced stage of neural maturation:

> This concept of the *Reizschutz* as a prototypic homologue of some defensive and *adaptive functions of the ego* [my italics], or perhaps even a true precursor in the sense of a co-determinant of one important but limited ego function, seems entirely plausible or even probable with respect to our "active stimulus barrier", but much less so with respect to the passive neonatal barriers. In the latter case one is at best dealing with an analogy without genetic continuity; in the former, with a phenomenon that, in one respect at least, is a true precursor, and beyond

that may conceivably have value as an indicator of other defensive and adaptive aspects of ego functioning (p. 63).

Benjamin interprets recent neurological findings to mean that between four weeks (the disappearance of the passive stimulus barrier) and eight weeks (the appearance of the active stimulus barrier), there is no mechanism at all for warding off stimuli, and the infant is so vulnerable that all protection must come from the mother. A good deal of Benjamin's paper is devoted to citing the pertinent neurological evidence for those physiological mechanisms which are central influences on afferent transmission.

The studies which involve the question of central influences on afferent transmission, or the physiological mechanisms pertinent to an active stimulus barrier, are available to the interested reader (Dawson, 1958a, 1958b; French, 1960; Galambos, 1955; Granit & Kaada, 1953; Hagbarth & Kerr, 1954; Livingston, 1958; Magni et al., 1959; Magoun, 1958; Perl et al., 1962; Satterfield, 1962; Scherrer & Hernández-Peón, 1955).

A number of works adopt a point of view which comes close to the position advanced in this paper: that stimulus barrier is an adaptive ego function, locatable somewhere in the hierarchy of other ego functions, and is comprised of various component factors. One such study is that by Murphy (1962), who provides some specific information, gleaned from a small sample of children, about the interrelationships of constitutional strength of the barrier and some other activities (in this case, strength of drive) that it affects. The children with average drive and marked sensitivity did not show the good capacity to struggle with deprivations as did those with marked sensitivity and high drive. Without high drive, high sensitivity tended to produce withdrawing tendencies and little effort to develop active, direct methods of dealing with the environment. With respect to devices used for the active management of stimulation, it is well to note Murphy's conclusion:

Shutting out stimuli that come at an unwanted time by turning away so as not to see, covering up ears, protesting, rejecting habitually stimuli that cannot be handled successfully, diminishing or terminating stimulation that is too much for pleasure, or after satiation; or in greater extremity, destroying or attacking painful stimuli. On the positive side of stimulus management, we see the beginnings not only of choice and selection, approach and seeking, but of techniques for evoking response, getting more of interpersonal stimulation as well as impersonal stimuli;

restructuring or merely organizing stimuli to enhance the satisfaction from exchanges with the environment ... (Murphy, 1962, p. 339)

For "successful and unsuccessful management" we need only substitute the terms "adaptive" and "maladaptive" to see how closely Murphy's ideas come to our own with respect to stimulus barrier as an adaptive ego function.

Waelder (1967) sees the stimulus barrier as an "active regulator", also implying an adaptive function. He feels that implicit in the idea of traumatic excitations powerful enough to break through the shield are the assumptions that the organism can deal with an onslaught of stimuli by either autoplastic adjustment (making an internal change so as to live with the external conditions without unbearable suffering) or by alloplastic adjustment (bringing about changes in the outer world to eliminate the source of tension). Both methods are used in the sense that the organism tries to eliminate as much of the outer disturbance as possible and to "accept and learn to live with the remainder". Only when the stimulus barrier is taxed by too much stimulation and the person cannot handle the tidal wave by the usual processes of autoplastic and alloplastic adjustment will there be a breakdown of the personality, analogous to physical diseases where a massive virulent invasion can break down even an otherwise immune organism. One more quotation documenting the basis for the present position comes from Goldfarb's discussion of the adaptive, integrating efforts of the ego in its attempt to master stimuli:

The term "hypersensitivity" may be confusing since sometimes it signifies lowered sensory threshold, and at other times it signifies manifestations of distress and defensive avoidance. These *two facets of ego response* [my italics] ought to be differentiated for: (1) threshold of sensory acuity, and (2) the child's integration of the sensory experience in terms of acceptance or exclusion, pleasure or distress, comfort or discomfort, and its meaning in terms of object relations ... (Goldfarb, 1961, p. 96) .

These "two facets of ego response" are essentially the two component factors of stimulus barrier which we are attempting to measure or scale, and are described in the final section of this paper.

## STIMULUS BARRIER AS A REFORMULATION:
## AN ADAPTIVE EGO FUNCTION

The complex and often contradictory ideas presented thus far require some new organization and context in which to understand stimulus barrier as not only a sensory or perceptual threshold measure, but one involving ego responses as well, with greater or lesser integrational–organizational aspects.

Let us now turn to some of these additional specific functions of the ego pertinent to *Reizschutz*: specific motor and sensorimotor responses other than direct sensory threshold indicators; defensive functioning; active ego efforts; and those aspects of the ego which reflect on object relations and stimulus barrier.

While measures of sensory threshold from which we may make inferences about the nature of the stimulus barrier are not always easy to obtain outside the laboratory, nevertheless it is often possible to make inferences about stimulus barrier from direct observations of such responses as motor discharge patterns. Holt (1965b) and Rapaport (1951), for example, claim that stimulus barrier is related to motor thresholds as well as receptivity to stimuli. Agitated or chaotic motor behaviour and sleep disturbances are among the most reliable indicators we have that the stimulus barrier tends towards the maladaptive, and these have been extensively considered in the literature. Among the many who have been concerned with specific aspects of motor discharge and stimulus barrier has been Bellak (1963), who describes some children who have been exposed to tremendous overstimulation of nearly all sense modalities. He feels that the person's system then gets a permanent overload, leading to a life-long inability for containment and the constant need for discharge. Benjamin (1965) notes how the overstimulated infant becomes prone to outbursts of undifferentiated affect expression. He also says that the mechanism for dealing with excessive stimulation through more directed motor action does not develop until much later than early infancy. Here he is obviously referring to the *adaptive, coping function of motor activity* in containing motor stimulation rather than to diffuse motor discharge as an expressive indicator of a maladaptive stimulus barrier.

Recent research on sleep, generally, has illuminated some aspects of sleep and the stimulus barrier. Cameron (1963) has observed that some adults fall asleep in the midst of excessive sensory bombardment. In referring to impingements produced by stimulus deprivations, Provence & Lipton (1962) found that infants in institutions slept longer than non-institutionalized babies. Discussing how falling asleep may be used defensively very early in life, Wallerstein (1967) sees sleep as an anlage of defence and, in his view, stimulus barrier.

## APPENDIX

Many psychoanalytic concepts suffer from a lack of adequate formulation and precise definition. A current study Bellak & Hurvich, (1969); Bellak et al., (1969, 1970); Bellak, (1969); Hurvich & Bellak, (1968), supported by the NIMH and conducted under the auspices of the New York University Postdoctoral Program for Study and Research in Psychology, provides the context for the definition, measurement and construct validity of stimulus barrier as an adaptive ego function. Stimulus barrier was also examined in terms of its various relationships to 11 other ego functions also explored in this larger research project.

To review briefly the general scope of this study, its main purpose is to evaluate and compare the ego function patterns of schizophrenic, neurotic and normal subjects by measurements evolved from clinical interviews, psychological test data and experimental procedures. The findings from these also would make it possible to address the interrelationships among the various ego functions, and would provide a good springboard for beginning to formulate an empirically based hierarchical order for ego functions. Thus we could see where stimulus barrier, for one, falls in the total picture of ego functioning. The 12 ego functions being studied are: reality-testing; judgment; sense of reality; regulation and control of drives, affects and impulses; object relations; thought processes; adaptive regression in the service of the ego; defensive functioning; stimulus barrier; autonomous functioning; synthetic-integrative functioning; and mastery competence. Definitions and component factors were worked out in detail for all 12 ego functions. They formed a basis for developing a *Manual for Rating Ego Functions*, which is keyed to questions from a *Guide for a Clinical Interview*. In constructing the Rating Manual, a seven-point (or modal stop) rating scale was developed to measure each ego function, with modal stop (1) representing the least adaptive manifestations and stop (7) representing the most adaptive. The functions, then, as defined for this study, could be scaled and then rated for interview data in terms of general adaptiveness–maladaptiveness, as well as in terms of the component factors unique to each function as they reflect the degree of adaptation.

I shall present the Interview Rating Manual definition, and component factors for stimulus barrier. High inter-rater reliability achieved in measuring stimulus barrier according to these scales adds credence to the construct validity of stimulus barrier, as well as other functions, as adaptive ego functions. It is defined in terms of its component factors: (*a*) *threshold* for sensitivity to, or awareness of, stimuli impinging upon various sensory modalities; (*b*) nature of *responses* to various levels of sensory stimulation, in terms of the extent of disorganization, avoidance, withdrawal or active coping mechanisms employed to deal with them. Both thresholds and response to stimuli contribute to adaptation by the organism's potential for responding to high, average or low sensory input so that optimal homeostasis (as well as adaptation) is maintained: (*a*) in the average expectable environment; and (*b*) under conditions of unusual stress. *Stimulus barrier* determines, in part, how resilient a person is, or how he readapts after the stress and impingements are no longer present.

Threshold, as described for component (*a*), refers not only to reaction to external stimuli, but also to internal stimuli which provide proprioceptive cues, or those originating within the body but eventually impinging on sensory organs. Light, sound, temperature, pain, pressure, drugs and intoxicants are the stimuli to be considered relevant to assessing thresholds.

Responses, other than threshold variables, referred to in component (*b*), include motor responses, coping mechanisms, effects on sleep and certain aspects of psychosomatic illness. In many ways component (*b*) would seem to overlap with the synthetic function of the ego.

Together, the two components represent a way of scaling the degree to which the ego effectively and adaptively organizes and integrates sensory experience.

## ACKNOWLEDGEMENTS

This paper was written in connexion with the New York University Postdoctoral Program for Study and Research in Psychology. Much of it relates to a study, "Ego Function Patterns in Schizophrenia", supported by NIMH grant 14260 to Leopold Bellak, M.D., Principal Investigator, carried out under the auspices of the Department of Psychology, Postdoctoral Program, New York University. I wish to extend thanks especially to Dr Bellak for his help in preparing and reviewing this material; and to acknowledge with appreciation the cooperation of the Psychiatry Department, The Roosevelt Hospital, N.Y.C., in making its clinical facilities available for the project. As this paper is an integral part of the whole research project, I would also like to acknowledge with thanks the various contributions of other members of the research team, especially Marvin Hurvich. Ph.D.

## SUMMARY

Stimulus barrier may be reformulated as a complex ego function measurable along a dimension of adaptiveness–maladaptiveness. It refers to those structures and functions which enable a person to regulate amounts of inner and outer stimulation so as to maintain optimal homeostasis and adaptation. The "receptive" and "protective" functions referred to by Freud have been elaborated here to include both sensory thresholds and also the organization of sensory experience. Together, these "component factors" of stimulus barrier as an ego function have been organized and developed into a rating scale keyed to interview questions (see Appendix). These scales have been used to rate data from clinical interviews and, along with similarly constructed scales for II other ego functions, may be useful in determining the relationship of stimulus barrier to other ego functions and in determining its place in the hierarchy of ego functions.

## REFERENCES

Amacher, P. (1965). Freud's neurological education and its influence on psychoanalytic theory. *Psychological Issues* monograph. 16.

Bellak, L. (1963). Acting out: conceptual and therapeutic considerations. *American Journal of Psychotherapy* 17:375–389.

——— (1969). The systematic diagnosis of the schizophrenic syndrome. *Dynamic Psychiatry* 2: 148–157.

———. & Hurvich, M. (1969). A systematic study of ego functions. *Journal of Nervous and Mental Disease* 148:569–585.

——— ——— & Crawford, P. (1969). Psychotic egos. *Psychoanalytic Review* 56: 526–542.

——— ——— Gediman, H. & Crawford, P. J. (1970). Study of ego functions in the schizophrenic syndrome. *Archives of General Psychiatry* 23:326–336.

Benjamin, J.D. (1959). Prediction and psychopathological theory. In L. Jessner & E. Pavenstedt (eds.), *Dynamic Psychopathology in Childhood.* New York: Grune & Stratton.

——— (1961). Some developmental observations relating to the theory of anxiety. *Journal of the American Psychoanalytic Association* 9:652–668. http://www.pep-web.org/document.php?id=apa.009.0652a

——— (1963). Further comments on some developmental aspects of anxiety. In H. S. Gaskill (ed.), *Counterpoint: Libidinal Object and Subject.* New York: International Universities Press.

———— (1965). Developmental biology and psychoanalysis. In Greenfield, N.S. & Lewis, W.C , eds. *Psycho-analysis and Current Biological Thought.* Madison and Milwaukee: University of Wisconsin Press.

Bergman, P. & Escalona, S. K. (1949). Unusual sensitivities in very young children. *Psychoanalytic Study of the Child* 3–4.
http://www.pep-web.org/document.php?id=psc.003.0121a

Bexton, W. Heron, W. & Scott, T.H. (1954). Effects of decreased variation in the sensory environment. *Canadian Journal of Psychology* 8:70–76.

Brazelton, T.B. (1962). Observations of the neonate. *Journal of Child Psychiatry* 1:38–58.

Bridger, W.H. (1962). Panel discussion: Symposium on research in infancy and early childhood. *Journal of Child Psychiatry* 1:92–107.

Brody, S. & Axelrad, S. (1966). Anxiety, socialization and ego formation in infancy. *International Journal of Psycho-analysis* 47:218–229.
http://www.pep-web.org/document.php?id=ijp.047.0218a

Brown, J. L. (1964). States in newborn infants. *Merrill-Palmer Quarterly* 10:313–327.
*Journal of Child Psychiatry.*

Cameron, N. (1963). *Personality Development and Psychopathology.* Boston: Houghton Mifflin.

Dawson, G. D. (1958a). The central control of sensory inflow. *Proceedings Royal Society of Medicine* 51:531–535.

———— (1959b). The effect of cortical stimulation on transmission through the cuneate nucleus in the anaesthetized rat. *Journal of Physiology*142:2P–3P.

Delgado, J.M.R., Roberts, W.W. & Miller, N.E. (1954). Learning motivated by electrical stimulation of the brain. *American Journal of Physiology* 179:587–593.

Eagle, M. (1962). Personality correlates of sensitivity to subliminal stimulation. *Journal of Nervous and Mental Disease* 34:1–17.
http://www.pep-web.org/document.php?id=zbk.003.0001a

Engel, G.L. (1962). *Psychological Development in Health and Disease.* Philadelphia: Saunders.

Escalona, S. K. (1962). The study of individual differences and the problem of state. *Journal of Child Psychiatry* 1:11–37.
http://www.pep-web.org/document.php?id=paq.031.0001a

Fenichel, O. (1945). *The Psychoanalytic Theory of Neurosis.* New York: Norton.

French, J.D. (1960). The reticular formation. In J. Field et al. (eds.), *Handbook of Physiology* vol. 2 Washington, D.C.: American Physiological Society

Freud, A. (1967). Comments on trauma In *S. S. Furst* 1967a.

———— (1892–9). Extracts from the Fliess papers. *S.E.* 1.
http://www.pep-web.org/document.php?id=se.001.0000a

Freud, S. (1895). Project for a scientific psychology. *SE.* 1.
http://www.pep-web.org/document.php?id=se.001.0000a

———— (1915). Instincts and their vicissitudes. *SE.* 14.
http://www.pep-web.org/document.php?id=se.014.0000a

———— (1920). Beyond the pleasure principle. *SE.* 18.
http://www.pep-web.org/document.php?id=se.018.0000a

———— (1925). A note upon the "mystic writingpad." *SE.* 19.
http://www.pep-web.org/document.php?id=se.019.0000a

———— (1940). An outline of psycho-analysis *SE.* 23.
http://www.pep-web.org/document.php?id=se.001.0000a

Furst, S.S. (ed.) (1967). *A Psychic Trauma.* New York: Basic Books.
http://www.pep-web.org/document.php?id=zbk.080.0029a

———— (1967b) Psychic trauma: a survey. In *S. S. Furst* 1967a.

Galambos, R. (1956). Suppression of auditory nerve activity by stimulation of efferent fibers to the cochlea. *Federal Procedures* 14:53.

Goldfarb, W. (1961). *Childhood Schizophrenia.* Cambridge, MA: Harvard University Press.

Granit, R. & Kaada, B. R. (1952). Influence of stimulation of central nervous structures on muscle spindles in cat. Acta physiol. scand. 27:130–160.

Greenacre, P. (1941). The predisposition to anxiety. *Trauma, Growth and Personality.* London: Hogarth Press, 1953.
http://www.pep-web.org/document.php?id=paq.010.0610a

Greenfield, N. S. & Lewis, W. C. (1965). Psycho-analysis and Current Biological Thought. Madison and Milwaukee: University of Wisconsin Press.

Guntrip, H. (1964). *Personality Structure and Human Interaction.* New York: International Universities Press.

Hagbarth, K.-E. & Kerr, D. I. B. (1954). Central influences on spinal afferent conduction. *Journal of Neurophysiology* 17:295–307.

Hartmann, H. (1933). An experimental contribution to the psychology of obsessive-compulsive neurosis: on remembering completed and uncompleted tasks. In: *Essays on Ego Psychology.* New York: International Universities Press, 1946.

———— (1939). *Ego Psychology and the Problem of Adaptation.* New York: International Universities Press, 1958.
http://www.pep-web.org/document.php?id=zbk.072.0001a

———— (1950). *Comments on the psycho-analytic theory of the ego Essays on Ego Psychology* New York: International Universities Press, 1964.

———— (1953). *Contribution to the metapsychology of schizophrenia Essays on Ego Psychology.* New York: International Universities Press, 1964. http://www.pep-web.org/document.php?id=psc.008.0177a

Holt, R.R. (1948). Some recent applications of Freud's concept of stimulus barrier to psychological research (Unpublished manuscript.)

———— (1965a). A review of Freud's biological assumptions and their influence on his theories. In N. S. Greenfield & W. C. Lewis 1965.

———— (1965b). Ego autonomy revisited. *International Journal of Psycho-Analysis* 46:151–167. http://www.pep-web.org/document.php?id=ijp.046.0151a

Hurvich, M. & Bellak, L. (1968). Ego function patterns in schizophrenia. *Psychological Reports* 22:299–308.

Jacobson, E. (1964). *The Self and the Object World.* New York: International Universities Press.

Khan, M.M.R. (1963). The concept of cumulative trauma. *Psychoanalytic Study of the Child* 18. http://www.pep-web.org/document.php?id=psc.018.0286a

Kris, E. (1956a). The personal myth. *Journal of the American Psychoanalytic Association* 4:653–681. http://www.pep-web.org/document.php?id=apa.004.0653a

————(1956b). The recovery of childhood memories in psychoanalysis. *Psychoanalytic Study of the Child* 11. http://www.pep-web.org/document.php?id=psc.011.0054a

————(1962). Decline and recovery in the life of a three-year-old; or: Data in psychoanalytic perspective on the mother-child relationship. *Psychoanalytic Study of the Child* 17. http://www.pep-web.org/document.php?id=psc.017.0175a

Kris, M. (1964). Discussion remarks: Symposium on infantile trauma. (*Psychoanalytic Research and Development Fund.*)

Lilly, J. C. (1956). Mental effects of reduction of ordinary levels of physical stimuli on intact, healthy persons. *Psychiatry Resources Reports* 5:1–9.

Livingston, R. B. (1958). Central control of afferent activity. In H. H. Jasper et al. (eds.), *Reticular Formation of the Brain.* Boston: Little, Brown.

Magni, F., Melyak, R., Monizzi, G. & Smith, G. J. (1959). Direct pyramidal influences on the dorsal column nuclei. *Archives of Italian Biology* 97:357–377.

Magoun, H.W. (1958). Non-specific brain mechanisms In H. F. Harlow & C. N. Woolsey (eds.), *Biological and Biochemical Bases of Behaviour.*

Madison and Milwaukee: University of Wisconsin Press.

Murphy, L.B. (1962). *The Widening World of Childhood.* New York: Basic Books.

Murray, H.A. et al. (1938). *Explorations in Personality.* New York: Oxford University Press.

Olds, J. & Milner, P. (1954). Positive reinforcement produced by electrical stimulation of septal area and other regions of rat brain. *Journal of Comprehensive Physiology & Psychology* 47:419–427.

Paine, R. S. (1965). The contribution of developmental neurology to child psychiatry. *Journal of Child Psychiatry* 4:353–386.
http://www.pep-web.org/document.php?id=paq.034.0001a

Perl, E.R., Whitlock, D. G. & Gentry, J.R. (1962). Cutaneous projection to second-order neurons of the dorsal column system. *Journal of Neurophysiology* 25:337–358.

Pribram, K. (1965). Freud's Project: an open, biologically based model for psychoanalysis. In N. S. Greenfield & W. C. Lewis, 1965.

Provence, S. & Lipton, R. C. (1962). *Infants in Institutions.* New York: International Universities Press.

Pumpian-Mindlin, E. (1967 Panel: Defence organization of the ego and psychoanalytic technique. *Journal of American Psychoanalytic Association* 15:150–165. http://www.pep-web.org/document.php?id=apa.015.0150a

Rangell, L. (1967). The metapsychology of psychic trauma. In *S. S. Furst* 1967a.

Rapaport, D. (1951). *Organization and Pathology of Thought.* New York: Columbia Universities Press.

——— (1967). The theory of ego autonomy: a generalization. *Bulletin of the Menninger Clinic* 22:13–35.
http://www.pep-web.org/document.php?id=psyche.021a.0001a

Rubinfine, D. L. (1962). Maternal stimulation, psychic structure, and early object relations: with special reference to aggression and denial. *Psychoanalytic Study of the Child* 17.
http://www.pep-web.org/document.php?id=psc.017.0265a

Satterfield, J. H. (1962). Effect of sensorimotor cortical stimulation upon cuneate nuclear output through medial lemniscus in cat. *Journal of Nervous & Mental Disease* 135: 507–512.

Scherrer, H. & Hernández-Peón, R. (1955). Inhibitory influence of reticular formation upon synaptic transmission in gracilis nucleus. *Federal Procedures* 14:132.

Shevrin, H. & Toussieng, P. W. (1962). Conflict over tactile experiences in emotionally disturbed children. *Journal of Child Psychiatry* 1:564–590.

―――― ―――― (1965). Vicissitudes of the need for tactile stimulation in instinctual development. *Psychoanalytic Study of the Child* 20.
http://www.pep-web.org/document.php?id=psc.020.0310a

Solomon, P. et al. (1961). *Sensory Deprivation.* Cambridge, Mass.: Harvard
Universities Press.

Spitz, R. A. (1945). Hospitalism. *Psychoanalytic Study of the Child* 1.
http://www.pep-web.org/document.php?id=psc.001.0053a

―――― (1946). Anaclitic depression. *Psychoanalytic Study of the Child* 2.
http://www.pep-web.org/document.php?id=psc.002.0313a

―――― (1950a ). Anxiety in infancy: a study of its manifestations in the first
year of life. *International Journal of Psycho-analysis* 31:138–143. http://
www.pep-web.org/document.php?id=ijp.031.0138a

―――― (1950b). Relevancy of direct infant observations. *Psychoanalytic Study
of the Child* 5. http://www.pep-web.org/document.php?id=psc.005.0066a

Waelder, R. (1967). Trauma and the variety of extraordinary challenges. In *S.
S. Furst* 1967a.

Wallerstein, R.S. (1967). Panel: Development and metapsychology of the
defence organization of the ego. *Journal of the American Psychoanalytic
Association* 15:130–149.
http://www.pep-web.org/document.php?id=apa.015.0130a

Winnicott, D. W. (1958). *Collected Papers.* New York: Basic Books.

―――― (1960). The theory of the parent–infant relationship. *In The
Maturational Processes and the Facilitating Environment.* New York:
International Universities Press, 1965.
http://www.pep-web.org/document.php?id=ipl.064.0001a

―――― (1963). From dependence towards independence in the development of the individual: *The Maturational Processes and the Facilitating
Environment.* New York: International Universities Press, 1965.
http://www.pep-web.org/document.php?id=ipl.064.0001a

Wolff, P.H. (1960). The developmental psychologies of Jean Piaget and psychoanalysis. *Psychological Issues* Monograph 5.

# Chapter 3: Actual Neurosis and Psychoneurosis

[Gediman, H.K. (1984). Actual neurosis and psychoneurosis. *International Journal of Psycho-Analysis* 65: 191-202. An earlier version of this paper was presented at the Freudian Track Colloquium Meeting of the New York University Postdoctoral Program for Psychoanalysis and Psychotherapy in the Spring of 1982. The paper was one of two on the topic of Actual Neurosis, and its companion paper was delivered by Donald M. Kaplan, Ph.D.]

## INTRODUCTION

The present paper will be concerned primarily with presenting an integrative psychoanalytic approach for understanding the place of the actual neuroses in psychoanalytic thought. Concern with their phenomenology has persisted as strongly as ever even though the nomenclature has changed, for when Freud's early "direct transformation" or first anxiety theory to explain the condition was discarded, so, by and large, was the term, "actual neurosis". At the same time that I shall be presenting an updated overview of the concept in its many guises, I shall be developing my main thesis that an integrative or unified psychoanalytic approach must appreciate how actual neurosis and psycho-neurosis may co-exist in one and the same individual. I shall develop my argument within the context of a critical review of that literature which is the relevant historical background to current psychoanalytic controversies about interpreting such states. Thus I shall look first into Freud's (1895a, 1895b, 1898) early position on the separate nosological status of the actual- and psy-choneuroses and then into Kohut's (1977) either/or view of narcissistic and neurotic disturbances as separate entities, a view which I believe is a traceable outgrowth of Freud's early, but not his later thinking. Next, I shall consider these positions which allow for viewing actual- and psychoneurotic phenom-ena as admixtures across the patient spectrum, notably those developed later by (Freud, 1926; Fenichel, 1945; Schur, 1955; Rangell, 1968: McDougall, 1980; and Gediman, 1982).

Along the way, I shall be returning to two major points. The first is that in the adult, there cannot be, except manifestly and transiently, a contentless mental state. The actual neurotic state always may be elaborated, symbolical-ly. That is, any "pure" affective or somatic experience must be potentially a cognitive-affective experience. The second major point is this: a re-appreciation of the quantitative[2] or intensity dimension along with the structural and dynamic points of view permits us to view actual neurotic states as phenomena that cut across the entire patient spectrum.

I shall close with some remarks on the implications of an integrative, non-polarizing theoretical understanding of psychopathology for the treatment of actual neurotic states while remaining within the same psychoanalytic framework we rely on for the treatment of the psychoneuroses.

It has often been implied that interest in the actual neuroses has waned and the concept has fallen into disrepute. If this is so, then the waning of interest has been more apparent than real. The phenomenon has not really been overlooked in the main, but has been called by many other names than actual neuroses since the early days of psychoanalysis. For a condition or syndrome really does exist, and always has, and it was this that prompted Freud to formulate the actual neuroses, and later prompted Fenichel to elaborate the "damned up state" of accumulated undischarged psychic tensions consciously experienced as more or less "contentless". Freud's early astute clinical observation was directed to this frequently encountered clinical syndrome.

Freud described a syndrome of anxiety due to frustrations. These frustrations were "actual" tensions due to specific sexual noxae ensuing from voluntary or involuntary abstinence: the tensions of frustration ensuing from coitus interruptus; masturbation as an inferior substitute for intercourse; the woman's frustration from the man's premature ejaculation; the man's frustration from fear of impregnating the woman. He was noting a general condition of the actual *sequelae* of insufficient satisfaction in the presence of excitement, and in that respect, his observations appear as valid today as ever. The validity is even more compelling if we shift our attention away from Freud's original limited focus on the specific sexual noxae and on to the broader arena of excitability and frustration in the face of any kind of internal and external stimulation of traumatic intensity.

The first reference to what was shortly to be called the actual neuroses (1898) occurred in Freud's 1895 paper on the anxiety neurosis. There he detailed a clinical syndrome involving the following: irritability and excitation; auditory hyperaesthesia or hypersensitivity to noise; and sleeplessness. In

---

2 While some psychoanalysts would characterize this dimension as the *'psycho-economic point of view'*, I prefer, for my purposes, the idea of a quantitative or intensity dimension. The concept of psycho-economics carries certain metapsychological assumptions about force and energy that my usage does not.

addition, there is anxious expectation, hypochondria, and free-floating anxiety which is "always ready to link itself with any suitable content". I will return to the latter remark of Freud's later on, in connexion with representability and secondary elaboration of tension states.

Fenichel (1945) classified as the actual neuroses the direct symptoms of psychological *conflict*, namely, inhibition of ego function and the associated painful feelings of tension. He said that the first clinical symptoms of the actual neuroses are, in a way that is very similar to those of traumatic neuroses, an automatic expression of the state of being "dammed up". This state is experienced subjectively as being flooded by uncontrolled amounts of increasing tensions and excitement. Sometimes discharge of this accumulated tension is involuntary and explosive, and sometimes it is blocked; in either case the tension often leads to physiological symptoms and the true organic changes of the organ neuroses or psychosomatic disorders. Fenichel also noted that actual neurotics are hypersensitive and irritable because their state of relative insufficiency of ego control makes them react to slight stimuli as though they are intense ones.

Blau (1952) and Rangell (1968) remind us that while the term, "actual neuroses", to designate these states, has fallen into disrepute, the states have been acknowledged all along by other names: terror, traumatic neuroses, anxiety neurosis, visceral anxiety neurosis, psychophysiological reactions, somatizing, and what Waelder (1960) designated as "frustraneous excitement". Now, one may add to this list what Kohut (1977) described as the dreaded anxiety experienced in narcissistic disorders as the anticipated annihilation of the self.

Greenacre (1967) referred to the same susceptibility to traumatic states which disorganizes mentation and other ego activities that later I (1971, 1983) referred to in my work, first on stimulus barrier and then on annihilation anxiety. In a departure from Freud's (1895) early position, I have been assuming an internal-world barrier as well as one for the external world. My position holds that the stimulus barrier concept is applicable to protection from inner as well as outer stimuli, including intensities of stimulation from instinctual drives and inner conflicts. Consequently the clinical state of the actual neuroses refers to an "endogenous replication" (Freud, 1898) of the traumatic neuroses and relates to stimulus barrier failures. References in my earlier work to such matters as overexcitation, flooding, overload, impingement, surplus excitation, and to such observable *sequelae* as torpor, shock, withdrawal, stunned reactions, agitated or chronic motor behaviour, frenzied overactivity, tantrums of rage, and sleep disturbances, were describing experiential *sequelae* of a *failure to dose and regulate stimuli, both internal and external.* I now believe that such *sequelae* are manifestations of the accumulated psychic tensions designated as actual neuroses. Clearly, this is to go beyond the sexual noxae of Freud's more limited vision, as has been done by others before me (Schur, 1955; Rangell, 1963a, 1963b, 1968). The tensions may relate to generally low thresholds, and may originate from a low stimulus barrier, determined either biologically or as the result of chronic early trauma. And a low stimulus barrier, may predispose to unusual intensities in the tensions inherent in psychoneurotic conflict as well as in the actual neurotic states themselves.

Let us now look closely at Freud's original toxic conversion or direct transformation theory that he used to explain the phenomena of the actual neuroses. In distinguishing anxiety neurosis and actual neurosis from "anxiety hysteria", a form of psychoneurosis based on repression, he said, "the affect [of anxiety] does not originate in a repressed idea, but turns out to be not further reducible by psychological analysis, nor amenable to psychotherapy ..." (1895, p. 97). He held that the affect of anxiety is a manifestation of undischarged sexual tensions. In keeping with his attempts to state the data of psychology in neurological terms, he regarded these noxae as somatic excitation deflected from the psyche and "expended subcortically in totally inadequate reactions". In his 1898 paper on "Sexuality in the aetiology of the neuroses", Freud used the term "actual neuroses", for the first time. The aetiology of the actual neurosis was thought to be physical and contemporary or present-day, as contrasted with the psychoneuroses whose origins are psychical and derive from the forgotten or repressed sexual events of childhood. Anxiety was then accounted for always by libido which has been deflected from its normal employment, whenever sexual tensions were increased and not adequately discharged, and it is this that accounts for the actual neuroses, regarded now as endogenous replicas of traumatic neuroses. Later (1915) Freud was to substitute "stimulus" for exogenous excitation, and "instinct" for endogenous excitation. It should be clear now how my reformulation of Freud"s stimulus barrier concept relates to Freud's thinking on these issues. In 1898, anxiety neurosis and neuraesthenia were named as the actual neuroses, to which list hypochondriasis was later added (1912). It was the actual neurosis, then, that was accounted for in Freud's first anxiety theory of the direct toxic transformation of repressed, dammed up libidinal excitations into the affect of anxiety. This anxiety was regarded as a substitute for libidinal discharge and an *organic process without psychic participation.*

Among those who have addressed the problem recently are (Schur, 1955; Rangell , 1968, Kohut 1977, 1978;, McDougall, 1980;, Freedman, 1982; and Gediman, 1983). Rangell renewed our interest in the syndrome as omnipresent, involving all intrapsychic tensions—libidinal, aggressive, intersystemic and intrasystemic. He saw the anticipation of actual neurotic states of traumatic helplessness as a signal function. Further, Rangell disagreed with Freud's early conception of the actual neurosis as a distinct nosological entity. He viewed it rather, and correctly, as a dynamic-economic state or a transient *psycho-economic* condition which sometimes does and sometimes does not accompany psychoneurotic symptom formation. The actual neurotic state involves all kinds of tension build-up and is not an entity but comprises a dimension of experience, related to intensity, quantity, and threshold, cutting across all conditions in all people.

One basis for viewing the condition as a quantitative dimension of experience for which there are individual differences comes from a developmental perspective. It is reasonable to assume that early biologically based thresholds or the neonatal stimulus barrier may be ego function precursors (Benjamin, 1965). As such, they may play a part in later susceptibilities. That is, they may predispose to greater or lesser degrees of susceptibility to actual neurotic states. I am referring here to more or less intense traumatic states, whether these are referable to environmental impingement or to those psychic tension states which are manifestations of intrapsychic conflict.

Kohut's (1957, 1978) work on non-specific "contentless" tensions induced by musical dissonance and resolved by musical consonance reflected his abiding interest in the discharge of actual neurotic tensions in a "soothing" setting. Unlike Rangell, he viewed the actual- and psychoneuroses as two distinct entities. Kohut's emphasis, in referring to the actual neurotic "symptoms", is on the absence or paucity of psychological elaboration of the tension states; that is, on the absence of neurotic or psychotic symptom formation. For him, it is the *absence of psychological or fantasy elaboration* of mounting tension that is the core of the musical listening experience *and* of the narcissistic disorders and actual neuroses.[3]

Here, then, is a concept of actual neurosis that is not rooted in a theory of the importance of human sexuality, as was Freud's, but in that of a "contentless state" in which pathology of the self is implicated. According to Ornstein, Kohut refers to increases and decreases of inner tensions as contentless because "the psyche [at this archaic level of organization] can neither register its needs (that is, experience them as wishes) nor provide for their relief: the

---

3   It is interesting that around the same time, Rangell had referred to the actual neurotic clinical state as involving a 'disturbance in poise', linking it, similarly, to narcissistic disequilibrium.

tensions remain, without psychological elaboration, on the physical level" (Kohut, 1978p. 15). By contentless, Kohut meant that the person feels subjectively uneasy, tense, anxious, irritated, or agitated, but with no thought or fantasy accompanying this vague distress. Hence, his emphasis on "therapeutic soothing". Kohut, says Ornstein, favours the psycho-economic point of view exclusively in postulating the contentless mental state, and sees it as preferable to "the construction of adultomorphic fantasies" which he feels analysts and analysands alike engage in.

Freedman (1982), like Kohut, also addresses higher and lower forms of tension regulation, but unlike Kohut, and more in line with my own thinking, sees the actual neurotic states as related to sensorimotor precursors which, throughout the life cycle, remain an accompaniment to, not a substitute for, symbolization, fantasies, and wishes.

As the issue of contentless mental states is related to the issue of separate nosological entities, some comments on nosology are in order here. I think it is accurate to say that Rangell's unificatory position of the actual- and psychoneuroses and my own views stand in direct contrast to the present either/or approach of Kohut and his followers. They adopt a polarizing approach, claiming separate pathogeneses and treatment plans for the narcissistic disturbances and the psychoneuroses. Some of Kohut's followers, notably Gedo & Goldberg (1973), even invoke complementary theories based on two models of the mind to account for two presumably separate nosological entities. This polarization is a present version of the early Freud's either/or considerations of the actual- and psychoneuroses.

An integrative approach which views both actual- and psychoneurotic phenomena as coexisting in one and the same individual does not require the principle of complementarity. For in the adult, there cannot be, for long, any such thing as a contentless mental state; the actual neurotic dynamic-economic state will necessarily be elaborated in conscious and unconscious fantasy and thereby be woven in with any or all of the components in the compromise formations of the psychoneuroses. That is, mounting tension states may be experienced as rage, punishment, forbidden excitement, anxiety associated with forbidden wishes, or stepped up measures to ward off worse dysphoria. Freud (1898) himself allowed that some, although not all, cases are mixtures of the actual neuroses and psychoneuroses; and he maintained that an actual neurotic current precipitant could reactivate a latent psychoneurosis of early origin. Nonetheless, he believed that when confronted with cases of this kind, it would be wise to separate the clinical picture proper to each neurotic illness.

As mentioned earlier, it was Fenichel who developed Freud's notion that the actual neurotic symptoms form the nucleus of all psychoneurotic conflict. The actual neurotic dammed up state could result from tensions inherent in psychoneurotic conflict itself. He also saw the actual neuroses as connected with symptoms, such as chronic fatigue, of manifold unspecific inhibitions of ego functions. He said that "the general neurotic inhibition due to quantitative impoverishment is an accompanying feature of all types of neuroses" (1945, p. 186). There, he was referring to ways in which the tensions inherent in the defensive struggle of the psychoneuroses may be experienced as an actual quantitative, "contentless" impoverishment, which secondarily could then become endowed with the "content" of the psychoneuroses. That is, the actual neurotic symptoms themselves become further elaborated in certain ways, or as Freud said, they are ready to be linked to any available content. For example, one can link chronic fatigue with a need for punishment or with a conviction of defectiveness.

Schur, however, cautions that because there is always secondary elaboration of symptoms, it is often difficult to flesh out the conflictual neurotic origins or even the primitive symbolic organ language of actual neurotic somatic symptoms. The patients he described with such symptoms did not comprise an entity with respect to neurotic symptom formation and did indeed span the spectrum of nosological diagnostic categories. However, he did find a prevalence of narcissistic and pregenital elements, a widespread impairment of ego functions, and an unusual amount of early traumatization. His findings are in keeping with Fenichel's observation that in cases with narcissistic fixations, the traumatizing effect of the actual neurotic symptoms, themselves, may include exaggerated self observation and form the core of a hypochondriasis which has meaningful latent content. Such narcissistic elaborations of the actual neurotic condition were always a concern of Kohut's, but in contrast to Fenichel and Schur, Kohut believed that the "contentless" affective tension states are characterized in the main by diffusiveness and lack of elaboration in fantasies. When associative fantasy formation with psychosexual content can be detected, it is relatively unimportant.

It is in just this area of the relative importance of unconscious meaning that we come up against a crucial difference between Kohut and today's mainstream Freudian psychoanalysts. These analysts would grant that such affective states might be experienced manifestly as contentless, but that they would be so only transiently. But they would wonder how the patient could not, if pressed, associate that affect with drive-derivative ideas, wishes, and fantasies related to one or the other classic calamities or danger situations. And they would see how the need for soothing, and for catharsis and discharge to restore psychoeconomic balance, would also get connected unconsciously with various psychosexual themes, such as fantasies of blissful union or of cleansing and purging. One need not take issue with Kohut's attribution of importance to the actual neurotic clinical state. To the contrary, one should take issue with an approach which plays down their significance. But one must take issue with Kohut's failure to appreciate fully the ramifications of the ways that fantasy content can be linked to these states. A balanced view is what is required.

Such a view has been offered by Glenn (1965) who relates "actual neurotic" sexual tensions to classical neurotic fantasy and symbolism. He shows how the symbol "three" becomes linked to the physiological sensations of excitement during erection and testicular congestion. He also refers to feelings of exploding which are augmented by sensations of impending orgasm. These physiological concomitants may give form to as well as determine castration fantasies. Glenn specifically alludes to the work of Masters & Johnson which he believes makes clearer just what physiological changes in the genitals result in "damming up" sensations which in turn could be a basis for symbolism.

Rangell (1968) correctly takes issue with the unpsychological nature of Freud's original accounting for actual neurotic states. He provides a bridge between the anxiety of Freud's first anxiety theory, the dammed up state, and the anxiety of the second anxiety theory, signal anxiety. He acknowledges a cognitive component when he says that the anxiety generated in connexion with the actual neurotic dammed up state "is not a toxic process without psychological meaning ... but is a signal of danger ... The dammed up state, or state of psychic helplessness ... is also a danger, the danger being that it will get worse and never stop ..." That is, an actual neurotic state can be anticipated and dreaded as an unabsorbable excess of stimuli, or state of excitation. And, most importantly, there can be psychic representations of the quantities and intensities of the so-called "contentless" mental state, what Anna Freud (1936) called "dread of the strength of the instincts". Here, one might elicit ideation about the actual neurotic state itself, having to do, for example, with extinction of life, stroke, the threat of madness (Freud, 1895b). Yet, if we press for further associations to this dread that something terrible will get worse and never stop, we also discover that the anticipation of quantitative accruals includes associated conscious and unconscious cognitive-affective content of all four of the classical danger situations of the psychoneuroses. *Both* the instinctual and the self-feeling aspects of such intense dreads would have to be addressed in an integrative approach.

Rangell's views on the signal function and its failure in the dammed up state formed the basis of my convictions in my work on annihilation anxiety (1983). There, I viewed annihilation anxiety as one particular manifestation of a *conscious mental content* associated with susceptibility to traumatic states and the sense of extreme helplessness. Since, unconsciously, such extreme helplessness is invested with variable specific meanings, I maintained that such an extreme dread need not be accorded the status of either a particular psychological entity or of a fifth prototypical danger situation, such as the shattering dissolution or annihilation of the "self". Such attribution is the predilection of those, like Kohut, who do not always look past manifest content for meaning. When Rangell says that the ego takes the early appearance of the dammed up state as a signal in anticipating the ceaseless continuation of a state of psychic helplessness, he is speaking of annihilation anxiety as I recently have conceived of it. Rangell links that actual neurotic state with the unconscious subjective sense of self-annihilation, sometimes chronic, but more often transient ego-dystonic episodes that can be experienced subjectively as feeling shattered, broken up, crushed, humiliated, fragmented, or mortified under certain specific conditions. That is, manifest content would be related to the intensity factor itself, which, to repeat, may be linked with *any* other fantasy content. Rangell implies the convergence of the two concepts of actual neurosis that I referred to above and am explicating in this paper: the one rooted in human sexuality and aggression, the other rooted in the pathology of the self. Most analysts are in agreement that there is an intensity or severity factor which is a variable or dimension in everything that we observe, and which they usually refer to as "economic". It is the ubiquitousness of this quantitative factor as a dimension of experience and the convergence of the two ways of conceptualizing actual neurosis that helps us to see how actual neurotic states and psychoneuroses co-exist in one and the same individual.

## SYMBOLIC REPRESENTATION OF
## THE ACTUAL NEUROTIC STATE

In my own attempted integration of the deficit and conflict models, I linked the instinctual and narcissistic dimensions of actual neurotic and psychoneurotic conditions as follows.

One non-polarizing way of looking at the problem is not to forget Freud's view that the anticipation of traumatic helplessness as a narcissistic catastrophe underlies all the danger situations. This dread becomes potentiated whenever instinctual drives associated with them involve an accumulation of need tensions beyond the current assimilating capacity of the individual. Waelder (1960) made a similar point in explaining that need tensions could lead to narcissistic catastrophe in anybody when they take on the meaning of the four great dangers which, for the very young child, can be all-round catastrophes ... [Narcissistic vulnerability] may also be potentiated by a low stimulus barrier, or psychoeconomic flooding, or relative if only transient ego weakness, resulting from drive intensity or rigid defences. These hallmark phenomena of accumulated undischarged psychic tensions lend a certain *experiential quality* to feelings of unreality and to dissolution anxiety, *whether or not these feelings are also neurotic compromise formations* (Gediman, 1983, p. 67).

It is important to note here that we really have no way of determining whether or not a mental state is contentless independently of our efforts at obtaining associations to it, i.e. by the psychoanalytic method of free association and construction. This hermeneutic view of the analytic process holds that the fantasy content of which I speak is not simply "uncovered" as something that is there and waiting to be discovered, but is something that is a product of the joint interpretive, constructive, and reconstructive efforts of the analyst and analysand working together in the psychoanalytic situation. If an analyst is committed to a view that mental states are contentless and so then never goes on to get the patient's associations, it could really appear as though the states are contentless. If an analyst does press for associations and gets them, we must face the question of whether the associated content is inherent in the state or whether it is a secondary elaboration drawn into the orbit of conflict. We can answer safely only that it is the latter.

There is yet another problem to contend with in our considerations of mounting tensions and representational content, and that relates to the tendency to neglect the importance of the *object representations* of instinctual drives. It seems as though pure deficit models such as Freud's early views and Kohut's contemporary ones about anxiety in the actual neuroses ignored the importance of drive-related content especially with respect to the *objects* —real or internalized—toward whom the accumulated need tensions could be directed. It is Joyce McDougall, perhaps more than anyone else, and in greatest contrast to Kohut, who has addressed the inevitability of object-related representational content being linked associatively to the actual neurotic states. Patients often experience these states, she says, in terms not only of archaic chaos and extinction dreads, but also of *persecutory internalized ob-jects* which must be got rid of or exorcized. We all recognize how the states of mounting tension may be endowed with such content as "I am tormented by demons", or, "My mother's curse makes me so horrible". In relation to actual neurotic states, McDougall says:

> The somatic event, invasion or explosion, will inevitably tend to at-tract the fantasy of a malevolent object to it as the result of the analytic process, with its stimulation to link primary and secondary modes of thinking, thus creating new ways of feeling and experiencing. These may provide the analysand with new pathways for dealing with psychic tension (1980, p. 353).

Schur (1955) showed how a somatic symptom may represent, among other things, punishment by an external but presumably internalized object. Fantasied or internalized objects also enter the picture, for example, as I point-ed out in my earlier work (1971), when non-specific tensions may be craved, as in stimulus hunger. These tensions may also be yearned for, nostalgically, when connected with fantasies and longing for an object of a past frustrated or thwarted love affair. In these instances, the experience of drive tensions them-selves can be represented in fantasy as fullness, fusion, the promise of contact with an object, and gratification through drive discharge (see also Winnicott, 1958). Or the states may be represented, as McDougall says, with various "malevolent object" fantasies: "I am filled with demons"; "Just look at what you've done to me!" Such tensions might also resonate with anal sadistic or rageful destruction, of "dumping", or with fantasies of relief from persecutory internalized objects, of coming clean, vomiting, and birth. In taking a position that actual neurotic symptoms may reappear when, despite the resolution of psychoneurotic conflict, there are no real life available objects to gratify de-sires, Fenichel leaves room, also, for the contribution to intrapsychic disequi-librium of the conscious and unconscious significance and fantasy elaboration of the unavailability of a need-satisfying object. For example, no one being around may be elaborated as abandonment by a bad, internalized object.

Writers such as Schur and McDougall do not equate the actual neurotic condition with an absence of conflict. Instead, they view it as a deficiency in the capacity to represent symbolically the related affective and tension states. And their therapeutic work is aimed at developing that capacity for symbolic representation and the construction of meaning. Somatic-affective manifes-tations always *signify* something. This is the essential psychoanalytic point of view, which is concerned with cognitive-affective experience, whether it be conscious, preconscious, or unconscious. To deal with the affective alone, or the somatic alone, is to scotomatize what is critical to human mental life and to the essence of psychoanalysis. McDougall and Schur exploit fully the heuristic potential of the psychoanalytic proposition that meaning may be imputed to all experience by psychoanalytic reconstruction and/or constructions. McDougall's position is that the symptoms of the actual neuroses are signs, not symbols, as in conversion hysteria, and that as such, they follow somatic and not psychic laws. But she has gone beyond Kohut in appreciating how meaning may be imputed to them and conveyed to the patient at increasingly higher levels of cognition and organization. Her position thus allows for unification of psychoanalytic data.

Freedman (1982), in his important discussion, expresses similar ideas in his appreciation of presymbolic meaning in "sensorimotor precursors". It seems to me that even if the actual- and psychoneurotic modalities are not linked developmentally, that is, even if presymbolic, pregenital, pre-objectal, prestructural tension states are merely precursors for tensions related to later-developed intrapsychic conflict, they certainly could be linked retrospectively in a given individual's mind. This is contained in the well known notion of secondary elaboration. It was also precisely this linkage that Freud (1918) speculated on in formulating his concept of *deferred revision* to account for the cognitive-affective shape and content that the Wolfman later gave to the diffuse and chaotic impressions occasioned by his exposures at the age of 1½ to primal scene overstimulation and by his malaria and other early traumata. Kris (1956) makes a similar point in speaking of the telescopic character of memory: that is, retrospectively, a single reconstructed memory of an early trauma comes to stand for a life-long accumulation of frustrating tensions. The latter were designated by Kris as strain trauma and do suggest the actual neurotic clinical state under scrutiny here.

## TREATMENT IMPLICATIONS

Current psychoanalytic controversy about the actual neuroses is no longer centred so much on whether or not they exist, but rather on what are the best modalities for their treatment. The main questions asked these days are: Are these states analysable? To what extent should they be "managed" and to what extent can they be interpreted? How one answers these questions depends on the extent that one views the states as invested with meaning; on how much one can determine their secondary elaboration; on how much one is convinced that they are significantly drawn into the orbit of conflict or that conflict can be "fleshed out" of them. My closing discussion on treatment represents no significant departure from many of the trends already referred to (Freud, Fenichel, Schur, Rangell, McDougall). It does aim to encourage a clinical application of the views presented in this paper by sharpening and clarifying within a psychoanalytic stance some guidelines for the flexible interplay of "holding", management and classical interpretation.

Implications for the broadening scope of psychoanalytic treatment do follow once this integrative view of the actual- and psychoneuroses is accepted, just as certain implications for restrictions of psychoanalytic applications followed from the more polarized early Freudian and contemporary Kohutian views. Freud's original position, in keeping with his direct transformation theory and his emphasis on catharsis and abreaction, was that since the affect of anxiety in the actual neuroses does not originate in a repressed idea, it is not reducible by psychological analysis and is not amenable to psychotherapy. "For such cases it has quite correctly come to be the therapeutic practice to disregard the psychoneurotic components in the clinical picture and to treat the 'actual neurosis' exclusively" (Freud, 1898, p. 279).

If we were to read that today as written by a contemporary, we would read an advocacy of some kind of psychotherapy short of psychoanalysis for the treatment of the actual neuroses. Freud, at that time, advocated a therapeutic method which emphasized the value of instinctual discharge through catharsis and abreaction; these are procedures which, as Rangell (1968) noted, were supported implicitly by the postulation of a mechanism of direct transformation without psychological motive or meaning. In 1910, even after the psychoanalytic method had replaced catharsis and abreaction for the treatment of psychoneuroses, Freud wrote that the actual neuroses merited some kind of "actual" therapy, that is, some alteration in the patient's current somatic sexual activity that was believed to cause the condition in the first place. So, abstinence and coitus interruptus were discouraged, and the effects on the woman of the man's premature ejaculation, or on the man of anxiety about the woman becoming pregnant were dealt with through direct suggestions for changes in sexual practices which would minimize frustration in the face of excitement. It is interesting how such prescriptive suggestions persist today in the folk wisdom of "All you need is a good fuck", and in some of the popular sex therapies which are often used as adjuncts to psychotherapy. If the pelvic congestion syndrome identified by Masters & Johnson is viewed as prototypical of the cause, or even as a good analogue of the actual neuroses; and if self- and object representations are disregarded, then catharsis, abreaction, and improved means of complete sexual discharge can easily be viewed as the treatment of choice, even today. As late as 1912, Freud still defended that position and predicted that he would never change it:

> The essence of the theories about the "actual neuroses" which I have put forward in the past and am defending today lies in my assertion, based on experiment, that their symptoms, unlike psychoneurotic ones, cannot be analysed. That is to say, the constipation, headaches, and fatigue of the so-called neuraesthenic do not admit of being traced back historically or symbolically to operative experiences and cannot be understood as substitutes for sexual satisfaction or as compromises between opposing instinctual impulses, as is the case with psychoneurotic symptoms (even though the latter may perhaps have the same appearance). I do not believe it will be possible to upset this assertion by the help of psycho-analysis.

He did, however, add the following:

> On the other hand I will grant today what I was unable to believe formerly—that an analytic treatment can have an indirect curative effect on "actual" symptoms. It can do so either by enabling the current noxae to be better tolerated, or by enabling the sick person to escape from the current noxae by making a change in his sexual régime. These would be desirable prospects from the point of view of our therapeutic interest (pp. 245–250).

This passage does not include Freud's belief that psychoanalytic treatment could resolve conflicts that kept the patient locked into noxious situations.

The Freud who wrote this had yet to write of the Wolf-Man, where he did find early antecedents to current chaotic states, and where he put forth his ideas on symbolic representation of that early experience that we now regard as implicated in actual neurotic conditions and which would render them amenable to psychoanalysis. Nor had he yet formulated the "signal" or second anxiety theory, whereby actual neurotic symptoms conceived as signals of the various anticipated dangers would then be amenable to analysis.

It was Schur (1955), in his work on the desomatization of actual neurotic symptoms who was to extend these later views in his hypothesis which "assumed the interdependence of the ego's faculty to use secondary process and to neutralize energy, and the desomatization of responses" (p. 124).

The views of Freud just quoted, do, however, provide the classical foundation for some of Kohut's ideas about a paradigm which differs from the classic psychoanalytic one for the treatment of the actual neurotic aspects of narcissistic transferences that evolve from traumatic origins. The views of early Freud and of Kohut also have provided some with a rationale for separating a psychoanalytic approach from other useful psychotherapeutic modalities which do not address unconscious processes. This rationale differs from the kind of integrative approach that I would envision as sometimes, even if not always, possible.

Let us look briefly at Kohut's views about treatment to see how they correspond with the early Freud and to see how they differ from the later Freud. Starting with his 1957 paper on music, Kohut advocated a therapeutic method which encouraged the discharge of actual neurotic tensions, which, it may be recalled, are not limited for him to the current and the libidinal but include the pregenitally based sexual and aggressive. He then laid the groundwork for his later suggestions for the treatment of narcissistic conditions, by recommending a primary psychotherapeutic strategy of "soothing". While his specific ideas on soothing as such are not to be found in Freud, the following passage shows his fundamental agreement with Freud's therapeutic prescriptions that I just quoted:

> Forms of therapy that seem to be concerned with the patient's structuralized personality can also help only indirectly, most often by creating the experience of being soothed by closeness, or of being comforted by a powerful therapist. The content of the verbal contact … is not by itself effective (1957 [1978], p. 245).

Yet in another place in that very same work, Kohut said that the therapeutic strategy should include teaching the patient to "listen to the content of the interpretations rather than being soothed by the sound of the analyst's voice". Would not this sound like an encouragement of psychological elaboration? However, the point of view later in Kohut's self psychology is that these contentless mental states are the hallmark of self-pathology and must be dealt with on their own as indicative of developmental deficit and self-fragmentation, requiring soothing and "holding". Any interpretation of content would be counter-indicated according to this view, because the traumatized patient will inevitably experience the analyst's interpretive activity as intrusive, as non-empathic, and as a revival of the original traumatic state.

In contrast to Kohut, mainstream Freudian analysts do believe that if one

asks the patient to associate to the contentless mental state, and if one estab-
lishes thereby a context for this state based on whatever associative potential
is at hand, symbolic linkages become evident or possible.

Schur (1955) offered a rationale for what I am here proposing when he
advocated the encouragement of secondary process thinking, even intellectu-
alization, in non-conflictual as well as conflictual areas to promote restoration
of ego functions in actual neurotic patients who somatize. Giving symbolic
form to the anxieties and other affects of the actual neurotic traumatic states
to pave the way for conflict analysis by interpretation, and "interpreting upward", supportively, during traumatic periods of affective turmoil to counteract or manage ego regression, may be called by some psychotherapy short
of psychoanalysis, and by others a flexible shift in stance within a psychoanalytic treatment. One is not compelled to adopt a rigid separation between
psychotherapy and psychoanalysis; one need not be in the position according
to which there should be one method, psychotherapy, for treating prestructural
conditions, and another, psychoanalysis, for treating others. And yet that is
just what Kohut seemed to be doing based on his assumptions about separate
nosological entities. Even within a traditional psychoanalytic stance, we are
true to the psychoanalytic attitude if we address transient, and, as Rangell
noted, "temporary and short-lived" states of mounting tension non-interpre-
tively. We might do this, from time to time, by soothing, "holding", empathic
communication exclusively, especially when our aim is to reduce the disorganizing effect of traumatic states on affect and ideation and restore those
manageable levels of functioning on which interpretations again would be
mutative. Refraining from interpretations is, according to this view, a matter of "dosage, timing, and tact" (Loewenstein, 1951) and not the tailoring of
technique to presumed discrete underlying nosological entities. The analytic
attitude manages endogenous stimulation by calling attention to the potential signal function of mounting tensions; verbalizing these tensions within
a meaningful context promotes a serene or composed setting in which useful
symbolic representation and the analysis of meaning may take place.

As for the value of offering interpretations in treating actual neurotic states,
there are two different summary points to be made. The first is that we do have
a point of *access* to neurotic conflicts through those derivatives that may be
manifested in these tension states. The second is the hermeneutic view that
symbolic meaning is *introduced* by interpretation, construction, and reconstruction, and that meaning has its own quieting effect. We would do well to
remember what Freud said about the indirect curative effect of interpretations
on the actual neurotic symptoms. Freud's point has too often been forgotten

of late. Maybe, as Kohut says, such constructions are adultomorphic fantasies. But that is not necessarily a bad thing, for providing, building, and analysing meaning through joint efforts at construction reduces the primordial chaos. Then, hopefully, the increased capacity for symbolic representation may help reduce the patient's tendency toward immediate "somatic" discharge via "actual" pathways. Additionally, all analysis of infantile conflict in adult language is inherently adultomorphic to some degree.

## SUMMARY

A comprehensive and unitary psychoanalytic approach must acknowledge the importance of the so-called "contentless mental state" of mounting psychic tensions. These states, once called the actual neuroses, are probably always further elaborated in fantasy. Once these states are endowed with meaning through free association and the joint constructive efforts of analyst and analysand, they may also be drawn into the orbit of neurotic conflict, if they have not already been drawn in by the patient alone, and then they may be dealt with analytically in connexion with the components of compromise formations which have interpretable meaning. Any person may be subject to traumatic states. Such states do not necessarily comprise a separate nosological category. What we are dealing with is a quantitative dimension of human existence that cuts across all conditions. Along with severe early traumata, weakness of the biologically determined stimulus barrier may predispose to later and life-long susceptibilities to traumatic states. If we substitute the notion of actual neurotic states for the older "actual neuroses", we come closer to a fully integrated psychoanalytic approach, to understanding and treatment of actual- and psychoneurotic conditions.

## REFERENCES

Benjamin, J.D. (1965). Developmental biology and psychoanalysis In: *Psychoanalysis and Current Biological Thought,* ed. N. S. Greenfield & W. C. Lewis. Madison and Milwaukee: University of Wisconsin Press, pp. 57–80.

Blau, A. (1952). In support of Freud's syndrome of "actual" anxiety neurosis. *International Journal of Psycho-Analysis* 33:363–372.

Fenichel, O. (1945). *The Psychoanalytic Theory of Neurosis.* New York: Norton.

Freedman, N. (1982). On psychoanalytic listening: the construction, paralysis, and reconstruction of meaning. Presented to Division 39, American Psychological Association, Rio Mar, Puerto Rico, March 1982. http://www.pep-web.org/document.php?id=pct.006.0405a

Freud, A. (1936). *The Ego and the Mechanisms of Defense.* New York: International Universities Press, 1946.

Freud, S. (1895a). Project for a scientific psychology. *Standard Edition* 1 1950. http://www.pep-web.org/document.php?id=se.001.0213a

———(1895b). On the grounds for detaching a particular syndrome from neuraesthenia under the description "anxiety neurosis." *Standard Edition* 3. http://www.pep-web.org/document.php?id=se.001.0000a

——— (1898). Sexuality in the aetiology of neuroses. *Standard Edition* 3. http://www.pep-web.org/document.php?id=se.001.0000a

——— (1910). "Wild" psycho-analysis. *Standard Edition.* 11. http://www.pep-web.org/document.php?id=se.009.0000a

——— (1912). Contributions to a discussion on masturbation *Standard Edition* 12. http://www.pep-web.org/document.php?id=se.011.0000a

——— (1915). Instincts and their vicissitudes *Standard Edition* 14. http://www.pep-web.org/document.php?id=se.014.0000a

——— (1918). From the history of an infantile neurosis *Standard Edition* 17. http://www.pep-web.org/document.php?id=se.011.0000a

———. (1926). Inhibitions, symptoms and anxiety *Standard Edition* 20. http://www.pep-web.org/document.php?id=se.020.0000a

Gediman, H.K. (1971). The concept of stimulus barrier: its review and reformulation as an adaptive ego function. *International Journal of Psycho-Analysis* 52:243–257. http://www.pep-web.org/document.php?id=ijp.052.0243a

——— (1982). Annihilation anxiety: the experience of deficit in neurotic compromise formation. *International Journal of Psycho-Analysis.* 64:59–70. http://www.pep-web.org/document.php?id=ijp.064.0059a

Gedo, J.E. & Goldberg, A. (1973). *Models of the Mind.* Chicago: University of Chicago Press.

Glenn, J. (1965). Sensory determinants of the symbol three. *Journal of the American Psychoanalytic Association* 13:422–434. http://www.pep-web.org/document.php?id=apa.013.0422a

Greenacre, P. (1967). The influence of infantile trauma on genetic patterns. In *Emotional Growth: Psychoanalytic Studies of the Gifted and a Great Variety of Other Individuals.* New York: International Universities Press, 1971 pp. 260–299.

Kohut, H. (1977). *The Restoration of the Self.* New York: International Universities Press.

———— (1978). *The Search for the Self.* New York: International Universities Press.

Kris, E. (1956). The recovery of childhood memories in psychoanalysis. *Psychoanalytic Study of the Child* 11:54–88.
http://www.pep-web.org/document.php?id=psc.011.0054a

Loewenstein, R.M. (1951). The problem of interpretation. *Psychoanalytic Quarterly* 20:1–14.
http://www.pep-web.org/document.php?id=paq.020.0001a

McDougall, J. (1980). *Plea for a Measure Abnormality.* New York: International Universities Press.

Rangell, L. (1963a). The scope of intrapsychic conflict: microscopic and macroscopic considerations. *Psychoanalytic Study of the Child* 18:75–102.
http://www.pep-web.org/document.php?id=psc.018.0075a

———— (1963b). Structural problems in intrapsychic conflict. *Psychoanalytic Study of the Child* 18:103–138.
http://www.pep-web.org/document.php?id=psc.018.0103a

———— (1968). A further attempt to resolve the "problem of anxiety". *Journal of the American Psychoanalytic Association* 16:371–404.
http://www.pep-web.org/document.php?id=apa.016.0371a

Schur, M. (1955). Comments on the metapsychology of somatization. *Psychoanalytic Study of the Child* 10:119–164.
http://www.pep-web.org/document.php?id=psc.010.0119a

Waelder, R. (1960). *The Basic Theory of Psychoanalysis.* New York: Schocken, 1971.

Winnicott, D.W. (1958). The capacity to be alone In *The Maturational Processes and the Facilitating Environment.* New York: International Universities Press, 1965 pp. 29–36.
http://www.pep-web.org/document.php?id=ipl.064.0001a

# Chapter 4: Seduction Trauma: Complemental Intrapsychic and Interpersonal Perspectives on Fantasy and Reality

[Gediman, H.K. (1991). Seduction trauma: Complemental intrapsychic and interpersonal perspectives on fantasy and reality. *Psychoanalytic Psychology* 8:381-401. ]

The recent publicized attention to Freud's abandonment of the seduction trauma theory to account for neurosogenesis has led to considerable re-examination of numerous interrelated psychoanalytic issues. Freud's complemental series principle serves to reconcile the apparent polarities: memory and fantasy, early experience and libidinal fixations, historical truth and psychic reality, and interpersonal and intrapsychic representations. I aim to show that although the importance of seduction and other trauma has never been rejected by psychoanalysis, the significance of such early experience has undergone historically important vicissitudes in our consideration of its place in our evolving and expanding theoretical and clinical contexts. The press coverage (see Gediman, 1985) of Freud's abandonment of the "seduction theory" has polemicized some of the subtlest areas of our theory and practice. A net effect has been an unfortunate muddying with obfuscatory, poorly informed, often ad hominem argumentation, masking difficult and controversial issues that responsible psychoanalysts have been tackling for some time.

Freud's critics insufficiently credit him and his followers as duly appreciating a real world of sadness, pain, misery, and cruelty. They fail to highlight or document Freud's and his successors' never-ending respect for the role of trauma—early or reactivating, shock or strain, actual or retrospective, real or psychic—in the psychogenesis both of the psycho- and the traumatic neuroses. I show how, in Freud's writings and in the history of psychoanalysis, interest in the importance of seduction and other traumatic influences was never abandoned. Further, the importance of such early experience can be understood only within the context of a complex view of psychic reality which includes multiple interrelationships and interactions between the inner life of fantasy, drive, and memory, on the one hand, and the outer life of external/ factual/ objective/material reality and historical truth on the other.

## CONFOUNDING OF THEORY WITH CLINICAL OBSERVATION

### FREUD ON SEDUCTION

That Freud abandoned a particular theory as explanatory does not imply that he ever gave up his conviction about the importance of seduction and other early trauma. Real trauma to this day is regarded as an important component in pathogenesis of the neuroses and of the more severe disturbances, just as the "kernel of truth" in paranoid delusions and day residues in dreams imprint importantly on the manifest content of psychic experience. And Freud never abandoned his "complemental series" (Freud, 1905b) principle, which is to this day central in accounting for neurosogenesis. Libidinal fixations and early experience both predispose.

The abandoned early seduction theory claimed that a real, traumatic seduction occurred in the childhood of every neurotic patient, particularly those suffering from hysteria. Freud did replace this belief in "exclusive traumatic pathogenesis" (Blum, 1986, p. 8), but retained his belief in the significance of seduction and other forms of trauma or nontraumatic external influences on development and neurosogenesis. And analysts, subsequently, have always assigned to experiential influences, a relative weight. They have never suppressed the fact that seductions of children occur frequently enough. It is critics like Masson (1984, 1990) who have suppressed the fact that Freud and his followers continued to recognize the sexual seductions of children, despite coming to understand that universally present sexual impulses in childhood no longer made seduction mandatory for eliciting a psychoneurotic outcome. Seductions were regarded as pathogenic if they occurred at a time when the psychic apparatus was too immature to deal with such stimulation or when the excitation was overstimulating and produced in the child a state of psychic helplessness, a state which defines psychic trauma. Where some analysts differ from Freud is on the importance of the quantitative factor for understanding trauma. All would maintain that the internalization of an original real event is critical, though some would underplay the importance of the actual intensity of stimulation at the traumatic moment.

Brenner (1986), for one, believed that one can define psychic trauma only with reference to its effects on the psyche, and that one can therefore dispense with any reference to the quantitative factor, such as an overwhelming influx of stimuli following a break in the hypothetical stimulus barrier or protective shield. In dispensing with the importance of the quantitative factor, Brenner's view that external stimulation is not a necessary factor in accounting for trauma, overlooks Freud's expanded view of trauma, as summarized by Strachey: "... the essence of [a traumatic situation] is an experience of helplessness on the part of the ego in the face of an accumulation of excitation, whether of external or of internal origin, which cannot be dealt with ..." (Freud, 1926, p. 81). My (Gediman, 1971) reformulation of the stimulus barrier as an adaptive ego function rested on Freud's inclusion of inner, or drive factors, as well as external ones, as responsible for ruptures in the protective shield and the resulting experiential state of psychic helplessness.

I believe that the parsimony of Brenner's exclusive intrapsychic emphasis, because it disregards the intensity of a traumatic impact from without and within upon the psyche, reduces rather than enlarges the explanatory power of his definition of psychic trauma as simply a compromise formation, identical in all important respects to any other. Specifically, his definition does not discriminate between seductions which at the moment of occurrence were experienced traumatically, in part because their intensity in and of itself was disorganizing, and those which were not experienced traumatically at the time but either activated latent fantasies or later fantasized elaborations of the real event, fantasies which in and of themselves carried terrifying meaning. I find it essential to make that distinction because there are different sequelae and correspondingly different therapeutic emphases, depending on whether or not a real external or internal event eventuated in an overwhelming of the ego, and a resulting state of psychic helplessness, and whether or not regression in ego functioning followed by obligatory repetitive phenomena can be linked to these real, historical occurrences.

A brief historical survey points to evidence for Freud's abiding interest in the role of seduction. In his earliest writings (1892b, 1893, 1896a, 1896b, 1896c), Freud evolved the notion that neurotic pathology was rooted in sexual experiences of early childhood. These involved literal, direct stimulation of the genitals by seduction and other forms of sexual excitement, such as that which might accompany the witnessing of intercourse between the parents.

Freud believed that traumatic seduction experiences could result from extended love relations over time as well as from occasional incidents with known or with strange seducers. It was on September 21, 1897, that the now well-known letter to Fliess was written, in which Freud said, "I no longer believe in my neurotica," that is, because reported seductions could not be established clearly as historical realities and were often mixed with fantasies. This statement constituted the linchpin in Masson's argument that Freud abandoned interest in real sexual trauma as etiologically important. Specifically, Freud confided to his friend that "... there is no "indication of reality" in the unconscious, so that it is impossible to distinguish between truth and emotionally charged fiction. (This leaves open the possible explanation that sexual fantasy regularly makes use of the theme of the parents)" (Freud, 1954 p. 216). E. Furman (Marans, 1988), in her splendid review of the topic of seduction, correctly interpreted Freud's statement to imply that external circumstances interact significantly with the child's personality, rather than merely acting upon it.

In the *Three Essays on the Theory of Sexuality* (1905b), though Freud saw psychic conflict—sexual drives and defenses against them—as more crucial than sexual trauma alone for the etiology of neuroses, he nevertheless still maintained that everything could be relevant for etiology, including direct and indirect noxious stimulation from accidental environmental factors. This conviction was best articulated in his postulation, then, of a "complemental series," where the diminishing intensity of the constitutional and predispositional drive factors is balanced by the increasing intensity of environmental and accidental factors and vice versa. In the Wolf Man case (1918), not only did Freud insist on the importance of early noxious sexual experience as interfering with development, but he entitled Part III of the work, dealing with the patient's real seduction by his sister, "The Seduction and its Immediate Consequences." As Blum (1986) pointed out, the Wolf Man's exposure to the parental scene when he was 18 months old has long been the model of sexual seduction and the traumatic effect of the primal scene.

In the *Introductory Lectures on Psychoanalysis* (1917), Freud noted three kinds of recurrent childhood experiences that are etiologically important for the development of neuroses: witnessing parental intercourse, seduction by an adult, and castration threats. Then, in a 1924 footnote to his 1896 "Neuropsychoses" paper, he said that he had attributed to the etiological factor of seduction a significance and universality which it does not possess. Freud acknowledged his former inability to distinguish between his patients' fantasies about seduction and their real recollections. "Nevertheless," he said, "seduction retains a certain aetiological importance, and even to-day I think some of these [presumably abandoned] psychological comments are to the point" (1896b, p. 168). Two years later (1926), he reiterated that seduction in childhood, in addition to the strength of the component instincts of the drives and their associated fantasies, retains a certain share in etiology. This formulation extends the complemental series paradigm of attributing more weight to fantasy when seductions were negligible, and less to fantasy when seductions preempted the picture.

The complemental series notion holds that the relationship between drive disposition and environmental events is a cooperative and not a mutually exclusive one, and that among the accidental factors, priority should be given to the experiences of childhood. The constitution and the accidental experiences of childhood interact in the same manner as do the disposition and the traumatic experiences in later life. Freud was to elaborate this principle:

> Disposition and experience are here linked up in an indissoluble aetiological unity. For *disposition* exaggerates impressions which would otherwise have been completely commonplace and have had no effect, so that they become traumas giving rise to stimulations and fixations: while *experiences* awaken factors in the disposition which, without them, might have long remained dormant and perhaps never have developed. (1914, p. 18).

## GASLIGHTING: A TRAUMA ON THE SENSE OF REALITY

The focus of psychoanalysis, even where real trauma is etiologically implicated, is mainly on psychic reality. We attend to those preexisting fantasies which are activated by trauma, as well as to the subsequent elaborations in fantasy of literal seductions as well as a wide range of other real trauma. This focus has never, I believe, led any competent analyst to tell a patient: "It never really happened. It's only in your mind." Masson (1984), in his parody, stated that all classical analysts do indeed say just that or its equivalent, in an assault on the patient's reality sense. He overlooked the fact that historical truth and material reality are concepts not alien to psychoanalysis, despite some current fashions which, in keeping with Masson's allegations, would view psychoanalysis as an exclusively hermeneutic discipline.

Hermeneutic analysts, notably Schafer (1983) and Spence (1982), have maintained that the goal of psychoanalytic interpretation is only to attain narrative fit within and among versions of reality and not to determine the historical truth of a patient's life history. Their view of psychic reality contains a heavy loading of inner constituents at the expense of the internalization of external-factual reality. The narrative truth is created and revised in the psychoanalytic dialogue by the two participants. A hermeneutic definition of trauma, then, is one which stresses the mind's interpretation of the meaning of an external event (see Rothstein, 1986). I think this disregard for objective reality is a valid way, perhaps the only way, for psychoanalytic literary critics to proceed in their efforts at psychoanalytic exegesis of texts. Coming to a consensus on the best storyline might be an appropriate model when we are interpreting and reconstructing unconscious motivations and the life histories of protagonists in drama and fiction, or in a psychoanalytically informed reading of visually presented art images. We are not applying to storybook characters or to pictures a therapeutic method which seeks to master psychic pain, to change and to cure. But when we as psychoanalytic psychotherapists try to put the life of a flesh-and-blood human being into historical perspective, we must sort out, as best we can, inner and outer constituents of psychic reality.

It is true that some patients find it seductive to use reality, even the reality of real seductions, as a resistance to understanding the place of fantasies or of later psychical elaborations of early experience in their idiosyncratically developing psychic economy. Telling patients that they only imagined that which really happened, or "that's just your version," may, as Masson (1984, 1990) claimed, eventuate in iatrogenic disturbances. A hermeneutic approach to psychoanalysis discounts the significance of external reality in its exclusive, if not fanatically interpretive focus on internal representations of others. Applying this approach to the truly traumatized is risky, for it may constitute a dangerous assault on the patient's sense of reality. Take, for example, the instance of an analyst who might suggest to a patient who remembers a past assault, "You must have thought you were being attacked." The patient might well respond, "I did think I was being attacked because I was in fact being attacked." This patient could be seen as being self-protective, sensing in that analytic situation a re-creation of past traumatic assaults on his or her sense of reality. If the analyst, true to a puristically hermeneutic conception of psychic reality, then says, "If it were really so," and the patient responds "It was really so," we must not necessarily conclude that the patient has no appreciation that psychic reality is the only legitimate purview of psychoanalytic work. The analyst who so concludes would exemplify and realize, par excellence, Masson's parody of the classical analyst. It is, rather, the not very self-protective patient whose reality sense is weak to begin with who surrenders to the analyst's influence by saying, "You're telling me that I really wasn't attacked, so I guess I only imagined it. Now I feel really crazy." This patient's already damaged reality sense is eroded further by the analyst's intervention.

This kind of interaction, sometimes called "gaslighting" (Calef & Weinshel, 1981), typifies the iatrogenic effect in question, whereby the analyst's suggestion is introjected by the patient and not adequately tested against his or her actual perceptions. The colloquial term, gaslighting, derives from the movie, *Gaslight* (1944), in which the husband, played by Charles Boyer, tries to drive his wife, played by Ingrid Bergman, crazy by shaking her confidence in her own perceptions of the level of brightness of the gaslights in the house. He alters the level, making them dimmer or brighter, and she remarks on the change. He, with a conscious and deliberate intent to have her believe she is crazy and thereby to drive her crazy, patronizingly tells her that the brightness level remains constant and that she only imagines, in her presumably demented mind, that it has shifted.

Transposing this prototypical, albeit exaggeratedly noxious, interaction to the analytic situation (without, of course, assuming any conscious intention on the part of the analyst to drive the patient crazy), I find it fitting to quote Hanly (1986) in his review of Malcolm's (1984) book which critiques *The Assault on Truth* (Masson, 1984):

> Certainly, it would be painfully humiliating, confusing, and profoundly detrimental to the progress of an analysis if analyst were to treat even a distorted memory of a real event as though it were a phantasy, let alone announce it to his patient who was struggling with the memory that he was lying. (p. 518).

Such iatrogenic occurrences are fewer, to be sure, than incidences of real early trauma. Psychoanalytic theory does not assign all the weight to fantasy and none to objective reality. So the notion that analysts always disregard historical truth or material reality is an ill-informed and consequently biased historical account of psychoanalytic theory development.

## DOES IT REALLY MAKE A DIFFERENCE?

Malcolm posed the question, does it really make a difference whether something really happened or not? To begin addressing her question, it is important to remember that a memory of a trauma should not be conceived in either/or terms: fantasy or reality. That false polarity has led, more than any other factor, to Masson's repeated innuendo of iatrogenesis: that psychoanalysts tell their patients who are convinced that something really did happen, "It's only in your mind." It could appear demeaning even to trouble to challenge Masson's statement that "ever since then analyst have been denying the reality of their patient's lives" (Malcolm, 1984 p. 50). However, in the light of the public outcries following Masson's published material, certain reminders may be in order.

The false polarity of reality or fantasy is paralleled by another, that of psychic reality or historical truth, and the two series, complemental series if you will, overlap considerably, conceptually speaking. A main thrust of this article is to show how most polarized dichotomies that have split analysts into theoretically divergent camps can be better understood by updated versions of the complemental series concept, a concept which should serve as a basis for complementarity in a unificatory position, healing the splits engendered in many current controversies.[4]

In a panel discussion of the seduction hypothesis (Marans, 1988), a major aim was to define psychic and external reality and the interactive relationship between them, as well as the relationship between reality—however composed—and fantasy. We are reminded that Freud, in the famous 1897 Fliess letter, said that fantasies include derivatives of impulses as well as factual and distorted experiences. Fantasies, in addition to expressing drives and wishes, also represent the real inner world of body and mind and serve as avenues to its exploration.

A proper understanding of the core psychoanalytic concept *psychic reality* is not that a fantasy is taken for the real truth, but that real recollections of psychic events are mixtures of fact and fantasy (Arlow, 1969). In their discussion of psychic reality, Wallerstein (1985) and Arlow (1985) both called for due respect for the weight of fact in psychic reality, which encompasses both of what are conventionally referred to as fantasy and reality, concluding that what people think really happened is always a combination, a complex intermingling of fantasy with perception of reality.

Arlow's (1985) position expands what Freud (1899) said in his "Screen Memories" paper: Not only is experience elaborated over time by fantasy construction, but later experience may be projected backward in memory, as in a deferred revision, whereby early memory undergoes distortion in accordance with later accruals in a false recollection of an early trauma. Kris (1956) introduced a similar idea in his consideration of the telescoping of past and present memories in one partially valent memory which serves to organize otherwise diffuse experience.

It seems to me that all of these views on the complex interrelationship of

---

4  My usage of the term *complementarity* does not subsume the meaning of that
   word as Kohut (1977) used it. Kohut borrowed the term from Bohr's "principle of
   complementarity" in physics to indicate that the explanation of psychoanalytic data may
   require not one but two (or more) theoretical frameworks, one of self psychology and
   one of conflict psychology. In contrast to Kohut, who used the term *complementarity*
   to characterize the two theories as co-existing but intrinsically incompatible, my usage
   of complementarity derives from Freud's complemental series notion and presumes
   a unified theory to explain all relevant psychoanalytic data, for example, trauma and
   conflict.

fantasy and reality are good applications of Freud's complemental series notion. Both Arlow and Wallerstein believed that although fantasy encompasses
the imprint of real factors, from the point of view of the experiencing human
being, there is no pure outer reality out there, unchanging and the same for
all. But, unlike the psychoanalytic hermeneuticists, their more balanced view
does not regard the real world of factual reality as a matter of indifference:
There is an intermingling of fact and fantasy at the core of experience.

Long before the recent upsurge of interest in the complex relationship between fantasy and reality for our understanding of trauma, Greenacre (1971)
elaborated very fully on fantasy and early trauma. She demonstrated how
severe and chronic trauma tends to produce falsification of memory—that is,
a confusion of memory traces with a characterological tendency to elaborate
in fantasy. Greenacre's major point about screen memories and the intermingling of fantasy and reality is that a real traumatic overstimulation leaves a
stronger imprint on experience when it is related to an associated fantasy is
more likely to serve as a significant motivating force in the personality if it has
been buttressed by early traumatic experience. For example, if a fantasy that
one's sibling would die is confirmed by traumatic experiencing of the sibling's
unexpected death, that experience contributes to traumatic fixation and vulnerability to repeated trauma. Whichever way one wants to look at it, I think
the most interesting point on intermingling that Greenacre made concerns the
reciprocal relation between real people—between the traumatized child and
significant interacting real figures who may be unconsciously provoked by
the child to really re-create the original traumatic occurrence, leading to a
mushrooming effect of the original trauma, all serving, in the child's mind,
to confirm drive-determined fantasy. I believe that Greenacre's observation,
confirmed in the experience of most clinicians, underscores the importance
of an intrapsychic model of psychic reality which also encompasses interpersonal relations in the representational worlds of self and other. This kind
of relational-intrapsychic model, like the one recently proposed by Benjamin
(1990), is particularly useful for comprehending the mutual relations of early
traumatic experience and later elaborations of that experience in keeping with
the notion of a complemental series.

The question which opened this section, "Does it make a difference?," has
by now been answered affirmatively. Analysts do not deny the reality of their
patients' lives, especially the reality of abuses suffered helplessly in childhood. In fact, they willingly suspend disbelief in all that the patient tells. They
are not solipsistically involved with fantasy at the expense of helping their
patients gain therapeutically valuable perspective on their own life histories.

It is for this reason that it seems important to take the time and make this effort to challenge Masson's extreme statement, for the general press coverage of the seduction trauma issue has been obliterating an important current in psychoanalytic thought. "The patient must know what he has suffered, at whose hands, and how it has affected him. The means he uses to not know, to deny, must be made fully conscious" (Shengold, 1979, p. 555). Malcolm (1984) incorrectly implied that Shengold stands alone among analysts when "he disagrees with the purists' contention that it doesn't matter what really happened" (p. 82). It really does make a difference to all concerned whether something truly traumatic and particularly, something abusive really happened or not.

## SOME REAL SEQUELAE OF REAL TRAUMA

The question, does it really matter whether a patient's recollections about infantile sexual or other trauma are fact or fantasy, is a spurious question, because fact and fantasy are always intermingled in psychic reality. But it is an entirely different matter to ask what are the sequelae of real, early seduction trauma; how can they be identified, both generally and in the treatment setting; and how may they best be dealt with therapeutically within the analytic situation. The gaslighting metaphor should prove useful at this juncture, as a reference point for understanding and treating the sequelae of seduction trauma. My own analytic observations are very much in line with E. Furman's (Marans, 1988) developmental research findings which indicate that reality testing, particularly the child's sense of reality—that is, a comfortable sense of confidence in his or her own perceptions even when others try to contradict them—is severely disturbed in those who have suffered childhood sexual and aggressive abuse. This is so because abusive parents tend not to empathize with the child's perception of external reality and often tell the young child that "It didn't happen" or "It was just a bad dream," contributing to a developmentally critical variant of gaslighting. Blum (1986) noted how the conspiracy of silence that often follows child abuse may continue in the analytic situation if the trauma is treated only as though it were a fantasy. A solid sense of reality is also impeded by chronic aggressive and sexual overstimulation; the consequent regressive patterns of drive and affect discharge, such as "narcissistic rage," are bound to have disorganizing effects on self-feeling and self-perception, and to lead to general failures in integrating all experience.

Being confused about what was done to one and what one only wished or feared might be done to one leads to chronic confusion over who is the initiator of an action, the self or the other. Projective and introjective defenses during strong, disorganizing arousal states compound the confusion about locus of action. And, as many have noted, the truly traumatized tend more than others to repeat with another the original traumatic situations and actually bring them about again. Furthermore, if the other has undergone similar traumatic experiences with subsequent development of introjective and projective defensive measures, the potential for traumatically disruptive interactions increases geometrically.

It is worth remembering Freud's words:

> The effects of traumas are of two kinds, positive and negative. The former are attempts to bring the trauma into operation once again— that is, to remember the forgotten experience or, better still, to make it real, to experience a repetition of it anew, or, even if it was only an early emotional relationship, to revive it in an analogous relationship with someone else. We summarize these efforts under the name of "fixations" to the trauma and as a "compulsion to repeat" ... A girl who was made the object of a sexual seduction in her early childhood may direct her later sexual life so as constantly to provoke similar attacks. ... The negative reactions follow the opposite aim: that nothing of the forgotten traumas shall be remembered and nothing repeated ... (1939, pp. 75–76).

These words were written a long time after the seduction theory was abandoned. The recent work on traumatic stress syndrome corroborates Freud's observations, where we see these two extremes in the sequelae of real trauma, which is defined as being helplessly overwhelmed by stimuli that could not be dealt with at the time. Among other well-identified sequalae are repetitive dreams, nightmares, repetitive reenactments, automatic anxieties, and rage. The past tendency among certain analysts since Freud to disbelieve that extremely deviant things really do happen is with us decreasingly in this era when we are confronted with the effects of massive social trauma, as among Holocaust survivors and Vietnam War veterans. Although Freud did not explicitly tie a history of real trauma to the recurrent experience of an assault on the sense of reality, I think he would have considered that particular ego vulnerability among both the positive and negative sequelae of seduction.

Calef and Weinshel (1981) described the reality sense confusion of gaslightees, "of victims who struggle with the feeling that their minds are being "worked over," their thoughts influenced, and the validity of their perceptions undermined. Meanwhile the victimizers perpetuate these distortions, disavowing them, and even claiming that they themselves are the victims" (p. 45).

Thus, these authors emphasized the interactional-interpersonal elements underlying the altered reality sense of individuals who were influenced by another or who influence another to doubt the validity of their own judgments. Their intrapsychic representations contain internalizations of actual interpersonal interactions, occurring from childhood on, which impact on significant present interactions, including the transference in analysis. Calef and Weinshel noted a particular condition in the paradigmatic gaslighting interactions which guarantees a seductive effect: The gaslightee succumbs to rather than questions or rejects the gaslighter's statements, in order to avoid risking a significant object loss.

The gaslightee, then, is seduced into accepting as so, that which flies in the face of his or her own reality sense, in order to hold on to the object. The child who was subjected to traumatic seductions by a loved family member would also be prone to repeated trauma involving a seduction away from his or her own reality sense. That child might introject what under normal circumstances would be rejected, for by accepting something as being so even though it defies the evidence of the senses, the child feels able to avoid an anticipated loss. An adult woman patient reported that as a young girl, she slept in a bed with her mother who clung to her in an effort to escape sexual abuse from her alcoholic husband. The daughter remembers being sent by her mother, in an apparent attempt to protect her from her father, to sleep at the home of her much older married sister when things got particularly bad. This frequent occurrence led to a bewildering sense of banishment and to grief over the loss of the blissfully experienced physical and emotional closeness with her mother. The patient recalls that from the age of 14, she received clandestine visits from her sister's husband, who regularly came into her bed, caressed her, and fondled her genitals. The patient, as an adult, could not remember whether or not she was sexually penetrated, explaining, in the analysis, that she never resisted her seducer until she was 14 and "realized what was happening." She passively submitted, remembering no fear, although "looking down upon myself as if from the outside, and as though it were not really happening to me but to someone else." Such dissociative reactions are quite typical among children who have been regularly seduced, and persist as an ego disturbance of the sense of reality well into adulthood. This patient, like many others who experienced similar disassociations, was enjoined by her seducer never to tell her sister (or mother, as the case may be) of the sexual seduction. In an effort to please her seducer, protect her sister, and save herself from some anticipated dire punishment, the patient's dissociative states were compounded by chronic confusion about what actually occurred, not only during the seductions, but in most other emotionally ambiguous situations from that time onward. One task of analytic treatment, in addressing the defective sense of reality and in a mastering the trauma, was to reconstruct as best as possible what really happened and what difference the real sequelae of the real trauma made in this woman's life.

## COMPLEMENTARITY OF REALITY AND FANTASY

### INTRAPSYCHIC REPRESENTATIONS
### OF RELATIONAL INTERACTIONS

An individual's internalization of the gaslighting interaction, as well as of a whole range of others, is a phenomenon which bridges the intrapsychic and interpersonal spheres. The psychic reality of all individuals, but particularly of individuals who have suffered the traumatic effects of the insidious intractions in a seductive assault on reality, must then include a heavy loading of representations of interpersonal reality. However, that interpersonal reality which is represented intrapsychically cannot be defined as a simple replica of objectively observable interactions between the patient and his or her primal object. It consists, rather, of *imagos*. For the victims of gaslighting and other seduction trauma, unconscious fantasies are activated along with more or less accurate representations of the potentially malignant interaction, providing an independent motive force for the victims to continue seeking out sexualized assaults on their reality sense.

It is this inner, predominantly drive-related aspect of experience that has been the concern, traditionally, of psychoanalytic investigations. Ever since Freud (1915) wrote "Instincts and Their Vicissitudes," psychoanalysis has provided a context for viewing that which is internalized as an object relationship related to drive vicissitudes. One cannot identify with the sadist without at the same time feeling what the masochist feels, and vice versa. One cannot exhibit oneself without identifying with the voyeuristic impulses of the one who actively looks. One cannot have survived abuse without internalizing the interaction of abuser and victim. These internalizations may or may not correspond to the objective reality of the real objects. There does seem to be an ever-growing trend, however, among psychoanalytic thinkers, particularly among infant-mother observation researchers, to think of the inner representational world as containing, in addition to defense and drive derivatives in fantasy, characteristic interaction patterns which, from the vantage point of an observer, have really occurred. Such a mutual influence model is proposed by Beebe and Lachmann (1988), whose empirical research, following that of Stern (1977, 1985), addresses certain specific "interaction structures" of derailment in the mother-infant dyad. I believe that such structured representations could serve as the proper *anlagen* for understanding the pulls or seductions of the typical gaslighting interaction. A history of upsetting derailments can account for the quantitative factor, the real and intolerable excitation or arousal levels in seduction trauma. Such a history often repeats itself in later dyads, specifically insofar as it provides the soil for unconscious motivation of each of two individuals to continue and perpetuate noxious and real interpersonal situations which afford compromised gratifications of multiple drives and wishes for each of them, separately, and both of them in interaction.

Like all the other either/or polarizations of objective and psychic reality, the forced choice of interpersonal or intrapsychic also implies a false dichotomy. There is always, by definition, an interpersonal matrix for seductions and their later elaborations in memory and fantasy. The inner constituents of psychic reality must encompass representations of the external reality of critical interpersonal phenomena. The complemental series paradigm serves well for integrating the intrapsychic or drive-defense aspects of conflict theory with the self and object representations data which have been the focus of self psychology and object relations perspectives. It should be clear that I do not regard this proposal as a mixed model where one theory suits one set of facts, the other, another set. It is, rather, an attempt toward a unificatory approach, organized by the complemental series principle (see Gediman, 1989). Restated in this context, the complemental series notion holds that when there has been severe early trauma, external influences are more prominently involved in pathogenesis, relative to the strength of the drives, than they are in the absence of early trauma. And strength of drive and related fantasies may be hypertrophied when external influences included premature sexual and aggressive stimulation. That is, we may sometimes expect to see in a child who has been sexually and/or aggressively abused more, and more intense, sadistic and aggressive drive-related fantasy than in one who has not.

Various observers have identified in the objective reality of the traumatically seduced child the particular interpersonal events that have been internalized and that have representations in psychic reality. I have been emphasizing gaslighting as a crucial derailment of dialogue in the histories of those suffering seduction trauma. Two other types of intrapsychic representation of interpersonal matrices involving derailment have been identified and reported by R. and E. Furman (Marans, 1988) in their study of patients who have been traumatically seduced. Their focus is on types of parental dysfunction or pathology that can predispose a child to being seduced repetitively. They have called one type *intermittent decathexis*, and the other *a pathological form of projective identification*, describing both as interactive relationships which can link to a range of neurotic disturbances in each of the interacting partners. In both types of dysfunctional interactions, overstimulation by the parents is a sine qua non. In intermittent decathexis, the parent fails to have a constant investment in the child. The child who is so recurrently decathected can easily be overwhelmed, in an instinctualized, provocative way. Such children are particularly prone to provoke the decathecting parent figure into an extended chase, followed by a need for distancing and withdrawal, similar to what Beebe and Lachmann observed and called the "dodge and chase" derailment. The children in turn identify with the parents' attitude and decathect themselves, losing interest in self-protection, thereby actively doing to themselves what they suffered passively at the hands of their parents. The Furmans concluded that one could not devise a better format for a seduction to occur, as the deeply craving child hungers for any kind of approach made to him or her.

The patient referred to earlier, who was regularly seduced as a child by her brother-in-law, appears to exemplify intermittent decathexis and hunger for any kind of approach, particularly those which are erotized. She later married, suffered emotional abuse from her husband, and fled back and forth between him and a lesbian lover, whose rejection of the patient in favor of her own husband and child led to the latter's seeking therapy. The patient chose a lesbian therapist, to whom her husband objected, so the patient terminated with her. To placate her husband, she then lied to him that she was a cocaine addict, a condition that he believed to be rapidly treatable. She then succumbed to his wish that she receive a brief course of behavioral modification for her "addiction." The behavioral therapist, on discovering that the patient had never used cocaine, and diagnosing the patient as an impostor, referred her for analysis to a heterosexual woman. The patient, fearing that the analyst might seduce her away from both her inconstant lover and her abusive husband, manipulated her husband into coaxing her out of treatment while she simultaneously begged the analyst to help her find clandestine ways to continue her sessions. Thus, the analysis could deal with the patient's actively repeating and provoking the passively experienced seductions in her identifiable pattern of the withdrawal and chase of intermittent decathexis.

The second interpersonal constellation described by the Furmans is a pathological form of projective identification in which parents deal with their anxieties by externalizing them and managing to make those anxieties a part of their child's experience. It is easy to imagine here how the assault on the child's sense of reality, and the subsequent excitability resulting from the parents' failure to shoulder amounts of stimulation that are beyond the child's capacities for mastery, could lead to perpetuation of a traumatic state, if not to seduction proneness per se. Projective identification, subsuming all the complexities of reversal, of passivity into activity, of confusion of locus of origination of an action, whether in self or other, of identification with the aggressor, and of actualizing what is projected (Sandler, 1976), may well serve as an umbrella concept to elucidate all of the interaction matrices involved in the psychic trauma of seduction.

## SORTING OUT INNER AND OUTER IN TREATMENT

This consideration of how some interpersonal-experiential realities of seduction come to be internalized leads us now to examine how the fact that something traumatic really happened makes a difference in the treatment setting, particularly affecting the transference and its interpretation. And here, in opposition to a hermeneutic approach, I maintain unequivocally that the essence of psychoanalytic treatment is to help a patient disentangle and sort out the real inner from the real outer constituents of his or her past in the interests of effective symptom, conflict, and character analysis. For the traumatically seduced, notably for those subjected to the perils of gaslighting, psychoanalytic treatment aims particularly to free reality testing and to strengthen the sense of reality. E. Furman discovered that difficulty in integrating all experience is a clue to the factuality of traumatic seductions in childhood. As child or adult analysands, individuals with this background would have specific troubles in integrating analytic interpretations, especially when the analyst is not good enough with dosage, timing, and tact. Searles (1965) astutely observed, in this regard, that the untimeliness of an analyst's interpretations could undermine patients' confidence in the reliability of their own emotional reactions and perceptions of external reality, and that such an unempathic analyst therefore could "drive patients crazy," a sometimes inadvertent though iatrogenic gaslighting trauma repeating the original in susceptible patients. These failures might at times reflect one degree or another of Masson's caricature of an insidious form of seduction by the analyst to a version of psychoanalysis which underplays the contribution objective reality to psychic reality.

The adult patient who was abused as a child often experiences interpretations, even those which are adjudged to be empathically timed, as assaultive intrusions when their content feels at odds with the patient's momentary experiences. There seems here to be a fusion of rape or other invasive, assaultive experiences, with memories of annihilative assaults on one's sense of reality, reminiscent of being told, "It didn't really happen, it couldn't really happen," when clearly something happened.

It is easy, E. Furman has told us, to reconstruct, via recapitulations and repetitions in the analysis, what was done to the abused child in the original traumatic situation. But far more difficult than reconstruction is the therapeutic task of dealing with the repeated assaults on that child's reality testing.

Blum (1986) noted how Freud (1905a) did just that in his treatment of Dora, whose father and Herr K. both attempted to convince her that their very real seductive behavior was all a figment of her imagination. Freud's correct therapeutic strategy of commenting on her reliability as an observer and reporter affirmed her reality sense while also allowing for an interpretive focus on the meaning in her fantasy life of her elaborations of her seduction experience.

Though I have not encountered a systematic study of transference manifestations among the traumatically seduced, the recent book, *The Reconstruction of Trauma*, edited by Rothstein (1986), does address various among them, as does the account of sequelae of trauma by E. and R. Furman (Marans, 1988). The Furmans noted a big difference in the way the analyst is seen as seducer when a real traumatic seduction has taken place in the patient's early life and the more usual, strictly neurotically based transference perceptions of the analyst as seductive. The difference centers on the failure of the patient who was traumatized as a child to integrate positive and negative aspects of his or her perceptions of the analyst. Although this failure of integration, perhaps splitting, is common to many other syndromes, for example, the borderline personality organization, it takes on a characteristic coloring for the particular group in question. For them, the intense negative responses to the analyst often center on ideas of being intrusively influenced for purposes of the analyst's personal gratifications.

I have observed several truly traumatized patients who had overwhelmingly negative reactions to their analysts' occasional persistence in interpreting. The patients failed to integrate their negatively toned perceptions with previous positive, trusting feelings. Repeated interpretations tended to be experienced as attempts to crush, to twist words, to recast thoughts in the analyst's terms, to pound into submission, to brainwash, to destroy identity. Under the immediate impact of the "anxiety of influence," that is, of the cognitive-affective, chaotic experiences of disorganization which follow even objective, well-timed interpretations, the truly traumatized patient might disavow ever having perceived the analyst positively, even though the positive feelings have in fact been strong. The more neurotic patient might also feel unduly influenced when interpretations do not correspond to consciously held self-perceptions, but would not react with such extreme disorganization, still able to retain positive good feelings about the analyst. The neurotic patient might fantasize that the analyst gets persistent in order to gratify his or her own needs (e.g., "analytic vanity") via seducing the patient into acceptance of interpretations. The patient may correctly identify the analyst's persistence as character trait, annoying but not threatening any long-term loss of emotional balance. Most important, the neurotic but relatively nontraumatized patient will not lose contact with his or her positive transferential feelings even while sporadically believing the analyst wishes to influence via interpretation. In contrast, the patient with a history of being traumatically seduced will crave a restoration of his or her sense of reality, of himself or herself.

One patient, a woman and only child, with a phobia that birds might swoop down on her unexpectedly, had shared a bed with her father for many of her early years. Her mother, who slept elsewhere, denied the import of this sexually seductive arrangement. She told the patient that she did not have to sleep with her husband any more because they had all the children they desired. The patient remembers being hyper-alert as a child to the possibility of her father's pajamas opening, but mostly she was never sure whether they were open or closed. Her fantasy was that his penis might fly out and touch, even impregnate her. This woman never could be sure about a lot of things and ambiguities about fact and fantasy were particularly disturbing. Each time her analyst encouraged her to share her fantasies about something, she would adamantly respond, "That was not a fantasy, it was a reality." The analyst's use of the word *fantasy* was experienced by her as a form of gaslighting, that is, as an attempt to influence her into thinking that there was no real basis to her experience. Interpretations were experienced as bewildering, sexualized seductions, flying out at her, as though the analyst were intentionally trying to shock her away from her convictions about the reality of her experiences.

Another patient, one who was definitely raped in puberty, could never be sure if she had been taken by force, or if she simply had consented while "spaced out" on marijuana, and had not been raped at all. Sequelae in her case included an obligatory and repetitive seeking out of dangers as she explored the "scuzzy" and seamy side of life. she suffered a pervasive abulia—a loss of will or sense of volition—and an inability to discriminate between instances when she was agreeing to things and instances of being unduly influenced. And that is how she felt about analytic interpretations during the treatment.

An important therapeutic aim in working with traumatized patients who have a strong fear of being influenced away from their reality sense by interpretations of their inner life, then, is to reintegrate disassociated and altered ego states with cognitive and affective working through of the traumatic experience. This is best accomplished through correct reconstruction of forgotten experiences of childhood, sorting out what really must have happened from what was fantasized. It is not accomplished by interpretation alone, nor is it accomplished by certain attempts at a non-interpretive stance on the part of the analyst, such as providing a corrective emotional experience.

## WHAT IS TRAUMA FOR ONE IS NOT FOR ANOTHER

Returning now to the ways in which real trauma makes a difference, it is not altogether impossible to be swept away by the passions aroused on learning of the realities of sexual and aggressive child abuse and lose analytic neutrality. That does not usually happen. But it did with Masson who said:

There are certain kinds of reality that are so overwhelming that they admit of only one interpretation.... I find it so sad that an analyst should support the position that a child can be raped by her father and have a positive experience. It's an awful position. (Malcolm, 1984p. 55).

Masson here is conflating an appraisal of an actual outcome with an analytic judgment which allegedly condones traumatically abusive practices. Real trauma has to influence, either by determining limits on or enhancing aspects of the shape, form, intensity, and content of drive-related fantasies. But what is traumatic for one individual may not be for another. The complemental series paradigm allows for the possibility of constitutional and learned varibility in proneness to the traumatic impact of seductions.

A child may experience an incestuous rape retrospectively with both pleasure, often guilty, and unpleasure, even though at the "traumatic moment" (Freud, 1896b, 1933) itself, it may indeed have been experienced one way predominantly. And the experience is by definition one of unpleasure if there is a psychological state of fright with more excitation than can be discharged and mastered, and a resulting state of psychic helplessness ensues. That is how we define psychic trauma. But maintaining that memory and its associated experience remains statically one way over time ignores transformations and elaborations in memory and fantasy. That narrow, archaic view also ignores the multiple and overdetermined effects of cumulative and strain trauma (Khan, 1963; Kris, 1956). We know that some traumas, upon recollection—which may be false recollection—gratify instinctual drives, a need for punishment, or serve other multiple functions.

We sometimes hear reports of the so-called beneficial effects of incest, the recognition of which has apparently tempted Masson out of an analytically neutral stance into a socially polemical one. The neutral analyst neither scotomatizes nor shrinks away in outrage upon learning that incest may be followed by increased capacity for orgastic pleasure accompanied by sado-masochistic fantasies (see Adams-Silvan & Silvan, 1983) or even, as Shengold (1979) reported, an increased sense of being protected. Such positive seeming outcomes and recollections on the part of patients undoubtedly reflect defensive adaptations to the trauma. That is, they may represent reversals, disassociations, or rationalizations of psychic pain. They may also, of course, express unconscious wishes, or some compromise formation between wish and defense. And Marans (1988) suggested that the psychic reality of a patient's present recollections of an early experience of seduction may serve ongoing experience and overshadow the etiological effects of pathology in the real child-parent relationship. Masson approached the truth in saying that certain overwhelming realities can be experienced in only one way. But that does not imply that they must, particularly as memories of the events become transformed, and as the events are recollected over time and past the occurrence of the traumatic moment. The ideas on the meaning of psychic trauma that I have just reviewed are encompassed by Brenner's (1986) perspective on trauma, derived from Fenichel (1945), which holds that stimuli are not traumatic for merely quantitative reasons. The varied and changing meanings of experience, and especially its unconscious meanings, are what is crucially important when it comes to psychic trauma, even when we accept Freud's quantitative view of trauma as a sense of helplessness in the face of over-whelming stimuli.

Transformations of meaning occur in reconstructive work during the course of a psychoanalysis itself. They also occur during individual development, as the child's mental capacities grow in more complex and diverse directions. Both processes enable the attribution of multiple and complex meanings to even the most overwhelming reality, limited as it may have been at the original moment to permitting only simpliform interpretation. Indeed, the remembered reality of seductions may exercise a seductive power in the direction of resistance to other issues. Masson was not right in claiming that Freud was never completely comfortable in giving up the historical truth value of early trauma no matter what its later elaborations in the representational world of the mind. Freud simply had not come to the point of integrating conceptually all of the various currents of experience influencing the development of psychic reality. That was to be the task of all of his followers, not just those in the so-called "avant garde." It does make a difference if something really happened or not, especially insofar as traumatic overstimulation makes its indelible imprint on the course of fantasies as powerfully motivating forces in the personality.

## ACKNOWLEDGMENTS

An earlier version of this article was presented to the New York Freudian Society in February 1986, New York City.

## REFERENCES

Adams-Silvan, A.S., & Silvan, M. (1983), December. *Sightings on the dark continent: Some speculations regarding the relation of sadism and oedipal displacement to the capacity in women to achieve orgasm.* Paper presented at the December, 1983, Meetings of the American Psychoanalytic Association, New York City.

Arlow, J.A. (1969). Fantasy, memory, and reality testing. *Psychoanalytic Quarterly* 38:28–51.

Arlow, J.A. (1985). The concept of psychic reality and related problems. *Journal of the American Psychoanalytic Association* 33:521–535. http://www.pep-web.org/document.php?id=apa.033.0521a

Beebe, B., & Lachmann, F.M. (1988). Mother-infant mutual influence and precursors of psychic structure. In A. Goldberg (Ed.), *Frontiers in Self-Psychology* Vol. 3, pp. 3–25. Hillsdale, NJ: The Analytic Press. http://www.pep-web.org/document.php?id=psp.003.0003a

Benjamin, J. (1990). An outline of intersubjectivity *Psychoanalytic Psychology* 7:33–46. http://www.pep-web.org/document.php?id=ppsy.007s.0033a

Blum, H. (1986). The concept of the reconstruction of trauma. In A. Rothstein (Ed.), *The Reconstruction of Trauma,* pp. 7–27. New York: International Universities Press.

http://www.pep-web.org/document.php?id=zbk.080.0007a

Brenner, C. (1986). Discussion of the various contributions. In A. Rothstein (Ed.), *The Reconstruction of Trauma*. pp. 195–203. New York: International Universities Press.

Calef, V., & Weinshel, E. (1981). Some clinical consequences of introjection: Gaslighting. *Psychoanalytic Quarterly* 50: 44–67.
http://www.pep-web.org/document.php?id=paq.050.0044a

Cukor, G. (Director), & Hornblower, A. (Producer). (1944). "Gaslight" [film]. Hollywood: Loews, Inc.

Fenichel, O. (1945). *Psychoanalytic Theory of Neurosis*. New York: Norton.

Freud, S. (1892). Extracts from the Fliess papers, Draft A. *S.E.* 1:175–280.
http://www.pep-web.org/document.php?id=se.001.0215a

——— (1893). On the psychical mechanism of hysterical phenomena: A lecture. *Standard Edition* 3:25–39.
http://www.pep-web.org/document.php?id=se.003.0025a

——— (1896a). Heredity and the aetiology of the neuroses. *Standard Edition* 3:41–156. http://www.pep-web.org/document.php?id=se.003.0141a

——— (1896b). Further remarks on the neuro-psychoses of defence. *Standard Edition* 3: 159–185.
http://www.pep-web.org/document.php?id=se.003.0157a

——— (1896c). The aetiology of hysteria. *Standard Edition* 3:89–221. http://www.pep-web.org/document.php?id=se.003.0187a

——— (1899). Screen memories. *Standard Edition* 3:01–322.
http://www.pep-web.org/document.php?id=se.003.0299a

——— (1905a). Fragment of an analysis of a case of hysteria. *Standard Edition* 7:3–122. http://www.pep-web.org/document.php?id=se.007.0001a

———. (1905b). Three essays on the theory of sexuality. *Standard Edition* 7:125–243. http://www.pep-web.org/document.php?id=se.007.0123a

———. (1914). On the history of the psycho-analytic movement *Standard Edition* 14:3–66. http://www.pep-web.org/document.php?id=se.014.0001a

——— (1915). Instincts and their vicissitudes. *Standard Edition* 14:105–140.
http://www.pep-web.org/document.php?id=se.014.0109a

——— (1917). Introductory lectures on psychoanalysis. *Standard Edition* 15 & 16. http://www.pep-web.org/document.php?id=se.016.0241a

——— (1918). From the history of an infantile neurosis. *Standard Edition* 17:3–123. http://www.pep-web.org/document.php?id=se.017.0001a

——— (1926). Inhibitions, symptoms and anxiety. *Standard Edition* 20:77–175. http://www.pep-web.org/document.php?id=se.020.0075a

——— (1933). New introductory lectures on psychoanalysis. *Standard*

*Edition* 22:3–182. http://www.pep-web.org/document.php?id=se.022.0001a

———— (1939). Moses and monotheism. *Standard Edition* 23:3–137. http://www.pep-web.org/document.php?id=se.023.0001a

———— (1954).*The origins of psychoanalysis. Letters to Wilhelm Fliess, drafts and notes 1887–1902* (E. Mosbacher & J. Strachey, Trans). New York: Basic Books.http://www.pep-web.org/document.php?id=zbk.051.0244a

Gediman, H.K. (1971). The concept of stimulus barrier: Its review and reformulation as an adaptive ego function. *International Journal of Psycho-Analysis.* 52:243–257.
http://www.pep-web.org/document.php?id=ijp.052.0243a

———— (1985, Spring). Point of view: Psychic trauma and the press. *American Psychoanalytic Association Newsletter*, pp. 1, 3–5.
http://www.pep-web.org/document.php?id=apa.033s.0003a

———— (1989). Conflict and deficit models of psychopathology: A unificatory point of view. In D. W. Detrick & S. Detrick (Eds.), *Self Psychology.* pp. 293–309. Hillsdale, NJ: The Analytic Press.

Greenacre, P. (1971). The influence of infantile trauma on genetic patterns. *In Emotional Growth: Psychoanalytic Studies of the Gifted and a Great Variety of Other Individuals,* Vol. 1, pp. 260–299. New York: International Universities Press.

Hanly, C. (1986). The assault on truth: Freud's suppression of the seduction theory. *International Journal of Psycho-Analysis* 67:517–519.
http://www.pep-web.org/document.php?id=ijp.067.0517a

Khan, M. (1963). The concept of cumulative trauma. *Psychoanalytic Study of the Child* 18:286–306.
http://www.pep-web.org/document.php?id=psc.018.0286a

Kohut, H. (1977).*The Restoration of The Self.* New York: International Universities Press.

Kris, E. (1956). The recovery of childhood memories in psychoanalysis. *Psychoanalytic Study of the Child,* 11:54–58.
http://www.pep-web.org/document.php?id=psc.011.0054a

Malcolm, J. (1984). *In the Freud Archives.* New York: Knopf.

Marans, A.E. (Reporter). (1988). Panel discussion: The seduction hypothesis. *Journal of the American Psychoanalytic Association* 33:759–771.
http://www.pep-web.org/document.php?id=apa.036.0759a

Masson, J.M. (1984).*The Assault on Truth: Freud's Suppression of the Seduction Theory.* New York: Farrar, Straus, & Giroux.

Masson, J.M. (1990). *Final Analysis.* Reading, MA: Addison-Wesley.

Rothstein, A. (Ed.). (1986). The reconstruction of trauma: Its significance

in clinical work. *Workshop Series of the American Psychoanalytic Association,* Monograph 2. New York: International Universities Press.
http://www.pep-web.org/document.php?id=zbk.080.0001a

Sandler, J. (1976). Actualization and object relationships. *Journal of the Philadelphia Association of Psychoanalysis* 3:59–70.
http://www.pep-web.org/document.php?id=paq.050.0694a

Schafer, R. (1983).*The Analytic Attitude.* New York: Basic Books.
http://www.pep-web.org/document.php?id=pct.002.0003a

Searles, H.F. (1965).*Collected Papers on Schizophrenia and Related Subjects.* New York: International Universities Press.

Shengold, L.L. (1979). Child abuse and deprivation soul murder. *Journal of the American Psychoanalytic Association* 27:533–559.
http://www.pep-web.org/document.php?id=apa.027.0533a

Spence, D. (1982). *Narrative Truth and Historical Truth.* New York: Norton.
http://www.pep-web.org/document.php?id=zbk.015.0001a

Stern, D. (1977). *The First Relationship: Infant and Mother,* Cambridge, MA: Harvard University Press.
http://www.pep-web.org/document.php?id=jicap.013.0024a

——— (1985). *The Interpersonal World Of The Infant.* New York: Basic Books. http://www.pep-web.org/document.php?id=zbk.016.0001a

Wallerstein, R.S. (1985). The concept of psychic reality: its meaning and value. *Journal of the American Psychoanalytic Association* 33:555–569.
http://www.pep-web.org/document.php?id=apa.033.0555a

## PART II. CONFLICT AND DEFICIT

## AUTHOR'S INTRODUCTION

I was asked by Arnold Goldberg, one of the best known and eminent self-psychologists in the world to contribute what is here Chapter 5, shortly after a most inauspicious meeting with him at an event in Chicago in the 1980s celebrating Heinz Kohut's life and work. Dr. Goldberg had the floor and shook me up some by quoting something I had written several years ago about Kohut, but without mentioning my name. At that time, he had never met me personally, so he had no idea that that woman he criticized and who was sitting right in front of him, looking at him straight in the eye as he spoke was none other than yours truly. "Someone," he said, quoting my article, "once said that Kohut's theories about conflict and deficit were interesting but not true." He then laughed, wondering who on earth could say of a theory that it was either true or not true since any educated person knew we could speak only to a theory's validity not to its truth. At the end of the session, I went up and introduced myself to Arnold as the person who had made that error in scholarship and apologized. Next I knew, he had invited me to contribute a chapter on Freud's structural model versus Kohut's deficit model in an upcoming book by Detrick and Detrick. I told Arnold that if I were going to write about my ideas of a Freudian take on Kohut's ideas about deficit, I would not want to limit my ideas to Freud's structural model alone, but would want touch on all of Freud's metapsychological points of view: the dynamic, economic, structural, genetic, and adaptive points of view (see Rapaport and Gill, 1959). Further, I did not see conflict and deficit as a versus matter—a false binary, that is, but would be willing to attempt to discuss Kohut's conflict and deficit models using Freud's metapsychological points of view in a comparative psychoanalytic context. I can see now that my life-long commitment to multiple perspectives clearly derived from extensive exposure to Rapaport's ideas thirty years earlier, during the time I had worked at The Research Center for Mental Health at New York University. Then, countless staff meetings were devoted to Rapaport's reading of Freud's Chapter 7 in *The Interpretation of Dreams*. The contract was signed, and my 1989 unificatory contribution, which has become Chapter 5 in this book, appeared in Detrick and Detrick's *Self Psychology* book, along with a life-long cordial relation with Arnold Goldberg.

The well-covered topic of empathy comes to mind in any consideration of self-psychology, especially in reference to the work of Kohut and his follow-ers. If I have not made it clear in the chapters in Part II that follow, I should like now to make it absolutely clear that I do not see the value of empathy in psychoanalytic treatment as related to a specific technique used only with patients who suffer from disorders of the self. Rather, I regard empathy as essential to any good psychoanalytic treatment of all patients regardless of the degrees of conflict and/ or deficit that brought them to seek help.

# Chapter 5: Conflict and Deficit Models Of Psychopathology: A Unificatory Point Of View

[Gediman, H.K. (1989). Conflict and deficit models of psychopathology: A unificatory point of view. In: D. Detrick and S. Detrick, Eds. *Self Psychology: Comparisons and Contrasts*. Hillsdale, N.J.: The Analytic Press.]

## CONFLICT AND DEFICIT MODELS

Conflict and deficit psychopathology must be understood within a broad, multiaxial psychoanalytic context. The structural model, alone, cannot fruitfully be compared and contrasted with the deficit model in the psychology of the self as put forth in the works of Kohut and his followers. To attempt that comparison, one would need to assume that the structural model per se is superordinate, all-inclusive, or able to embrace all relevant other points of view. I cannot make that assumption any more than I could view a "structure" of self as superordinate to the traditionally designated structures, id, ego, and superego (see Richards, 1981, 1982). If one's theoretical approach to psychoanalytic material is perspectival, and I believe mine is, then one must look at the value for integrating conflict and deficit models, of multiple points of view. Only then can we hear multiple themes in the clinical material we listen to and observe, themes which in the past have been obscured by unidimensional theoretical perspectives. And only then can we engage in timely shifts in technique geared to the material which emerges. New views on old and new perspectives permit new ways of grasping and of applying psychoanalytic interpretations insightfully. The position I am developing is not uniquely mine, nor is it held by all Freudian psychoanalysts. It derives from Freud's (1915) idea that any psychical process can be described from various points of view, in which case we speak of a metapsychological presentation. Freud's multiaxial position was expanded by Gill (1963) and is, I believe, still, to this day, the better model for understanding the complex relationships of conflict and deficit than the structural point of view, alone. In its attempts at parsimoniously explaining everything, the structural point of view alone runs the risk of collapsing important distinctions which a metapsychological presentation as Freud originally conceived it, broadly, though not so specifically as to include such anachronisms as the original notions about cathexis and excitations, does not do.

There are important aspects of self psychology which may be incorporated into the psychoanalytic corpus as a whole. That corpus, that body of knowledge which is recognized as psychoanalytic, would have to include not just the structural model of classical psychoanalysis, but the topographical, economic, genetic, dynamic, adaptive, developmental, and environmental points of view as well. This expanded scope of metapsychological viewpoints would, in addition, have to address those real clinical phenomena formerly designated by the rubric "actual neuroses" (see Rangell, 1968; Gediman, 1984). That is, it would acknowledge the importance of stimulus regulation and the antecedents and sequelae of generalized tension states of all kinds: sexual and aggressive, preoedipally and oedipally linked. It would also have to deal with psychic trauma, carefully sorting out the contributions to psychic reality of not just fantasies, but also of material reality and historical truth. It would take particular note of the way in which fantasy makes use of real, traumatic historical occurrences, such as seductions, abuses, and failures in maternal empathic attunement, and it would note how real traumatic abuse, say, impacts on all areas of psychic functioning, including but not limited to fantasy formation. That is, an inclusive, perspectival psychoanalytic point of view requires an appreciation of the various admixtures of fantasy and reality, and centers on a concept of psychic reality which includes intrapsychic representation of real interpersonal events (Gediman, 1987). And here is where the psychology of the self also enters into what the reader will by now recognize as a unificatory effort at integrating multiple points of view dealing with multiple aspects of human psychic functioning.

The self states which Kohut has succeeded in *recalling* to our attention are, I believe, embedded in the very clinical phenomena which receded from psychoanalytic illumination when specific but inadequate theories relating to actual neuroses and psychic trauma were abandoned in favor of newer developments in psychoanalytic theory. An attempted integration of the deficit and conflict models within a general psychoanalytic theory would reflect, in my view, a resurrection of aspects of all these worthy viewpoints which the structural model, when conceived in isolation from the rest, has cast into relative oblivion. The spotlight is once again on these neglected phenomena and their pathological manifestations. And it is to Kohut that all psychoanalysts owe a special debt of gratitude, for it is he who in large measure revived their importance through his selective emphases on both the clinical manifestations themselves, and on the timely shifts in technique which, to my mind, may be included within the basic treatment model, for dealing with them psychotherapeutically.

## A PLEA FOR A UNIFICATORY THEORY

A while ago I (Gediman, 1980) wrote a book review essay on *The Search for the Self: Selected Writings of Heinz Kohut: 1950-1978*, edited by Paul Ornstein. Its purpose was to show how the scope and sweep of Kohut's central issue provides a perspective on the development of his now well known self psychology, and how it promised an unprecedented opportunity for raising to the level of consciousness those aspects of human psychology, referred to above, which the tendency toward exclusive reliance on the structural model, to the relative exclusion of even the topographic and economic points of view, had downplayed. I now feel more strongly than ever that the value of Kohut's contributions lies not in their replacing of a conflict model which relies only on the structural point of view, but on an understanding of how the phenomena addressed by self psychology interdigitates with those addressed by a conflict psychology informed by *all* relevant points of view. For our particular aim of comparing and contrasting conflict and deficit, I think we need first to pay particular attention to some valuable aspects of the controversial psychoeconomic point of view.

Just as contemporary classical analysts have recently redirected their attention to the importance of the psychoeconomics of stimulus regulation, even among people suffering from neurotic structural psychopathology (id-ego- superego conflicts), so too did Kohut emphasize the economic point of view. In that 1980 paper, I noted that Paul Ornstein (Kohut, 1978) correctly concluded that Kohut always embraced the psychoeconomic point of view to account for increases and decreases of tension, and for imbalances of narcissistic libido. What is probably less well known is the application, in Kohut's earlier papers, of the psychoeconomic point of view in affirming the importance of the traumatic and actual neuroses for an understanding of the creative process, generally, and the enjoyment of music and literature in particular. Kohut attributed pleasure in listening to music to relief from psychological tension via the release of energy required to withstand the influx of a chaotic situation, or to overcome the threat of a traumatic stimulus bombardment. This relief occurs, he said, when the form of music transforms chaos into orderly stimulation that can be dealt with comparatively easily. Later, reasoning similarly, Kohut attributed narcissistic equilibrium to the relief from psychic tensions which are induced by traumatic failures in empathy. In the final triumphant mastery of the musical task, the transformation of unpleasurable, dissonant tension into consonance, the peak of enjoyment is reached via regression to a primitive ego state in which, according to Kohut, the ecstatic listener does not clearly differentiate between himself and the outside world. The regressive experience of a primitive narcissistic equilibrium, along with the preservation of complex ego functioning to master the influx of sound, creates the experience of being soothed by closeness.

I view Kohut's early attempts to unify the more classical psychoeconomic and structural points of view with a developmental object relations perspective as critical underpinnings for understanding the relationship of a conflict model to self psychology. Ornstein stated that Kohut *added* self psychology to id and ego psychology. Yet, in comparing and contrasting, certain important differences are clear. Kohut, for example, minimized the role of aggression as id-derivative, just as he found relatively dispensable psychoanalytic drive theory generally, because he believed it treats aggression as a biological drive configuration and not as a psychological construct. What he saw as omnipresent and as meriting psychological construct status is rage, a "disintegration product" following shameful submission. This rage encompasses revenge, .destructiveness, and sadism, all secondarily employed, like Goldstein's "catastrophic reaction," to soothe or stimulate a narcissistically injured, humiliated, or damaged self. Thus, he saw defensive activity as motivated primarily by shame, a defect in the grandiose self, and not by anxiety or guilt over unconscious forbidden sexual or aggressive wishes. Despite his superb phenomenological understanding of narcissistic rage, Kohut's emphasis would strike the Freudian psychoanalyst as one-sided and neglectful of clinical manifestations of psychic structure and conflict as generally understood. The anxious and the guilty also suffer from escalating shame propensity and hurt pride—the pathology of the self. And conversely, it may be that narcissistic personalities have a relatively poor capacity for guilt over aggressive oedipally related impulses, but they hardly can be totally free of related conflicts. It is always a matter of degree and relative weight.

From Kohut's earliest papers, it is easy to detect his dissatisfaction with all previous attempts within psychoanalysis to articulate a unified approach for understanding and treating patients with structural conflicts and psychoneuroses, on the one hand, and those suffering from ego defects, ego modifications, or borderline psychopathology, on the other. Although his expressed purpose was to create a unified theory of psychopathology, I believe that he succeeded more at differentiating two models: a developmental defect model for the psychology of the self, and the standard conflict model, which was retained to account for psychological formations in the neuroses. What started around 1950 as a much needed attempt to expand the theory of the therapeutic action of psychoanalysis to areas beyond the classical transference neuroses had, by 1976, evolved into a dichotomization of people, a dichotomization more rigid, I believe, than the one that the original modifications set out to soften. In the 1950s, Kohut stated how all patients, even narcissistic personality disorders, formed transferences, and his efforts were then directed more toward differentiating transferences than toward differentiating patients. He came to conclude later that some people develop transferences based exclusively on relationships toward objects perceived as autonomous and independent, while others develop transferences, especially those involving archaic selfobjects, based on projection onto others of parts of the self.

Kohut's requirement of two different transference paradigms for conflict and deficit pathology suffered from its bifurcation of two aspects of transference: that which involves the repetition of a past relationship with a significant figure; and that which involves the projection of a repudiated aspect of the self onto others. In fact, both aspects of transference phenomena are to be found in all individuals.

Additionally, Kohut's view is, I believe, at odds with a developmental understanding of preoedipal, prestructural conflicts as well as oedipal conflicts, as universal motivators of compromise formation and psychopathology. After a while, Kohut no longer implied merely two types of transference paradigm, but two types of people. He proceeded as though two major nosological entities, neurotics who are structurally conflicted and narcissistic personality disorders suffering from pathology of the self, require two different *theoretical* as well as therapeutic approaches. I think we are indebted to Kohut for calling our attention to self psychology and articulating its distinction from structural pathology, but I sense that most mainstream analysts would tend rather to see both phenomena—the neurotic and the so-called borderline narcissistic—and their underlying intrapsychic and prestructural or preoedipal conflicts in all patients, in varying degrees.

Kohut distinguished nonspecific as well as specific narcissistic forces, particularly defenses and resistances. Nonspecific narcissistic phenomena accompany all forms of anxiety, the frustration of instinctual drives, and the frustration, particularly, of oedipal wishes. Here, narcissistic injury may be secondary to a core neurotic conflict. Specific, primary narcissistic pathology, on the other hand, relates, said Kohut, to a specific genetic trauma: the insufficient mirroring or traumatic withdrawal of phase-appropriate mirroring of the child's self. This position feels right, clinically, and is consistent with classical psychoanalytic theory, even though one might identify other patho-gens in the development of narcissistic disorders, such as mutual derailments in attunement which may or may not relate to mirroring. What feels wrong, clinically, is a tendency to polarization. Kohut once again implied two sep-arate, *mutually exclusive* groups of individuals. The first he called "Guilty Man," which is composed of individuals suffering primarily from structural conflicts and compromise formations constituting the neuroses. The second he called "Tragic Man," and this is composed of those suffering primarily from developmental conflicts involving pathology of the self, constituting mainly the narcissistic personality disorders. These groups correspond to Kohut's two paradigmatic forms of psychopathology: nuclear oedipal pathology that is hidden by a broad cover of narcissistic disturbance; and narcissistic disorders that are hidden by seemingly oedipal pathology.

I believe that mainstream psychoanalytic theory as well as Kohut's self psychology has suffered from a tendency to polarization, but that many recent integrative efforts, such as the one I am attempting, have been made. There *are* these two paradigmatic forms of psychopathology which seem to apply in cer-tain cases, but there is a broad spectrum in between and overlapping as well. Therefore, they do not require us to *split* mankind, as Kohut appears to have done, in order to understand and treat them. Rather, their existence dictates a shift in emphasis, technically, to deal with different facets of psychopathology in one and the same individual, as well as in different individuals. We should speak, rather, of the pleasure-seeking Guilty Man *sector* and the shame-prone Tragic Man *sector*, a position implied in Kohut's earlier work, but which he abandoned in favor of his so-called cohesive theory of the self that, ironically, implies a false split, a "vertical split," whereas the abandoned position was more true to phenomenological reality. Both phenomena, the neurotic and the narcissistic, and their underlying intrapsychic, prestructural and preoedipal and oedipal conflicts may be seen as essential features of all patients, granted in varying degrees.

Since all patients, neurotic or otherwise, are shame-prone, especially in treatment, *all* interpretations of unconscious and/or ego alien material inevita-bly provoke narcissistic resistances against all psychoanalytic interpretations because the very discovery of unconscious processes dethrones, as Freud told us, man's narcissism, and such resistances do not necessarily confirm the cor-rectness of the analyst's interpretation of conflicts in the area of object-instinc-tual drives. Similar ideas have been proposed by Sandler and Sandler (1983, 1984, 1987), who claim that a universal content in the "present unconscious" of *every* individual is the presence of feelings of shame, embarrassment, and humiliation. They believe that the second censorship of the *topographical* model, that between the systems Conscious and Preconscious, has as its fundamental orientation the avoidance of or resistance to these feelings. Sandler and Sandler, unlike Kohut, do not propose a new theory to account for shame resistances; rather, they revive the importance of some of the metaphors of the topographical model, integrating that approach with the structural point of view. But it was at the heart of Kohut's technical recommendations that the unspecifically as well as the specifically narcissistic resistances require empathy from the analyst, who must show the patient that he or she understands the feeling of shame and helplessness and lack of omniscience at a sudden revelation over which the patient has no conscious control. I believe that these resistances are amenable to interpretation as well as requiring empathy in a uniquely important way. Kohut had therewith added centrality to these issues by raising the consciousness of all practicing analysts to the emphasis that this kind of empathy must be accorded. It is here, in the attention that is being paid to shame-proneness in our daily clinical analytic work, that the potential for rapprochement between Kohut's self psychology and new developments in conflict models is to be found.

## THE PROBLEM OF ANNIHILATION ANXIETY: A TEST CASE

In 1983, I (Gediman, 1983) took the phenomenon, "annihilation anxiety," as a test case to try to document the views on the unfortunate polarization of people that the conflict and deficit models, when viewed as mutually exclusive, could lead to. I turn once again to a consideration of "annihilation anxiety," for the various ways in which that phenomenon has been conceptualized can tell us much about comparing and contrasting self psychology with a conflict model which subsumes the multiple points of view of a broadly conceived perspectival psychoanalytic approach.

"Annihilation anxiety" has been described in the psychoanalytic literature variously, as fear of the ego's own dissolution; fear of fragmentation of the self; fear of unreality of the self; and the disintegration products of narcissistic trauma. It also covers the range of "existential anxieties." Kohut (1977) believed that the primary anxiety of the oedipal child was not castration anxiety, but what he viewed as a more basic anxiety, "disintegration anxiety," a fear of psychological death, a fear of loss of the human self, deriving from the "loss of the self-cohesion-maintaining responses of the empathic subject..." (Kohut, 1984, p. 19). It is referred to, in the structural model, as the overwhelming of the ego, or the "dread of the strength of the instincts" (Freud, 1923; A. Freud, 1937).

There is something about the subjective experience of annihilation anxiety that is right at the heart of what I regard as a major polarization in psychoanalytic theory today: the deficit versus the conflict model. Perhaps one reason for the polarization is the failure to understand that the rubric term, annihilation anxiety, conceals multiple referents in its various meanings: a manifest experiential content; traumatic intrusions of stimulation; the anticipation of psychically traumatic helplessness. It could be said that the deficit model of Kohut's self psychology has been employed largely to account for psychopathology associated with the *conscious* experience of annihilation or disintegration anxiety and its associated manifest content.

For Kohut and his followers, annihilation anxiety has been regarded as an archaic, "prestructural" prototype of the more familiar poststructural anxiety developments. They would see its manifestation in adults as a unique anxiety "form." In fact, Kohut (1984) stated that none of the "forms" of anxiety described by Freud are equivalent to the basic experience of psychological disintegration posited by self psychology. Kohut is not quite right in assuming that Freud referred to "forms" of anxiety. And the conflict model, as understood today, has generally regarded all anxieties, including those with the manifest content of annihilation fears, not as four separate forms, but as relating to the four prototypical danger situations of childhood: loss of the object; loss of the object's love; castration; and, loss of the superego's love and approval. In viewing annihilation anxiety as a class of anxiety experience different from what is subsumed under the traditional danger situations, Kohut states:

> Whatever the trigger that ushered in or reinforced the progressive dissolution of the self, the emphasis of the experience lies...on the precarious state of the self and not on the factors that may have set the process of disintegration into motion... (1977, p. 102).

The nucleus of the patient's annihilation anxiety, according to Kohut, and to Stolorow and Lachmann (1980), is his experience that his *self is undergoing an ominous change*. This postulation of annihilation anxiety as a fifth and transcendental danger situation is one that self psychologists regard as requiring a so-called complemental deficit model or theory.

In looking at some interrelations of conflict and deficit, in an attempt to integrate the two models, I would say that one nonpolarizing way of looking at the problem is not to forget Freud's view that the experience of the anticipation of traumatic intensity of excessive stimulation and the corresponding feeling of psychic helplessness as a narcissistic catastrophe underlies *all* the danger situations. And these situations, when there has been a history of psychic trauma, tend to get repeated in the present, constituting a trauma in their own right:, called variously, depending on whether we are speaking conceptually or in terms of experiential states, the overwhelming of the ego, the fear of disintegration of the self, annihilation anxiety. This dread becomes potentiated whenever instinctual drives or narcissistic tensions associated with it involve an accumulation of need tensions beyond the assimilating capacity of the individual. Waelder (1960) made a similar point in explaining that need tensions could lead to narcissistic catastrophe in anybody when they take on the meaning of the four great dangers which, for the very young child, can be all-around catastrophes.

Narcissistic catastrophe, then, as manifest content or latent fantasy of self-annihilation, as traumatic state, or as susceptibility to traumatic states, is not fruitfully conceived as a separate anxiety form or a fifth prototypical danger situation, but refers to the vulnerability of the psychic structure, of the person, in the face of undischarged accumulated need tensions in situations of psychic helplessness (Freud, 1926). The unconscious or the manifest experiential content known as annihilation anxiety refers to powerful affects, i.e., the quantitative intensification of anxiety, associated with representations of all four of the traditional danger situations. That the emphasis in *understanding* the process shifts to what Kohut describes as the threat to the cohesive, integrative psychic structure, to the sense of self, does not, to my way of thinking, in any way reduce the importance of the danger situations that trigger this threat, for in order to master the traumatic *sequelae* of the vulnerability or the belief that one is vulnerable, one must know what potentiates it. Whatever its various and consistent unconscious or manifest experiential qualities, annihilation anxiety does also signify a psychoeconomic state, or as Kohut said, a self state, to which I shall return shortly. These hallmark phenomena of accumulated undischarged psychic tensions lend a certain *experiential quality*, such as feelings of unreality and dissolution anxiety, *whether or not these feelings are also neurotic compromise formations.*

My reconciliatory position contains two basic assumptions. (1) Both narcissistic and neurotic manifestations of anxiety, in the broadest sense, are implicated in conflict and compromise formation, although these manifestations may differ with respect to the relative preponderance of preoedipal or oedipal conflicts. (2) Both narcissistic and neurotic annihilation anxiety reflect a certain degree of traumatic excitability, deriving either from traumatic failures in empathy and any other trauma, or from other factors such as rigid defenses, that could be held responsible for unusual drive intensities or which, metapsychologically, could be characterized as a "flooding" of the psychic apparatus, an "overwhelming of the ego." Note here that the formulations are both structural and psychoeconomic, as well as genetic and developmental-environmental. The structural point of view alone will not suffice, just as the psychoeconomic point of view did not suffice when Freud (1923, 1926) attempted to integrate the psychoeconomic theory of the traumatic and actual neuroses (the first anxiety theory) with that of signal anxiety in the psychoneuroses. His second anxiety theory did accomplish that integration. Thus, Freud's "problem" of anxiety was analogous, I believe, to the problem of integrating the deficit and conflict models with respect to annihilation anxiety: both may be resolved through a unificatory approach embracing multiple viewpoints.

Whether the traumatic excitability of annihilation anxiety was originally conflict-free (as deriving from a low neonatal stimulus barrier) or deriving from preoedipal conflicts between the child and his environment (as in the mother's failure as "protective shield" or "holding environment," or as in the fear of annihilation during the "rapprochement crisis"), it may play a part in the development and content of the intrapsychic conflict, for the psychoeconomic state of excessive excitability is *capable of being psychically represented*, or being given experiential content. A patient's experiential descriptions of intense anxiety may be just that: or they may be used defensively or in the service of resistance. For example, a patient may claim the fantasy content or the affective state generally subsumed under annihilation anxiety defensively, as in "I feel annihilated by your interpretations," a claim with which the analyst often colludes by modifying his analytic stance, unreflectively. Such presentations are not always insusceptible to motivational analysis.

These ideas are not original to me but may be traced back to the work of Freud (1926) and particularly to Ernest Jones (1927, 1929, 1936) in his work on "aphanisis," which he conceived as a dread of the ultimate danger situation of "total annihilation of the capacity for sexual gratification." Jones said that the fear of a permanent extinction of this capacity is a primal trauma underlying all the neuroses as well as psychotic states, and is expressed by different contents in different conditions. For example, the manifest content of the dread of aphanisis among obsessionals is the fear of loss of the personality. In hysterics, the dread takes the form of being overcome by sadistic excitement. The phenomenon was also referred to by Anna Freud (1937) in her discussion of instinctual anxiety, as "the ego's fear of its own extinction" when there are excessive instinctual accessions. Winnicott (1958) advanced similar ideas about "extinction" anxieties produced by a lack of id tension following orgastic discharge after intercourse. The vast literature from the Kleinian school on the universal "psychotic core" in everyone's personality makeup is also relevant. The phenomenology discussed by these authors does not seem too different from that emphasized by Kohut. But in my view, a new theory, a different model is not so much required as is a resurrection of certain aspects of the psychoeconomic and other points of view and their integration with the structural.

Thus, in distinction to self psychology, a contemporary conflict model, along with its coordinate other viewpoints within mainstream psychoanalysis, maintains that annihilation anxiety is not "contentless," is not simply the accumulated, undischarged psychic tensions of the actual and traumatic neuroses. The so-called conflict theorists would understand fears of annihilation or disintegration as a content experienced *manifestly* and often described *metaphorically* by patients and theorists alike in such terms as splitting, vulnerability, fragmentation, dissolution, disintegration, and fragmentation of the self. These, I maintain, are the subjective side, the experience of what is explained by the theoretical constructs of either id-ego or narcissistic tensions of extreme degree. In my view, these phenomena, as I stated before, do not warrant a new conceptualization of a different form of anxiety, but understood as self states, they do warrant special *attention* and specific therapeutic stances such as those proposed by Kohut and his followers.

Thus, the value of calling attention to what has variously been called annihilation or disintegration anxieties lies, I believe, not in investigating whether those clinical phenomena can best be accounted for by a conflict *or* by a deficit model, but rather in focusing on important aspects of the clinical phenomena themselves. Bach (1985) has referred explicitly to narcissistic states of consciousness, a form of an altered self state which may be appreciated on its own terms. Transitory modifications in technique which address altered states therapeutically need in no fundamental way contradict the traditional approach to conflict resolution through the basic model of psychoanalytic treatment. Subjective states of extreme anxiety, dissolution, disintegration, annihilation may indeed require noninterpretive interventions, and interventions which are variants of holding or soothing, but so too do other "momentary" occurrences in the course of psychoanalytic treatment. But that is not all that altered ego states require, for they may serve multiple functions as compromise formations which are attempts at conflict resolution as traditionally understood. That is, a self-image as fragmented may serve id wishes, e.g., of anal explosive pleasure; may serve superego needs for punishment for forbidden gratifications of sexual and aggressive wishes, and may serve defensive purposes as well, for one's focus of attention on an altered state of consciousness within oneself may protect from knowing how angry or enraged one may be toward an important person upon whom one is dependent. Ultimately, it should be possible to interpret all of these aspects of an altered state of consciousness, of a self state, in a way that results in a more successful compromise formation than one that eventuated in such painful subjective experiences. Attention to conflict alone, or to deficit aspects alone, is inadequate. What we attend to is the patient's psychic reality.

Freud's first anxiety theory, a purely psychoeconomic one, revolved around the traumatic state as responsible for anxiety. Freud's second theory focused on the traumatic anxiety that all four danger situations signaled—a portent of the original state of psychic helplessness that, for Freud, was not conflict-based, but that loomed significantly as a component of intrapsychic conflict *as soon as the individual was capable, developmentally speaking, of investing helplessness with varied representational content.* Thus, traumatic states are interpretable in the terms they take on of the patient's psychic reality. The flooded or overwhelmed psyche, the quantitative factor, that featured so prominently in Freud's first anxiety theory is essentially that which Kohut identifies as the contentless mental state of annihilation anxiety. But, as I have been attempting to show, these accessions, themselves, are not devoid of psychic content.

The original, mechanistic view of the actual neuroses ignored the importance of both conflict and of objects toward whom accumulated need tensions were directed. Similarly, a pure deficit model of self psychology ignores the role of conflict and the object of instinctual drives. It does not, for example, refer as Freud in effect did in his paper, "On Narcissism" (1914), to how even a selfobject may also be an object of sexual or aggressive instinctual drives. The build-up of sexual and aggressive tensions in the traumatic experiential state of psychic helplessness implies, in essence, an object relations point of view. An aggressive or libidinal drive derivative, especially when traumatically intense, requires an object not only for its satisfaction, but for the reduction of trauma. An object, as understood in the evolving context of psychoanalysis, does more than gratify a need associated with an instinctual drive. The object or "other" also reduces trauma by affirming the person's reality sense, thereby restoring a state of well-being and self-continuity. This is important because a prototypical outcome of traumas of seduction, or of failures in maternal empathy, is, in addition to chaotic self states, an alteration in the sense of reality. Therapeutic care addresses the functioning of the ego *and* the restoration of the self. It also may provide libidinal gratification. The principle of multiple function is hereby applicable to the effects of technique. The presence or absence of the object, the degree and quality of the object's availability thus play an important role not only in the continuation or the lessening of the trauma, but in the mental content, the psychic representations of the annihilation anxiety experience.

One reason why annihilation anxiety poses a problem is that attempts to understand it lead to a common conceptual error committed by analyst and analysand alike, as in what I (Gediman, 1983) have called "the fallacy of parallel importations." This error occurs when the analyst offers metaphor as concrete, and the conceptual is confused with the clinical level of thinking for both analyst and patient. Reed (1985, 1987) made a similar point in recognizing, in the tendency of self psychology to draw parallels between the restoration of the self and the restoration of meaning, a tendency to concretize understanding, to "transform it into substance." She also found this tendency responsible for the confusion, in self psychology, between theoretical language and language in the clinical process. Despite his call for clearer conceptualization of psychic structure, Kohut often used the kind of metaphorical language that reflects a mixing of conceptual levels (see Grossman, 1982). Thus, when he talked of penis envy in girls, or of fellatio, or of perversions generally as a "need to fill in a structural defect," he was, as Slap and Levine (1978) have pointed out, using "hybrid concepts," and implying, as in the case of girls, that the fantasy of being defective is based on a reality. When Kohut said that children who do not acquire internal structure because of sudden narcissistic trauma form a life-long object hunger, he is correct clinically and developmentally. However, when he said that these children intensely search for objects who may serve as a substitute for the missing segments of psychic structure, he tended to confound metapsychological constructs with clinical phenomenology, despite his disclaimer that self as superordinate structure is just a metaphor. Grossman and Stewart (1976) present cases where "penis envy" is concretized as metaphor by both analyst and analysand in a similar manner. The authors argue that penis envy, whether inferred or interpreted as unconscious wish, or stated openly as experiential content during analysis by the patient, must be treated like the manifest content of a dream. It is not to be regarded as an ultimate irreducible truth, impenetrable to further analysis. I believe, analogously, that *we also must not regard as "bedrock" or not further analyzable* such clinical contents as reported or inferred experiences of self-dissolution, annihilation anxiety, and feelings of unreality.

Slap and Levine adopt a similar point of view, arguing that Kohut's central concern that narcissistic psychopathology is caused by the patient's

119

realistic perception of deficiencies in ego structure exemplifies a trend of using metapsychological terms as though they refer not to abstractions but to substantial entities that the individual can perceive directly. This reification of metapsychology thus gives apparent reality to patients' and, I would add, analysts' fantasies.

## CONFLICT, DEFICIT, AND THERAPEUTIC TECHNIQUE

One reason for choosing the subject of annihilation anxiety as a test case for the type of analysis I (Gediman, 1983) proposed was that it seems to lend itself both to therapeutic interventions aimed at addressing "deficit," and to interpretations addressing conflicts and compromise formations for a broad range of cases. Like Wallerstein (1982), I believe that the same kinds of psychotherapeutic interventions employed in self psychology can be found in classical analysis as well. To this end, I discussed annihilation anxiety in two "pure" and two "mixed" neurotic and narcissistic cases, trying to account for it by showing how traditional psychoeconomic formulations may be used conjointly with structural and dynamic formulations for a given patient without adopting a bipolar schema, such as Kohut's, for diagnosing and therefore treating the narcissistic and neurotic disorders.

Narcissistic and self states and their potentially disorganizing feelings of helplessness require analytic efforts to provide the patient with a means of representing, symbolically, the underlying preverbal trauma and its currently associated affect. But offering empathic understanding as a substitute for interpreting conflicted wishes, say for exceptional entitlement, could reflect a nonneutral collusion by the analyst with only one side of a complex conflict. These narcissistic tensions and their underlying conflicts in cases of the more narcissistic patients require interpretation, just as interpretation of conflicts is required in the case of the more neurotic patients.

I believe that in accounting for structural, dynamic, *and* psychoeconomic aspects of mental events, in this instance annihilation anxiety, conflict theorists would explain their therapeutic strategy differently from the way Kohut did when he evoked the principles of self psychology as guidelines for technique. Kohut would, I believe, have seen disintegration anxieties as a component of neurotic symptom formation only rarely, but often as simply an accurate, endopsychic perception of the self. Kohut also said that often the four familiar anxiety danger situations are but the individual patient's attempts to give a circumscribed content to a deeper, unnamable dread, experienced when the patient feels that his or her self is becoming enfeebled or disintegrating. This may, of course, happen. However, I believe that if one continues to explore analytically and avoids "incomplete" interpretations, one needs not necessarily be strengthening defenses against danger anxieties. Even when material expressing conscious castration concerns, for example, is being used defensively against the deepest annihilation fears, perhaps a psychotic core of the personality, it does not follow that the genesis of that defense for a given individual patient and its manifestations are to be ignored or discounted. But before we can deepen our interpretive attempts, we must succeed in our aim of the eventual expansion of the patient's contextual understanding of his or her subjective reaction. For this treatment phase, the analyst's attempts are not necessarily interpretive, but aim to help the patient represent symbolically, through reconstruction, the early, preverbal, precognitive, preoedipal trauma (e.g., seduction, abuse, failures in maternal empathy) which have resulted in susceptibility to traumatically tinged self states which may be experienced as annihilation anxiety—*as though* the self were disintegrating. Only then, when there is the possibility of investing later revivals and revisions of early states with representational content, will interpretive attempts be meaningful.

Like Brenner (1976, 1979), I believe that even when ego deficit is present, it, like any other mental phenomenon, may play a part in compromise formation once it is invested with meaning or representational content by the patient. Unlike Brenner, I do not regard such deficits as are manifest, say, in altered self states as simply another compromise formation, just like any other. We owe Kohut a debt of gratitude for raising our consciousness to an empathic appreciation of altered self states as clinically important above and beyond the functions they serve in compromises. I would regard these states, when encountered in the analytic situation, as requiring shifts in technique, although I do not see these shifts as an alternative to the basic psychoanalytic treatment model. Rather, they expand and enrich its contextual applicability.

I believe that therapeutic strategy must assume the presence of conflict whether or not some degree of deficit is also present. To do otherwise would risk questionable reinforcement of deficit feelings and possibly a consolidation of narcissistic defenses, both at the expense of insight and conflict resolution. When the dissolution of the self metaphor is contained in interpretations which the analyst offers to narcissistic patients, the patients often tend to respond narcissistically, with any one of a number of narcissistic "entitlement" fantasies. Of the two narcissistic patients whom I studied in connection with annihilation anxiety, one felt "entitled" to restore his self-esteem by holding his creditors at bay and recklessly spending money in pathological esteem-building ways. The second felt "entitled" to resist analytic interpretations because, he in effect claimed, he deserved self-restoration by a symbiotic, orally fulfilling, noninterpretive restorative stance on the part of his analyst. If the analyst were to neglect latent content and the role of conflict in the kind of incomplete, one-sided interpretations aimed only at addressing developmental arrests, he or she could produce an "iatrogenic effect" in helping along the patient's expectation of being treated either as defective or as an "exception." However, once the analyst is aware of the potential effect of his or her use of metaphor, he or she can deal with the consequences, analytically.

Self psychology has tended to regard shame resistances as noninterpretable. One hears a case made for avoiding too much interpretation of aggression or sadism as instinctually gratifying, because the patient then internalizes a self-image as too hostile, too sadistic. Resistances to such interpretations are taken, in self psychology, not so much as indications of unconscious conflicts, but more often as self-dystonic feelings of shame. The aggression and sadism are then presumed to be only expressions of narcissistic rage, or the disintegration products of a damaged-feeling self resulting from the analyst's failures of empathy in his or her attempts to link such rage with instinctual gratification. There is no doubt that we frequently observe narcissistic rage when a patient feels misunderstood by an analyst believed to be unempathic. However, consistent with Sandler and Sandler's revival of the metaphors of the topographical point of view, I contend that the shame resistances at the more "superficial" level censorship between the systems Conscious and Preconscious are also subject to interpretation, just as the resistances between the systems Preconscious and Unconscious are customarily interpreted in all conflict and compromise formation analysis.

The analyst must sometimes address the material in a *sequence* that assumes compromise formation and conflict is more likely than ego deficit. By sequential analysis, I do not mean literally that at any given moment in time we would not choose to address transitory disorganization and chaotic self-feeling empathically and by offering some representational contents, perhaps by reconstruction of the past, for understanding its genetic roots, in preference to interpretation—which often has to avoid diminution of traumatic excitability. The patient's momentary state with regard to relative panic or serenity would dictate flexibility in the tactics of our timing, in order to avoid an early crystallization of narcissistic entitlement resistances. But sometimes, as in the case of Mr. Z. (Kohut, 1979), the "deficit" issues must be addressed before meaningful work on conflict can proceed.

By sequence, then, I am referring to an overall strategy and its related hypotheses and assumptions—it is a sequence of thinking through the problem of technique. I am not attempting to offer specific technical recommendations which are closely correlated with any cohesive theoretical framework, but only to suggest the way we must think of working when we do not rigidly dichotomize our patients into the clearly conflicted and the clearly developmentally arrested. In fact, the purpose of this chapter is to show that prescribing one treatment strategy for one "type," another for another type, prematurely attempts to settle an issue by precategorizing individuals rather than by developing a unificatory, multiaxial, psychoanalytic theoretical context which can guide our understanding and treatment of all psychic disorders.

## CONCLUSION

In attempting to bring together the conflict and deficit models, I draw attention once again to the issue of false polarities. The false polarities deficit and conflict are paralleled by other false polarities: reality *or* fantasy; historical truth *or* psychic reality. Rather than think of polarities, we might think of two series, complemental series, as Freud (1905) called them, which overlap considerably, conceptually speaking. According to Freud (1905), the complemental series paradigm holds that the diminishing intensity of constitutional and predispositional drive factors is balanced by the increasing intensity of environmental and accidental factors and vice versa. Restated in this conflict and deficit context, the complemental series paradigm holds that when there has been severe early trauma and subsequent deficit, external influences are more prominently involved in pathogenesis, relative to the strength of the drives and subsequent conflict than they are in the absence of early trauma and subsequent deficit, and vice versa.

Most polarized dichotomies which have split analysts into theoretically divergent camps can, I believe, be better understood by updated versions of the *complemental series concept*, a concept which should serve as a basis for complementarity in a unificatory position, healing the splits engendered in many current controversies. My use of the term "complementarity" (Gediman, 1987) does not subsume the meaning contained in that word as Kohut (1977) used it. Kohut borrowed the term from Neils Bohr's "principle of complementarity" in physics to indicate that the explanation of psychoanalytic data may require not one but two (or more) theoretical frameworks, one of self psychology, one of conflict psychology. In contrast to Kohut, who then used the term "complementarity" to characterize the two theories as coexisting but intrinsically incompatible, my usage of "complementarity" derives from

Freud's *complemental series* notion and presumes a unified theory to explain, compatibly, all relevant data, e.g., deficit and conflict.

Like all other either/or polarizations of objective and psychic reality, the designations interpersonal or intrapsychic; deficit/trauma or conflict imply a false dichotomy. There is always, by definition, an interpersonal matrix for seductions, for failures in maternal empathy, as well as for other traumatic contexts of deficits, and their later elaborations in memory and fantasy. The inner constituents of psychic reality must encompass representations of the external reality of critical past and present interpersonal phenomena which relate to issues of deficit. The complemental series paradigm serves well for integrating the intrapsychic or drive-defense aspects of conflict theory with the self and object representations data which have been the focus of self psychology and object relations perspectives. It should be clear that I do not regard this proposal and others embedded in this chapter as a mixed model, where one theory suits one set of facts, another another set. It is, rather, an attempt toward a unificatory approach, organized by various psychoanalytic principles which have withstood the test of time: the complemental series principle; the principle of multiple function; and a perspectival metapsychological approach which subsumes multiple points of view: the structural, dynamic, economic, topographic, genetic, adaptive, developmental-environmental, object relations, and self psychological. I have hoped, like Wallerstein (1985).

> that the clinical insights of self psychology could have been integrated into the mainstream of classical psychoanalysis—as an enriching supplementation—rather than being directed off (Kohut's choice) into new theory formation and yet another separate theoretical perspective and "school" within the corpus of psychoanalysis... (p. 103).

## REFERENCES

Bach, S. (1985). *Narcissistic States and the Therapeutic Process*. New York: Jason Aronson.

Brenner, C. (1976). *Psychoanalytic Technique and Psychic Conflict*. New York: International Universities Press.

———— (1979). The components of psychic conflict and its consequences in mental life. *Psychoanalytic Quarterly* 48:547–567.

Freud, A. (1937). *The Ego and the Mechanisms of Defense*. New York: International Universities Press, 1946.

Freud, S. (1905). Three essays on the theory of sexuality. *S.E.* 7.

———— (1914). On narcissism: an introduction. *S.E.* 14.

———— (1915). The unconscious *S.E.* 14.

———— (1923). The ego and the id. *S.E.* 19.

———— (1926). Inhibitions, symptoms and anxiety. *S.E.* 20.

Gediman, H.K. (1980). Special book review: "The Search for the Self, Selected Writings of Heinz Kohut." *Psychoanalytic Review* 67:503–514.

———— (1983). Annihilation anxiety: the experience of deficit in neurotic compromise formation. *International Journal of Psycho-Analysis* 64:59–70.

———— (1984), Actual neurosis and psychoneurosis. *International Journal of Psycho-Analysis* 65:191–202.

———— (1987), Seduction trauma: complemental intrapsychic and interpersonal perspectives on fantasy and reality. Presented at the December 4, 1987, meeting of the New York Freudian Society, New York, N. Y.

Gill, M.M. (1963). Topography and systems in psychoanalytic theory. Psychological Issues Monograph 10. New York: International Universities Press.

Grossman, W.I. (1982), The self as fantasy: fantasy as theory. *Journal of the American Psychoanalytic Association* 30:919–938.

———— & Stewart, W. A. (1976). Penis envy: from childhood wish to developmental metaphor *Journal of the American Psychoanalytic Association* 24: (Suppl): 193–212.

Jones, E. (1927). The early development of female sexuality. In: *Papers on Psychoanalysis*, ed. E. Jones. Boston: Beacon Press, 1961, pp. 438–451.

———— (1929). Fear, guilt and hate. In: *Papers on Psychoanalysis*, ed. E. Jones. Boston: Beacon Press, 1961, pp. 304–319.

———— (1936). Love and morality. In: *Papers on Psychoanalysis*, ed. E. Jones. Boston: Beacon Press, 1961, pp. 196–200.

Kohut, H. (1977). *The Restoration of the Self.* New York: International Universities Press.

———— (1978). *The Search for the Self. Selected Writings of Heinz Kohut: 1950–1978*, ed. P. Ornstein. New York: International Universities Press.

———— (1979). The two analyses of Mr. Z. *International Journal of Psycho-Analysis* 60:3–27.

———— (1984). *How Does Analysis Cure?* Chicago: The University of Chicago Press.

Rangell, L. (1968). A further attempt to resolve the problem of anxiety. *Journal of the American Psychoanalytic Association* 16:371–404.

Reed, G.S. (1985). Psychoanalysis, psychoanalysis appropriated, psychoanalysis applied. *Journal of the American Psychoanalytic Association*

30:939–958.

—— (1987). Rules of clinical understanding in classical psychoanalysis and self psychology: a comparison. *Journal of the American Psychoanalytic Association* 35:421–446.

Richards, A. (1981). Self theory, conflict theory, and the problem of hypochondriasis. *The Psychoanalytic Study of the Child* 36:319–337.

—— (1982). The superordinate self in psychoanalytic theory and in the self psychologies. *Journal of the American Psychoanalytic Association* 30:939–958.

Sandler, J. & Sandler, A-M. (1983). The "second censorship," the "three box model" and some technical implications. *International Journal of Psycho-Analysis* 64:413–425.

—— (1984). The past unconscious, the present unconscious, and interpretation of the transference. *Psychoanalytic Inquiry* 4:367–399.

—— (1987). The past unconscious, the present unconscious, and the vicissitudes of guilt. *International Journal of Psycho-Analysis* 68:331–341.

Slap, J.W. & Levine, F.T. (1978). On hybrid concepts in psychoanalysis. *Psychoanalytic Quarterly* 47:499–523.

Stolorow, R. & Lachmann, F. (1980). *Psychoanalysis of Developmental Arrests: Theory and Treatment.* New York: International Universities Press.

Waelder, R. (1960). *The Basic Theory of Psychoanalysis.* New York: Schocken, 1971.

Wallerstein, R. (1985). How does self psychology differ in practice? *International Journal of Psycho-Analysis* 66:391–404.

Winnicott, D.W. (1958). The capacity to be alone. In: *The Maturational Processes and the Facilitating Environment,* ed. D. W. Winnicott. New York: International Universities Press, 1965, pp. 29–36.

# PART III. LOVE AND DEATH

# AUTHOR'S INTRODUCTION

Perhaps it is hardest for me to fathom what it was about my past interests that led to my writing of this group of papers, and how my struggling with them influenced my subsequent writings. When I began to apply my clinical observations of love and death to the "Tristan and Iseult" myth and legend, I had been immersed in Kohut's Self Psychology and tried to extend my understanding of loving oneself to an understanding of narcissistic modes of loving another person as though that person were oneself. Thus, my interests moved from narcissism as generally understood to "twin narcissism," one condition that formed the basis of my interpretation of love and death in "Liebestod Fantasies." John Updike 's New Yorker series (1963) about Denis de Rougemont's work on *Love in the Western World* had also captivated me. My interest in "Liebestod Fantasies" grew out of my study of the distinction between "loving," "being-in-love," and "falling in love."

I had a chance to look further into "Liebestod Fantasies" during my personal travels some years after these publications but before writing my 1995 book, *Fantasies of Love and Death in Life and Art*. For several years, from 1984 through 1987, I was a member of a traveling summer study group called "Psychoanalysis and the Arts," which was formed and convened largely by Bruce Sklarew and that relied heavily on the knowledge and talents of co-traveler and mentor, Ellen Handler Spitz. We visited Tuscany, Rome, and St. John, U.S. Virgin Islands to combine pleasure and the study of fine arts in relation to psychoanalysis. I had become particularly interested in what made one person in a couple feel unable to go on with life after the other member of the couple had died, and came up with ideas for a series of works on "Liebestod Fantasies." That interest led me to look carefully into the recurrence of the love-death theme in opera and in art, particularly in Renaissance Art. Simultaneously with our trips, I had been working with an older patient who had fantasies of "dying in the saddle," which appeared to be his only way of coming to terms with loss of function and pleasure during the last phases of his life. His fantasy was, that if he died while making love, he would achieve immortality. In the course of my researches, I had come across some interesting papers by Ernest Jones, including one that dealt with a couple that was determined to die together when their lives were at risk in the course of going over Niagara Falls. Through Jones, I had also come upon the works of Heinrich von Kleist, to which I had referred in my book, *Fantasies of Love and Death in Life and Art*. Von Kleist was one of Germany's greatest dramatists, whose life ended in a suicide-murder pact, an enacted Liebestod fantasy. Von Kleist had also interested Theodore Jacobs, who invited me to discuss a paper about von Kleist's life and work in one of his discussion groups on *Psychoanalysis and the Arts* at a meeting of The American Psychoanalytic Association. By the time my book was completed, my ideas on love and death bridged the initial ones deriving from Self Psychology to the role of a wide variety of unconscious fantasies about love and death, as more traditionally understood.

# Chapter 6: Reflections on Romanticism, Narcissism, and Creativity[5]

Gediman, H.K. (1975). Reflections on romanticism, narcissism, and creativity. *Journal of the American. Psychoanalytic Association* 23: 407–423. Also in Gediman, H.K. *Fantasies of Love and Death in Life and Art.* New York: New York University Press, 1995.

Kohut's (1966) theory that narcissism unfolds as a developmental sequence in its own right suggests new dimensions for the resolution of certain old controversies. One such controversy, of interest to poet and psychoanalyst alike, is embedded in the polarity of "loving" versus "being in love." Being in love is a transitory state, often experienced as an irrational, stormy "grande passion"; loving is a rational, more durable, "mature genital object relationship" (Bak, 1973). If we agree that the establishment of a narcissistic self is a maturational achievement paralleling that of object love, then it is easy to see how states of loving and being in love both recapitulate earlier ego states and may co-exist in the mature adult.

The contrasting views of two literary critics provide a springboard for the reflections put forth in this paper. In *The New Yorker* magazine (1963), John Updike wrote a scathing and beautiful critical essay on two books by Denis de Rougemont—*Love in the Western World* (1956), and *Love, Declared: Essays on the Myth of Love* (1963). The controversy that sparked my interest was inherent in the discrepancy between Updike's and de Rougemont's views on narcissism as depicted in the myth of Tristan and Iseult. Updike's review was written nearly a decade before the upsurge of psychoanalytic interest in the many facets of narcissism. Today, his ideas are all the more salient in the light of our present understanding of a spectrum of phenomena encompassed by narcissism.

The essence of Kohut's (1966, 1971) position is that there is a separate narcissistic developmental line, which is never outgrown but is, rather, transformed. According to this view, the narcissistic line of development parallels the object-libidinal line of development. Kohut's position, therefore, requires that we abandon the old view that narcissism is merely a precursor of object

---

5  I thank Drs. Phyllis Ackman, Sheldon Bach, William I. Grossman, Martin L. Nass, and Fred Schwartz for their valuable suggestions.

relations and object love and, thereby, a developmental stage to be outgrown. Instead, we must regard narcissistic libido, like object libido, as normally undergoing progressive transformations which are developmental accomplishments. This newer view can account for the simple observation that certain people who fall romantically in love—an expansion of the idealized, or narcissistic self—are also capable of object love. The older, and, I believe, "straw man" view cannot explain this fundamental fact of love.

What are some of the transformations of narcissism with adaptive potential? Kohut enumerates them as man's creativity, his ability to be empathic, his capacity to contemplate his own impermanence, his sense of humor, and his wisdom. And what is the relationship between romantic idealization of another and creativity? Kohut tells us that for the average individual, idealization, a transitional point in the development of narcissistic libido, survives only in the state of being in love. The *gifted* individual idealizes—and despairs—about his work as well. For the creator, his work is a transitional object, invested with transitional narcissistic libido (Kohut, 1966p. 261).

## A CONTROVERSY BETWEEN CRITICS

I shall attempt now to elaborate the critical position taken by Updike on the important relation between certain narcissistic elements in dyadic relationships and the creative process. It should be kept in mind that de Rougemont's position throughout this paper is presented as seen through Updike's eyes.

De Rougemont, a Swiss theologian and essayist has examined the classical French myths underlying the plots of the love ballads produced by the troubadours of Languedoc. He announces that his purpose is "to describe the inescapable conflict in the West between passion and marriage." He analyzes the Tristan-and-Iseult legend[6] to delineate the conflict between honorable marriage and unlimited, romantic, over-idealizing, passionate love. He sees the occidental obsession with romantic love as the major cause of decline in civilized values. Such a love, if consummated, he says, opposes the realms of soul and spirit, and man's only escape from the temptations of the flesh is through asceticism and mystical "knowing." The religious function of the romantic ballads was to present a mythology of a fundamentally asexual, obstacle-ridden love that served at once to satisfy and check the "baser" demands of the populace. De Rougemont holds Romanticism responsible for

---

6 For a comprehensive retelling of the legend, the reader is referred to the version by Bédier (1945).

the "fact" that happy love has no history in western literature. The negative values he attributes to the Tristan myth are described as pathetic inventions to propagate a prototype of the "Unattainable Lady," a prolongation of a state of mind—passion—whereby Eros is allied with Death and destroys marriage, social stability, and international peace.

Updike, on the other hand, contends that de Rougemont has been blinded to the essence of the romantic legends. Sexual passion *is* their essence. The sword between the sleeping Tristan and Iseult does not, as de Rougemont maintains, symbolize simply a civilization-preserving obstacle to ensure chastity, but also the parallel current of the lovers' sexual union. Updike adds that certain features that accompany Tristan and Iseult's narcissistic over-idealization of each other provide the essential conditions upon which particular manifestations of creativity are honed. Happy, unobstructed love is the possibility that animates all romances. Updike explains de Rougemont's failure to recognize the possibility of passion co-existing with civilization as his captivation by a rather Thomistic faith in and religious insistence on a total, uncompromising supremacy of mind over instinct. Incestuous modes, de Rougemont says, must be kept from the masses: a man cannot marry an Iseult, "the woman ... of his most intimate nostalgia," his mother. But Freud tells us that a man must come to terms with his fantasies of incest with mother and sister before he can be really free and happy in love.

It might be useful to think of de Rougemont as talking, in Kohut's terms, about the relations of the self to the *libidinal object,* whereas Updike is attempting to add the complementary point of view of narcissism and to deal with the relations of the self to the *selfobject* which is the basis of creativity as well as of romantic love.

In keeping with Updike's interpretation and positive evaluation of romanticism realized, I should like to elaborate on certain narcissistic modes of relating and the process of inspired creativity. My intention is to illuminate the positive and creative values of certain narcissistic modes of relating and the concomitant early ego states they may reactivate in the over-all context of object relatedness.

## EARLY EGO STATES AND TWIN NARCISSISM

Twin narcissism is a term I borrow from de Rougemont who uses it somewhat pejoratively to characterize the "being in love" aspects of Tristan and Iseult's unlimited passion: they are in love with their love. I prefer to delete the judgmental connotation and to define it simply as a more or less transient fusion state in which the libidinal investment of the self is transferred to the object. Self and object are loved as one because both share a love for a commonly esteemed activity, feeling state, or object. Like Bak, I believe that "the state of "being in love" tends to draw imagery and sensations from these very early ego phases and aims towards fusion of self and non-self, even with an integrated and intact ego" (1973, p. 4). Twin narcissism is a term for fusion of self and object that is evocative of an early ego state common both to lovers and some creative artists.

The temporary sharing of his own judgments about his work by projecting them onto the image of an empathic, sometimes adoring audience forms the narcissistic element in the core of the artist's fantasies, and constitutes a re-enactment of the earliest being in love with his own creation. The creative urge is often triggered by a mutually empathic experience with an "other," and, subsequently, when creative activity requires solitude, the other may, in fantasy, be dismissed or beckoned at will, according to the requirements of the creative process unfolding. Mutual acknowledgement of the worth of the process and the product between creator and alter ego enhances feelings of self-regard which are indispensable for creativity. The twin narcissism of creativity, in short, has as its precursor that developmental stage characterized by, among other things, attachment to the transitional object (Winnicott, 1953). The empathic bliss of symbiotic union with the "good enough" mother is partially renounced for the tentative but ecstatic glimpses of the burgeoning of one's separate, individuated development, and the expansion of the autonomous ego functions: function pleasure in being the "true self." To correlate this simplified description with Updike's ideas on Romanticism, it may be said that the happy, passionate love of which he speaks has as its precursors a developmental stage and associated ego state that are also prototypical of creativity: the transitional-object developmental phase and its associated phenomena.

What are some of the critical relationships between twin narcissism and the creative process? Winnicott (1953) first described the transitional object as an essentially normal phenomenon arising from a particular need for support, or "holding" during a period of marked growth involving early stages of individuation and separation from the mother. He emphasized that the transitional object is created by the child and loved in its own right as his creation, and is thus not simply a crutch to move from symbiosis to individuation.

Greenacre (1970, p. 343), too, lends support to the notion that the artist in a spell of creativity is recapturing the early ego state of when he was attached to a transitional object—the nostalgic juxtaposition of blissful reunion with the good mother and the ecstatic pleasure which accompanies the first autonomous steps away from her. In a Panel (1972) discussion on creativity, it was noted that there might be a certain type of artist for whom the developmental process crucial to his artistry is to be found in the transition from infantile primary omnipotence to secondary omnipotence, the latter deriving from identification with the idealized parent. Additionally, the prototypical artist had, as a child, experienced extreme sensitivity and inventiveness, especially at this change point from what we may call single to twin omnipotence or narcissism.

Let us turn now to what Jacobson has to say about certain normal, yet vacillating mood states that seem to repeat the early ego states under consideration here. She offers the example of a young man who felt good after pleasant esteem-raising experiences with his girl friend, and bad after unpleasant ones. He felt like a different person with a different relation to the world, and the world in turn looked different to him. "It appears that an experience causes a change of mood only if it can bring about qualitative changes in the representations of the self and of the object world ... (1971, p. 73). " . . . the moods transfer the qualities of the provocative experience to all objects and experiences; thus they impart a special coloring to the whole world and hence also to the self . . . " (p. 80). This might well be applied to narcissism, creativity, and the perceptual style of the artist. The relation of mood to object love is well put by Jacobson (1971) who said that a relieving "sweet sadness" may break through for people who have suffered a loss at the moment when they are achieving a libidinal recathexis of their lost objects and of pleasant memories relating to them. Kohut elaborates this relationship to encompass creativity and narcissism in saying that humor and creativity do not present a picture of grandiosity and elation, but of a quiet inner triumph admixed with melancholy. Kligerman too, (Panel, 1972) summarizes that insofar as the creative process implies *change,* there must be a mourning for old structures and old aspects of the self. Thus, every creative act is specifically based on the working through of depressive fantasies aiming at the reparation of early lost objects which one feels are damaged.

## TWIN NARCISSISM AND CREATIVITY

Twin narcissism, as conceptualized here, is a valuable developmental milestone implying high-level transformations of primary narcissism. Greenacre (1971) speaks of the way Kris facilitated her creativity, and we are all familiar with how Freud was, for a time, nourished by his relationship with his "self-created object," Fliess (Schur, 1972). And so, returning to the critics' controversy, I shall consider a particular aspect of creativity which, though it may occasionally involve a transient surfacing of regressive components, is, like Kris' regression in the service of the ego, essentially nonregressive.[7] This view, like Kohut's, regards creativity as a healthy, adaptive transformation of certain vagaries of narcissism.

The spectrum of narcissism is particularly well illustrated by the transitional-object fetish contrast and also, on another level, by the contrast between Updike and de Rougemont in their different interpretations of the Tristan myth. De Rougemont's proclamation that love takes the form of romantic inaccessibility logically leads to his negative ideas about passionate love feeding on denial, and to his contention that the love myth as expressed in the romantic troubadour songs states that avidity for possession is more delightful than possession itself: "to possess her is to lose her." Freud (1914) characterized "the purest and truest" feminine type as narcissistic. The condition of women loving themselves with an intensity comparable to that of the man's love for them, and of one person's narcissism having a great attraction for another's is not solely regressive. We know that mutually being "in thrall" may precede and persist contrapuntally with object love, sustaining it over time. In fact, the two modes of loving co-exist precisely because they radiate from narcissistic and object-libidinal lines of development respectively. The posthumously published paper on *The Dual Orientation of Narcissism* by Lou Andreas-Salomé (1922) considers some of the positive aspects of twin or shared narcissism, especially as they affect the creative process. According to Andreas-Salomé the creative direction of narcissism, aided by the ego, contains vitally important residues of the primal, unambivalent union of mother and child, implying an object relation from the start. That Andreas-Salomé was, on the other hand, also greatly influenced by the elements de Rougemont pejoratively attributes to romanticism is evident in her ideas about narcissistic love in its other orientation, ending in the annihilation of the object:

---

7   Dr. Martin L. Nass has helped me to formulate the crucial position of nonregressive elements in the creative process. He himself recently emphasized the nonregressive aspects of creativity in his work on music and psychoanalysis (1971), stating that the capacity for shifts in ego states and temporary dissolution of ego boundaries is most common among the creative, and that the structural point of view permits such cognitive shifts to be understood as part of normal functioning. The presence of early modes of ego organization does not necessitate the postulation of a regressive process.

"With the progress of ecstatic love, as the object is more and more un-
reservedly magnified, the more does the object behind its manifest symbolic form remain undernourished and devitalized. The more fiery the
fanaticism of love, the more cooling is the effort of its distortions—until
climactically fire and frost are one" (pp. 12-13).

She contrasts such narcissistically "self-destruct" forms of passionate love
with another, narcissistically productive friendly love of two who "are at one
in God, or only in collecting or going fishing." In both types of love, there is
a narcissistic overestimation of the love object. But here,

... The heart of the matter is this: whatever love, honor, even trans-
figuration the friend may attain in our eyes comes from this "third,"
which is able to forge bonds stronger than those of personal erotism.
Detached from the goal of sexual possession, everything imaginable
seems attainable to the libido thus elaborated, and with the sublimation
of the most archaic autoerotism it arrives at a confusion of self and
world experienced à deux. In exchange for the narrow scope imposed
by the genital love of a particular person, the broadest compass is permitted to narcissism that has successfully developed outside the range
of genitality (pp. 13–14).

This particular quotation implies that the narcissistic self-other dyad or
creativity "à deux" requires sublimation, which, in turn, depends on the eternal promise of reunion with the primary maternal object.

The relation between external sources of self-esteem regulation and the
autonomous function of the ego as it is directed toward creativity is set forth
compassionately:

... no autonomous ethical stand can exist without the promise of the
mother's warm embrace. Everything that we call sublimation depends
on this possibility—that we can retain something of that last intimacy of
the libidinal attitude toward even the most abstract and the least personal things. This alone prompts the process whereby "sexual energy, all or
in part, abandons the sexual route and is drawn to other goals" (p. 18).

This paper, written in 1921, predates theoretical developments in ego psychology, object relations, and child development, and would appear to reflect
both Updike's and de Rougemont's perspectives by virtue of the emphasis on

the dual orientation. In discussing the essential duality of narcissism, Andreas-Salomé stresses two elements. One has to do with self-love, which, when excessive, annihilates both self and object (the validity of de Rougemont's position). The other has to do with the "persistent feeling of identification with the totality" (p. 5), or fusion with an Other and with shared values, ideals, and loves, which, she says underlie "narcissistic transformation to artistic creativity" (p. 5) (the validity of Updike's and Kohut's position).

Turning once more to Kohut, this time on twin narcissism, we note his statement, "The creative individual, whether in art or science, is less psychologically separated from his surroundings than the noncreative one; the "I-you" barrier is not as clearly defined" (1966, p. 259).

Updike, like Andreas-Salomé and Kohut, rejects the negative view of idealization of the love object, and of the narcissistic state the Tristan myth implies, whereas de Rougemont clearly attributes pejorative values to such idealization: "Tristan and Iseult are, de Rougemont concludes, in love not with one another but with love itself, with their own *being* in love; their unhappiness thus originates in a false reciprocity, which disguises a twin narcissism" (Updike, p. 90). Updike also rejects de Rougemont's gloomy pronouncements on romanticism, celebrating instead the positive and affirmative aspects not only of the myth but of the Tristan-and-Iseult mode of loving, of the creative aspects of twin narcissism which may not only survive but even flourish within the range of genitality.

The adaptive aspects of transformed narcissism parallel object constancy and genitally mature heterosexuality. Being in love thereby might be regarded as a transiently revived "state," and loving as a structuralized, constant mode of object relatedness. Updike concludes his critique of de Rougemont on narcissism:

> Again, the charge of narcissism that de Rougemont levels against lovers of the Tristan-and-Iseult type seems dubiously fair, for, as Freud in his essay on narcissism points out, "the human being has originally two sexual objects: himself and the woman who tends him." That is, in feeling or making love, the lover shares in the glorification—the "overestimation"—of the beloved; his own person becomes itself lovely. These selfish and altruistic threads in these emotions are surely inseparable (p. 94).

It is worth recalling Freud's actual words:

We have, however, not concluded that human beings are divided into two sharply differentiated groups, according as their object-choice conforms to the anaclitic or to the narcissistic type; we assume rather that both kinds of object-choice are open to each individual, though he may show a preference for one or the other. We say that a human being has originally two sexual objects—himself and the woman who nurses him—and in doing so we are postulating a primary narcissism in everyone ... (1914. p. 88).

Thus Freud, though referring to primary infantile objects rather than to later self-created ones, nonetheless laid the groundwork from which Kohut later developed his thesis. As for the relationship between twin narcissism and object love, Freud said: "... it seems very evident that another person's narcissism has a great attraction for those who have renounced part of their own narcissism and are in search of object-love" (1914, p. 89).

## STIMULUS HUNGER AND ROMANTICISM

With recent conceptual delineation between the ego and the self, we may bypass easily the arguments about positioning creativity somewhere on the polarity between asceticism and self-abnegation, on the one hand, and gratification and self-indulgence on the other. The internalization of self-esteem touches on both the object-libidinal and narcissistic lines of development. When these are regarded as parallel rather than mutually exclusive, it makes pointless the tired debates about whether creativity thrives better on starvation or satiation. The psychoanalyst and the poet each may appreciate the effects on the creative process of stimulus hunger, stimulus seeking, and stimulus manipulation.

I submit that illusion-formation during the transitional-object phase bears a critically important kinship to the overvaluation, the overidealization of the self-created love object, a normal narcissistic component of attachment behavior generally, and of the romantic prelude to constancy and mutuality in object relations. Greenacre has suggested that such illusion formation is particularly related to the creative process in sensitive and especially gifted individuals. With the onset of walking, the child's perception changes in the direction of an obligatory enrichment of the range and combinations of sensory ingredients and therefore an increased exploratory capacity:

My point here is that the introjective-projective relation to the outside *is by no means an inability to distinguish the boundary between the self and the other, or even a simple mirroring...* This flexibly changing interplay of sensorimotor responses to the external object must furnish the possibility for myriad illusions to occur, before the exploratory experiences have been repeated sufficiently that a central core of reliable expectancy has formed, *permitting the perceived object gradually to settle down to a recognizable entity or identity of its own ...*(Greenacre, 1970. p. 347; italics added).

Here we see that the merging, fusing processes of both introjective and projective mechanisms have an adaptive potential. What have traditionally been regarded as only the most primitive defense mechanisms may in good situations form the basis for empathy. At such times they may be regarded as highly adaptive precursors to both creativity and object relations—an idealization of self-created work and self-created objects.

We are familiar with that quality of narcissism which, if not reinforced or mirrored by someone, produces a lowering of self-esteem which stimulates rage and depression of such intensity and durability as to be ended only and temporarily by the next external mirroring of the "ideal self." Freud described the relationship between self-regard and object-cathexes by stating:

... Loving in itself, in so far as it involves longing and deprivation, lowers self-regard; whereas being loved, having one's love returned, and possessing the loved object, raises it once more... The return of the object-libido to the ego and its transformation into narcissism represents, as it were, a happy love once more; and, on the other hand, it is also true that a real happy love corresponds to the primal condition in which object-libido and ego-libido cannot be distinguished (1914, pp. 99–100).

Whether from the mother, the lover, the psychoanalyst, or from fortuitous and serendipitous life circumstances, the *constant* flow of external sources of narcissistic supplies becomes superfluous following the developmental process of internalization, leading to object constancy—the stable internalized image of the object and, of course, the internalization of self-regard. Yet, clearly, certain longings do not disappear even with a life of reasonable instinctual satisfaction and routine work productivity. To work in a better-than-pedestrian manner there must be some glorification, adoration, idealization of people and products, while the healthy grasp of reality's more severe limits are temporarily suspended. Andreas-Salomé's "no autonomous ... stand can exist without the promise of mother's warm embrace ..." fittingly applies. Updike speaks of how "eternal" relationships hope to preserve original passion and thereby creativity, contrasting the position that the more abstinent modes of loving are more qualified to achieve this end with his own belief that sexually passionate love may be equally effective. He faults de Rougemont's interpretations of such well-known myths as *Phèdre* and *La Princesse de Clèves,* which would have those myths representative of the more abstinent modes.

I question Updike's endorsement of the verdict delivered by the Comtesse de Champagne in 1174 when the favorite question about courtly love proposed in a Court of Love was, "Can true love exist between married people?" She stated and affirmed by the tenor of those present that love could not extend its rights over two married persons. Updike explains the extramarital prerequisite for creative narcissism in the Tristan-and-Iseult mode of loving as an escape valve from the hazards to creativity of too much biological contentment. A less extreme, less literal approach is, I believe, required to reconcile the demands of a long-term routinized relationship with the romantic-erotic conditions required for creativity, and Updike himself is onto it, linking the essential condition to the quest for variety in the stimulus or love-object. This approach correctly bypasses sociological considerations and brings to mind Schachtel's (1959) views about man's craving for stimulation in infinite variety. Freud, Schachtel, Greenacre, and others regard the quest for change as an important aspect of love not related to "varietism" or immorality. Updike ties in the quest for variety with the mechanism of sublimation: "The body's chronic appetites can be satisfied by repetition, but, merged with the mind's quest for new knowledge, they become insatiable. Fickleness is the price we pay for individualizing one another" (p. 102). Similarly, Jacobson (1971) reminds us that Goethe's statement, "nothing is harder to bear than a series of good days" evidently was meant to convey that "in a prolonged specific pleasure experience we become gradually aware of unpleasure feelings indicating the 'urge for a change' in the situation" (p. 27).

Greenacre provides us with a conceptual bridge between love, stimulus hunger, and creativity. She, like Bergman and Escalona (1949) acknowledges that, in the specially gifted person there may be an unusual sensitivity to all sensory and kinesthetic stimulations. The second year of life

is a time of infinite stimulating surprises, which are invigorating under good-enough mothering conditions but may be desperately frightening in states of distress and deprivation. The transitional object based on the good mother-me dyad relationship when the distinction between the mother and the infant is not clearly defined, can then carry multiple reassuring illusions, and in this way consolidate the stable perceptive appreciation of many new objects both animate and inanimate. It is then a period of burgeoning discovery, and its conquests have such an impact as to open up the surrounding but unexpected universe (p. 351).

Greenacre has thus helped put to rest the near eternal debate about the relative importance of tension reduction versus stimulus seeking. The principles do not in any way contradict one another viewed in an over-all context of development of the total personality, and especially of the regulatory potential of homeostasis. Contemporary psychoanalysis would perhaps view normal gratification of instinctual needs as a necessary but not sufficient condition for maximum productivity and creativity. Perhaps the sufficient conditions are added to by some kind of sublimated living out of the Tristan myth.

Kohut (1971) has dignified narcissistic transference relationships. With special reference to creativity, he notes that the solving of an intellectual or aesthetic problem always leads to a feeling of narcissistic pleasure. Empathic, merging contact, quite outside the realm of pathology, may also be observed as

when certain creative personalities appear to require a specific relationship (as in a narcissistic transference) during periods of intense creativity. This need is especially strong when discoveries lead the creative mind into lonely areas that had not previously been explored by others... we are dealing either with the expansion of an active, creative self, or ... with the wish to obtain strength from an idealized object (idealizing transference), but not predominantly with the revival of a figure from the past which is cathected with object libido (pp. 316–317).

## SUMMARY

Certain transformations of narcissism and idealization contribute to the creative process. A consideration of some forms and transformations of narcissism discussed by Kohut is offered here as applied to the Romanticism of the Tristan-and-Iseult legend, with specific reference to a revival of early ego states. Andreas-Salomé's views on the dual orientation of narcissism are presented as a particularly helpful way of reconciling the apparent contradiction between the "new" and "old" views of narcissism.

## REFERENCES

Andreas-Salomé, L. (1922). The dual orientation of narcissism. *Psychoanalytic Quarterly* 31:1–30.

Bak, R.C. (1973). Being in love and object loss. *International Journal of Psycho-Analysis* 54:1–8.
http://www.pep-web.org/document.php?id=ijp.054.0001a

Bedier, J. (1945). *The Romance of Tristan and Iseult.* New York: Pantheon. Also Doubleday Anchor Paperback.

Bergman, P. & Escalona, S. K. (1949). Unusual sensitivities in very young children. *The Psychoanalytic Study of the Child* 3–4:333–352.
http://www.pep-web.org/document.php?id=psc.004.0333a

de Rougemont, Denis (1956). *Love in the Western World.* New York: Pantheon.
——— (1963). *Love Declared: Essays on the Myth of Love.* New York: Pantheon.

Freud, S. (1914). On narcissism: an introduction. *S.E.* 14:67–102.
http://www.pep-web.org/document.php?id=se.014.0000a

Greenacre, P. (1969). The fetish and the transitional object. In: *Emotional Growth: Psychoanalytic Studies of the Gifted and a Great Variety of Other Individuals.* New York: International Universities Press, 1971, pp. 315–334.
http://www.pep-web.org/document.php?id=psc.024.0144a

——— (1970). The transitional object and the fetish: With special reference to the role of illusion In: *Emotional Growth: Psychoanalytic Studies of the Gifted and a Great Variety of Other Individuals.* New York: International Universities Press, 1971, pp. 335–352.
http://www.pep-web.org/document.php?id=ijp.051.0447a

Jacobson, E. (1971). *Depression.* New York: International Universities Press.

Kligerman, C. (1972). Panel: Creativity. *International Journal of Psycho-Analysis* 53:21–30.
http://www.pep-web.org/document.php?id=ijp.053.0021a

Kohut, H. (1966). Forms and transformations of narcissism. *Journal of the American Psychoanalytic Association* 14:243–272.
http://www.pep-web.org/document.php?id=apa.014.0243a

——— (1971). *The Analysis of the Self.* New York: International Universities Press. http://www.pep-web.org/document.php?id=zbk.049.0001a

Nass, M.L. (1971). Some considerations of a psychoanalytic interpretation of music. *Psychoanalytic Quarterly* 40:303–316.
http://www.pep-web.org/document.php?id=paq.040.0303a

Schachtel, E.G. (1959). *Metamorphosis: On the Development of Affect,*

*Perception, Attention and Memory.* New York: Basic Books.

Schur, M. (1972). *Freud: Living and Dying.* New York: International Universities Press.

Updike, J. (1963 *More love in the Western World. The New Yorker* August 24, 1963 pp. 90–104.

Winnicott, D.W. (1953). Transitional objects and transitional phenomena In: *Collected Papers: Through Pediatrics to Psychoanalysis.* New York: Basic Books, 1958 pp. 229–242.

http://www.pep-web.org/document.php?id=ijp.034.0089a

# Chapter 7: On Love, Dying Together and Liebestod fantasies

Gediman, H.K. (1981). On love, dying together and Liebestod fantasies. *Journal of the American Psychoanalytic Association* 29: 607–330. Also in Gediman, H.K. *Fantasies of Love and Death in Life and Art*. New York: New York University Press, 1995.

"MY LORDS, IF YOU WOULD HEAR a high tale of love and death," starts the troubadour version of the legend of Tristan and Iseult, "how to their full joy, but to their sorrow also, they loved each other, and how at last they died of that love together upon one day; she by him and he by her." The love-death, or *Liebestod* motif of the story condenses multiple fantasies and invites a general psychoanalytic study of the legend's meaning. In particular, one might aim to illuminate the phenomenon of being in love and its various outcomes, only one of which is the relatively unexplored but clinically important yearning to die together. Let me summarize the Celtic legend's plot.

Tristan is born in misfortune. His father has just died and his mother dies in childbirth. He is raised by King Mark of Cornwall, his loving and beloved uncle, and performs feats of prowess at an early age, continuing his heroics throughout life. At puberty, he kills the giant Morholt of Ireland, who had been exacting unending tribute of local maidens and youths, and becomes mortally wounded. This giant was the brother of the queen of Ireland, and the queen's daughter, Iseult, nurses Tristan back to health with a magic cure, not knowing that he was her uncle's slayer. Some years later, Tristan is sent by King Mark to bring back Iseult to be Mark's bride. After killing a dragon to save the populace, he is wounded once more, and once more Iseult nurses him back to health, this time learning that he is her uncle's killer, whereupon she threatens to kill him, but decides to spare him once she learns of his mission to bring her back as his uncle's bride. On sailing for Cornwall, Tristan and Iseult are tricked into drinking the magic love potion whose effect, although they do not know it, is to render them forever in love with one another and to commit them to a fate from which they can never escape, *for they have drunk their destruction and death*. One cannot live or die without the other. They consummate their love. Notwithstanding his betrayal of his uncle, Tristan delivers Iseult to Mark, and the King and Iseult wed.

Tristan and Iseult remain lovers, and successfully contrive to meet secretly for some time, until the felon barons, Tristan's rivals for Mark's favor and love, report the adultery to the King. For a while, the lovers trick Mark into believing their innocence, but the felons finally confront Mark with incontrovertible evidence of their adultery. Mark hands over Iseult to one hundred lepers, and sentences Tristan to the stake. Through heroic efforts, Tristan escapes his fate and rescues Iseult from hers, and for three years they lead a harsh and hard life as exiles in the forest. At the end of that time, Mark comes upon them while they are asleep, and deceives himself that they are innocent.

According to most versions of the legend, it is at this point that the potency of the love potion wears off, Tristan repents, and Iseult wishes she were queen again. Tristan surrenders Iseult to Mark, who promises forgiveness. Now separated, the lovers pledge to reunite whenever either shall wish it, and so they part and come together, overcoming obstacles of the felon barons and their own making alike. Subterfuges, disguises, and ordeals abound. Finally, after a self-created agony that Iseult no longer loves him, Tristan marries another Iseult. Wounded in a final grand feat, Tristan is about to die and sends for Iseult his lover, for only she has the power to save his life, if the ship which brings her hoists a white sail. Tristan's wife, Iseult, tormented by jealousy, tells him the boat's sail is black, and Tristan dies. Iseult lands, lies down beside her dead lover, and clasps him close. Then she dies too.

I believe that most psychoanalysts today would see this legend as a vehicle to express certain vicissitudes of being in love. I shall rely, therefore, on the legend as myth to generate hypotheses and formulations about the psychology of love, and will not attempt a psychoanalysis of the work as a piece of literature. A major purpose of this paper is to offer an approach to the psychology of love which avoids polarization—for example, of loving *versus* being in love; of symbiotic *versus* oedipal genesis; of repressed ego state *versus* ego capacity— which has characterized much of the psychoanalytic literature on that subject.

Current works (Bak, 1973; Bergmann, 1971; Gediman, 1975) have presented being in love as a "state," derived primarily from the earliest impressions and memory traces of the blissful symbiotic stage, the stage that precedes a sense of separateness from the mother. It would not be at all difficult to deduce from the legend, as summarized above, that yearning for the lost bliss, fusion, and merging feelings of symbiosis underlies the movement of the lovers toward eternal reunion through death together. However, to reduce the quest for being in love to revived symbiotic longings, alone, is to commit the "genetic fallacy," whereby to explain all facets of complex adult patterns of love as derivatives of impressions of the earliest infantile state and of universal fantasies about it is to explain nothing at all. I propose to illuminate the nature of loving and being in love by analyzing the multiple fantasies expressed in the legend, with particular emphasis on the *Liebestod* motif.

In the course of this discussion, I shall also take up a number of themes which must occupy a place in any psychoanalytic discussion of love: object loss; passion and obstacles to its fulfillment; sadomasochism; symbiosis and separation-individuation; identification; dying together, and death and rebirth.

## THEMATIC ANALYSIS OF THE LEGEND

The version of the Tristan legend on which my inferences will be based is in fact a composite of five, separately authored, tellings.[8] Therefore, it would not be correct to offer strictly genetic hypotheses as if we were looking at an actual case study. We may take this legend as a statement about some important facets of human existence, and we may develop an understanding of this statement by speculating about critical events in the life of the legendary Tristan and then go on to generalize toward an expanded psychology of love. I focus primarily on Tristan's and not Iseult's life because the legend provides us only with a vague, sketchy notion of the woman, whereas it approaches more of a three-dimensional characterization of the man. Some believe the sketchy depiction of Iseult as a real person reflects the secondary status of women at the time of the legend's evolution. Others feel the sketchiness is consistent with the characterological remoteness in the romantic idealization of the prototype of the unattainable lady, which typified the romantic view of women. The reasons, whatever they may be, are not the main emphasis of this paper.

## TRISTAN'S CHILDHOOD

Tristan's parents both died by the time he was born, and this double loss might predispose any child to develop fantasies of atonement, of regaining

---

8   The version by Bedier (1945) is the comprehensive retelling of the legend incorporating the five separately authored versions by Robert of Rheims, Thomas de Bretagne, Eilhart von Oberg, Gottfried von Strassburg, and Beroul. I am indebted to Dr. Judith Isaac for providing me with a historical chart depicting sixteen different transformations of the legend occurring between the seventh-century Celtic fable and the 1945 Bedier version, including Wagner's 1857 opera, *Tristan and Isolde*.

the lost parents, and of reunion through death. In fact, the troubadour version holds these deaths responsible for Tristan's chronic "yearning for dying." The parents' deaths may be the trauma that Tristan is trying to master throughout his life, providing the context out of which the *Liebestod* leitmotif develops. Here we note a legendary representation of what real life is all about even when the parents do not actually die: the yearnings and attempts to refind the lost idealized parental image of each developmental phase.

Tristan, like all Celtic youths, was raised only by men—by King Mark and by other father surrogates—and sheltered from women. He was trained to perform magnificent feats, and then, at puberty, was knighted by Mark for his many heroic deeds and miraculous rescues and escapes from death, which were to continue throughout his life. These feats would eventually earn him the right to marry. Tristan was revered prematurely as a lord, not merely loved as a son by his father surrogates. This aggrandizement would, in a child, tend to predispose to precocity and to a narcissistic sense of entitlement, which is implied in Tristan's grand and grandiose heroics throughout the legend.

Tristan's passion to assert his prowess in moments of peril always involves suffering and courting of death, the "beloved pain of the troubadours," which is perhaps masochistic, perhaps counterphobic, and most likely a forerunner of the love-death through attempts at active mastery of the passively feared death. Here again, his life may be understood to be a repetitive reliving of the trauma of loss in order to master it.

## THEMES AND FANTASIES IN THE TRISTAN LEGEND

Among the fantasies embedded in the legend are those deriving from the drinking of the fatal love potion which permits "passion and joy most sharp, and Anguish without end, and Death." The crucial enactment of drinking the same love potion embodies, reflects, and organizes many themes. Instead of condemning the lovers for their guilt and transgressions, the troubadours' audience, or the masses, admired them, for the love potion provides an alibi which permits their claim to innocence in the eyes of God and frees their passion, which is superimposed by fate, from any connection with human responsibility. The issue of Tristan's guilt or innocence in the eyes of God, an issue that pervades the troubadours' questioning within the legend, hinges on the drinking of the philtre, and on the rules of chivalry, where the fair conqueror always wins. The lovers are not the authors of their actions, so they cannot help gratifying their passionate yearnings that the potion's magic imposed. The potion, originally provided by Iseult's mother, who intended it for her daughter and King Mark, also appears to dissolve Iseult's former hatred of Tristan, whom she had nurtured only when his true identity was unknown to her. So Iseult's hatred is transformed into love. It would seem reasonable to suggest that they both are quite repelled by each other, as they were in fact before they drank of the magic, together. Tristan, who loves Mark above all, is forced, despite his will, to love Iseult. Iseult, who hates Tristan because he slew her uncle, is forced to love him now. The legend thus reflects bisexual currents in Tristan's personality. His presumed homosexual motivation is also used to declare innocence—it was all for the love of Mark that the lovers are smitten, for Tristan sacrificed his life to bring Iseult to Mark to gain more of Mark's love and admiration.

There are numerous other indications in the legend that Tristan's primary tie is to King Mark and not to Iseult. Denis De Rougemont (1956), a Swiss theologian and essayist who has provided a thorough literary analysis of the legend, informs us that an Arthurian knight, like a troubadour, regards himself as the vassal of some chosen lady when he actually was the vassal of a lord. Tristan's quest for Iseult, before the influence of the potion, is clearly undertaken to please Mark, with whom his loyalty lies. His heroic feats are designed to seduce her falsely, to present her to the King. The felon barons, who constantly erect obstacles to thwart Tristan's passion, are not so much jealous of his love for Iseult, but are envious of Tristan because he is Mark's favorite. Because of his love for Tristan, Mark does not desire a wife and heir, but agrees to wed only to pacify the felon barons, never intending it seriously. Even after his marriage, Mark has Tristan sleeping in his chambers where he has free access to the queen, and would apparently never have entertained any objection to this arrangement if not for the pressures exerted on him by the envious felon barons.

Other evidence for Tristan's strong loyalty to Mark is to be found in the text describing the lovers' banishment to the woods. Here, Tristan prays to God to give him the strength to give Iseult back to Mark, so that he may serve his beloved King again. Iseult also wishes to return to her husband, but primarily to restore Tristan's status with Mark. They have a writ prepared, declaring their innocence. The King considers the writ with the felon barons, and pardons Tristan, concluding that Tristan wants to prove his right in arms that he never loved Iseult with a love dishonorable to the King.

One might wonder if the manifest content here serves to mask guilt over oedipal victory and incestuous consummation. The oedipal themes in this story are atypical with respect to outcome. Tristan, because he never participated in the oedipal triangle, was exempt from the usual oedipal and incestuous prohibitions of childhood. It is not surprising, then, that to be an "oedipal winner," as it were, is part of his fate. This victory is recognizable as a continuation of the theme of Tristan's narcissistic entitlement—a wishful, grandiose fantasy that transgression for him, the favored son, will be understood rather than punished. Indeed, the lovers' banishment to the forest is ended by Mark's erroneous belief, based on the sword's being between them, that they are innocent. They are thus not only exceptions to the laws banning incest, but they may proceed with the blessings of the wronged father—a classical fantasy of narcissistic entitlement.

It is important at this point to note that one of the five versions of the legend, Gottfried's, on which Wagner's opera, *Tristan and Isolde*, is based, has the lovers chaste: their union is never consummated. This version, unlike the others, does not mask the critical superego prohibitions, for it appears to express certain oedipal features of traditional courtly love whereby the idealized but unattainable lady is admired and adored only from a distance. Because she represents an incestuous object, Tristan's adoration is compromised by his regarding sexual contact with her as low and debased, not compatible with tenderness. In all four other versions of the Tristan legend, Tristan starts with a sin against courtly love, traditionally chaste, by actual physical possession of a real woman. This sinfulness, representing oedipal and incestuous enactment, is painfully redeemed, despite Mark's forgiveness, by the long penance the lovers undergo.

The belief and proclamation of the populace that the lovers are innocent of incest, even when guilt is too visible to be denied, may be understood as an instance of mass denial, and would appear to be related to primal-scene disavowal and the wish to live the lives of Tristan and Iseult vicariously. That the King and the people are fooled by the sword between them is, on their part, sheer falsification of the facts, like the child's insistence on the parents' chastity, but the falsification is welcomed by all as an opportunity to deny the feelings of painful exclusion inherent in witnessing the primal scene. So long as Tristan and Iseult can prove their innocence by ordeals and the painful overcoming of obstacles, arbitrary as those may seem, they are happily exonerated by all.

The twin fantasy, the merger fantasy, or the fantasy of the double relates to an aspect of being in love that seems to characterize the Tristan and Iseult type of relationship: each is a "selfobject" (Kohut, 1971) for the other. De Rougemont noted that each loves the other from the "standpoint of the self." From this observation, he reasoned that their unhappiness originated in a false reciprocity which disguises a "twin narcissism." I elaborated the twin narcissism concept in another paper, Chapter 7 in this book (Gediman, 1975) where, although I borrowed the term from De Rougemont, I questioned his pejorative or *exclusively* narcissistic characterization of Tristan and Iseult's unlimited passion, and his assertion that they are in love *only* with their love. Self and object, I believe, often may be loved as one when both individuals share a love for a commonly esteemed activity, feeling state, or object. In that paper, I also spoke of the frequent coexistence in one and the same individual of the twin narcissism of *being in love* with the object-relatedness of *loving*. De Rougemont believes that loving the other from "the standpoint of the self" is also the essence of the state of nostalgia, which he views as incompatible with true dialogue between two people who perceive each other distinctly as separate individuals. It should be clear that I do not see nostalgia and dialogue as mutually exclusive any more than I see being in love as ruling out loving. Therefore, I disagree with De Rougemont's position that the usual fate of the twin narcissism of being in love is the destruction of the love relationship and of life itself. He implies that Wagner's *Liebestod* motif depicts the twin nostalgia for oneness, and that the leitmotif music conveys the ecstatic release of dying together: "The love of Tristan and Isolde was the anguish of being two." He describes twin narcissism as "foundering in a twin down rush," "being cast into a headlong swoon," alluding to phenomena which we as analysts would regard now as sensations deriving from early ego states.

Of all the themes of this legend, the *Liebestod* motif or the theme of fatal love is the most powerful. I shall devote the remainder of this paper to examining it in detail.

## ROMANTIC LOVE AND THE LIEBESTOD: MASOCHISM OR RAPPROCHEMENT CRISIS

The romantic love songs of the troubadours are nearly all characterized by (1) an idealization of the state of being in love, (2) putting obstacles in the way of fulfillment of passionate longings, and (3) the death from grief of one lover upon the death of the other. A study of some of the manifest contradictions in the myth will be used to shed some light on the intrapsychic function of obstacles to the fulfillment of love, and how it relates to the love-death.

### THE FUNCTION OF OBSTACLES IN THE LEGEND

De Rougemont feels that the manifest contradictions reflect the author's intention to describe the lovers' secret quest for the "obstructions that foster love." Passion, he says, is inevitably linked with self-destruction for anyone yielding uncompromisingly to it; it leads ultimately to death, and that is the primary disguised content of the myth. I agree with him that it is precisely the manifestly arbitrary character of the obstructions introduced into the tale that may reveal its latent content and elucidate some aspects of the passion it is concerned with. After all, Tristan the giant and dragon slayer, with all his prowess and cunning, is in an unquestionably favorable position to carry on his affair with Iseult unimpeded, and without King Mark's interference. De Rougemont says that objectively not one of the barriers to the fulfillment of their love is insuperable, yet each time they give up, never missing a chance of being parted. When there is no obstruction, they invent one in order to intensify their passion, which requires coercively imposed obstacles in order to be perpetuated. His major thesis is that the legend is primarily about partings in the name of passion in order that the lovers may intensify their love even at the cost of their happiness and their lives. I agree with De Rougemont on the function of struggles and obstacles in maintaining the intensity of passion. However, he is talking only of drastic kinds of obstacles which ultimately destroy love, while I would like to underscore the importance of those more "normal" obstacles which can also enhance regard and loving concern for the object.

## SADOMASOCHISM

The classical explanation of obstacles, suffering, and maintaining the intensity of passion is that the romantic love of the troubadours and of the nineteenth-century romantics is essentially sadomasochistic.

The phenomenon of lovers' self-creation of obstacles when none are in fact imposed from without is what has been called the masochism of romanticism. The theme of all the romantic plots is that passion must mean suffering. Evans (1953) tells us that the main characteristic of troubadour love is that the lady is worshipped from a *distance*. She is cold, disdainful, and aloof, while the lover is abject. The strength of his love is demonstrated by his capacity to suffer. He sees the haughty, aloof mistress, the abject lover, and the technique of avoidance as the basic ingredients of the troubadour concept of love, and this, he says, is the masochistic prototype. The woman who is idolized is the *femme fatale* who, he feels, represents the preoedipal mother. The romantic love themes of the troubadours convey the man's desperate attempt to repudiate his succumbing again to the originally passive role which, as a boy, he had managed to escape. When a man does not surrender himself in emotional attachments, according to Evans, it is because this involves succumbing to his deep masochism of the preoedipal period. If the *femme fatale* derives from the preoedipal mother imago, and if that imago is nonspecific as to gender (Pollock, 1975); (Bergmann, 1980), I would add that there could also be a male equivalent of the *femme fatale* in adult relationships who would also represent the preoedipal mother to whom the woman either submits or fears to submit masochistically. Clinically, this seems to be the case.

In the legend of Tristan and Iseult, masochism is clearly presumed in the following summary I have prepared of self-imposed obstacles:

The lovers have been apart for two years, and Tristan, not hearing from Iseult, his love, assumes she does not love him. In his misery, he marries another woman, also named Iseult, whom he does not love. Finally, he receives a report that with all the time and distance between them, Iseult, his love, is pining away. Somehow Iseult learns that Tristan did not face a foe conjured in her name. She feels this is a betrayal, so when Tristan finally finds a way to meet with her, she sends a message that she will not see him. Tristan sends a messenger back to tell Iseult that he really loves her, but she does not believe what she hears. Tristan, disguising himself as a leper, tries to see her, but she spurns him—although in private, she pines away. Tristan, downcast, sails away. Iseult repents, realizing she has been unjust. To punish herself, she puts on a hairshirt. Tristan, now home again, languishes because Iseult has driven him away. He wants to die, but also wants Iseult to know that it is for love of her. He returns to her, disguised as a beggar. As a ruse, he simulates madness, shaves his head, dyes his skin, and gets into court. In this condition, he says his name is Tristan and that he loves Iseult. He asks Mark to give her to him. At first Iseult refuses to believe he is Tristan, but when he proves his identity, they resume their love trysts once more. But a felon baron is on to them. Tristan flees, but only after he and she agree that he will summon her to die with him when his death becomes inevitable.

This summary illustrates the legend's central emphasis on repeated self-creation of obstacles that Evans and others view as essentially masochistic. The greater the belief of one that the love is unrequited, or that the lover is indifferent, the greater the yearning for the apparently withholding one. The lovers take turns acting and feeling first in control and then victimized, all on the basis of their illusions. This is the prototype of masochism in romantic literature.

So we see throughout the story numerous "degradation trips." Does this two-year development of the lovers' mutual distrust reflect, as Evans and others contend, only the pathological form of love, sadomasochism, or does it contain other important implications? It is my belief that suffering and pain as part of the human condition, and the need for punishment of oedipally related transgressions do not always or exclusively imply sadomasochism. However, since the oedipal issues in romantic love have received reasonably extensive coverage in the classical psychoanalytic literature, I have chosen to give priority, in my discussion, to certain relatively neglected preoedipal features. I believe that rejection, scorn, suffering, and the wish to die are *pathological variations* of the conditions normally required for arousal in all love relationships: pathology enters an otherwise normal picture when attempts to increase the intensity of passion escalate to sadomasochistic extremes.

Freud (1912) said that obstacles are normally required to heighten libido, and "where natural resistances to satisfaction have not been sufficient men have at all times erected conventional ones so as to be able to enjoy love" (p. 187). This normal increase in intensity stands in contrast with the torments depicted by the troubadours. An optimal degree of self-imposition of obstacles is, as Freud implied, a normal technique of love-making, enhancing the entire experience and facilitating maximal pleasurable orgastic discharge. However, when there are significant sadomasochistic predispositions in the partners, a seeming readiness for this normal technique emerges manifestly as the sadomasochism depicted so persuasively in the romantic novels. And that very sadomasochism may sometimes serve a restitutive function for vulnerable individuals, helping to restore self-object differentiation when boundaries between self and other have even transiently suffered in a state of being in love or during passionate sexual arousal. The lovers' self-imposed obstacles may also function as devices aimed at ensuring an unambivalent state of union. Heightening of passionate intensity, by creating external obstacles, permits a "split" whereby love is preserved in a passionate unity and hatred directed toward the obstacle-ridden outer world.

The important relation between love and hate in the being-in-love state is discussed by Bergmann (1971) who says that in order to be able to love, early object representations must be benign and cathected more with libido than with aggression. In a later work (1980) he develops the theme of masochism along lines that I agree with. Namely, the state of longing and yearning is not painful *per se*, but only under certain conditions: when it is self-perpetuated, as in a prolonged state of unrequited love; when the feelings of yearning and longing are cathected more than the object is; and when it precludes, because of its intensity, any integrative efforts of the ego to respond to the reality of the other person and thereby maintain object constancy.

## DISTANCE REGULATION AND THE RAPPROCHEMENT CRISIS

I propose that the apparent sadomasochism attributed to the Tristan and Iseult mode of loving also reflects an attempt at distance regulation and, therefore, may be conceptualized, even reformulated, in terms of a particular resolution of the rapprochement crisis (Mahler, 1972); (Mahler, Pine, and Bergman, 1975) which embodies the typical conflicts of the preoedipal phase. Intensifying passion by obstacles to its fulfillment may be viewed as a way of mastering separation anxiety, but more particularly, of mastering the anxiety of achieving individuation and separateness when they conflict with the desire for a sense of oneness (Kaplan, 1978). The swooning and revival waves of Wagner's *Liebestod* leitmotif evoke memories and reminiscences of life-long rhythmic patterns, of feeling states connected with arousal and relaxation, of approaching and distancing, merging and separation, as they are echoed in the later developed patterns of passionate sexual arousal and orgasm. That is, the musical leitmotif captures what is also depicted in the written legend: the comings and goings of the rapprochement crisis.

The "exquisite anguish" in the yielding swoon of the lovers casts its spell because it is evocative not only of sexual passion, but also of the early ego state of fusion and merging. The swoon without the effort of the mind—the ego's work to achieve individuation and separateness—could be understood as psychological death, as opposed to psychological birth, or living. In this way, then, I find it useful to view the rhythms of parting and coming together, the theme of all courtly love myths, as derivatives of the rapprochement rhythms of establishing optimal distance between two people, both literally and intrapsychically (see Bouvet, 1958).

Fitting here, too, are the ideas of Hermann (1936) who speaks of clinging and going in search—a pair of contrasting instincts that are precursors of sadism and masochism—of roaming and wandering as derivatives of yearning to re-establish the original union with the mother. The sadism and masochism, as well as the propensity toward suffering for other reasons, that are represented in Tristan and Iseult's many partings and returnings, could also be viewed usefully as derivative of these early trends, as Hermann feels many such intense relationships are. Tristan's urge to roam, especially, is not simply counterphobic, simply a form of "heroic masochism." We may also see in the Houdiniesque elements of adventure and escape, the tidal wave feel of coming perilously close to danger followed by heroic escapes and then aimless wandering attempts to escape from the dreaded primary maternal engulfment which threatens each time the yearning for blissful reunion is enacted. Tristan's adventures suggest a fusion fantasy, fantasies of death and denial of death through rebirth and the fantasies of a "great escape artist." The theme of repeated partings, wandering far and then returning, also suggest the wish-fear of the claustrum, or the conflicts specific to the oral triad (Lewin, 1946). The "masochism," the suffering attendant on the placement of obstacles in the way of fulfillment of passion, serves the lovers in their attempts to regulate distance, to find the optimal balance of "oneness and separateness" in boundary formation.

The lovers repeat these echoes of preoedipal trauma and conflict in endless variations, which they then attempt to master by alternating rhythmically their self-created obstacles and distrust with their blissful reunions. From this point of view, the comings and goings of Tristan and Iseult and the obstacles they place between themselves express both the wish and the fear of symbiotic fusion and merger. The wish may reflect a defensive regression prompted by oedipal anxieties and/or a repetition of the bliss of original symbiosis; the fear may reflect the drive to advance to new libidinal positions, and the thrust of the drive for ego autonomy and growth which preserve the sense of self and separateness.

## SYMBIOSIS AND SEPARATION-INDIVIDUATION IN THE LIEBESTOD

The term *Liebestod* fantasy was coined by Flugel (1953). It refers to fantasies of love and fantasies of death, which condense into fantasies of "dying together." Such fantasies express a wish not for a cessation of life, but, he says, for "intrauterine omnipotence," for Nirvana, a life of peace after death. There is very little in the psychoanalytic literature about dying together. Freud (1913) states that if a man is faced with the necessity of death, he tends to deny it with a woman's love, suggesting a *Liebestod* motif, if not precisely the dying-together phenomenon. Later (1917), however, he states: "In the two most opposed situations of being most intensely in love and of suicide the ego is overwhelmed by the object, though in totally different ways." Suicides in the state of melancholia which represent a dying together may also reflect this pathological introjection into the ego of the ambivalently loved lost object, where the lost loved and hated one lives on as a part of the self.

It was Ernest Jones who wrote specifically on dying together in two separate papers. The first (1911) makes reference to Heinrich von Kleist's suicide. In it Jones concludes that most psychoanalysts would probably agree that the wish to die together is the same as the wish to sleep and lie together, originally, of course, with the mother. He also reminds us of the primal connection between ideas of travel and of death which relate to fantasies of dying together.

The second Jones paper (1912) concerns an actual event of a man and a wife who perished together in Niagara Falls in a dangerous situation which nonetheless could have been escaped were it not for the woman crying, "I can't go on! Let us die here!" whereupon neither made an effort at self-preservation or to rescue the other. Jones explains the double suicide as representing birth, where the childless couple, making use in the unconscious of the connection between the womb and the grave, equate their wish to have a child with death: it is a suicide with no suicidal intent, but where the wish to die in the arms of the beloved represents a wish to beget a child with the loved one, and at another level, a return to the mother's womb.

Zilboorg (1938) said that in "murder-suicide" pacts,

... the drive toward death, always with the flag of immortality in hand, carried with it the fantasy of joining the dead or dying, or being joined in death. The latter is particularly prominent among the double suicides of lovers. There is hardly a primitive race which does not have a lovers' volcano (Japan), a lovers' waterfall (Bali), or a lovers' rock from which the lovers jump so that they may be joined in the beyond (p. 197).

Pollock's (1974) paper, "Homicide and Suicide Following the Death of Another," surveys documented double suicides throughout the world's history and cultures, concluding that each bears the hallmark of a significant reaction from the past, reflecting uncompleted and pathological mourning. Pollock believes that what may look like identification in the suicide may be more reflective of the wish to reunite with the one from whom the separation occurred. He invokes Kohut's (1971) concepts of the merger, the mirror, and the twinship to account for the phenomenon.

Suicides attempting reunion in a life after death are explicitly linked by Brodsky (1957) to *Liebestod* fantasies. In describing a case of a woman's wish to die after the death of her brother, he says:

In some of the material from this case it seemed clear that the brother was really a substitute for the unsatisfying mother. The fantasy of being eternally asleep in the grave with a surrogate of the maternal object suggests that Lewin's oral triad of wishes is at the basis of *Liebestod* fantasies ... Lewin has in this connection equated good death with good sleep ... (p. 15).

Bergmann (1971) states that the *Liebestod* in the great love stories is chosen in preference to separation, and is a poetic rendering of the emotions that belong to the symbiotic phase when separation means death. Because love revives emotions that once belonged to the symbiotic phase, it is often feared as endangering the boundary of the self.

The hypothesis of *Liebestod* fantasies as derivative of the symbiotic phase is an intriguing one. Because affects deriving from early symbiosis and fusion are evocative of the love-death aspects of being in love, it may be said that some adults fear the altered state of consciousness and the sexual passion and other intense feelings being in love brings about, because this threatens their sense of separateness and integrity of the self. These feelings and fears may evoke *fantasies and dim, repressed memories* of having "experienced" engulfment and merger, but they cannot be said to revive the early ego state exclusively. Oedipal pressures, frustrations, and anxieties may be responsible for fear of loving, serving as a warning signal for regression to early ego states. But the resultant "state" in the adult is far more complex than a simple revival of the infantile symbiotic state. Bergmann (1980) says that the state of symbiosis in being in love is a state *sui generis*: it is neither regressive nor pathological *per se.* This is a view I share. That is, there may simply be temporary suspension of certain ego functions, analogous to creative or "controlled" regressions. In such instances, being in love in and of itself does not necessarily preclude a loving concern for the object, although it may. When it does, we are dealing with a condition that appears to characterize the relationships depicted in many of the great romantic love stories.

Freud (1914) said that "a real happy love corresponds to the primal condition in which object-libido and ego-libido cannot be distinguished" (p. 100). That is, in a state of being in love, one loves the object as if he or she were oneself. It does not seem quite right, however, to say that a *correspondence* to the original state of primary narcissism implies a revival of only that state, nor is any significant self and object dedifferentiation implied. Too much has intervened developmentally. It seems, too, that Freud was not referring as much to "boundary fusion" as he was to identification—especially to cross-identifications and the interchanging of identifications.

I consider the process of identification pivotal to an understanding of being in love and loving, for it subsumes a hierarchy of experiences, originating in the subjective sense of merging and proceeding up through a differentiated capacity for empathy.

Pathological identification with one who had died, or with whom one wishes to die, is a concept which has been used to explain those variants of the *Liebestod* where there is either a suicide pact or a suicide-murder pact.

The mechanism of pathological identification may be broken down into its more familiar components of wishes to die and reunite, of self-neglect in the service of realizing a fantasy, and introjection of an ambivalently loved figure of great importance. The fear of getting too close in relationships, the fear of becoming engulfed or of psychic death, is only the other side of the coin of the wish to die together in timeless death.

Pollock (1975) says that most conceptions of heaven, paradise, and the ideal state of afterlife imply a regression to a beginning state of symbiosis and provide the basis for the belief in immortality. Such conceptions also include fantasies of rejoining the dead via a symbiotic reunion with a figure, nonspecific as to gender, who represents the first omnipotent, omniscient parent, or maternal being. Paradoxically, then, symbiotic fantasies of dying or killing oneself ward off the fear of death, for they express the wish not for ending life, but for its new and perfect beginning. He thus provides a helpful understanding of *Liebestod* fantasies, although he does not refer to them by that name.

It is of greatest importance to emphasize that *fantasies* of rejoining are not to be equated with the *experience* of symbiotic merger, even though, in dreaming or dreamlike states, they may revive certain dim memories and impressions of early states. This formulation is consistent with those of Isakower (1938) and Lewin (1946) who stay close to the clinical data of dreams and sensations of adult patients. Their formulations do not confuse these clinical data with the data gleaned from infant observations. Pollock, too, appears to refer not to literal revival or archaic infantile ego states, but rather to internalized ideals and object representations, to later developed and elaborated fantasies about what intrauterine life, or early oral symbiosis, must have been like.

Mention must be made of the important phenomenon of idealization, which often reflects merger, bliss, or symbiosis fantasies. At the height of the normal being-in-love state, as at the height of sexual passion with its concomitant normal idealization of the love object, the boundary between ego and object threatens to "melt away." In Kohut's terms (1971), the love object becomes the idealized self-object. In Freud's terms, ego libido and object libido cannot be distinguished. Freud (1930) also said that "against all evidence of his senses, a man who is in love declares that 'I' and 'you' are one, and is prepared to behave as if it were a fact" (p. 66). Idealization of the loved object occurs, said Freud, because the lover tends to see in the object the image of some *previously* loved person who, by means of nostalgic revisions of early memories, becomes loved unambivalently. The loved object is thus overestimated and romanticized as perfect. The condition of "normal" romantic love, then, is *not*, I maintain, a symbiotic regression, although it involves the investment of a considerable quantity of narcissistic libido in the object who then replaces the ego ideal.

Symbiosis, a potentially serious regression in any adult, may be conceptualized as psychological death insofar as it precludes separateness and the individuation of various ego functions. Paralleling the normal and pathological modes of recapturing symbiotic representations in the being-in-love state are normal and pathological modes of achieving separateness and individuation. The prototypical pathological modes are beautifully illustrated by Tristan's driven and repetitive adventures and escapes which have a life-or-death quality to them. People who seek out such trials and ordeals are not simply exercising the autonomous functions of the ego in their adventures, but often are enacting maladaptive repetitive patterns of avoidance and escape from the feared representation of the engulfment state. The alternation, or fragmentation, of seeking merger during heightened passion, and fighting off commitment and engulfment fears by exaggerated self-sufficiency and efforts to achieve autonomy in ways that to the casual observer appear masochistically self-defeating are, I believe, the hallmark of unresolved preoedipal conflicts.

The distinction between symbiosis, pathological identifications or boundary fusion in the being-in-love state, and normal being in love—when there is full separation-individuation, boundary-crossing (Kernberg, 1977), and flexibility in ego functioning—is crucial for understanding the outcome of *Liebestod* fantasies: whether they eventuate in real or symbolic death, e.g., a suicide pact, as in the Tristan legend, or whether they lead to creative mastery and object love. The troubadours tell us that romantic love is inevitably blind, and that because it blinds judgment, anticipation, and routine reality contact, it can survive only in a passionate state, one which, in this context, sounds split off, fragmented, or dissociated. The sometimes irreconcilable-seeming split between being in love and loving represents a more pathological than normal state of affairs, for normally passion necessitates a relation to an object, a relation that implies the ego's capacity to respond to the realities of the object. Normally the two states—passion on the one hand and reality testing or object constancy on the other—alternate or blend, and their reconciliation is achieved when the level of the ego's functioning oscillates between controlled regressions and adaptation.

The relation between loving, being in love, and passion have rarely been well thought out in psychoanalysis. Winnicott (1958), however, has come very close to an appreciation of important distinctions when he contrasts the quiet loving and liking of "ego-relatedness" with the more passionate loving of "id relatedness." It is possible, says Winnicott, that "id relationships strengthen the ego when they occur in a framework of ego relatedness" (p. 34).

I believe that the polarization between passion and loving concern for the object should be regarded as a split or fragmentation into two or more relationships of something that cannot be managed within one. But intense passions need not seek outlet only in "eternal" relationships where there is not let-up in intensity and no opportunity for the ego to regain its equilibrium and resume mastery of the drives. Passion usually culminates in "death" from which one returns to life—"le petit mort" (Bak, 1973). The altered ego state of orgasm gratifies and renews regularly the need for intensity of a grand passion, for the temporary suspension of many ego functions, and for a living out of the fantasy of death through reunion via the ever-returning illusion of immortality and blissful merger. The passion with which Tristan loves, in contrast, is savored for its own sake, and is heightened to a painful intensity of sentiment, indifferent to its living and external object. It is no accident that we know virtually nothing about Iseult as a real person.

My main point here is that passion, in and of itself, is neither pathological nor adaptive. It may or may not escalate into sadomasochism or "lethal" narcissistic indulgence at the expense of self-regard and regard for the object. It may be considered pathological when critical ego functions, such as reality testing or object constancy, do not co-exist or reliably alternate with it. Thus, from the side of the id, as in full orgastic experience, and from the side of the ego, as in the development of the capacity for loving, there is hope for lovers that they may enjoy the intensity of passion and being in love (the narcissistic libidinal cathexis) while at the same time preserving the object-relatedness of loving (the object-libidinal cathexis).

This integrative position is consistent with Freud's point that "The finding of an object is in fact a refinding of it" (1905, p. 222). This refinding could now be understood as a rapprochement between nostalgic idealization and object constancy in love relationships. Bergmann (1971) states that certain ego functions, such as reality testing, must be temporarily suspended if the necessary *idealization* prerequisite to the *capacity* to fall in love is to take place. Yet he says, paradoxically, this very reality-testing function must simultaneously be operative to make possible the selection of a good mate. The apparent paradox may be resolved by noting that the ego may maintain an equilibrium, oscillating in all its functions, variably, in levels of regression, adaptation, or dominance. And here I emphatically agree with Bergmann that falling in love or being in love is a capacity of the ego, and not always a pathological aberration; it is compatible with the development of object constancy and with loving concern for the object.

## SUMMARY

The study of the legend of Tristan and Iseult in terms of the multiple fantasies it might express adds to our understanding of the psychology of love. In a previous paper (1975), I delineated, via allusion to the Tristan legend, the romantic-erotic conditions sometimes involved in creativity. In this one, I have approached the question of love from the other direction and have tried to delineate the creative-adaptive conditions required for integrating the experiences of loving and being in love. The "High tale of love and death," the *Liebestod* fantasy realized, is still with us, but the happier ending may be a realistic, viable alternative.

## REFERENCES

Bak, R.C. (1973). Being in love and object loss. *International Journal of Psycho-Analysis* 54:1–8.

Bedier, J. (1945). *The Romance of Tristan and Iseult.* New York: Pantheon.

Bergmann, M. S. (1971). Psychoanalytic observations on the capacity to love In: *Separation-Individuation: Essays in Honor of Margaret Mahler*, ed. J. B. McDevitt & C. F. Settlage. New York: International Universities Press, pp. 15–40.

——— (1980). On the intrapsychic function of falling in love. *Psychoanalytic Quarterly* 49:56–77.

Bouvet, M. (1958). Technical variations and the concept of distance. *International Journal of Psycho-Analysis* 39:211–221.

Brodsky, B. (1957). Liebestod fantasies in a patient faced with a fatal illness. *International Journal of Psycho-Analysis* 38:13–16.

De Rougement, D. (1956). *Love in the Western World.* New York: Pantheon.

Evans, W.N. (1953). Two kinds of romantic love. *Psychoanalytic Quarterly* 22:75–85.

Flugel, J.C. (1953). Death instinct, homeostasis and allied concepts. *International Journal of Psycho-Analysis* 34 (suppl.):43–74.

Freud, S. (1905). Three essays on the theory of sexuality. *S.E.* 7.

——— (1912). On the universal tendency to debasement in the sphere of love. *S.E.* 11.

——— (1913). The theme of the three caskets. *S.E.* 12.

Chapter 7: On Love, Dying Together and Liebestod fantasies

—— (1914). On narcissism: an introduction. *S.E.* 14.

—— (1917). Mourning and melancholia. *S.E.* 14

—— (1930). Civilization and its discontents. *S.E.* 21.

Gediman, H.K. (1975). Reflections on romanticism, narcissism, and creativity. *Journal of the American Psychoanalytic Association* 23:407–423.

Hermann, I. (1936). Clinging and going-in-search: a contrasting pair of instincts and their relation to sadism and masochism. *Psychoanalytic Quarterly* 45:5–36, 1976.

Isakower, O. (1938). A contribution to the patho-psychology of phenomena associated with falling asleep. *International Journal of Psycho-Analysis.* 9:331–345.

Jones, E. (1911). On "dying together." With special reference to Heinrich von Kleist's suicide. In: *Essays in Applied Psychoanalysis* 1 99–105 London: Hogarth Press, 1951.

——(1912). An unusual case of "dying together." In *Essays in Applied Psychoanalysis* 1 106–111. London: Hogarth Press, 1951.

Kaplan, L. (1978). *Oneness and Separateness.* New York: Simon & Schuster.

Kernberg, O.F. (1977). Boundaries and structure in love relations. *Journal of the American Psychoanalytic Association* 25:81–114.

Kohut, H. (1971). *The Analysis of the Self.* New York: International Universities Press. http://www.pep-web.org/document.php?id=zbk.049.0001a

Lewin, B.D. (1946). Sleep, the mouth, and the dream screen. *Psychoanalytic Quarterly* 15:419–434.
http://www.pep-web.org/document.php?id=paq.015.0419a

Mahler, M.S. (1972). Rapprochement subphase of the separation-individuation process. *Psychoanalytic Quarterly* 41:487–506.
http://www.pep-web.org/document.php?id=paq.041.0487a

—— Pine, F. & Bergman, A. (1975). *The Psychological Birth of the Human Infant.* New York: Basic Books.

Pollock, G.H. (1974). Manifestations of abnormal mourning: homicide and suicide following the death of another. In *Annual of Psychoanalysis* 4:225–249. http://www.pep-web.org/document.php?id=aop.004.0225a

—— (1975). On mourning, immortality, and utopia. *Journal of the American Psychoanalytic Association* 23:334–362.
http://www.pep-web.org/document.php?id=apa.023.0334a

Winnicott, D.W. (1958). The capacity to be alone. In *The Maturational Processes and the Facilitating Environment.* New York: International Universities Press, 1965 pp. 29–36.
http://www.pep-web.org/document.php?id=ipl.064.0001a

Zilboorg, G. (1938). The sense of immortality. *Psychoanalytic Quarterly.* 7:171–179.

# Chapter 8: Resurrection Themes in Life: A Case Study

[Gediman, H.K. (1995). Resurrection fantasies in art and the love life of an older man. In Gediman, H.K. *Fantasies of Love and Death in and Life and Art*. New York: New York University Press, 1995.]

Dr. D was a surgeon who had engaged in a lifelong pattern of passionate, compulsively driven, extramarital, "dangerous" sexual liaisons with women he regarded as "femmes fatales." In his later years, this pattern was overwhelming him with symptomatic anxieties. He entered treatment with me in his sixties because of a tormenting inability to extricate himself from a painful relationship with a woman who had fallen in love with him, as he had with her. Her relentless pursuit of him bore uncanny similarities to the portrayal by Glenn Close of the seemingly surreal "vampire" lady in the film *Fatal Attraction*. She pursued not only him, but me as his analyst as well, harassing both of us with suicide threats, letters, phone calls, message taping, and persistent "hang-up" calls in her driven efforts to verify his whereabouts. She pleaded with me to let her join him in sessions and tried to intimidate me into persuading him to leave his wife because she had proof he loved her more. The patient, who was "hopelessly" in love, felt helpless to deal with these pressures and tactics. He felt unable, by and large, to resist his own underlying temptations to submit to the potentially "fatal" but sexually exciting pulls of their liaison. His symptomatic chronic panic states over his lack of control in the face of her seductiveness became the focus of the treatment.

These severe anxieties took the form, manifestly, of a fear of being caught and of death. It soon became apparent that he hoped to ward off his own death in a number of mostly superstitious ways. In seeking out "illicit" forms of intercourse with certain perverse aims, Dr. D lived out fantasies of being masochistically beaten, flagellated, and particularly of "dying in the saddle" with the femme fatale to whom he felt attracted. In his imagination, these events were spectacles witnessed by others and remembered eternally. Yet, he superstitiously warded off death in a wide variety of symbolic ways. In tending to his garden, he hoped to exhume from the soil his vision of recurrent blooms and eternal life. By sleeping in an upright position, he hoped to ward off death, which he feared would be prematurely visited upon him should he succumb to the yielding sleep of the prone position. In restoring old junk to become original and new beautiful objects, he enacted a wish to revitalize inanimate, decayed, and decaying substances to life and perpetuity. He would retrieve old castaways from the gutters of the rich: a sled, a flowerpot, a toilet bowl chain from which he forged a modern abstract sculpture, and restore them to a new form, resurrecting them from the trashed-out dead. He pursued his sexual escapades, his work, and his avocations of gardening, art appreciation, and restoration of discarded objects with a drivenness that betrayed overriding wishes to leave his mark and memories, to resurrect himself so that others would remember him, as outstanding in all of these spheres. Dr. D was a "would-be-artist," warding off his fear of the "bad death" through the pursuit of illicit and what he fantasized as eternal sexuality, as well as through his avocational art pursuits, both of which he enacted compulsively to grant him a new lease on life. Yet, the more he feared the "bad death," the more inextricably bound he became to his femme fatale, and the more bound to her, the more terrified he became of submitting to his masochism, a pattern that could be read as a male version of the *Hörigkeit* scenario.

Dr. D's concerns about death appeared to surface only late in life, in connection with the deadly consequences he anticipated in response to his uncontrolled sexual indiscretions. He also had to contend with a mild cardiac condition and other medical problems which undoubtedly are not rare among the elderly or aging patient in analytic therapy. However, Dr. D's worries actually started in childhood and by the age of seventeen they had become an obsessive preoccupation. At that time, he entertained morbid thoughts about his grandparents' visible signs of bodily deterioration. However, we must not confound these existential, conscious preoccupations with their dynamically unconscious motivations, for he remembered those adolescent years as .a time of severe beatings by his father for what sounds to be age-appropriate sexual experimentation. Memories of decomposition of the flesh thus were condensed with masochistically gratifying fantasies of being beaten for forbidden sexual forays.

Dr. D's obsession with his femme fatale stimulated him to attempt to realize his fantasies of immortality. As he would tell me of his illicit sexuality, an erotic transference developed as he drew me into his circle of fatal attractions. He languished in fantasies of seducing me, of sinning lasciviously and carrying through these activities in Purgatory, where he would have liked to stay indefinitely. God's punishments were, he said, the price he paid in his bargain with the devil to continue his earthly delights in whatever locale he would occupy in the afterlife.

With advancing age, illness, diminution of potency, and accumulating social slights in response to his uncontrolled exhibitionistic sexual indiscretions, and, not incidentally, in his transferential feelings toward me, Dr. D chose to shift to relative abstinence as a new way of life. He began to identify with the martyred Christ in many ways. Resurrection fantasies became more apparent and driving forces than they were at the start of his analysis, when he was hardly abstinent but very active sexually in his dangerous liaisons. When he felt forced by age, illness, and feared social slights to limit his extramarital sexual activity, Dr. D thought he knew chastity as Christ did, and this belief fostered his Christ identification and the accompanying resurrection fantasies, which contained elements of both the resurrection of Christ and the Last Judgment.

It became clear in the course of the analysis that Dr. D's resurrection fantasies, like the images of resurrection in Renaissance art, condensed a multiplicity of unconscious fantasies. Prominent among them was a wish to recreate himself, parthenogenetically, through his idiosyncratic oeuvre. The oeuvre of this "would-be-artist" consisted, for one, of his fantasy of the legacy he would leave to the next-generation doctor, whom he fantasized as his replacement and who would inspect and admire the reconstructive work that he had performed on his former patients. The man who would continue Dr. D's practice would view Dr. D's unsurpassed, perfect record of exquisite surgical incisions and restorations, praising his work and promoting his immortality. It also consisted of some very concrete representations of all the art knowledge that he had accumulated and had "poured into his head," which he would then pour into the heads of his children, grandchildren, and anyone who wished to read his autobiography, which he was dreaming of writing for them. His oeuvre extended to his select collection of antiquities and primitive art, to his perfectly crafted carvings, all of which he kept polished and shiny in anticipation of their becoming part of his estate. Additionally, he had a collection of old discarded literal junk, which he had restored by rubbing down and bringing out the original finishes, for posterity to admire. As much as anything else, his oeuvre consisted of his memory traces of all the world's greatest art that he liked to imagine that he had created, himself. In fanciful moments, he imagined that a brain autopsy could preserve his mental acquisitions forever. His oeuvre was epitomized by his ever-renewable garden, of which more shall be said shortly.

Dr. D had been told by friends that he can be quite crude and offensive to women, that he defiled them through excessive "womanizing." One is reminded of a passage in Lifton's (1979) book, where Norman Mailer is quoted. Mailer is quite explicit about the male quest for immortality via the encounter with the female and her "seat of creation." This quest, Mailer says, is a cause for such a man to detest women, to "defile them, humiliate them, defecate symbolically upon them, do everything to reduce them so that one might dare to enter them and take pleasure of them" (Lifton 1979, 32, citing Mailer 1971). In this reference to man's envy of women, Lifton says that the envy of which Mailer speaks is a life-creating envy, an immortality envy. Out of that envy man degrades woman, for she is seen as the source, possessor, and guardian of the life process itself, "and of the sexual union as an absolute expression of centering in which the immediate blends with the ultimate and the present with a sense of timelessness" (33). Dr. D's fear/wish of "dying in the saddle" related in this way to his degradation of the women he got close to.

It became clear in the course of his analysis that Dr. D's resurrection fantasies, like the images of Christ's resurrection in Renaissance art, condensed a multiplicity of unconscious fantasies, all accompanying the proliferation of death anxieties which increased with age, illness, and curtailment of sexual activities. Prominent among them was a wish to achieve immortality and recreate himself in various ways that would force others to remember him. He memorized all he could of the world's great art, wishing he had created it himself. A favorite haunt for seducing women was a local art museum where his personal attractiveness, he believed, would be enhanced as women idealized his stored knowledge of immortal art and art immortals.

One particular preoccupation was expressed in his belief that only artists can be immortal: "I wish I could reinvent the safety pin, or something like it. That would be enough for me." That is, he would accept this variation of creative accomplishment as an adequate substitute for attaining the creative perfection of his lifelong ego ideal, who was Picasso. He chose Picasso because of the longevity in both the sexual and artistic spheres of his life. Our would-be-artist also admired art that carries messages of immortality and of the possibility of the afterlife. He always liked Thornton Wilder's *Our Town* (1938), a play that takes place in a graveyard, in which the protagonist meets all the people of her childhood who had predeceased her. In fact, Dr. D referred to this play in the eulogy he delivered at his father's funeral. He was also intensely interested in Florentine Renaissance artists. At the age of fourteen he had read Benvenuto Cellini's autobiography, and was so impressed with the miracles that the Italian craftsman had sculpted out of gold that one cannot help but wonder if Dr. D's choice of surgery, which involves intricate handiwork in "resculpting" body parts, was in part motivated by this early enchantment. In adolescence, he kept track of the lives of the Italian artists, the Medicis and Popes who were their patrons, and the donors who appear in the paintings they commissioned as a way of assuring their own immortality by resurrecting themselves in the memories of their viewers. The patronage system captured his imagination so that he seemed to have enacted a Renaissance-age drama in the terms of the cultural and economic condition of his own lifestyle. Adolescent fantasies about being sponsored by great men of power seem to have influenced his seeking and finding, as if this were the only sensible route to marriage, the equivalent of a patron in his father-in-law. Dr. D bought out the practice of an older doctor who promised to bequeath to Dr. D, once the younger man would replace the older, many wealthy and famous acquaintances as patients, most of whom were prominent in the worlds of the performing and creative arts. The murderous wishes stirred up in Dr. D, as his senior achieved unanticipated longevity and a long delay of the promised referrals, were later, and during analysis, projected onto his own potential replacements. His fear that they might wish to polish him off led to significant inhibitions in planning for his own eventual retirement.

Unconscious resurrection fantasies were also to be found in Dr. D's efforts to restore and preserve the body. The bones in particular, he was convinced, are immortal, for they alone are preserved over time in skeletal remains of the dead, just as he had preserved them in life. But Dr. D was not a mere preserver of the corpus. He regarded each and every surgical incision and reconstruction with the respect and devotion of an archaeologist who aims to preserve forever a relic from antiquity. He preserved, restored, and reconstructed with methodical care, patience, and pride. He explained to me, in accounting for his perfectionism (which in fact annoyed some of his patients and frightened away others), that if any of his deceased patients were to be autopsied, or their graves exhumed, the surgical reconstruction that was the object of his painstaking labors, the perfect artistic creation, would be immortalized in testimony to his professional perfection and scrupulous conscientiousness. These were the conscious fantasies. Unconsciously there was a web of others.

Dr. D fancied himself a true Renaissance man, though he knew he fell short. Like his boyhood idol, Cellini, he was more of a consummate craftsman than an imaginative artist. Our knowledge of his resurrection fantasies, together with our knowledge of some of his inner conflicts, helps to interpret the art he would aspire to create: the safety pin, the immortal phallic imagery of a Picasso, or the craftsmanship of the Florentine goldsmiths, each of whom had his patron and an apprentice to carry on the great tradition, assuring that any art to be judged as great through posterity would be the same now as, say, during the Sumerian era. As with a Wagner opera, we can identify leitmotifs in the life of this man. In this instance, they are resurrection subthemes that recur repetitively, and because of the drivenness of this man's preoccupations, we would categorize them as pathological despite their normative and universal roots.

## LEITMOTIFS OF BLASPHEMY, EXHUMING, AND DECAY

Just as Steinberg's erection-resurrection equation might evoke in the minds of people of delicate sensibility protests of too much vulgarity, sacrilege, and blasphemy, so too might Dr. D's eccentric life style evoke a host of epithetic reactions.

Throughout his life, Dr. D displayed a pattern of behavior in which one might identify secular versions of religious defamation, profanation, sacrilege, and blasphemy. As a young man, he attempted to "purify" himself by changing his Jewish last name to one that sounded elegant and Christian to him and represented his counteridentification with aspects of his father's aggression and sexuality which he repudiated as being crude and vulgar. Yet, the vulgar infiltrated his everyday behavior in the form of symptoms. He regularly offended certain of his patients by invasive questioning when they were getting ready to go on the operating table, or when they could not talk; he degraded and defiled the women he made love with by treating them roughly and inconsiderately when they expected more tact and consideration than he was inclined to offer; he high-mindedly betrayed his trust as an officer and a gentleman in the army by taking on a fraudulent identity and illegally maneuvering a pleasure trip to Paris in order to view great art and to visit some prostitutes during the height of the Nazi occupation. His trip to Paris for purposes of illicit sexual adventure was a conscious and deliberate attempt to achieve in reality what he had imagined in his adolescence to be the forbidden delights of a city that brought to life the lasciviousness he found in Lautrec's paintings of prostitutes. When he sought out the seedy and vulgar, however, it was usually in a context of wishing to defame the more sacred images he knew of in the many pictures of Paris that he had clipped and collected. The images that particularly impressed him in these secretly kept collections involved the juxtaposition of profane and sacred contents, suggesting to him the very vulgarity and crudeness that he repudiated in his father, but which gave him secret pleasures. On the illegal wartime trip, he headed straight for the neighborhood near the Church of Le Sacré Coeur where he photographed, with Le Sacré Coeur as backdrop, an artist with his nude model, thereby actualizing his boyhood thrill of thinking of Parisian whores as the only source of models for artists. He designated this photograph as part of his legacy, hoping it would be viewed by posterity as part of his "oeuvre." The would-be-artist hoped then to be associated in people's minds with the artists represented in his ego-ideal, such as Cellini or Picasso, whose privileged illicitness, when expressed in their eternally admired works, would guarantee immortality. Idealizing of the vulgar, a leitmotif in the life of this would-be-artist, was always to be found in a context of both identifying with and defensively trying to undo and repudiate the strong unconscious identification with his father's vulgarity which he came to repudiate, consciously. Since childhood, he anticipated punishments, whippings, even arrest as a criminal for all of his own vulgarity. He masochistically wished to provoke reprimands, as in sessions. Often, he blew his nose vigorously, wiping it, putting the soaking tissues on a chair in my office where I and others sit. This apparent disregard of cleanliness and hygiene appears as a manifest contradiction of his meticulous cleanliness and quest for purification in his surgical practice.

This compulsive activity can be understood, then, as a repetitive enactment of certain scenes he had witnessed, and which irritatingly excited him, such as that of his vulgar father blowing his nose into a dinner napkin and then wiping his mouth with it. Dr. D did exactly that in his wife's presence. With me, in addition to the vigorous nose blowing, he "licked his chops" often as he told me of his illicit sexuality, his fantasies of seducing me, and his lifelong preoccupations with sinning lasciviously and of carrying through the activity in Purgatory, or limbo, where he hoped to stay indefinitely.

I regard his repetitive, compulsive "blasphemous" acts as reflecting a resurrection fantasy, especially as he changed his name from a Jewish to a Christian one, a change that unconsciously signified rebirth into a faith which held a belief in the afterlife, and where men, who were not circumcised as boys, need not live in shame. He had given a good deal of thought to the burial customs of different religions. He was troubled by the Jewish belief in the idea that bodies simply decomposed into dust following death, being more comfortable with the Christian ideas of purity in the possibility of resurrection. His fantasies contain the same sort of juxtaposed elements of vulgarity and divinity as appear prominently in the images of Christian theology selected by Steinberg (1983) from Renaissance art works to convey the sexuality of Christ and the erection-resurrection equation.

Related to blasphemy is Dr. D's preoccupation with decay and exhumation of dead substances. Juxtaposed with the lofty and glorious aspirations toward the aesthetic were a fascination with rotting, decayed, fecal, and necrotic substances and their symbolic equivalents. This juxtaposition has already been referred to in his perseverative, driven behavior in transforming junk into valuable restorations, and decaying skeletal supports into monuments of per-manently resurrected bone, in testimony to his consummate skills as a surgeon and craftsman. His absorbing passion to dig deep into his patients' bodies to resurrect tissue and life might be characterized as variations on a theme of alchemy, or the wish to transform feces into gold, death into life. In Dr. D's personal fantasy life, in this variant of necromancy and perpetual revival, particular emphasis was directed to the place of hair, nails, urine, and feces. These substances, because they are infinitely renewable, lend themselves in conscious and unconscious fantasy as suitable material out of which one can forge an image of a self that can endure well into perpetuity. They thus can easily be appropriated to express resurrection ideas.

In his idealized body image, Dr. D made use of his own waste products in his wish to preserve his body as forever young, renewed, and never de-cayed and wasted. That is, his image of his glorious body suffused with a narcissistically enhancing self-feeling was not restricted to what have cus-tomarily been associated with the body as pure phallus. It extended beyond the phallic narcissistic imagery to accompany excreta as well. He relished the thought of spraying his urine throughout the world, imagining it evaporat-ing and becoming part of the timeless cosmos. His feces could fertilize food supplies that others would ingest and then excrete, at which time they would generously transform into new food for new generations, and thus contribute to the chain of immortality. Dr. D continuously yearned for resurrection of his own precious bodily substances and this fantasy motivated a corpus of symptomatic compulsive behaviors which substantiated the notion that his resurrection fantasies incorporated pathological elements. He had indulged for years in certain compulsive toileting rituals of wiping himself spotlessly clean and flushing the toilet between each stool production of a given bowel movement, as though cleaning both the toilet bowl and his own anal orifice in an honoring manner, preparing them for a pristine state in which to receive the next produced stool. From time to time, he overblew his nose, belying a compulsion to rid it of all exudate. Although this compulsion to purify body orifices received sublimated outlet in his daily work of cleaning out wounds, antiseptically, he approached this task with perfectionistic zeal bordering on violence, which had threatened and alienated some of his patients.

His treatment of money, the nonorganic fecal equivalent, was, as would be expected, similar. Until his penuriousness was analyzed, he kept his holdings in a safe-deposit box where, although they earned no interest, he could touch and feel the cash as real, fearful of investing in a way that would inform him only on paper of accruals of his assets. Monthly statements from a broker, even those indicating growth of his assets, were not palpably real like growing piles of money that he could count and recount. An important aspect of his superstitious use of money and the collection of junk to be restored was their designation as inanimate, dead substances, like feces or mucus. He confessed to a (conscious) fear that the medical examiner at his death and at his autopsy would find the dirt, and that was one reason he offered for the compulsive cleaning and polishing of his own oral, aural, anal, nasal, and dermal orifices. Similarly, he explained that his perfectionism in performing antiseptic cleansing procedures on his patients was a way of assuring that they would go to their graves in a state of purification, and would therefore be a credit to his reputation should they ever be examined by the Department of Health. These purification rituals, then, were clearly related to some narcissistic aspects of immortality concerns. The purifying obsessions seem in large measure to be attempts to purify himself from the guilt of his indiscretions: "When I die, I don't want the doctor to see any dirt on me." All of these rituals illuminated his preoccupation with the revitalization of dead and inanimate substances, and reflected, along with the wish to be rid of guilt, his powerful resurrection wishes. The fantasy of his own resurrection in the form of a perfectly clean, polished, and repolished restoration of inanimate and decaying matter was acted out in countless ways. In one particularly fanciful version, he became obsessively preoccupied with discovering what restorative substance he imagined to be inside of a strange bottle kept by a collegial rival in his office. Although it looked to him to contain an ordinary solution, he was plagued by the possibility that it contained a secret elixir of life. That potion would enable his rival to prevent his own patients' bodies from ever decaying, while Dr. D, on the other hand, would have to risk the very shameful (to him) failures of an ordinary surgical practice. His patients would carry for all the world to see the evidence of their surgeon's falling short of professional perfection, which translated for Dr. D into the evidence of mortal decay. He fantasized that his own patients would, after his death, be examined by other surgeons, his successors, who would discover how he fell mortifyingly short of his fantasized accomplishments. *(Mortify:* to subdue or deaden, as the body or bodily passions, by abstinence or self-inflicted pain or discomfort; to become necrotic or gangrenous. How close the dictionary definition comes to, captures, this man's equation of shame with death and decay, and underscores the existence of unconscious resurrection fantasies.)

These preoccupations accompanied memories referred to earlier, of his father and uncle vulgarly blowing their noses into their dinner napkins in public, suggesting an identification which he repudiated yet at the same time felt compelled to enact in my presence during the sessions. Interestingly, it was Dr. D's job as an army medical officer to "short-arm" the men, to pull back their penile foreskins, to detect excrescences that might be related to venereal disease. He also compulsively avoided or removed perspiration, and picked out all possible pimples and blackheads. Nothing was to be seen leaking from any orifice, even the tiniest pore. So he was constantly wiping his face, hands and neck. He often dwelled on the horror of the gas-chamber victims defecating and urinating and standing in their own excrement. These concerns were exacerbated when he involuntarily urinated during a mugging and also when he was interrogated by police for speeding, incidents he regarded as his closest brushes with death.

One reason that Dr. D was so fascinated by museums, and from a very young age, is that in them, the inanimate and the dead are preserved as immortal. He was constantly preoccupied with where his possessions, clean, restored, well-kept, as well as his body exudate would go after he dies, and was fascinated with the Egyptians, especially Tutankhamen who took all his gold and other possessions to the grave with him. Those concerns were evident also in Dr. D's attachment to such memorabilia as the man who was immortalized in Madame Tussaud's wax museum with his preserved nails and hair put into the wax figure that was made into an exact replica of himself. This fascination relates to his preoccupations with his own feces and nasal exudate, both of which suggest an obsessional interest in inanimate matter that is infinitely regenerable. His compulsive surgical cleaning, repairing, and rebuilding were related, in that he believed that the cleaned out rot, flesh, and blood participated in the life-death cycle of appearance and disappearance with each procedural cleaning-out. These preoccupations sometimes verged on the macabre, as when a close relative died. He would not leave the hospital where she died nor take his eyes off the corpse until the morticians came. He waited for them for hours although his presence was in no way required. After the cremation, he held onto the remains, obsessed with what substances other than ashes, such as teeth and bone remnants, might be in the urn. He had been unable to get rid of the cremated remains, mainly because he took so to heart the symbolic meaning of whatever place he might have chosen to dispose of them. Thoughts of disposal were associated with other thoughts, mainly of the cremated gas-chamber victims whose gold teeth fillings stand as mementos in holocaust museums. He longed to plant his relative's ashes in his garden, as though they would grow to full fruition as he wished would happen to him after his own death. These fantasies contained elements of resurrection symbolism to be found in artistic renditions of themes of both the Resurrection of the Dead and Christ's Resurrection.

Because Dr. D customarily and energetically invaded with potentially lethal instruments, body parts and orifices generally regarded as forbidden territory, his compulsive surgical cleaning and the compulsive cleaning out of his own fecal matter can be regarded as compromise formations. Good hygienic practices would realistically guarantee a longer life, permitting as well a continuous invasion, for purposes of pleasure, of the forbidden depths of the body and what they symbolize, perhaps mother earth. The very same behavior also represented a purification ritual to pacify the superego following these frequent forays into forbidden spaces.

Additional manifestations of his yearning to penetrate forbidden places proliferated transferentially, as he would intrusively pick up things to read from my desk, always curious about my private life. Extra-transferentially, these invasive longings took the lifelong form of an obsession to go to Africa, the dark and forbidden continent. As with his literal sexual activity, his fatal attractions, this obsession with symbolically penetrating the forbidden woman was so overriding that with good opportunities to take the trip, he found reasons not to be able to go. Often, the rationalizations boiled down to a fear that any journey was to be his last, and in his neurotic efforts to ward off death and extend his life, he superstitiously avoided traveling to all the places that were, in his mind, associated with oedipal transgressions as well preoedipal fears of the engulfing, forbidden maternal object—the femme fatale.

In sum, all of the eccentric habits in relation to the decayed and the inanimate seemed to be expressing a simple message: each gesture, each flower planted, each operation of flesh cleaned and repaired, the self-scrubbing during and after each surgical intervention and each bowel movement, each day of work, each postponement of taking a trip, each instance of sexual intercourse—all were equated with extending his life by another day, culminating in his desperate and absurd attempts to postpone the end of his life indefinitely, or at the very least, to avoid the bad death. Thus, he sought to increase the chances of being resurrected in the minds of others, if only to be remembered for his eccentricities, which he deemed to be singular, unique. It was indeed amazing how his facial mien actually reflected his eccentric death and rebirth preoccupations, and at times invited attention and commentary. Typical reactions were such incidents as a man stopping him in the street, whispering, "You look like death warmed over," or a man outside a movie house saying, "You're not supposed to be alive again yet."

A psychoanalytic interpretation of Dr. D's pathological concerns with decay, exhuming, and perpetuity would, in addition to the compromise formation described earlier, also have to address the condensation of multiple fantasies in any particular enactment. In his wish for a perpetual renewal of body parts, his body itself and what goes in and out are representations of himself, whether of the body phallus, or variations on the body fecal column. This fantasy of perpetual renewal via the incorporation into himself of outside bits and pieces expresses a compromise between both fecal and castration anxiety on the one hand, and making reparation for the anticipated loss of representations of himself either as a whole or by parts. When he referred to meat-eating as "eating the body parts of animals" and as devouring raw flesh, he was expressing an aspect of this fantasy. I would designate this resurrection-fantasy variant as belonging in the general category of "parthenogenesis," or fertilizing and giving birth to a representation of oneself without benefit of intercourse with the opposite sex. Much in this resurrection fantasy with its oral incorporative and phallic narcissistic components reflected a conscious wish. The fantasy is narcissistic, to repeat, in that the parthenogenetic wish involved a drive to recreate himself without connection to a specific object, or woman. The femme fatale is simply a means to this cosmic end: a "sex object."

To repeat, these fantasies were conscious. It was the gratification of oral and anal sadistic wishes that were unconscious. It should not be forgotten that he chose surgery as a profession, one in which he could perpetually repair decay in his, elderly patients, over whose bodies he had complete control to open, invade, exhume, and resurrect. So, his forbidden "fatal" sexuality found its parallel in his other obsessions and compulsions. Clearly, his concerns were to ward off the bad death and not to seek the good one. Reunion and merger fantasies with another were not part of his aim, which appeared restricted to perpetuating himself, narcissistically, in perpetuity. He would ruminate about the way precious substances are decanted out of purified waste matter, destined to be resurrected as eternal substances in our streams, rivers, oceans, and evaporating into the atmosphere, and are bound to be breathed in or ingested and renewed, perpetually, in some bond of cosmic oneness between the universe and man, particularly himself. This narcissistic variant of a resurrection fantasy, then, would appear to exclude the elements of the Liebestod as I understand the latter class of fantasy: it is not concerned with the good death via reunion and merger with an object where two are as one. Instead, the incidental object is purely instrumental in attaining the narcissistic goal of avoiding the bad death. In that sense, it would appear to reflect more pathology than a universal wish for oneness with a loved one or the cosmos in an eternal good death.

## LEITMOTIFS OF GARDENING AND RESURRECTION

As the years went by and age overtook her, there was something comical yet touching in her bedraggled appearance on this awesome occasion—the small hunched over figure, her studied absorption in the implausible notion that there would be yet another spring, oblivious to the ending of her own days which she knew perfectly well was near at hand, sitting there with her detailed chart under those dark skies, in the dying October, calmly plotting the resurrection.

— E. B. White, Introduction to Katharine S. White's *Onward and Upward in the Garden*

It would be natural, after considerations of perpetuity, decay and exhuming, to look to Dr. D's passion for gardening as a concrete representation of these and other resurrection wishes. As close an illustration of the erection-resurrection equation as one might expect to encounter could be interpreted from the conscious fantasies that he entertained in connection with a most significant portion of his avocational "oeuvre," his garden, and what it represented in his psyche.

By way of introduction to Dr. D's gardening obsession, I return once more to Lifton (1979) on immortality. In speaking of the "natural mode" of immortality, Lifton referred in a footnote to

the longstanding Anglo Saxon preoccupation with vigorously confronting the infinite dimension of nature and with "cultivating one's garden." In that last image, the idea of nurturing and communing with one's own small plot of land becomes a metaphor for tending to one's own realm, whether of domestic national policy or the individual psyche. (23)

Dr. D longed to have his ashes, after cremation, planted in his garden, where, somehow, they would help fertilize and promote the growth of a rose bush which, in his fantasy, would be no less than himself, reborn. Not only did he obsessively tend his garden, he would steal seedlings from other places to make it the best ever. On occasion he committed the reverse infraction. When he would see a plot of someone else's land unplanted, he would dig up the barren earth under cover of darkness and plant something on the property he had trespassed, excited over both the idea of violation and of promoting fecundity. He would then replace the soil, as though in mimicry of both a burial and a rebirth. He became obsessed with who would tend and perpetuate his garden when he dies, and wrote and rewrote his will so that now his wife, now his children, would inherit it, depending on who he thought would most likely preserve it exactly as he had cultivated it. He had even considered willing it as land in the public trust as a memorial to himself, where he would request burial, his monument to be the rose bush that would rise from the soil, fertilized by his cremated ashes. The fantasy ended with his wife looking at the thorns in the bush, wistful about the various women whom he had penetrated sexually during his life, and who are now passing by his flowery reincarnation. As each woman leans to touch the thorny bush, his wife puns to the assembled tribute-payers, "Pricked by D again." So his gardening represented digging and exhuming his own grave in preparation for his resurrection as a phallus-prick, eternally active, sexually.

Once again, as in his vocational work of surgery, there seemed to be echoes of wishes to invade forbidden places, like the dark continent, Africa, and wishes to remain phallically erect after death, wishes that in large measure accounted for his pattern of passionate fatal attractions. His gardening mania condensed ideas about death and rebirth to a life of perpetual erection and romance. In this one man's version of the erection-resurrection equation, a gardening mania condensed many late-life preoccupations with intercourse, fathering, and generativity in general. He showed the same passionate zeal in his death-defying gardening as in his "fatal" sexual encounters.

Steinberg (1983) said that according to legend, the Tree of Life planted in the Garden of Eden was predestined to yield its wood to the cross. He was referring here to the 1511 Baldung Grien woodcut *The Fall of Man* in which we see a dead tree hosting a vigorous vine, which Steinberg called "a rectifying fresh vine that mounts the dry trunk behind St. Anne" (p. 118). Such an interpretation would have Adam resurrected as Christ, as the Fall prefigures the Passion. The iconology that informs most art historians' interpretations of Grien's imagery does not lead generally to the kinds of conclusions that are customarily drawn in psychoanalytic interpretations of the dynamic unconscious. Those very images and what they symbolize in primary process thinking, however, would appear to have an important point of contact with Dr. D's fantasies of rebirth as a tree. Dr. D became obsessed with planting trees, each a memorial to himself; he wanted to take home a small tree in my office in order to repot it and then return it so as to guarantee him immortality, by at least serving as a reminder to me of his existence, ensuring his place in my thoughts about him. His continual planting, whether in his own or others' gardens, appeared to express nothing of the frequently encountered romantic theme of the red rose and the green briar that entwines in a true lovers' knot-a fantasized reunion *with an object* after death. Dr. D's fantasy was, rather, a self-preoccupied image of a loner, of solitary perfection, risen, on a stake, akin to one of many possible psychoanalytic readings of Grien's imagery as autonomous text: a narcissistic fantasy of the body-self as phallus, of perpetual erection memorialized into perpetuity.

A resurrection fantasy of coming back to life by growing out of the very soil of one's burial and birth place seemed in Dr. D's case to be a reaction to early but traumatic awareness of death, decomposition, and mortality which he dated to an organized memory of himself at age seventeen. It was then that he wrote a story of an old man contentedly warmed by the rays of the sun while sitting on a park bench. The indigent man was destined for interment in Potter's Field, and the adolescent writer concluded with the line, "Too bad they can't bury you exactly where you die, where the good things happen." In later life, of course, the good happening was to be "dying in the saddle."

## LEITMOTIFS OF ORAL INCORPORATION
## AND PHALLIC PARTHENOGENESIS

Before elaborating further on the phallic-narcissistic elements which, as we have seen, are to be found frequently in the way that resurrection ideation figured in Dr. D's fantasy life, I should like to note the elements of oral incorporation that also played their part in motivating the vocational and avocational interests he pursued so intensely. In keeping with Oremland's (1989) notion that ideas of oral incorporation, or of taking-in aspects of another that enhance one's narcissism, play an important part in resurrection fantasies, it can be shown that Dr. D also thought that a greedy taking-in of the good that others possess could guarantee him immortal recognition.

His fear/wish of dying in the saddle and the related envy, anger, and degradation of women also related to his ever-desperate but failed attempts to recreate himself, parthenogenetically, with absolutely no dependence on a woman, as in trying vainly to take control of his childrens' lives by pouring all the world's knowledge from his head into theirs. However, in a particular fantasy variant of oral incorporation, that of parthenogenesis, the emphasis on narcissistic concerns is more prominent. In a typical parthenogenetic fantasy, a man wishes to perpetuate himself without benefit of intercourse with a woman, consistent with negative oedipal longings. Oremland (1989) in particular emphasizes the oral incorporative elements in his exegesis of the resurrection motifs in Michelangelo's Sistine Chapel ceiling. Like Steinberg, Oremland, basing his inferences upon Michelangelo's Sistine ceiling images, interprets Adam's parthenogenetic birth and the Fall as prefiguring Christ's immaculate conception and crucifixion, and also interprets Christ's resurrection as a continuation of Adam's life on earth. Oremland holds that oral incorporation motifs inhere in resurrection ideation which always implies a wish to perpetuate a lost object by taking it into the self, as the self becomes perpetuated by being taken into others, ad infinitum, into perpetuity. He notes the parthenogenetic, particularly the auto-fellatio aspects of oral incorporation in several Sistine Chapel images of self-fertilization, birth, and rebirth.

On the day that Dr. D expressed a wish for me to look at and take in as fully as he had Katharine White's book (1981) with its explicit reference to gardening and resurrection, he expressed greed to "eat up" everything written. He was sure that I knew everything there was to know about psychoanalysis and it was just a matter of my discretion when I would pour it all into his head. He would then be in a position to pour all of his ingested knowledge into the head of his grandchild and all of his professional knowledge into the head of whichever young man was to replace him in his practice. However, to recreate himself by transferring his wealth to a chosen individual in the next generation led to conflict because it was contingent on his dying. Many of his unconscious fantasies and conflicts were based on cannibalistic wishes to devour another person's power, and on the wish to resurrect himself in the image of the all-knowing one whose phallic power he has incorporated, orally. This form of greed is precisely what motivated his relationship to the mentor whose practice he had bought out early in his own career. When the older man did not die as soon as Dr. D anticipated, Dr. D harbored murderous wishes toward him, and because he anticipated similar motives on the part of whomever was to buy out his practice prior to his retirement, his fear of being drained by his successor alternated with oral expulsion wishes to pour everything he knew into his replacement. The conflict led to paralysis of his will in arranging for someone to buy out his practice in preparation for retirement. Related are marked filicidal fantasies toward his own children, fueled by his projections onto them of his wishes to steal and then incorporate the paternal phallus. Dr. D at times seemed concerned about their wellbeing after his death, but was tormented by ideas of how they would probably misappropriate and abuse his possessions, unable to love and cherish them with an intensity equal to his own. In retaliation for the parricidal treachery he expected from them, he disappropriated his children from time to time in impulsive rewritings of his will. His projections onto them paralleled a disregard for his own father after the latter's death. It would be just as futile to expect that his children would be the ones to resurrect him as it was futile to believe he wanted to resurrect his own father.

While my focus here is on the oral incorporative elements of resurrection fantasies, these wishes also contain clearly negative oedipal and homosexual implications, as in Dr. D's wish to orally incorporate the idealized parental phallus. In keeping with his negative oedipal fantasies of submission to a powerful but benevolent father, is Dr. D's expressed "nostalgia" for Renaissance art history, the time when such artists as Michelangelo had patrons. He had the conscious fantasy of making himself the favored "pet" of senior members of his profession who would patronize him, and whose practices he dreamed of inheriting upon their deaths in return for the favor of his obsequies. As I mentioned earlier, he lived out his Renaissance man fantasies, taking for granted his unusual attractiveness, skills, and knowledge. I should interject here that in a pathographical consideration of the psychological determinants that may have influenced the individual Florentine artists' paintings of certain images, such as the father's hand on the groin of the dead son, we may be onto something beyond the Christological creed as understood by Steinberg. I am referring to the breakthrough of homosexual, negative oedipal thematic material that might well have been very prominent in the personal lives of many of the Florentine painters who thrived in the patronage system just as it was prominent in Dr. D's living-out of his idiosyncratic patronage fantasies.

As termination of his analysis drew near, Dr. D seemed to be experiencing that ending in the very terms of impending death: each new session represented to him a chance to buy more time to live. He fantasized having the wisdom of all my books and all the books ever written on psychoanalysis poured into him as I, in the transference, represented the paternal phallus to be incorporated and then passed on. The desperation for me to read his gardening book with its reference to resurrection suggested to me that because he knew of my interest in writing, he may have wanted me to immortalize him in a book. He denied this, but did imagine I might write up my case to present to my classes, making of his case history the immortalizing biography he had always dreamed about. It was as though he wanted me to eat his book and thereby incorporate him, keeping him with me after his death, just as he wished to pour knowledge down the throats of his issue. There was a poignancy in his wish to have me eat, preserve, and resurrect him in myself, sexually as well. He felt a sense of sexual excitement as he cannibalistically ingested the world's art into himself and then poured it into a woman so that she would impress his image upon her father and sons, thereby guaranteeing his resurrection in the minds of those who were vitally important to him.

## LEITMOTIFS OF PHALLIC BODY NARCISSISM

Most of the psychoanalytic literature on death preoccupations gives priority to fantasies of rebirth, reunion, and merger with a lost other and provides lesser emphasis on the phallic narcissistic aspects of resurrection via self-perpetuity. Blacker (1983) believes that the idea of rebirth indicates starting life anew without blemish, whereas resurrection fantasies express the wish for another chance to live but with the same defective body. The idea of defect and the phallic castration anxieties underlying it, are at the root of many of Dr. D's resurrection fantasies. His self-image as an immortalized body-phallus is evocative of Steinberg's erection-resurrection equation, and his preoccupation with immortality and resurrection cannot be understood readily in terms of merger with the lost object. That his resurrection fantasies are more narcissistic than object-related was noted earlier, in connection with his wish to reincarnate as a lone rose bush, not as one entwining with the green briar. There is a conspicuous absence of an other in his resurrection fantasies, with the exception of the mirroring audience, a selfobject (Kohut). This patient sustained no significant early losses and no significant early identifications with a lost object. He did, however, experience significant narcissistic losses, both of his physical prowess and attractiveness and of living up to a perfectionistic and esteemed idealized self-image. In his case, one may speak of identifications with a lost part-object, the phallus, as opposed to the loss of a whole person, as his ideas of death related primarily to detumescence, while those of tumescence represent the coming to life again. I did learn late in the treatment that his mother had been hospitalized in a psychiatric hospital for "premature senility" and his preoccupations could be seen in part as a late-life identification with her during her waning years. Mostly, though, his fantasies were narcissistic dreams of glory and everlasting sexual and artistic might.

Dr. D wished he could be a character in a Molière play where everyone is around his deathbed and, unbeknownst to them, he comes back to life to hear what they have to say about him. He, like Blacker, but for different reasons, was intrigued by people who had died, technically speaking, and then come back to life, as after cardiac arrest or in drowning and resuscitation. Themes of the raising of the dead and the curing of cripples, such as those that appear in Renaissance art, fascinated him. He hoped that he might upon his death achieve a moment of peace, representing the alleged transmigration of souls.

The patient, the would-be-artist, felt convinced that there was a special connection between Picasso's creativity, his longevity, and his phallic preoccupations. Picasso was Dr. D's ego ideal, because the artist lived to a ripe old age. Dr. D was convinced that an obscene enjoyment of perverse and illicit sex in his old age permitted Picasso his immortal fame. The lascivious content of the artist's perpetually surviving paintings, particularly those painted in old age, were a sign to this patient that Picasso's active sexual life promoted both his art and his immortality. Because Dr. D did not possess Picasso's artistic gifts, and because he found his sexual activity to be on the wane, he felt less likely to be immortalized in glorious ways, and was more and more preoccupied with avoiding the unwelcome fate of a "bad death," of the humiliating death of fading into insignificance and oblivion. He therefore resorted, sometimes consciously, sometimes unconsciously, to various measures that were intended to ward off the bad death, measures which, as he got older, were stepped up with a drivenness and intensity, followed by frustration. It was the chronic and cyclical nature of these swings that lent the stamp of the pathological to an otherwise normal phase in the life cycle. One special way that Dr. D attempted to ward off death was to buy clothes, endlessly, the unconscious fantasy being that each newly purchased garment buys an extra day of life. He was obsessed each morning with how to put together a unique ensemble. There was never any repetition of shirt, pants, sweater, and jacket combinations, or of any given color combination. That would be the death of him. When I quipped that we ought to get him together with Imelda Marcos, he remained serious, convinced that she replenished her stocks, aiming for an unlimited supply of shoes because she knew she could not possibly get around to wearing everything, thus expressing her effort to stay alive, forever. It is of interest that he was bequeathed, and nostalgically cherished, the overcoat of his most adored patient, a man famous as a patron of the arts.

Dr. D in fact compulsively collected shirts and pants to hang in his closet as he got older, unconsciously believing that each article of clothing wards off death as it extends his life and promotes a phallic self-image. Shortly following a point at which new purchases became a near daily affair, he lapsed into a depression at the thought that his wife might, after his death, donate the garments to a thrift shop where, in the patient's words, "they would hang limp like a dead, detumescent penis." If his sons, the fruit of his loins, would only inherit the garments and wear them, he would have some hope of resurrecting himself, his immortality guaranteed. Dr. D's worst fears were that his sons would discard the clothing as being too big for them to fill out, and he literally imagined himself sentenced to that fate of hanging limp in a thrift shop.

The leitmotifs of phallic narcissism and of immortality could be discerned in the patient's chronic bouts of insomnia when he would sit up, refuse to prepare for bed, and then attempt to reassure himself by compulsively masturbating, falling asleep erect or at the table, all the while attempting to maintain a phallic-erect posture. One reason he gave for fear of going to sleep, and particularly of sleeping lying down in bed, is that he would wake up without his habitual morning erection, and he wanted to avoid facing that disturbing event. Here, we see a literal enactment of a resurrection wish via concrete behavioral and postural representations of the body phallus, where the state of arousal functions as a defense against some wish to be eaten, to fall asleep, and to die a death merged with his wife in their marriage bed. For Dr. D, such merger which to many individuals would epitomize the "good death" connoted only the bad. Therefore, he counterphobically avoided the possibility of losing the firm self-feeling of imagining the body as a phallus: he avoided any attempt at intercourse that might lead to a lost erection, for he unconsciously equated the normal detumescence, and the relaxation and sleep following orgasm with being merged with, identified with, and transformed into a woman.

These profound castration and merger anxieties were echoed in Dr. D's fantasy of a primal, guiltless, perpetual erection. He started his analysis by elaborating on a fantasy that he had made a bargain with the devil to extend his life, indefinitely. He was willing to go to hell and suffer all the torments if in his perpetual life he could enjoy a very exciting, even terrifying sexuality. As he aged, however, he was guilt-ridden to the point of abstinence dictated by growing fears of impotence and death.

His sexual life took on more and more of a masochistic coloring as he advanced in years. Bondage and beating scenarios were enacted in actual sexual encounters, and could be discerned as unconscious motivators of some of his more eccentric habits. In his illicit affairs, he often consciously fantasized a flagellation, even asked to have his hands tied, "like Christ on the Cross." When he fantasized his flagellation and crucifixion, he would get a "tremendous erection" and then he overtly fantasized about "dying in the saddle, what a way to go." Such fantasies suggest the connection between crucifixion fantasies and beating fantasies proposed by Edelheit (1974). For this particular patient, the fantasies seemed to increase his feeling of differentiation from the potentially dangerous woman of merger and to increase the phallic narcissistic body feeling as a defense against castration anxiety.

## CONCLUDING REMARKS

Freud (1926) said that the conscious fear of death, in addition to signifying the fear of castration, condenses all the danger situations as well as signifying failures in the protective shield, as when excessive amounts of excitation impinge upon the mental apparatus. There is no doubt that Dr. D scared himself with the overstimulation of excessive excitement which he felt put him constantly in danger of being abandoned by the powers-that-be, upon whom he depended. These conscious fears gratified his masochism and blended into flagellation and crucifixion fantasies with an increasing identification with the figure of Christ in the Passion of his last days. We recall in this connection the patient's illicit activities in the army, some of which violated his professional vows, and his extramarital indiscretions that risked considerable moral approbation, or so he thought. Death, with its particular unconscious meaning of castration, was to be a punishment for a lifelong accumulation of literal and symbolically illicit actions, the latter including his very career. He considered his courses in anatomy and pathology to be the ecstatic pinnacle of his training and could not imagine how they could be anything but thrillingly pleasant to anyone lucky enough to have had the experience of dissecting a cadaver. He feared discovery, however, for having performed an illicit excavation, of penetrating the dark and forbidden continent with any slip of his scalpel or other surgical equipment. Freud (1915) also said that we dare not contemplate a great many undertakings which are dangerous but in fact indispensable, such as attempts at artificial flight, expeditions to distant countries, or experiments with explosive substances. Indeed, it was with the onset of conscious death anxieties that my patient stopped all travels, which he formerly loved as among his favorite illicit preoccupations, tied in not just with literal violations of sexual mores but with the symbolic invading of the territories of forbidden bodies of land and other space.

Dr. D was constantly on guard about being found out, usually for he knew not what. One of his most terrifying moments came on the occasion of his being audited by the Internal Revenue Service. Although in fact not guilty of any of the tax violations under investigation, he feared that his tax-deductible fees paid to me over the years would be deemed illegal and that he would be jailed or professionally admonished so as to be unable to work again. That is, he masochistically fantasized taking a beating from me for his transferential feelings, as he made not too subtle but very provocative attempts at introducing tones of illicitness into the treatment. For example, he had begun woefully pleading to me, using my first name, to complain about his wife's lack of understanding. He attempted to woo me in this stylized manner as he had wooed in all of his extramarital relationships. What the IRS was doing was in fact tantamount to no more than a slap on the wrist (he had listed one large personal liquor bill as a professional expense), but he would use these slaps to gratify beating fantasies, working himself up into a chronic anticipation of the worst possible type of punishment—his version of the flagellation and the crucifixion. These doom anxieties were related to his neurotic fears of poverty, as though when the supply of money, clothes, garden innovations, and most important, the treatment itself would run out, he would die.

It is of interest that Dr. D had been preoccupied with circumcision and its connection with extended or aborted life spans. He remembered vividly a World War II incident in which the Germans asked a group of French hostages to pull down their pants, whereupon they killed all of the circumcised, presumably Jewish men, in a terrible blood bath. A dramatic incident related to these preoccupations occurred during the first few weeks of his treatment, when I noticed a trickle of blood seeping through his trousers around the groin area. His explanation was that he had to run to get to his appointment with me promptly, knowing he would be charged and chastised for the missed time, and in his haste he collided with an open taxi door which ripped his flesh, later requiring seventeen stitches to repair. During the session, he endured his pain, martyred yet proud of his ability to bear it. It was not until later in the analysis that he was able to associate the blood to the blood on Christ's groin in Renaissance paintings. This in turn related to the many beating, flagellation, and crucifixion fantasies he had, and to his comparison of the blood signifying life to the bloodless death state he feared. One might well conclude, based on a pathographical study of Dr. D's "oeuvre," that the circumcision prefigures the resurrection not only in art but in life as well.

The analysis of Dr. D ended on a note of highlighted Liebestod and resurrection fantasies combined. Although he gave up the dangerous death-dealing fatal attraction that brought him to treatment in the first place, he replaced that enactment with a newer version of his fantasies. It was his wish that his analyst resurrect him in memory through a biographical narrative study to become part of the psychoanalytic literature. Did the analyst, too, drawn to the stories of fatal attraction of the Liebestod and the Resurrection, share many fantasies in common with her analysand, wishing, as he did, that their joint endeavors be resurrected through "immortal" preservation, analogous to the way a work is preserved in a museum? Being "fatally" attracted to their work, they thus transform the fatal to the eternally viable, and hopefully, the pathological to the normative.

## REFERENCES

Blacker, R.S. (1983). Death, resurrection, and rebirth: Observations on cardiac surgery. *Psychoanalytic Quarterly* 52:56–72.

Edelheit. H/ (1974). Crucifixion fantasies and their relation to the primal scene. *International Journal of Psycho-Analysis* 55:193–199/

Freud. S. (1915). Thoughts for the times on war and death. *S.E.* 14:273–300.

——— (1926). Inhibitions, symptoms, and anxiety. *S.E.* 20:75–174.

Lifton', R.J. (1979). *The Broken Connection.* New York: Simon and Schuster.

Oremland, J.D. (1989). *Michelangelo's Sistine Ceiling: A Psychoanalytic Study of Creativity.* Madison, CT: International Universities Press.

Steinberg, L. (1983). *The Sexuality of Christ in Renaissance Art and Modern Oblivion.* New York: Pantheon/October.

White, K.S. (1981). *Onward and Upward in the Garden.* New York: Farrar, Strauss, Giroux.

Wilder, T. (1938). *Our Town.* New York: Harper Perennial.

# PART IV. SEX AND GENDER

## AUTHOR'S INTRODUCTION

It is easy to think of the diverse connections between sex and gender, on the one hand and certain ideas about love that relate to identifications, identity, and sexual object choice. As for the place of my thinking about sex and gender within the totality of my enterprise, what is probably original is its relation to my ideas about imposture and deception, which I hope will become clear in Chapter 9, below.

Newer and current generations, the Millennial generation in particular, and those active in postmodern critical thinking and in third wave feminism of the 1990's have certainly influenced my ideas on sex and gender as false binary. Those who grew up with me in the now bygone "classical" psychoanalytic era, and during the period of second wave feminism in the 1960s and 1970s of my earlier days would have considered sex and gender synonymously, or as one phenomenon. The scientific researches as well as the politics of LGBT developments of my later years have been among the psychoanalytic advances that have guided me toward parsing out the differences and interrelationships between sex and gender. There are other papers I have written, such as "Male Object Choice in Women with Female Sexual Desire," (2003) that are not included in this collection, but which embrace the fact of probably even broader nuances on thinking through sex and gender than what I have argued for in this book.

When I presented my first version of Chapter 11, below, on sex and gender mixes, I had the pleasure of working closely with Adrienne Harris, who discussed an early version of that paper, which I had presented at the American Psychoanalytic Association in Boston in 2003. Then, my focus was on "Gender Benders," and Adrienne picked up on and contributed her own ideas that eventually became the substance of her book, *Gender as Soft Assembly* (2005). That collaborative experience, more than any other, convinced me that although sex must be distinguished from gender, those two aspects of one's psychological makeup could not fruitfully be thought of as dichotomous, or as binaries. For example, one's sexual orientation does not determine the many facets of one's gender identity. Although the jury is still out on how to bridge our grasp of sex and gender in their totality, I hope my contributions on the false dichotomy: male equals active and female equals passive, will help the endeavor along.

# Chapter 9: Men Masquerading as Women: Imposture, Illusion, and Dénouement in the Play, M. Butterfly

[Gediman, H.K. (1993). Men masquerading as women: Imposture, illusion and dénouement in the play, "M. Butterfly." *Psychoanalytic Psychology* 10:460-479. Also in Gediman, H.K. and Lieberman, J.S. *The Many Faces of Deceit*. Northvale NJ and London: Jason Aronson, 1995. An earlier version of this article was presented at the meeting of Division 39 of the American Psychological Association, New York, April 1990.].

In the play, *M. Butterfly* (Hwang, 1989), the experience of being duped by a man masquerading as a woman is shared by protagonist and audience alike. In a parallel process, both simultaneously know and do not know the realities of the impostor's gender. Cross-dressing, as a variety of imposture, is explained by expanding on Freud's (1927) contribution of the "fantasy of the phallic woman." A full psychoanalytic understanding of perverse and fetishistic resolutions of early developmental conflicts about the nature of gender requires a consideration of the fear of the vagina along with the wish for a woman with a phallus. This approach to a study of imposture suggests that fantasies shared in common by all people help to account for the success of even gross impostures.

As a psychoanalyst, I have always been intrigued by the topic of imposture in its many degrees and variations (see Gediman, 1985, 1986), as have analysts before me, notably Abraham (1925/1955), Deutsch (1955/1965), and Greenacre (1958/1971a, 1958/1971b). Therefore, when I had the pleasure of viewing *M. Butterfly*, I was able to expand my psychoanalytic understanding of a particular form of imposture, that of cross-gender dressing, involving men masquerading as women.

Cross-gender imposture, though one of several themes, is the most central and dramatic element in David Hwang's (1989) play, *M. Butterfly*, which is based on the true story of the Bernard Boursicot-Shi Pei Pu affair (see Wadler, 1988). In the play, René Gallimard, a French diplomat, is fooled by his male lover, the transvestite opera singer and spy, Song Liling, who posed for 20 years as a woman. A psychoanalytic understanding of the protagonist's and the audience's responses to the type of cross-gender imposture depicted in *M. Butterfly* may enhance our understanding, appreciation, and enjoyment of the play while it provides new perspectives on gender and sexuality.

The contribution that psychoanalysis has made to understanding the success of certain kinds of imposturous caricatures in fooling others is to be found in what Freud, in 1927, referred to as the fantasy of the phallic woman. This seminal contribution needs to be enriched by integrating it with the more recent psychoanalytic observations of the fear of the vagina. It seems clear from the truths embodied in this play that the living out of this fantasy in certain guises may be regarded as one important variety of imposture. I cannot make any assumptions about the playwright's or the actors' knowledge or intentions to portray, either consciously or unconsciously, the psychoanalytic views I present. But I can assume that the insights provided by psychoanalytic thinking derive from universal wishes, fantasies, anxieties, and conflicts, shared "communally" at some level of consciousness, in the psyches of author, protagonist, actors, and audience alike. In this article, I elaborate on the fantasy of the phallic woman as universal and, I believe, as embedded in the message of this play. To do so, I have to include certain updated views of gender.

The power of the play derives not only from our fascination with the psychology of imposture but from the skillful interweaving of its plot of duplicity and domination with the similar plot of Puccini's 1900 opera, *Madame Butterfly*. The true-to-life staged spy story of Liling, the impostor, dovetails in a dramatic analogy with the actual libretto and plot of the opera. Whereas the imposture theme emerges gradually as the plot of the play unfolds, parallels with the opera are drawn early on. In the opera, the relationship between Pinkerton and Butterfly is depicted as one in which the man epitomizes imperialist domination by Western nations over weak Eastern societies. Puccini's work gives particular emphasis to the counterpoint of West as equated with the dominant male and East as equated with the passive, submissive, helpless female. In the opera, Butterfly is enthralled with Pinkerton and his Western male domination, and this subjugation leads to her ultimate destruction by suicide. In Hwang's play, Gallimard is a French diplomat in the People's Republic of China, beginning in 1960 when France was a world power with strong colonial interests and when China was still relatively undeveloped. Gallimard meets Liling, a leading soprano in the Beijing opera at a time when all female roles were sung by men, just as Liling was performing the title role in *Madame Butterfly*, and enters into a long, total, and intimate love relationship with "him," whom he assumed was "her." As a theme within a theme, Liling often tauntingly and ironically confronts Gallimard with the issue of Western domination over Asian peoples. Motifs of global politics and sexual politics are contrapuntally expressed. The second theme, which develops slowly and emerges fully only much later in the play, concerns Liling's double imposture.

By cross-dressing in a gross and successful impersonation of a woman, on and off stage, and by being a spy, Liling dupes Gallimard both sexually and politically for 20 years.[9] A true impostor is defined as one who passes herself or himself off incognito, often in delinquent, psychopathic, sociopathic, and other criminal ways, as actually possessing an identity of someone other than himself or herself. Song Liling, of course, did just this, in the variant of imposture known as crossdressing and female impersonation. And his espionage certainly involved the assumption of an outright false identity. Almost all psychoanalytic studies of the true impostor, as well as those dealing with lesser imposturous tendencies— ranging from outright lying, through mild deceptions, to playacting an identity on or off stage—note the absolute necessity of an audience to the impostor. Abraham (1925/1955) was especially aware of how the impostor requires a cooperating, colluding, gullible audience to guarantee the success of the imposture. Gallimard's self-deception indeed enabled him to fulfill this role for the doubly-deceitful Liling. And in viewing the play, we as audience are also deceived. Gallimard's passion for Liling is rooted in his compassion for Puccini's Butterfly, and in all of the tender, guilty, protecting feelings that her domination by Western imperialism stirred up in him. The stage for the double-duping involving sexual and international politics is further set by Liling's teasing discussions with Gallimard about the sexual, racial, commercial, and political domination of the East by the West. And at some point during the performance, we the audience will also feel teased by the playwright and actor.

The part of Liling is played by a male actor (B. D. Wong in the production I saw), who cross-dresses imposturously in two stunning female impersonations: one on the operatic stage in his role as Liling singing Butterfly and the other off the operatic stage, in his role as Liling being his imposturous self. We the audience are both witness to and "willing victims" of the double deceptions, depicted on stage artfully and skillfully by the playwright and performers.

---

9   After completing my manuscript for this article, my attention was directed to Garber's (1992/1993) book, *Vested Interests*, in which a chapter is devoted to a "deconstructivist" analysis of Hwang's play. Although Garber attempts some psychoanalytically based analysis of crossover and deception in the play, her approach is primarily that of well-documented literary criticism emphasizing the cultural politics of gender and transvestism. She concludes that cross-dressing such as Liling's proves that gender is constructed and not essential or innate—a view that is, for the most part, alien to psychoanalytic thinking. What I find psychoanalytically useful in her fascinating argument is the idea that acting, spying, spying, diplomacy, and transvestism are forms of border-crossing, which is compatible, I believe, with my ideas on their connection with imposture and deception.

Our gullibility thus parallels that of Gallimard as the various threads of the dramatized duplicity interlace with our willing suspension of disbelief in the double deception. And we remain gullible despite the obviousness in the ruses of gender impersonation and espionage that are unfolding before our very eyes. At this point, I attempt to explain this ironic parallelism.

Although the dramatist and performers make bold attempts to sustain the gender deception for the audience, press releases, some program notes, and published essays have prematurely exposed the facts of the imposture to many members of the audience. Whereas earlier audiences were often fooled, more recent playgoers are frequently aware of Liling's (and Wong's) gender reality. Nonetheless, we too are gulled by the unfolding drama, though preconsciously aware from the beginning, of that which is to be gradually unraveled and finally exposed fully as bold truth during the play's most climactic and dramatic moment: the visually startling dénouement of Wong-as-Liling's naked male body, previously disguised as female. Can we assume a parallel process in Gallimard, that he is aware, like us, of the truth behind Liling's exposure of the naked truth? It is this visually traumatic exposure of two truths that Gallimard had long denied—that is, Liling's true gender and then his own (in fact homosexual) behavior—that culminates in his final mortification and suicide by the ritual disembowelment of hara-kiri. Gallimard's suicide follows a humiliating confrontation of Liling's double deception of espionage and gender as well as of his self-deception—a confrontation with his changed self-perception from having been the one who dominated to becoming the one who is dominated, both politically and sexually. In the opera, it is the woman, Butterfly, who commits suicide following her abject shame and grief on hearing of Pinkerton's deception and sexual betrayal of her. Gallimard, in his final act of self-immolation, now feels totally merged as one with the "inferior," Eastern, submissive, subjugated woman, and he literally masquerades as the shamed, dishonored Madame Butterfly as he dons the wig and kimono worn by Liling when the opera singer played that role. He is united with her by becoming her symbolically.

It is an amazing thing to be a member of the audience viewing this production, knowing in advance the very twist of plot that builds to the climactic "surprise" moment of revelation in the play's last act. Throughout the play, leading up to the dénouement, at the same time that one *knows*, one *does not know*. For example, a colleague who knew of the outcome before seeing the play told me that she "forgot" it totally while watching the play and was shocked by it. This simultaneous perception and disavowal of apperception must be the very psychological mechanism that enabled the protagonist, René

Gallimard, to cohabit intimately with Song Liling for 20 years and not know that the opera singer was a man, not a woman. In the mind of every member of the audience must hover some version of the obvious question, "How could he have been Liling's lover and not know the true nature of Liling's genitals?" Or "How did Liling manage his sexual contacts so as to hide the fact of his gender?" That is, we assume that the audience's questions mirror Gallimard's and that there is a parallel process going on in the minds of fictionalized character and audience alike, a process that is familiar to psychoanalysts, and that enables a denial or disavowal of the perception of what in fact is really there. And this denial proceeds despite what must be all the evidence of the senses.

In this case, what is disavowed is the presumed knowledge of the true anatomical difference between the sexes. What is in fact really there, yet denied by Gallimard, is the presence of his lover's male genitals. Therefore, the parallel—let us say "illusionary"—experience of audience and protagonist is that it is not *really* there. Also denied is the absence of the female genitals, so that what Gallimard presumably knows is not there is responded to, wishfully, as though it really were there. Such illusionary experiences have long been of great interest to psychoanalysts in their attempt to elucidate many instances of overt and latent homosexuality, of fetishism, and of other forms of sexuality commonly referred to as "the perversions." In all of them, but particularly in cases of men cross-dressing as women or as caricatures of women, men may convince themselves through clothing or fetishistic objects that a woman, if only an illusionary woman, does indeed possess a penis, albeit an illusory penis, while denying the fact that she does instead possess a vagina. Transvestism, cross-dressing, and related forms of imposture are variations on enactments of the fantasy of the phallic woman, a fantasy considered by Bak (1968) to be universal in the sexual perversions.

Freud introduced the notion of the phallic woman fantasy in his 1927 work on fetishism. He believed that at some time, all very young boys refuse to take cognizance of the fact that a woman does not possess a penis. "No, that could not be true," Freud said of the little boy's disavowal of this critical piece of reality, "for if a woman had been castrated, then his own possession of a penis was in danger" (1927, p. 153). The idea that a woman has a penis "remains a token of triumph over the fear of castration and a protection against it" (p. 153). It should be noted that Freud's emphasis on denying the absence of the penis in women was accompanied by his ellipsis of the little boy's need to deny the presence of the vagina. Freud has been rightly criticized for neglecting this important aspect of the phallic woman fantasy, but his omission should be regarded as a consequence of his own "phallocentrism" and should be rectified in light of our current understanding of the anxieties and terrors that the positive knowledge of the female genital can evoke in very young boys. Kaplan (1991) regarded Freud's omission both as consistent with a 4-year-old boy's anxious imaginings about gender and as a use, in itself, of the perverse strategy. "*Fetishism*," she said, is in itself a "fetishistic document" (p. 55). Although most boys outgrow this fantasy, it remains a potent organizing force in certain personalities, determining the sexual preference of some fetishistic and/or latent to overt homosexual men as well as among men with heterosexual object choices. In their various enactments of the fantasy of the phallic woman, then, these men attempt to overcome persisting childhood castration fears either by masquerading as or by choosing as sexual partners women (or "women") who are symbolically endowed with the characteristic that makes them tolerable as sexual partners.

It is well-known that a perception may be simultaneously acknowledged and disavowed, even among the nondelusional and nonpsychotic. Crossdressing, the case in point, prototypically permits both partners to maintain the illusion of the woman with the penis. The fantasy of the phallic woman is gratified in these conditions, insofar as something that one wishes were there but that in reality is not there—that is, a real male genital on a real woman—is responded to illusorily, or by various degrees of self-deception, as though in fact it really were there. I refer to this self-deception as the first layer of a disavowal.

Liling was one such "woman" with a penis in his imposturous caricature; thus, the imposture in this case may be understood as a variant of the fantasy of the phallic woman. If we apply the insight of psychoanalysis to the play, *M. Butterfly*, we encounter an apparent reversal of the fantasy's usual content. In what we presume to be Gallimard's unconscious fantasy life, the penis is first perceived, and then that perception is disavowed. Usually, that which is disavowed is the absence of a penis on a real woman and not, as in this case, the presence of a penis on an impersonated woman. Fetishism is the clearer case, where the fetish is the substitute for the woman's penis. We presume that the fetishist, like Gallimard, has been traumatized by the sight of the female genital as having no penis. The fetishist *adds* something—a piece of leather, a garter belt—filling in the gap with, as it were, a *positive* hallucination. Gallimard, in a reversal, *subtracts* something. He presumably sees no penis where there actually is one, creating a gap with something akin to a *negative* hallucination. Something, then, that is really present, the male genital, is responded to illusorily, by protagonist and audience alike, as though it were not there. Gallimard's psychological blind spot or negative hallucination of his lover's actual penis protects and defends against the double demons of castration and homosexuality. We might further speculate that the very blind spot that defends against castration also expresses a wish to castrate.

How well Freud (1927) understood this compromise formation in the fetishism specific to Chinese culture! He said:

> a parallel to fetishism in social psychology, might be seen in the Chinese custom of mutilating the female foot and then revering it like a fetish after it has been mutilated. It seems as though the Chinese male wants to thank the woman for having submitted to being castrated. (p. 157)

And it is as though Gallimard were saying to Liling, "You are my submissive, inferior, Chinese, Eastern lover; therefore, there is no way that you can possess a penis and its accompanying powers. Only I have that." By means of his scotomization, Gallimard was also able to disavow the fact that his lover did possess a penis, and he could thereby promote the illusion that his lover was a woman and that he was not engaging in homosexual activity. In the usual version of the fantasy, the fetishistic man, for instance, or one choosing a transvestite love object, "has it all"—a woman with a penis—by creating in his mind a real woman with an illusory penis. In this play, the (at least latent) homosexual man has it all, as denial and tricks of imagination enable him to possess an illusory woman with a real penis.

One might take this analysis one step further and assume, for the sake of argument, that Gallimard also was guided unconsciously by the universal fantasy of the phallic woman and that he was beset with castration anxiety. The play provides ample evidence for his fear of the genitally female woman and its connection with his homophobia and subsequent massive repression of his male lover's true gender. The playwright explicitly includes material delineating a personality with a lifelong history of shyness and reluctance to make contact with women. Gallimard avoided most opportunities provided by a college chum to carouse with women, with the exception of one brief date with a young and fawning American "bimbette." In his marriage, his wife complained of their having no children. We are given to believe that the marriage had not been consummated through genital intercourse and had persisted for only practical and never sexual reasons. We wonder if Gallimard had been a virgin. As suave and worldly as Gallimard was with Liling, he was shy and retiring with women from his own cultural milieu. We feel quite comfortable, then, in assuming that he was able to consummate a union with his transvestite lover only because that lover did have a penis, sparing him the horrifying contact with the female genitals of his persisting 4-year-old's imagination. Then again, we might wonder if perhaps the affair were never truly consummated. Gallimard knew but he did not know, just as the audience knew but did not know. These parallel reactions of audience and protagonist involve a double disavowal: To defend against the knowledge that all women do not have penises—the usual version of the phallic woman fantasy, and what I earlier referred to as the first layer in Gallimard's double disavowal—our protagonist also had to disavow that his male-lover-impersonating-a-woman did in fact have a penis, the reversal in the second layer of Gallimard's disavowal. In the artistic depiction of this double-layered disavowal lies the heart of the play's mystery and its success in engaging the audience's willingness to be "fooled."

In general, whether the disavowed is the presence of the penis, as in the case at issue, or its absence, as in instances of fear of the vagina, is not particularly relevant for our understanding of the kind of self-deception in which Gallimard must have engaged. I think that most contemporary psychoanalysts would agree with Bak (1968) who believed that the fantasy of the phallic woman is ubiquitous in all perversions and that what is relevant is the ambiguity and uncertainty as to gender and not simply the presence or absence of a penis. Due to equivocal perceptions and the lack of intimate knowledge of the female gender, the boy's ego suspends decision about the presence or absence of a penis and leaves it uncertain, neither denying nor accepting his own perception, so that the question of what is more important—the absence or the presence of the penis—is a moot one. One imagines that such uncertainty persisted in Gallimard's ability to remain "unknowing" for some 20 years. And it is this very ambiguity of perception that is reflected in the "M." of the play's title. Although in France, "M." stands for "Monsieur," in America it might well be the mode of address for either, any, or both genders—a "unisex," leveling form of address.

The de facto relationship between René Gallimard and Song Liling is homosexual. The homosexuality is not to be confused with the perverse. It is the fetishistic solution for dealing with homosexual and other anxieties in both men and women that constitutes the perversion. If Liling's gender had been known to Gallimard, and if Gallimard had been fully conscious of his object gender choice, the relationship would have been both homosexual and fetishistic, for from Gallimard's point of view, his lover's cross-dressing and female impersonation would be among the conditions or requirements for sexual satisfaction. Such an overt, conscious choice of a homosexual man who crossdresses would, according to the psychoanalytic view just summarized, represent an enactment of the phallic woman fantasy as a way of avoiding castration anxiety. On that view, the appearance—whether by art, artifice, illusion, or fantasy—of the phallus or its symbolic equivalent (as in a fetish) on someone who in all other respects is visibly a woman levels the differences between the sexes, eliminating the anxiety that such differences may call forth in those men, homosexual or heterosexual, who have not resolved childhood conflicts centering on castration anxieties. In this instance, the fetishistic solution, a perversion, is a way of dealing with homosexual anxieties.

In the program notes in a 1988 playbill, we learn of the difficulties experienced by John Lithgow, who originally played Gallimard, and by playwright Hwang in coming to terms with the leaks to the audience through the press and by word of mouth, that B. D. Wong and Song Liling, whom he portrays, are both men. Lithgow concluded that it was all right to reveal the plot line publicly because "even if you know the premise, there is still great excitement at seeing the information gradually disclosed." Hwang noted that by the end of the evening, only a few people still cannot accept the idea that a man could live with another man for 20 years and not know that he was not a woman. He contended that the production was successful in persuading the majority of people to suspend their disbelief. That seems to happen, but it must take some doing as the sensitive audience member cannot be fooled for too long by Wong's portrayal of Liling's vocal and verbal mannerisms. The gullible viewer might hear those speech mannerisms as typical of the submissively and exaggeratedly feminine Oriental woman, but the sophisticated listener is more apt to identify them correctly as containing the typical innuendo of a man in drag, caricaturing a woman's speech and intonations. One may suspect, in this connection, that the playwright wrote Liling's part with the specific intention of teasing the audience, of "pulling its leg." And Lithgow concluded in the playbill: "The play asks how anybody can fool himself that drastically, and yet the world is full of examples of delusions that extreme." But I must interject at this point that illusion formation, allowing boundary crossing in gender identifications, is a most common normative as well as pathological phenomenon. Playful identificatory interchanges between man and woman are required for maximum sexual pleasure.[10] Innate bisexual tendencies in every man and woman enable cross-gender identifications, empathy, and playful, imaginative, illusory sexual interchange. We are dealing in our case with an extreme version of self-deception about gender that transcends normal creative illusion

---

10 Dr. Sheldon Bach, in his discussion of an earlier version of this article, elaborated extensively on this theme.

formation. However, the universality of normal illusion formation with refer-ence to gender is most important for explaining the ubiquitous gullible reac-tion of audiences witnessing cross-gender impersonations.[11]

Within the play itself, characters are baffled by the success of the sexual duplicity, and the judge at the spy trial presses for details of how the imposture was in fact carried out. But to focus on such details risks obliteration of the artifice of the imposture as well as the artistry of the playwright in conveying the subtleties of imposture and illusion to the audience. To repeat, I have no knowledge of the author's and actors' conscious or unconscious intentions in structuring the portrayals to achieve their effects, but it might be of in-terest to learn of them. A psychoanalytic understanding of the simultaneous knowing and not knowing the true nature of his lover's genitals could well explain Gallimard's 20 years of cohabitation with someone he believed to be a woman, yet at the same time "knew" was only masquerading as one. Along with the audience, he saw a man before him only when clear-cut gen-ital identity was unveiled and ambiguity was erased in the deadly climactic dénouement. His lover's complete undressing and genital exposure on stage was the psychically traumatic moment for the hero and was the moment of maximum dramatic shock for the already-knowing audience. Knowing the facts in advance apparently mitigates little or none of the startling emotional impact of visual confrontation of the reality that had previously been denied and the subsequent painful process of stripping away the protective, defensive disavowal and denial of the imposture. The full knowledge that he had been duped by his imposturous lover/impersonator put Gallimard in fatally full contact with his previously defended sense of shame and literal mortification, eventuating in his suicide by disembowelment. It would seem to me to be no accident that disembowelment was the chosen method of self-annihilation,[12] above and beyond its being facilitated by Asian traditions of suicide. The bowels are internal organs, often symbolizing, for men, the inner genitals,

---

11 Gender ambiguity is central to Garber's (1992/1993) explanation of the success of the deception, just as it is to mine. However, our positions differ in one fundamental respect. She takes the hermeneutic view that ambiguities, conundrums, and undecidability in gender perception are inevitable because gender is always a construction or interpretation and never refers to anything innate. She concludes, therefore, that both real and fictionalized. individuals are gendered only in representation or performance and never in reality. I, on the other hand, believe that the critical ambiguities are due to innate bisexuality, to empathy, and to other psychologically real capacities for cross-gender identifications.

12 I am grateful to Dr. Adria Schwartz for suggesting this line of interpretation to me.

the inner sense of one's femaleness in universal potential for cross-gender identification. With this symbolic equation in mind, we could then conclude that it was Gallimard's hatred of his own feminine gender identification, a hatred internalized from centuries of cultural oppression and from individual attitudes toward women resonating with developmental misconceptions about women as genitally defective, that enabled his 20-year blindness to the gender reality of his masquerading partner as well as the final act of deadly self-mutilation. The ridicule of the burlesque was internalized in his final act of deadening when blindness no longer served its purpose. His fate, and that of Madame Butterfly, were as one: to die with honor when one can no longer live with honor.

## REFERENCES

Abraham, K. (1955). The history of an impostor in the light of psychoanalytical knowledge. In *Clinical Papers and Essays on Psychoanalysis* (Vol. 2, pp. 291-305). New York: Basic Books. (Original work published 1925)

Bak, R.C. (1968). The phallic woman—The ubiquitous fantasy in perversions. *Psychoanalytic Study of the Child* 23:15-36.
http://www.pep-web.org/document.php?id=psc.023.0015a

Deutsch, H. (1965). The impostor: Contribution to ego psychology of a type of psychopath. In *Neuroses and Character Types* (pp. 319-338). New York: International Universities Press. (Original work published 1955)
http://www.pep-web.org/document.php?id=paq.024.0483a

Freud, S. (1927). Fetishism. *S.E.* 21:149-157.
http://www.pep-web.org/document.php?id=se.021.0001a

Garber, M. (1993). *Vested Interests*. New York: HarperCollins, (Original work published 1992)

Gediman, H.K. (1985). Imposture, inauthenticity, and feeling fraudulent. *Journal of the American Psychoanalytic Association.* 33:911-935
http://www.pep-web.org/document.php?id=apa.033.0911a

Gediman, H.K. (1986). The plight of the imposturous candidate: Learning amidst the pressures and pulls of power in the institute. *Psychoanalytic Inquiry* 6:67-91. http://www.pep-web.org/document.php?id=pi.006.0067a

Greenacre, P. (1971a). The impostor. In *Emotional Growth: Psychoanalytic Studies of the Gifted and a Great Variety of Other Individual,* Vol. 1, pp. 93-112. New York: International Universities Press. (Original work published 1958.)

Greenacre, P. (1971b). The relation of the imposter to the artist. In *Emotional*

*Growth: Psychoanalytic Studies of the Gifted and a Great Variety of Other Individuals*, Vol. 2, pp. 533-554. New York: International Universities Press. (Original work published 1958)
http://www.pep-web.org/document.php?id=psc.013.0521a

Hwang, D.H. (1989). *M. Butterfly*. New York: New American Library.

Kaplan, L. (1991). *Female Perversions*. New York: Doubleday.
http://www.pep-web.org/document.php?id=sgs.001.0349a

Wadler, J. (1988). For the first time, the real-life models for Broadway's "M. Butterfly" tell of their very strange romance. *People* 30(6):91.

# Chapter 10: Premodern, Modern, and Postmodern Perspectives on Sex and Gender Mixes[13]

Gediman, H.K. (2005). Premodern, modern, and postmodern perspectives on sex and gender mixes. *Journal of the American Psychoanalytic Association,* 53: 1059–1078. An earlier revised version of the paper was presented in March 2004 in Miami Beach at the yearly meeting of Division 39 of the American Psychological Association. Submitted for publication August 2, 2004.

## PREMODERN, MODERN, AND POSTMODERN PERSPECTIVES ON SEX AND GENDER MIXES

Postmodern sensibilities, generally associated with relational psychoanalysis, are applicable also in traditional and contemporary Freudian psychoanalytic contexts. Historically speaking, views of femininity and female sexuality may be ordered according to positions designated as premodern, modern, and postmodern. This temporal continuum provides a basis for incorporating aspects of postmodern feminist approaches to deconstructing gender into a more traditional yet contemporary psychoanalytic framework. The postmodern "crisis of category" is addressed through a critique from a modern psychoanalytic point of view of the gender stereotyping inherent in certain false binaries and either/or thinking of premodern psychoanalytic thinking regarding female (as well as male) sex and gender. The cultural changes brought about by the consciousness-raising of postmodern feminist and contemporary psychoanalytic thinking contribute significantly to evolutionary changes in the understanding of gender that are further internalized and represented intrapsychically. That is, sequential transformations in the internalization of new cultural norms influence the development of still more new cultural norms, so that progression in these identificatory markers of gender can be observed over successive generations.

Historically speaking, views of gender and sexuality may be ordered according to positions that I designate as premodern, modern, and postmodern.

---

13 The author expresses her appreciation to Adrienne Harris, whose ideas in her discussion of an earlier version of this paper, presented in June 2003 at the American Psychoanalytic Association meetings in Boston, have helped shape this significantly revised version.

This temporal continuum provides a basis for incorporating aspects of post-modern feminist approaches to deconstructing gender into a more traditional yet contemporary psychoanalytic framework. I address, from a contemporary psychoanalytic point of view, the postmodern "crisis of category" by critiquing the gender stereotyping inherent in certain false binaries and the either/or thinking of premodern psychoanalytic thinking regarding female, (as well as male) sex and gender. The century-long historical sweep starts with Freud's false binary of masculinity-active/femininity-passive, and moves on from the phallocentrism of the premoderns through the primary femininity of the moderns, to deconstructionism and postmodern radical feminism.

The cultural changes brought about by the profound impact of feminist and contemporary psychoanalytic thinking have themselves contributed to changes in the understanding of sex and gender, and these have in turn been further internalized and represented intrapsychically and interpersonally. My aim here is to invite responses from psychoanalytic thinkers I would identify as premodern, modern, or postmodern, and who see themselves at various, perhaps overlapping points along the temporal-historical continuum at the forefront of my presentation.

I identify myself as a feminist who holds to the notions of innate yet variable core gender identities, universal bisexuality, and the centrality of empathy in cross-gender identifications and boundary crossings to account for new ways of constructing personal understandings of gender and sexuality. Once we acknowledge multiplicity in sex and gender mixes, traditional psychoanalytic interpretive strategies centering on the conscious and unconscious fantasy lives of individuals add significantly to postmodern approaches for appreciating the crisis of category in regard to both male and female sexuality. We no longer simply amalgamate sex and gender into simple male/female, masculine/feminine, man/woman dichotomies. Rather, we speak of sexual desire, sexual orientation, sexual object choice, sexual aims, gender identity, transgender cross-dressing, and sex change, and the many permutations and combinations among these components that lead to myriad consistencies and conflicts in one or another individual. When older notions of sex and gender are recontextualized, new configurations, referred to in the vernacular as "gender benders," meet the eye and affect our theoretical and clinical commitments.

Where are we today in our thinking, psychoanalytically, about sex and gender? Let us start by pondering the recent *New Yorker* cartoon depicting a young woman bending over a baby carriage cooing and admiring the baby and asking its mother the quintessential postmodern question: "And how is it gendered?" The cartoon's caption captures it all. So much for the old-fashioned "Is it a boy or a girl?" The postmodern mission to deconstruct gender grew out of the modern feminist movement and has now taken hold in ways that affect our psychoanalytic views of both female and male psychology.

Psychoanalysis has a lot to say about the "politically correct" affectation that caricatures, as does the cartoon caption, current attempts to avoid the pitfalls of gender stereotyping. It took a long time, on a hard and bumpy road, for this postmodern view to capture the popular imagination. For psychoanalytic theorists studying female psychology from a postmodernist, deconstructionist point of view (Benjamin, 1996; Butler, 1990; Dimen, 1991; Garber, 1992; Harris, 1991, 1996; Hoffman, 1991; Kristeva, 1986; Rivera, 1989; Weedon, 1987), old categories and false binaries no longer suffice. While most ideas on gender diversity and multiplicity have been confined to studies of women, an important exception is to be found in the work of Person (1976, 1983; Person and Ovesey, 1974) in relation to transvestitism and transsexualism. However, and this is my major point, once we recognize multiplicity in sex and gender designations, traditional psychoanalytic interpretive strategies can add significantly to postmodern approaches to the crisis of category.

## AN HISTORICAL OVERVIEW

Historical changes in psychoanalytic concepts of sex and gender began with an exploration and radical revision of ideas about femininity. I hope this historical overview will illuminate changes that have occurred in thinking about the psychology of men, as well as of women. I begin with the caveat that much that I am about to review may sound familiar to the psychoanalytic scholar who has kept up with recent historical trends in the sex and gender literature, as epitomized in the 1996 supplement of the *Journal of the American Psychoanalytic Association*. However, I believe that what I have to say, while appearing at times deceptively simple, nonetheless opens up new perspectives on premodern, modern, and postmodern views of sex and gender that can inform psychoanalytic thinkers of various persuasions.

The revolutionary movement in the history of female sexuality might be said to have begun when analysts questioned Freud's signature premodern implicit syllogism (1905b), whose basic premise rings patently false to both modern and postmodern feminists, and to many other psychoanalytic thinkers. Freud's flawed logic went something like this: all that is active is masculine; libido is always active; therefore libido is always masculine. In a corollary implicit syllogism, women have sexual desire; sexual desires are masculine;

therefore women with sexual desire are masculine and not feminine. In the early days of psychoanalysis, since there was no such thing as feminine libido, all female sexuality was believed to be patterned on a putative active male libido. Since passivity was equated with the feminine and activity with the masculine, women who are active and empowered had to be regarded as masculine. Repudiation of this logic, based on the false premise that all activity is masculine, and its corollary that all femininity is passive and therefore not sexually motivated, was largely responsible for an entire revamping, if not deconstruction, over time, of Freud's theories of female sexual development. It seems fair to say that the first person to demonstrate that feminine women possess active sexual desires of their very own, and are actively engaged in empowered living, stretched our minds and imagination by creating a "gender bender." Now that we no longer equate feminine with passive, masculine with active, the business of characterizing gender has become much more complex than was once the case.

As compelling as present-day revisions may be, nothing in the way of advances in our understanding of female sexuality may be taken for granted, for nothing in the way of reasonable progression of ideas came easily. The positions that we have more or less consolidated today were hard-won and followed an oscillating though distinct evolutionary path. Difficult labors, struggles, and hard-won victories have brought credibility to positions that without this historical perspective would today seem mere truisms. There is a primary femininity; there are primary genital anxieties typical for girls that are not built on the anlagen of male castration anxieties. Although subsequent female sexual identity as simply "lack" may be the case in certain pathological developmental outcomes, such as extreme penis envy, a woman developing normally is not simply a man manqué. Penis envy in women is not rooted in what postmodernists would regard as an arbitrary category, Freud's "bedrock" (1925) of concrete anatomical structure. The myopically crafted phallocentric cultural lens through which early psychoanalysis viewed female sexuality once obscured some additional realities that most of us can see clearly now: that women enjoy sex, and have always derived pleasure from their bodies; that women love men's bodies not simply because they idolize their masculinity as something to be coveted, but because men's bodies turn them on.

Of course, one does not have to be a postmodernist interested in presenting gender benders by deconstructing false binaries to know that the little girl is not basically a little boy, and that she wishes for a child not simply to compensate for her lack of a penis. Recently we have been so overloaded with presentations that document primary femininity and primary female anxieties (for a comprehensive review, see Bassin, 1999; Gediman, 2001) that we might be tempted to assume that the idea of primary femininity is today universally accepted across all schools of psychoanalysis. Putting women on a par economically, socially, politically, intellectually, and sexually with men is now the norm rather than the exception. That female sexuality must be understood on its own terms; that women, anatomically speaking, are not "have-nots" and men "haves"; that the girl's identity is not based on absence and "lack" but on presence as positively feminine are ideas well assimilated into present-day psychoanalytic thinking. Modern psychoanalysts hold that the little girl's sense of herself as sexual and gendered must obviously derive from her own body and its representation in her psyche, and not from notions of how she stacks up to the little boy's. Nonetheless, as unquestionable as these assumptions may be to the moderns, postmodern psychoanalytic thinkers have developed new challenges to this modern view.

## FROM PHALLOCENTRISM TO DECONSTRUCTION AND POSTMODERN RADICAL FEMINISM

Historically, views of female sexuality may be ordered according to the positions I designate as premodern, modern, and postmodern. The premodern position (Freud, 1905b, 1925, 1931; A. Freud, 1922) takes male development as the norm for understanding female sexuality, and equates femininity with passivity and masochism. I designate the psychoanalysts who originally questioned this position and who postulated a primary female sexuality as modern (Horney, 1924, 1926, 1933; Jones, 1927, 1933, 1935; Riviere, 1929). In the 1976 *JAPA* supplement, a major break from the old premodern position foreshadowed the modern views which, though introduced by Horney and Jones, were developed mainly in the 1990s. The 1976 supplement contained articles that confirmed Freud's basic discoveries while amending certain of his hypotheses. Most emendations were based on child observations and clinical data from the psychoanalyses of adults (Kleeman; Galenson and Roiphe; Parens et al.) that acknowledged penis envy in the feminine castration complex while at the same time emphasizing the innate and fundamental differences between male and female sexual and gender development. The volume also contained articles that more boldly question the premodern view by virtue of a decidedly modern cast on issues of primary femininity that rejects masochism and universal penis envy as endogenously feminine (Stoller; Blum; Grossman and Stewart; Kestenberg). They and many more contemporary modern psychoanalysts (e.g., Balsam, 1996; Bernstein, 1990; Mayer, 1995; Chodorow, 1996;

Richards, 1996; Elise, 1997; Kulish, 2000) have concluded that there exist a primary femininity, female genital anxieties that are not derivative of male castration anxieties, and primary feminine activity that includes agency and subjectivity. Those identified as postmodern question the categories male and female, masculine and feminine, viewing them as either/or false binaries to be discarded in keeping with a contemporary deconstructionist zeitgeist (see Harris 1991, 1996). The postmodern deconstructionist thinkers include radical, or what are sometimes called "third wave" feminists (Benjamin, 1996; Dimen, 1991; Rivera, 1989; Weedon, 1987), as distinguished from the feminists of the women's liberation movement of the 1970s. These third-wave feminists tend to reject the notion that there is any such thing as innate gender, whether primary femininity or primary masculinity. They would hold that gender is always and only constructed politically, socially, and psychologically.

Unlike these postmodern psychoanalytic thinkers, both premoderns and moderns maintain that there is something that is distinctly male and something distinctly female, although the two approaches have differed markedly as to what the distinction might be. For example, premodern phallocentric thinkers, following Freud (1925), regarded the girl's sexual development as based originally on what was assumed to be the little boy's. They believed that her castration anxieties were appropriated from the boy's, in that they mimicked his uniquely male fear of harm to his genitals. The girl's castration anxieties were thought to culminate in penis envy once she took note of the concrete anatomical difference between the sexes. Premodern psychoanalytic thinking held that the girl had no sexual desire qua sexual desire, odd as that may seem to present-day men and women. By contrast, in the modern view of sex and gender, a woman is seen as possessing her own body, as having her own genital representations from the start, and as having her own set of anxieties and mastery modes. The moderns, in stark contrast to the premoderns, believe that a distinct female sexuality is present from the very start, based on the little girl's mental representations of the full genitalia she actually has, and not simply on fantasies emanating from what she thinks it means to be lacking what the boy has. She is not simply a penisless being; she obviously possesses her own genitalia and all that that may come to signify for her in terms of acquiring her own representations of her sex and gender. Additionally, her sexual desire is a primary, normal part of female development and not some coquettish wish to placate the sexually dominant male, an idea frequently encountered among premodern phallocentric monists.

## HORNEY AND PRIMARY FEMININITY

Karen Horney was not the only analyst to introduce nuanced changes on the topic of female sex and gender, but she was probably the most courageously groundbreaking among those who did. It was Horney who, in "The Flight from Womanhood: The Masculinity-Complex in Women" (1926) and "The Denial of the Vagina: A Contribution to the Problem of Genital Anxieties Specific to Women" (1933), launched the most frontal challenge to Freud's premodern doctrine of femininity: she was the first to explicitly identify the masculine or patriarchal underpinnings of Freud's thought, that is, his phallic monism. Horney's revolutionary perspective marked her as unique in fore-shadowing most contemporary thought on the topic of female psychology. In a dazzlingly modern feminist statement for her time, Horney took the mind of the girl on its own terms, discarding the mind of the boy as a model, and proceeded to honor one feminine mental function after another. Girls, she said, felt guilty for triumphing not only over the men they envied, but over the women whom they successfully rivaled: "It is this guilt that inspires woman's flight from womanhood and made her acquiesce in the man's scornful version of femininity" (p. 91). Adaptation and accommodation to the wishes of men were no longer believed to be cardinal traits of femininity, or a woman's true and predestined nature.

Horney (1926) spearheaded a shift in our thinking that has culminated in some very interesting ideas: first, that there are biological differences between the sexes other than genital differences; that women's physiological superiority, as manifested in the capacity for motherhood, leads to intense envy of women in the boy's unconscious psyche; and that "the capacity of women for coitus is not less but simply other than that of men" (p. 331). As familiar as we are with these ideas today, they are nonetheless amazing reminders of where we were and where we have arrived. It seems amazing now that women were actually believed in early psychoanalytic doctrine to have less interest in sex than men have. (See Deutsch [1930, 1944–1945] on what she believed to be a common if not universal connection between masochism and frigidity in women.) And it is amazing that it took so long to figure out that the oedipal fantasies specific to women potentiate primary female genital anxieties. Horney's belief that defensive flight into the male role would be reinforced and supported by the actual disadvantages under which women labor in social life, though certainly borne out, has unfortunately led some to regard her views as simply culturalist. Horney, a woman way ahead of her time, was in her day dismissed from mainstream psychoanalytic thought

and organizations. She was spurned by traditionalists, despite her careful consideration of the role of drive and defense in conflict theory terms, her deep
understanding of the relation of the outer to the inner world, and her grasp of
the nuances in relationships between the intrapsychic and the interpersonal
realms of the mind.

## FROM MODERN TO POSTMODERN

Primary female anxieties include dread of internal vaginal injury, as well as of
injury to the clitoris, because mental representations of both these parts of the
female genitalia critically shape the early infantile and later genital organization of women. The primary fear of vaginal injury has come to be regarded as
only secondarily and defensively transformed into a fantasy that mimics the
male's conception of castration. The gender binaries of the moderns, which
postmodernists have been trying to deconstruct, are most succinctly delineated in the work of Doris Bernstein (1990), who held that the genital anxieties
that are primary to women, that women call their very own, center on access,
penetration, and diffusivity: "As the bodies are different, the nature of the
resulting anxieties, the developmental conflicts, the means of resolution, and
many of the modes of mastery must of necessity be different as well" (p. 152).
Yet even when we acknowledge, as primary femininity theorists do, an inevitable, bodily based primary cathexis of the female genitals and specific fears
of injury to them, a caveat is in order. As Chodorow (1996) has noted, such
specific representations are more essential in the psyches of some women than
they are for others: "the meaning of the body is never self-evident, but always
imbued with individual fantasy and conflict ... in the case of femininity we
assume that female embodiedness inevitably generates particular meanings
and that it is always salient in the construction of gender ..." (pp. 219–220). In
addition, Elise (1997) reminds us that primary femininity and an intrapsychic
mix of bisexuality coexist. Thus, although Bernstein's position on the difference between the sexes has been embraced by many moderns, others, along
with the postmodernists, fault it as simply another version of the categorically
questionable "anatomy is destiny" premise of the premodern Freud (1925).
The controversy still rages.

## GENDER AS FALSE BINARY

The cartoon caption that introduced this presentation ("And how is it gendered?") shows what a substantial foothold the postmodern feminists have

gained, at least in the upscale media. Dimen's serious doctrine (1999) parallels this humorous cartoon. "It is only in the triangle created by psychoanalysis, feminism, and postmodernism that we have a shot at understanding the dynamics of gender, psyche, and power. Having it all, that is to say, gender-multiplicity, means moving beyond the splitting tendencies implicit in theories of psychic bisexuality" (p. 415). Although both premoderns and moderns hold views of men and women as sharply differentiated with regard to gender, as well as to sexuality, the two views of what it is that differentiates them are entirely different. At the other extreme, postmoderns, whether they hail from psychoanalysis, women's studies, or literary criticism, argue that any conclusions, whether premodern or modern, that regard something as distinctly male or distinctly female when it comes to sex and gender are fictive, and derive from a "false binary." Such false binaries, stereotypes, or either/or thinking, even when such polarizations have heuristic value, exemplify for them a category crisis that requires deconstruction of outdated, mostly "sexist" constructs.

Certain postmodern thinkers (Bassin, 1996; Harris, 1991, 1996) find the poststructural feminist approach appealing because it dissolves impasses and disciplinary walls by defining gender, gender identity, sexuality, sexual orientation, and their various facets and interactions as simultaneously psychic and social. Feminine identity, they say, cannot be subordinated to Freud's model, in which all sexual desire comes under the sway of genitality. They substitute a model that provides for heterogeneous aspects of gender, as well as varied representations of self in diverse gendered and sexual mixes. Their view dispenses with false binaries and pleads for tolerance for gender ambiguity, as well as for bisexual psychic structure. Taken to its extreme, it would rule out the question "Is it a boy or a girl?" and substitute the de-sexed "How is it gendered?" For these theorists, gender is subjective in that it is not defined by any objectively identifiable substrates in an individual, such as drive endowment and genitalia as determinants of psyche, but rather can be located in a field of multidirectional power relations: that is, not only does body determine psyche, but psyche determines the body's vicissitudes. Here we have a postmodern, psyche-soma version of the age-old grasp of the mutual influence of body and mind.

Some postmodern feminists believe that because there is no such thing as primary femininity (so-called "real" femininity has been deconstructed), there can be only a masquerade or caricature of some abstract ideal of womanliness. The moderns, however, because they believe that there is a primary femininity, would view the caricature or masquerade as a form of pathology in gender identification and not some dubiously normative cover-up for an absence of any primary gender identity at all. Riviere (1929), in contrast, felt that masquerading was a reaction formation against female aggression toward both men and women, and can take the form of a periodic obsequiousness and servile coquetry. I think we are all familiar with this strange but not so uncommon behavior of women "dumbing down," caving in, or taking care of what they claim is a man's fragile ego. Riviere, a feminist ahead of her time, but still somewhat burdened with the premodern phallocentric monism of her day, believed that these masquerades help the woman avoid the retribution she expects from both men and women for her covetous identification with the phallus. Because Riviere never fully emerged from her phallocentric psychoanalytic milieu, she had not yet conceived a primary femininity. Although postmodernists repudiate her phallocentric grounding, they tend to embrace her view of caricature as a way of highlighting what they believe is the absence of any true, innate, or objective, culture-free femininity. Caricature stands for them as absence of category, and is well suited to mock false binaries.

Kaplan (1991), by contrast, regards the masquerade of femininity by subjugation and extreme submission to men as the hallmark of "female" perversions, gender stereotypes, and caricatures: it is compulsively driven sexuality, whether heterosexually or homosexually oriented. A perversion, she says, involves bondage to a stereotype, "a mental strategy that uses one or another stereotype or caricature of masculinity and femininity in a way that deceives the onlooker about the unconscious meanings of the behaviors she or he is observing" (p. 9). I think that both modern and postmodern analysts would agree that gender stereotypes constitute false binaries. But moderns differ from postmodernists in that they assume bodily and innate determinants of mental representations of gender, including a primary femininity that may or may not be caricatured into a misleading stereotype, perhaps in the service of a perversion, perhaps in the service of other functions, such as an evangelical adherence to the zeitgeist of deconstructionism.

The roots of my own modern position are clearly classical and derive from Freudian drive theory, which has always embraced sex and gender multiplicity in such concepts as bisexuality (Freud 1905a, b) and the polymorphously perverse disposition (Freud 1905b, 1906) as normal in the sexual development of children. In fact, the concept of multiplicity, so much favored by the postmoderns, was used by Freud himself in *Three Essays* (1905b): "in general, the multiplicity of determining factors is reflected in the variety of manifest sexual attitudes in which they find their issue in mankind" (p. 146 n). Unlike deconstructionist radical feminists, who discard any notion of innate core gender identity, I identify myself as a feminist who does not. I understand femininity as including characteristics that in the phallocentric psychoanalytic view (by now, I hope, defunct) were customarily regarded as masculine, phallic, or at the very least normally bisexual. The group of outer-directed activities, of promoting oneself, accepting and enjoying positions of power, propelling oneself ahead assertively and competitively, are intrinsic aspects of female genitality and sexuality. In fact, they are every bit as intrinsic as the more traditionally designated inner-directed qualities of receptivity and nurturance. Distorted or incomplete notions about sexual attributes and functions of the female body have clouded our understanding of primary female genital function and pleasure, as well as of primary female genital anxieties. Sherfey (1966) recognized the essential importance of clitoral sensations, and at least one contributor to the 1976 *JAPA* supplement, Lerner, regarded clitoral sensations no less than vaginal as quintessentially feminine. Un-conflicted realization of femininity involves the pleasures and accompanying fantasies of outer-directed clitoral sensations, as well as the accompanying anxiety of being cut down. It involves as well the pleasures and accompanying fantasies of inner-directed vaginal sensations of being entered, penetrated, filled up, and the corresponding anxieties of being invaded, pierced, and mutilated within.

Now that we no longer equate feminine with passive, masculine with active, the business of identifying gender has become more and more complex. Not only have we discarded Freud's false premise as the scaffold for a theory of sexuality, but we also cannot fail to emphasize the mutual influence of cultural and psychological changes on the way we identify gender. The consciousness-raising attributable to feminist and psychoanalytic thinking, both modern and postmodern, has in turn altered what is internalized intrapsychically by individuals regarding the nature of sex and gender. Persistent efforts by women and men to actively change their cultural environment vis-à-vis sex and gender have successfully produced an evolved set of ideas and constructs that have been internalized, and are effectively modifying the contents of psychic reality. Cultural changes come to be represented intrapsychically and contribute significantly to evolutionary changes in the cultural understanding of sex and gender that come to be further internalized and represented intrapsychically. That is, sequential transformations in internalization of new cultural norms influence the development of still more new cultural norms, so that progressions in these identificatory markers of gender can be observed over successive generations. The changes have been so vast in our time that it is little wonder that "gender benders" seem to be coming at us from all directions.

## GENDER BENDERS AND SEXUAL CONUNDRUMS

I merely summarize here some extremely brief examples of gender benders, which I have elaborated elsewhere (Gediman 2003a, b) with extensive
psychoanalytic data. The object choices of one woman with predominantly homosexual desires are primarily men. I noted that "heterosexual object
choice in lesbian women" may be construed as an oxymoron, but if that is
so then let it stand, because ambiguity, complexity, and uncertainty in the
meaning of that choice are the hallmarks of my position, which calls for a
complex view of gender and sexuality in women as well as in men. I am
using the words *choice* and *preference* fully aware that the politically correct
position currently is that homosexual women, or homosexual men, have no
choice—they are simply oriented in a particular direction, which fulfills some
powerful, irreversible inclination. This position completely ignores the influence of unconscious dynamics on object choice. It also ignores bisexuality
and the polymorphously perverse disposition, as well as the potential in all
individuals, male or female, for identifying with both men and women, as
complex motivating factors in sexual desire, sexual orientation, sexual object
choice, and gender identity. Early developmental phase-specific factors, such
as thwarted oedipal longings, penis envy, and other explanatory stereotypes
once believed to be pathognomonic of later-developing specific outcomes in
gender identity and sexual orientation in fact lead to multiple outcomes. Once
we unpack the meanings of this gender bender, we can understand its multiple
determinants and functions. Traditional psychoanalytic methodology serves
to construct the various meanings of the gender bender, while deconstruction
of the false binary—homosexual women choose women, heterosexual women
choose men—can serve as a means to this end.

A particular homosexual man's development is characterized by positive,
not negative, oedipal fixations. He was and still is more beset with troubled
rivalries than he is with a compulsive quest for libidinal attachments with
father figures. Libidinal attachments to the father, or the negative oedipal,
traditionally have been considered the hallmark of homosexual development
in boys, and libidinal attachments to the mother and the wish to get rid of
the father, or the positive oedipal, the hallmark of heterosexual development
in boys. Examination of that assumption suggests yet another false binary.
Homosexual men have been known to feel rivalrous with their fathers for
the mother's love, and for achievement and approval. Once we separate
sex from gender, or sexual orientation from gendered self-representations,
we can see how a homosexual man's object choice may be modeled on

positive, as well as negative, oedipal attachment. A male drag queen is seriously involved in a "heterosexual" relationship with a lesbian "butch." A "macho" male homosexual prefers women for long-term sexual attachments but experiences more sexual excitement when "cruising" with what he calls effeminate or stereotypically demure and girlish homosexual men. A heterosexual man whose favorite position during intercourse is for his wife to be on top fantasizes, pleasurably as he penetrates her, that she is a homosexual man penetrating him.

In all fairness, we must credit the premodern Sigmund Freud with introducing the foundations of the kind of gender benders outlined above. In a 1920 footnote to *Three Essays* (Freud 1905b), he endorses Ferenczi's distinction between "subject homo-erotics," who feel and behave like women, and "object homo-erotics," who are completely masculine and who have merely exchanged a female for a male object. Consistent with my gender bender examples is his statement: "While granting the existence of these two types, we may add that there are many people in whom a certain quantity of subject homo-erotism is found in combination with a proportion of object homo-erotism" (p. 147 n). In his overt rejection of a monolithic approach to an understanding of homosexual men, Freud was far more au courant and correct than he was in his understanding of heterosexual women. One could say that his early groundbreaking discoveries were a gender-bending deconstruction of the sex and gender stereotypes of his day.

From film comes another vignette. In *Boys Don't Cry* (1999) a young teenage woman, Teena Brandon, who wishes she were a boy, prepares for a sex-change operation. She experiences her gender as clearly male, her sex as female, and her sexual orientation as male. After adopting the name Brandon Teena, she impersonates a "he," falls in love with a heterosexual woman, becomes sexually involved with no conflict about his gender, but is always at pains to keep her sex hidden from both of them. Local rednecks finally rape and kill her when they discover that he is a she. Note the way I interchange pronouns here in an effort to convey the confused relation between sex and gender objectivity and subjectivity from the points of view of both the protagonist and the audience.

The last gender conundrums I will deal with involve deconstruction and the attack on reality in gender and social deceptions. Marjorie Garber (1992), the feminist literary critic, devotes a good part of her book, *Vested Interests*, to a "deconstructivist" analysis of crossover and deception in literature. Her approach is primarily that of well-documented literary criticism emphasizing the cultural politics of gender and transvestitism. She concludes that

213

cross-dressing proves that gender is constructed and is not essential or innate, a view for the most part alien to traditional psychoanalytic thinking. According to Garber, "the fact of transvestitism is both a personal and a political as well as an aesthetic and theatrical mode of self-construction" (p. 236). Referring to the play *M. Butterfly* (Hwang 1989), Garber notes that "the figure of the cross-dressed 'woman,' the transvestite ... functions simultaneously as a mark of gender undecidability and as an indication of category crisis. Man/woman, or male/female, is the most obvious and central of the border crossings in *M. Butterfly* [and] ... indicates the play's preoccupation with the transvestite as a figure not only for the conundrum of gender and erotic style, but also for other kinds of border-crossing ..." (pp. 238–339).

Gender ambiguity is also central to Garber's explanation of the success of the deception of transvestites and other cross-dressers. Although her argument is persuasive, our positions differ in one fundamental respect. Garber takes the postmodernist, hermeneutic view that ambiguities, conundrums, and undecidability in gender perception are inevitable because gender is always a construction or interpretation and never refers to anything constant or innate. She and other postmodern critics risk being construed as believing that all gender designations are imposturous. By contrast, my position (see Gediman 1990) is that the critical ambiguities are due to innate bisexuality, to empathy, and to other psychologically real capacities for multiple within-gender and cross-gender identifications. The deconstructionist, hermeneutic approach seems to allow for gender to be defined fictitiously and, I would argue, deceptively. Those who regard gender as only a construct, and cross-dressing, say, as simply one variety of deconstruction of gender, are guided by postmodern, deconstructionist, and hermeneutic approaches. Deconstruction and hermeneutics are currently fashionable disciplines that downplay the objective or material reality of all matters, including that of the actual genitals and other innate or "real" gender markers. These views pervade the current academic zeitgeist and reflect trends that some would want to incorporate into psychoanalytic theory. These trendy intellectual currents allow for many versions of the truth, and often compromise significantly the traditional psychoanalytic concepts of material reality and objective truth-values, against which to check shifting versions of historical, subjective, intersubjective, and narrative truth.

Postmodern, deconstructionist, radical feminist thinkers, whether psychoanalysts, artists, writers, or others, have been interested in gender benders such as these discussed here, taking them as proof of the ineluctable separation between sex and gender. For example, many believe that being biologically or anatomically female conveys nothing about gender and gender identity outside of social and political context. These thinkers elaborate no stereotypical gender markers to demonstrate that there are no innate givens but only constructed ones when it comes to sex and gender. Gender, and gender-related personality implications, can, they say, be constructed and co-constructed hermeneutically in as many ways as there are individual subjectivities developing in social, political, and other contexts.

In contrast to the postmodernists, I believe that such open-ended possibilities for constructing gender, without the counterbalance of universal bodily markers, lead to omnipotent, solipsistic gender conceptualizations too broad to convey specific meaning. I believe that the objectively real correlates of gender, of sexuality, and of identificatory processes do in fact generally exist, alongside the subjective correlates. My interest lies primarily not in deconstructing gender, but in opening up our sensitivities to evolving new ways of understanding and interpreting all of the objectivities, subjectivities, and newly discovered interactions between the two that we come across clinically with regard to sex and gender. I am skeptical about our being able to come up with gender bender vignettes that prove there is no objective or psychobiological substrate of gender, but I am convinced that the clinical realities of complex sex and gender connections underscore the fact that our old notions do not always hold up and that the assumptions on which they are based are now subject to question. Just as postmodernists rightly question old categories, I too am questioning old categorical assumptions in order to free myself to hear and understand things differently from the circumscribed ways I did early on in my journey as a psychoanalytic observer of sex and gender. My attention is drawn to the kinds of workaday psychoanalytic data that question old basic assumptions and open up new if not limitless perspectives on various sex and gender mixes.

## CONCLUSION

I have tried to bring together academic feminist critical discourse and clinical psychoanalysis in order to broaden our understanding of gender complexity and multiplicity. Postmodern sensibilities, generally associated with relational psychoanalysis, are appreciated here as applicable also in traditional and contemporary Freudian psychoanalytic contexts. Flexibility, diversity, and multiplicity have in this postmodern era replaced the rigid categorizations of many premoderns and arguably many moderns in how one recognizes and experiences sex and gender, one's own and that of others. I hope I have conveyed that one does not need to be exclusively a postmodern deconstructionist to appreciate flexibility and multiplicity, just as one does not have to have exclusively one or another set of gender characteristics and sexual bents to declare whether psychically one is basically male or female, masculine or feminine, man or woman.

## REFERENCES

Balsam, R. (1996). The pregnant mother and the body image of the daughter. *Journal of the American Psychoanalytic Association* 44 (suppl.): 410–427.

Bassin, D. (1996). Beyond the he and she: Toward the reconciliation of masculinity and femininity in the postoedipal female mind. *Journal of the American Psychoanalytic Association* 44 (Suppl.): 157–190. http://www.pep-web.org/document.php?id=apa.044s.0157a

——— ED. (1999). *Female Sexuality: Contemporary Engagements*. Northvale, NJ: Aronson.

Benjamin, J. (1996). In defense of gender ambiguity. *Gender & Psychoanalysis* 1: 27–44. http://www.pep-web.org/document.php?id=gap.001.0027a

Bernstein, D. (1990). Female genital anxieties, conflicts, and typical mastery modes. *International Journal of Psycho-Analysis* 71: 151–165. http://www.pep-web.org/document.php?id=ijp.071.0151a

Blum, H.P. (1976). Masochism, the ego ideal, and the psychology of women. *Journal of the American Psychoanalytic Association* 24 (Suppl.): 157–191. http://www.pep-web.org/document.php?id=apa.024s.0157a

Butler, J. (1990). *Gender Trouble and the Subversion of Identity*. New York: Routledge.

Chodorow, N. (1996). Theoretical gender and clinical gender: Epistemological reflections on the psychology of women. *Journal of the American Psychoanalytic Association* 44: (Suppl.):215–238. http://www.pep-web.org/document.php?id=apa.044s.0215a

Deutsch, H. (1930). The significance of masochism in the mental life of women. *International Journal of Psycho-Analysis* 11:48–60. http://www.pep-web.org/document.php?id=ijp.011.0048a

——— (1944–1945). *The Psychology of Women*. 2 vols. New York: Grune & Stratton.

Dimen, M. (1991). Deconstructing difference: Gender, splitting, and transitional space. *Psychoanalytic Dialogues* 1:335–352. http://www.pep-web.org/document.php?id=pd.001.0335a

——— (1999). From breakdown to breakthrough. *Female Sexuality: Contemporary Engagements*, ed. D. Bassin. Northvale, NJ: Aronson, pp. 407–420.

Elise, D. (1997). Primary femininity, bisexuality, and the female ego ideal: A re-examination of female developmental theory. *Psychoanalytic Quarterly* 66:489–517. http://www.pep-web.org/document.php?id=paq.066.0489a

Freud, A. (1922). The relation of beating fantasies to a daydream. In *The Writings of Anna Freud*. Vol. 1. New York: International Universities Press, 1974, pp. 137–157. http://www.pep-web.org/document.php?id=ijp.004.0089a

Freud, S. (1905a). Fragment of an analysis of a case of hysteria. *S.E.* 7:1–122. http://www.pep-web.org/document.php?id=se.007.0001a

——— (1905b). Three essays on the theory of sexuality. *S.E.* 7:130–243. http://www.pep-web.org/document.php?id=se.007.0123a

——— (1906). My views on the part played by sexuality in the aetiology of the neuroses. *S.E.* 7:269–279. http://www.pep-web.org/document.php?id=se.007.0269a

——— (1925). Some psychological consequences of the anatomical differences between the sexes. *S.E.* 19:248–258. http://www.pep-web.org/document.php?id=se.019.0241a

——— (1927). Fetishism. *Standard Edition* 21:149–157. http://www.pep-web.org/document.php?id=se.021.0001a

——— (1931). Female sexuality. *S.E.* 21:223–245. http://www.pep-web.org/document.php?id=se.021.0221a

Galenson, E., & Roiphe, H. (1976). Some suggested revisions concerning early female development. *Journal of the American Psychoanalytic Association* 24 (Suppl.):29–57. http://www.pep-web.org/document.php?id=apa.024s.0029a

Garber, M. (1992). *Vested Interests*. New York: Harper Collins, 1993.

Gediman, H.K. (1990). Men masquerading as women: Imposture, illusion, and denouement in the play M. Butterfly. *Psychoanalytic Psychology* A10:469–479. http://www.pep-web.org/document.php?id=ppsy.010.0469a

——— (2001). Review of D. Bassin, ed., Female Sexuality: Contemporary Engagements. *Psychoanalytic Psychology* 18:602–611. http://www.pep-web.org/document.php?id=ppsy.018.0602a

——— (2003a) Gender benders: Premodern, modern, and postmodern perspectives. *Precirculated paper presented to the American Psychoanalytic Association*, Boston, June 2003.

——— (2003b). Male object choice in women with homosexual desire. In *Sexual Faces*, ed. C. Schwartz & M. Schulman, New York: International Universities Press, pp. 93–114.

Grossman, W.I., & Stewart, W.A. (1976). Penis envy: From childhood wish

to developmental metaphor. *Journal of the American Psychoanalytic Association* 24 (Suppl.):193–212.
http://www.pep-web.org/document.php?id=apa.024s.0193a

Harris, A. (1991). Gender as contradiction. *Psychoanalytic Dialogues.* 1:197–224. http://www.pep-web.org/document.php?id=pd.001.0197a

———. (1996). The conceptual power of multiplicity. *Contemporary Psychoanalysis* 32:537–552.
http://www.pep-web.org/document.php?id=cps.032.0537a

Hoffman, I. (1991). Some practical implications of a social constructivist view of the psychoanalytic situation. *Psychoanalytic Dialogues* 2:287–304.
http://www.pep-web.org/document.php?id=pd.002.0287a

Horney, K. (1924). On the genesis of the castration complex in women. *International Journal of Psycho-Analysis* 5:50–65.
http://www.pep-web.org/document.php?id=ijp.005.0050a

——— (1926). The flight from womanhood: The masculinity-complex in women as viewed by men and women. *International Journal of Psycho-Analysis* 7:324–339.
http://www.pep-web.org/document.php?id=ijp.007.0324a

———. (1933). The denial of the vagina: A contribution to the problem of genital anxieties specific to women. *International Journal of Psycho-Analysis* 14:57–70. http://www.pep-web.org/document.php?id=ijp.014.0057a

Hwang, D.H. (1989). *M. Butterfly*. New York: New American Library.

Jones, E. (1927). The early development of female sexuality. *International Journal of Psycho-Analysis* 8:459–472.
http://www.pep-web.org/document.php?id=ijp.008.0459a

——— (1933). The phallic phase. *International Journal of Psycho-Analysis* 14:1–33. http://www.pep-web.org/document.php?id=ijp.014.0001a

——— (1935). Early female sexuality *International Journal of Psycho-Analysis* 16:263–273. http://www.pep-web.org/document.php?id=ijp.016.0263a

Kaplan, L. (1991). *Female Perversions*. New York: Doubleday.
http://www.pep-web.org/document.php?id=sgs.001.0349a

Kestenberg, J.S. (1976). Regression and reintegration in pregnancy. *Journal of the American Psychoanalytic Association* 24 (Suppl.):213–250.
http://www.pep-web.org/document.php?id=apa.024s.0213a

Kleeman, J.A. (1976). Freud's views on early female sexuality in the light of direct child observation. *Journal of the American Psychoanalytic Association* 24 (Suppl.):3–27.
http://www.pep-web.org/document.php?id=apa.024s.0003a

Kristeva, J. (1986). *The Kristeva Reader*, ed. T. Moi. Oxford: Blackwell.

Kubie, L. (1978). The drive to be both sexes. *Psychoanalytic Quarterly* 43:349–426. http://www.pep-web.org/document.php?id=paq.043.0349a

Kulish, N. (2000). Primary femininity. *Journal of the American Psychoanalytic Association* 48:1355–1379.
http://www.pep-web.org/document.php?id=apa.048.1355a

Lerner, H. (1976). Parental mislabeling of female genitals as a determinant of penis envy and learning inhibitions in women. *Journal of the American Psychoanalytic Association* 24 (Suppl.):269–283.
http://www.pep-web.org/document.php?id=apa.024s.0269a

Mayer, E.L. (1995). The phallic castration complex and primary femininity: Paired developmental lines toward female gender identity. *Journal of the American Psychoanalytic Association* 43:17–38.
http://www.pep-web.org/document.php?id=apa.043.0017a

Parens, H., Pollock, L., Stern, J., & Kramer, S. (1976). The girl's entry into the Oedipus complex. *Journal of the American Psychoanalytic Association* 24 (Suppl.):79–107.
http://www.pep-web.org/document.php?id=apa.024s.0079a

Person, E. (1976). Initiation fantasies and transvestitism: Discussion. *Journal of the American Psychoanalytic Association* 24:547–551.
http://www.pep-web.org/document.php?id=apa.024.0547a

——— (1983). Review of Alan P. Bell & Martin S. Weinberg, Homosexualities: A Study of Diversity among Men and Women. *Journal of the American Psychoanalytic Association* 31:306–315.
http://www.pep-web.org/document.php?id=apa.031.0306a

——— Ovesey, L. (1974). The transsexual syndrome in males: Primary transsexualism. *American Journal of Psychotherapy* 28:4–20.

Richards, A.K. (1996). Primary femininity and female genital anxiety. *Journal of the American Psychoanalytic Association* 44:(Suppl):261–281.
http://www.pep-web.org/document.php?id=apa.044s.0261a

Rivera, M. (1989). Linking the psychological and the social: Feminism, poststructuralism, and multiple personality. *Dissociation* 2:24–31.

Riviere, J. (1929). Womanliness as a masquerade. In *The Inner World and Joan Riviere*, ed. A. Hughes. London: Karnac Books, 1991, pp. 133–153.
http://www.pep-web.org/document.php?id=ijp.010.0303a

Sherfey, M.J. (1966). The evolution and nature of female sexuality in relation to psychoanalytic theory. *Journal of the American Psychoanalytic Association* 14:28–125. http://www.pep-web.org/document.php?id=apa.014.0028a

Stoller, R.J. (1976). Primary femininity. *Journal of the American Psychoanalytic Association* 24 (Suppl.):59–78.

http://www.pep-web.org/document.php?id=apa.024s.0059a
Weedon, C. (1987). *Feminist Practice and Poststructuralist Theory*. Oxford: Basil Blackwell.

# PART V: DECEIT AND THE DECEPTIONS OF EVERYDAY LIFE

## AUTHOR'S INTRODUCTION

I thank Fred Pine for crediting me with an eye-opening quality for my use of the term, "gaslighting" as a traumatic assault on a person's sense of reality of the self. I must credit those who were aware of the importance of such assaults on one's subjective sense of what is real, particularly Calef and Weinshel (1981), who introduced the widely quoted term into the psychoanalytic literature as a specific form of introjective defense. My interests have moved toward the interpersonal traumatic nature of imposturous forms deceitful influence of one person on another. Once again, I attempt to bridge the gap between the more classical intrapsychic understanding of manipulatively fooling and being fooled, or duping and being duped, and a more relational understanding by toggling between one perspective and another. At the time I wrote the papers in Part V, Chapters 12 and 13, I had been drawn to the topic of imposture for another reason in addition to its being a particularly noxious form of traumatic assault. I believed that all individuals could be characterized by one degree or another of imposturous tendencies, those ranging from the imposture of everyday life, through the "as-if" personalities through the psychopathy of the true impostor. Leonard Shengold had been an important influence on my thinking, not only for his deep respect for real trauma, such as "soul murder," but for his honoring of a continuum on which many varieties of psychopathology in everyday life could be placed. I was fortunate to have reviewed his book on the delusions of everyday life (Gediman, 1996) at a time when imposture, along with other forms of deception and self-deception were very much on my mind as I was co-authoring with my friend and colleague, Janice S. Lieberman, *The Many Faces of Deceit* (1996).

# Chapter 11: Imposture, Inauthenticity, and Feeling Fraudulent

[Gediman, H.K. (1985). Imposture, inauthenticity, and feeling fraudulent. *Journal of the American Psychoanalytic Association*, 33: 911–935. Also in Gediman, H.K. & Lieberman, J.S. *The Many Faces of Deceit*. NJ and London: Jason Aronson.]

> The world is crowded with "as if" personalities, and even more so with impostors and pretenders. Ever since I became interested in the impostor, he pursues me everywhere. I find him among my friends and acquaintances, as well as in myself.

The epigraph introduces Helene Deutsch's (1955, p. 337) famous paper on the impostor. Her words imply the universality of imposturous tendencies. This present paper aims primarily to take a new look at the concept, imposture, by studying its various manifestations in the psychoanalytic situation. I shall include three case summaries that will be viewed in the context of a continuum, or spectrum, of imposture, which could broaden our understanding of that problem and perhaps lead toward increasing recognition of important clinical variations.

The continuum idea should be particularly compelling for analysts who have experienced difficulties in coming to definite diagnostic conclusions in assessing certain manifestations of inauthenticity in their analysands. Consider a patient who appears "shifty." Is the patient a "true" impostor, assuming multiple false identities in order to deceive, deliberately? Or, is the patient an "as-if" personality suffering from unstable, shifting, unintegrated identifications along with a preponderance of imitative tendencies? Or, does the "shifty" patient tend to *feel* fraudulent and imposturous when to the objective observer he is not? Or, is the deceit we think we see not deceit at all, but related rather to more or less normal promotion of illusion, as in art and play? Apparent lies and deceit may also function defensively to disguise unconscious wishes and fantasies, that is, "something untrue may be represented as something true, to make it possible to represent something true as untrue" (Fenichel, 1939p. 130). Such apparent "lies" may be looked upon as genuine lies by some in that they seek to conceal by presenting something other than that which would be most useful analytically. I aim to illustrate particular and important variations of imposturous tendencies, including that variation where the psychoanalytic enterprise, because of its inevitable focus on illusion and disguise inherent in psychic reality, poses certain problems for individuals suffering from conflicts around authenticity.

The continuum implied by these questions, ranging roughly from the most to the least pathological forms of imposture, covers the pathology of the psychopathic impostor who may assume a false identity for conscious and deliberate purposes of deception, through a heterogeneous variety of individuals who are vulnerable to a shaky identity sense. It includes those who are particularly vulnerable when empathy and multiple, shifting identifications are required by certain situations, such as being an analysand or learning to do analysis. And finally, it refers to those who have problems with illusion and disguise within the range of the psychopathology of everyday life. Most of the psychoanalytic literature to date approaches the problem of imposture from the viewpoint of pathology. I would like to add the perspective of approaching the problem from the other direction of the more average expectable end of the continuum as well [14]

## DIAGNOSTIC ISSUES

Important distinctions have been made customarily between the impostor and the "as-if" personality with imposturous tendencies. The impostor is one who passes himself off incognito (which is often the only way he can function) in delinquent, psychopathic, sociopathic, and other criminal ways, as actually possessing an identity—a literal name—of someone other than himself. True impostors (Deutsch, 1955; Greenacre, 1958a; Ross.1967), do not show a proclivity for multiple, unconsolidated identifications as do the "as-if" personalities with serious disturbances in their sense of reality of themselves and of the world. The latter take on, even exist, by multiple, shifting, superficial identifications. They may "role-play" facilely, but generally do not come to the attention of the law for any reason. One might say that the impostor pretends under the literal cover of someone else's name, while the imposturous, or the "as-ifs," pretend, with great interest in mimicry, imitation, and gesture, under someone else's style and role, taking on

---

14 I am grateful to Dr. Charles Brenner for his suggestions for approaching the concept imposture from these two directions in his thoughtful discussion of an earlier version of this paper.

the color, imitatively, and in the absence of cohesive identifications, of those who are admired. The "as-if" personality resembles Winnicott's "false self," which feels more "real," subjectively, than the nonexperienced potentially better integrated "true" one.

A particular problem lies in differentiating the psychopathic from the nonpsychopathic. There is an illusory quality to "created experience" which stands in the borderland between reality and authenticity, on the one hand, and unreality, inauthenticity, and outright lying, on the other. That makes for difficulties in certain differential diagnoses. In identifying psychopathy, we are prone to make "false positive" as well as "false negative" assessments. That is, it is easy to be "conned" by real psychopathy into overlooking something psychopathic that is present, just as it is easy to assume falsely the presence of psychopathy where it is not present. Abraham (1925), in the very first psychoanalytically informed study of an impostor, an imprisoned criminal, concluded the man's temporary and repeated successes at deceiving "were associated with strong unconscious guilt feelings which had to bring about a rapid end to his happiness as an act of self-punishment."

Another problem is that of distinguishing elements of neurotic pathology, such as the hysterical symptom formation of that form of "lying" called *pseudologia fantastica* (Fenichel, 1939, 1945), from the deceit characteristic of the "true" impostor. Yet another differential diagnosis issue lies in teasing out the more serious ego pathology from the structural transference-neurotic elements in both the true impostor and others with imposturous tendencies. In our focus on the neurotic aspects, we would be concerned with possible unconscious needs for punishment involved in lying, forgery, swindling, and so forth. These "criminal acts" are sometimes motivated by a neurotic need for punishment, as among "criminals from a sense of guilt" or "those wrecked by success" and in other neurotic character problems. Some masochistic characters and obsessional neurotics under the domination of the repetition compulsion are also to be found among impostors and the imposturous. The drive, among the imposturous, to produce illusion rather than substance may contain a neurotic fear of commitment to well-developed and sustained interests when such responsible commitments are unconsciously equated with monstrous crimes for which they would not want to risk being caught. Better to be caught at the lesser crime of imposture, as uncomfortable as that may be. Such neurotic conflicts were found among Freud's criminals from a sense of guilt. Related are those who consciously feel and fear they are fraudulent when they are not.

## NEUROTIC AND DEFICIT ASPECTS OF IMPOSTUROUS TENDENCIES

There are those who might argue in either-or terms about what is more central to imposturousness: is it a "deficit" or fundamental ego pathology, such as a fragmented identity sense due to developmental arrest; *or*, if not that, then is it the neurotic need for punishment for excessive forbidden gratifications of whatever nature? But I believe it is best to examine the problem from multiple, complementary viewpoints.

In considering developmental arrest or deficit and neurotic conflict as complementary points of view, it is important to recognize how ego function disturbances such as failures in internalization, identity diffusion, and ego fragmentation may also serve multiple functions in neurotic compromise formation. So let us now turn to five important related attributes of an altered subjective sense of reality of the self which appear to be aspects of imposture in many of its variations. These attributes range from what is behaviorally observable to what may be inferred about complex dynamics and psychopathology.

The first is verbal fluency, facility, and fluidity; the second is a hypertrophied development of a limited kind of empathy; the third is a quality of dilettantism, involvement in esoterica and artifice; the fourth is an intense disturbance in the sense of identity manifested in multiple identifications and fragmented, largely imitative, noninternalized roleplaying; the fifth is a paradoxically heightened sense of reality accompanying what Eidelberg (1938) has called imposturous ego states.[15]

As for the first, the astounding verbal mimicry and fluency, Greenacre (1958b) notes that impostors conspicuously utilize words with punning variations and substitutions, often with names through which nuances of change of identity may be implied. Among the imposturous, that fluency may deteriorate, under pressure, into fluidity, glibness, or disjointed and confused speech.

---

15 These attributes of an altered subjective sense of reality of the self, along with disturbed self and object representations, have also been discussed extensively in the literature on narcissistic and borderline personalities. While *some* of the individuals I am discussing may be diagnosed as belonging in these categories, my emphasis is decidedly not on placing imposturous tendencies within any one specific diagnostic category. My perspective here, which also has a history in the literature, is on ego function disturbance as dimensionalized on a continuum along which *any* individual may be assigned a place, according to the degree of disturbance. (See Bellak, Hurvich, and Gediman, 1973, for a comprehensive review of this tradition.)

Chapter 11: Imposture, Inauthenticity, and Feeling Fraudulent

Anais Nin (1959) in her novel about artifice, *A Spy in the House of Love*, portrays such gibberish so well in her heroine, Sabina's, verbal stigmata: "she behaved like someone who had all the symptoms of guilt: ... her unpremeditated talk, without continuity; her erratic and sudden gestures, unrelated to her talk; the chaos of her phrases ..." (p. 3). "And when in desperation he [the lie detector] clung to the recurrences of certain words, they formed no design by their repetition, but rather an absolute contradiction" (p. 5). The "lie detector" could not, after hours of detection, tell whether she was an actress, or wanted to be one, or was pretending.

These attributes of an altered subjective sense of reality of the self, along with disturbed self and object representations, have also been discussed extensively in the literature on narcissistic and borderline personalities. While *some* of the individuals I am discussing may be diagnosed as belonging in these categories, my emphasis is decidedly not on placing imposturous tendencies within any one specific diagnostic category. My perspective here, which also has a history in the literature, is on ego function disturbance as dimensionalized on a continuum along which *any* individual may be assigned a place, according to the degree of disturbance. (See Bellak, Hurvich, and Gediman, 1973, for a comprehensive review of this tradition.)

The second common feature characterizing the disturbed reality sense of the imposturous appears as an "excessive" empathy, or, more accurately, empathy-like responses, limited to areas of highly selective, often beautifully attuned in a circumscribed way, telepathy-like forecasting of what the person believes the other expects of him or her. This excessive, even uncanny attention to the expectations of others has been noted by Krohn (1974), who described how certain patients regularly put into words the private associations of the therapist just as the therapist is having them. They show a heightened vigilance to both the superficial peripheral aspects *and* the primitive unconscious of others. Further, he says that this so-called "borderline empathy" is not unique to borderlines, but occurs among many others who have difficulty perceiving the more enduring, characteristic, consolidated ego attitudes of others. I believe that many people with imposturous tendencies do appear to catch on extraordinarily quickly to what they believe the other is thinking and feeling, both at the most superficial and at the most unconscious levels. Their own shaky and fragmented identity sense would account for difficulties in perceiving the ego-integrated aspects of others. As keen and as sharp as their responses may be in picking up details and certain nuances in the lives and activities of others, particularly those they simulate, they may be, at the same time, utterly obtuse in other areas. That is, they show a failure in empathy.

The third characteristic, the unmistakable artifice and inauthenticity in the typical failure of empathy that is so characteristic of imposture, is often masked behind esoterica. The imposturous person, as well as the "true" impostor, then can count on not being discovered because of an ability to pass himself or herself off, consciously or unconsciously, as having expertise that the average listener could not be expected to evaluate with respect to genuineness or authenticity. We are familiar with glib talkers working in certain fields, sometimes including psychoanalysis itself, where the area of expertise may be esoteric enough, or where the linguistic conventions are so idiosyncratic, as to permit "creative" deviations from the ordinary. Such esoteric fields do provide a haven in which inauthenticity may nestle unnoticed for long periods of time.

The fourth characteristic, an intense and circumscribed disturbance in the sense of identity, is manifested in multiple, imitative, fragmented, and shifting identifications on an imitative level. It was Deutsch (1964) who pointed out that the "as-if" personality can exist only by identifications. Ross (1967) suggests that such shiftiness in identifications is not merely an ego function deficit, involving pathology of the self, but also serves adaptive and defensive functions. For example, agreeing with everyone ingratiatingly may serve as imagined protection from attack; the rapid sequence of identifications may be a means of appeasing objects.

Paradoxically, many people with the disturbances in the sense of reality just reviewed experience themselves as most authentic, subjectively, when they are acting imposturously, and often feel as though they are presenting to others with artifice and phoniness when they are in fact functioning at integrated, higher levels, reflecting more consolidated identifications. Some people, for example, are unable to acknowledge real giftedness as their own, imagining instead that they are inauthentic plagiarizing swindlers of other people's ideas; they themselves are unable to distinguish their authentic from their inauthentic being. The "true" impostor described by Deutsch (1955) never feared exposure when he was a swindler, but felt like an impostor and inauthentic when he did honest work. Various explanations have been offered for this paradox. Greenacre (1958a, 1958b), believes that a narcissistically heightened sense of reality may derive, for some, from the sadomasochistic excitement of imposturous states. Others (Deutsch, 1942; Ross, 1967) suggest that guilt related to oedipal conflicts accompanies the imposturous individual's attempts at higher-level functioning. Therefore, such a person feels subjectively more "real" with a "false self" presentation than as a "true self," for defensive reasons.

It goes without saying that with the typical failures in ego functioning, particularly of object cathexis and the subsequent failures of internalization seen in identifications which never progress beyond the early stages of imitativeness, there would also be serious lacunae in superego formation (Jacobson, 1964). Like ego attitudes, the morals of the imposturous are poorly internalized or consolidated. They tend to be simply imitative reflections of good and bad, the content of which varies with the momentary object of identification.

All of the aforementioned disturbances in the sense of reality of the self and the world usually have been attributed, in developmental terms, to a fixation at the two- to three-year-old developmental level of imitativeness and primary identification, with a persistence of simple mimicry of that very early type of identification. No one, however, has suggested what maladaptations during that phase are *specific* to the development of imposturousness. One finds as a rule, in the phase-appropriate ways in all object-relations development, the same processes one finds among the imposturous: multiple identifications, the self and object poorly differentiated, and object constancy not yet established—at one time or another. Such processes also characterize a *range* of later outcomes. Thus, those conditions may be necessary, but hardly sufficient to account for the specific outcome in question.

### THE ANALYSAND AS IMPOSTOR

I turn here to a requirement of the analytic situation whereby the analyst and the analysand *must* focus on multiple shifts from inner to outer reality, *must* aim toward constructing multiple and changing life histories, and *must* adopt multiple points of view and perspectives for understanding current life problems and conflicts. Such required shifts in perspective often involve shifts in identifications that are essential for empathy and insight and for the process to move on. The fluidity of perspective *required* in learning to be an analysand, an analyst, and a supervisor might in itself constitute a "pull" for a certain, it is hoped transient and reversible, "as-if" behavior, phenomenologically speaking. It perhaps could even encourage the average participant to *feel* like an impostor from time to time. In those with significant imposturous tendencies, the "pull" could constitute a more serious danger.

In dream analysis, for example, we encourage our analysands to see multiple and complex aspects of themselves as represented in their various roles and other self-representations as portrayed by various characters in the manifest dream content. There may be disturbances in the sense of reality as the analysand contemplates his or her self-created dreams and fantasy interpretations. It is not too far-fetched, I believe, to think of the patient as feeling somewhat imposturous as he or she has certain reactions to these self-creations, which may or may not precipitate a troubling sense of identity, according to how potentially fragile that function might be.

Turning to literature, I am reminded of the writing strategy of D. M. Thomas (1981), author of the novel, *The White Hotel*, which featured shifting versions of reality, representing shifting versions of narrative truth, depending on the viewpoint of the particular protagonist. It was my perplexity about that very facility of portraying shifting versions of the truth, the so-called "Rashomon" phenomenon, that, in large measure, inspired me to study imposture with particular emphasis on differentiating the sort that could be called psychopathological from the more "creative," whose work requires perspectivism but not necessarily psychopathology.

In the following case summaries, each analysand shows significant disturbance in one or more aspects of the sense of reality discussed above.

## PATIENT A.

Mr. A. was brilliant and facile with the surface meaning of words and ideas, and gave the impression that he had a capacity for depth of understanding as well. He learned very quickly what was expected of him as an analysand and brought in dreams with the kind of symbolism that nearly always appeared to confirm my tentatively offered speculative hunch about his unconscious conflicts. He, himself, became an "expert" at responding in an "empathiclike" manner to his own primitive unconscious, but did not have much insight into the ego and superego aspects of his functioning. For example, in a typical early session which dealt mainly with his fear of there being" nothing there" if he were to associate freely, he reported a dream he entitled "Premature Pontification" in which female genitals on a screen merged from light into dark into nothingness. "Ah," he said, "I concede with relish to your analytic prowess in connecting 'nothing there' with castration. You have a point, and I become more diffuse and blobby." The more playful he became at punning, the more he became obtuse to whatever meaning could be attributable to his failure to make more than small payments on owed fees. This delinquency, he insisted, was irrelevant analytically, and the problem was that I was too "uptight" about it.

As an analysand, he seemed a "natural" until one discovered that his associations to and his glib interpretations of his dreams and symptoms were replete with ridicule of psychoanalysis, as in the example above. His fantasies of writing literary treatises for esoteric periodicals on the unconscious meanings of his symptoms and dreams included wishes to expose the analytic process as fraudulent. He initially sought treatment because of a serious writing inhibition, for although he had ambitions to write in his area of expertise, he could not write, but would verbally infuse others with his esoteric ideas. Although a teacher in a department of a prestigious college, he was hired without ever having taken the requisite graduate courses, an almost unheard of feat in his field and in his school, where all teachers are required to maintain certain standards through continuing education and written work. It became apparent to me in the course of the work that he had misrepresented himself by offering false credentials to both me and his employers. When confronted with this deception, he suffered acute anxiety about being exposed as a "psychological" fraud and impostor. That is, he insisted such fears were neurotic and should be analyzed away.

Why was he kept in analysis for as long as eight months? He expressed conscious concern, anxiety, and guilt about his superfluency of language and dialect, which he correctly believed was a sign of his instability as well as a talent. He was concerned about some real-life tangles that his predilection for the illusionary over the work-a-day and his outright deceptions through artifice had led him into. He worried that he lacked solidity, believed he assumed various roles too well and convincingly. He complained of a compulsive quest for ambiguity about who he actually was because of "a fear of consequentiality." These potential motivational inroads kept me interested in analytic work with him. Additionally, he was accustomed to having others *wish* to take him seriously, and I was no exception.

Meanwhile, the analysis itself was being ridiculed in having to be experienced as inconsequential, and the analyst ridiculed for taking him or anything in the world as serious, solid, or real. A series of fantastic coincidences had made it impossible for him to pay his bills on time, to write checks that did not bounce, or to get to the bank before it closed. It must be said that in the beginning he managed enough part payment for me to believe the matter was analyzable, *especially as he would link it to apparently meaningful psychological content.* He would wax philosophical that all the coincidences preventing payment must be further evidence for the uncanny feeling with which he started analysis: it was "irresponsible" for him to be in such a luxurious, truth-focused treatment modality because he did not deserve it as a person. He felt like an impostor to be working at anything so genuine when he himself suffered from *painful but apparently self-serving feelings of unreality.*

After a while, however, this motivational inroad itself proved inaccessible. Not only did he disclaim all responsibility for his financial swindling of me, but thought if I would simply trust that the money would materialize without a plan, the treatment would proceed much better. It felt so prosaic to him, so bourgeois, so opposed to a greater sense of morality to plan about money, for after all, as psychoanalysts all know, money is equated with feces and his values were set at a higher level. He prided himself on his sense of true as opposed to my trivial morality: he would not kill or cause physical harm. To be concerned with a payment was not part of his enlightened moral code, while to cleverly fool others was. Mr. A. held that if he were going to commit an infraction of consensually held moral and ethical codes, it had better be a *big one*, to be done in excess. This, according to his value system, would lend it some esthetic credence so that, philosophically speaking, it would be on a higher plane than a mere petty malfeasance. Thus, what others might question on moral grounds and consider as arrogance, grandiosity, even criminality, this patient rationalized as meeting elitist esoteric standards of excellence, reflecting an ego ideal not atypical for impostors. He patronized my insistence that he look into these matters analytically.

Why did I let things develop to the point where I not only could identify him with confidence as an imposturous psychopath, but countertransferentially, I began to see him as the incarnation of that very evil he had been proclaiming as his ego ideal? Without, for now, going into possible personal countertransference reasons, it is important to wonder whether something less individual was involved in my being that willing an *audience*, hoodwinked into denying his psychopathy by his obvious pain, his motivation, by his eagerness to be an analysand, by his eagerness to attend sessions, and by his attempts at small payment from time to time. He must have known that *unconsciously, I, like many others, wanted to believe him*. After all, he suffered, was potentially creative, appeared to understand about analysis. He learned the language quickly. He knew I did not want to believe he was psychopathic, but he also knew I would not continue to work with him if I came to believe that this were truly the case.

An interesting aspect of this case was that Mr. A. became more verbally fluid as the problem with the owed fees continued. He would offer garbled and contradictory accounts of his financial situation, tending toward the deteriorated verbal fluidity of unsuccessful imposture. His view of *himself* shifted more to the criminal and away from the troubled. From the beginning, he expressed fears that he labeled neurotic: the entire analysis would be an attempt to unmask and punish him for a crime he felt guilty of.

While Mr. A. conveyed the impression at first that he suffered from a neurotic "criminality from a sense of guilt," a classic success neurosis, and quest for talion castration associated with his "fear of consequentiality," he was unable to sustain that impression. Some aspects of a repetition compulsion underlying neurotic repetitive criminality from a sense of guilt did indeed seem to be present and, in the beginning, made the differential diagnosis between psychopathic impostor and masochistic character with self-punishing tendencies difficult to make and at times arbitrary. Much of the associative material he presented turned out to be based on some recent readings of Freud, which he understood superficially, and appeared as part of an imposture at being simply a neurotic patient as well as a planned mocking of psychoanalysis. But more than that, those tendencies expressed his fears and the corresponding conflicting wishes of being unmasked as illusory, empty, only role playing, both in his profession and in being an analysand. He was gifted, as well as a pretender, but when expected to follow through with the "responsibilities" attendant on acknowledgement or acceptance of the giftedness as his own, he imagined himself to be what he at times did indeed become: a swindler, plagiarist, and, like Woody Allen's Zelig, a "chameleon" man of the world.

Operant here were *both* the dynamic reasons connected with the wish-fear conflict of being wrecked by success, as well as the "prestructural" pathology of self-fragmentation, of too many hacked-up identities. It would be difficult to settle the differential diagnosis question of what is primary, the structural defect *or* the need for punishment. We are dealing here with the fluid linguist, the person of nonconsolidated identities who aimed to set this liability to his own advantage, deceptively. And he was not entirely without guilt, despite the primitive form and the convoluted content of his idiosyncratic morality, for he feared being wrecked by his deceptively earned success. It is we who tend to dichotomize our patients who do not clearly fall into either-or categories. Mr. A.'s failure to complete his job requirements and his subsequent falsification of his credentials were related to his failure to take analysis seriously, to his need to see serious responsible work and roles as something superficial—a game, a fad, an illusory indulgence of the idle rich. As his status as teacher and as analysand both stimulated grandiose fantasies, it simultaneously provoked unbearable humiliation and fears of inconsequentiality.

The moments of seriousness and commitment to our work were troubling mainly in that they seemed to interfere with his capacity for maintaining illusions he required for a reasonably cohesive subjective sense of self. He had a genuine panic reaction about an extra-analytic indiscretion and wished to hold me responsible as a magic mover for self-endangering actions he wished to disclaim in order to keep the whole analytic endeavor on an illusory, unreal plane. His failure to commit himself seriously to the work of analysis and to obtaining credentials for his profession, while partaking in some respects of the coloring of a transference "success neurosis," also reflected a profound need to only marginally negotiate life's hurdles. In this way he could maintain an illusory identity, but one which held him together. As Greenacre (1958a) noted, a heightened subjective sense of both reality and identity accompanies the success of the fraudulence of imposturous claims. Mr. A. appeared compelled to sabotage the analytic work as it moved in the direction of strengthening a subjective sense of authenticity of both himself and his relationship with the analyst. These problems, along with the delinquencies around the fee, made it impossible to continue with him in treatment.

Before going on to the next illustrative case, I must introduce a particular variant of the role of illusion in the lives of the imposturous that relates to fantasies that their fragile sense of emptiness and incompleteness can be completed by some symbolic representation of an "illusory phallus." Greenacre (1958a), in particular, has noted that the impostor feels incomplete, anxious, and fearful when not involved in acts of imposture, reflected in an "ego hunger" and a need for completion in a particular way: union through identification. Patients with imposturous tendencies often feel incomplete and complain of there being "nothing there," even when functioning well, objectively speaking. I regard their characterization of these "self-states" not simply as an endopsychic perception of emptiness, worthlessness, and defectiveness, which would motivate what Greenacre called "ego hunger," but also as clearly referable to a sense of genital inadequacy, usually unconscious, as well. That is, individuals with deficiencies in their sense of identity also experience themselves, consciously or unconsciously, as being deficient with respect to genital adequacy. Imagery suggesting an illusory but "harmless" phallus accompanies inauthentic actions which, in those with imposturous tendencies, are not threatening to subjectively experienced self-integrity. It is the more genuine acts, symbolic of nonillusory self-assertion, or of exhibitionism (see Conrad, 1975) at any psychosexual level which, because they spark castration anxieties, also threaten the integrity or the subjective sense of reality of the self. This subjective sense of both personality and genital "deficit" seemed to pervade the feelings of a woman whom I shall call Miss B.

### PATIENT B.

Like Mr. A., Miss B. suffered a writing inhibition that, upon analysis, could be understood as related to a deep-seated fear of writing under her own name. When she did put her name to her work, she feared she was imposturous. Her symptom could be understood, more so than for the other two analysands I am presenting, in classical oedipal terms. The active claim of authorship on her part was for her unconsciously tantamount to a parricide, for she was deeply guilty about her high literacy level which her less educated mother had promoted self-sacrificially. Competent performance was also related to castration anxiety around "phallic exhibitionism," whereas stagy dramatic playing at being smart or smart-alecky did not unconsciously stimulate fantasied dangers of castration or loss of love. She yearned for a male analyst, one who would require nothing of her and from whom she could soak up the analytic mystique in safety. With me, she felt doomed to hard work and to analytic "stupidity." This woman was creative, inventive, a brilliant teacher of graduate students whom she assisted in accomplishing their writing aims. But she could only put pen to paper with her own ideas if "forced," symbolically raped into delivery by a strong male figure from whom she craved completion and mirroring acceptance and whom she could imagine as the true author. Mostly, she "played dumb" with one particular male colleague with whom she carried on an active correspondence, who was for her an alter-ego. His affirmation of each and every sentence was her condition for adequate performance. He served as an illusory phallus, an imaginary companion, a symbiotic parent, a narcissistically invested mirroring partner whom she actually provoked, like a ventriloquist, into putting her truly original thoughts and words on paper, as though they were his, not hers.

I saw her manifest craving for this man's validation in one respect as an expression of a kind of "twin fantasy"—that is, the wish for completion through primary union and identification—while in another respect it expressed her need for an illusory phallus. Analysis revealed this twinship or merger condition for performance to be a particular version of feeling imposturous; in psychic reality, she was unable to affirm writing under her own name alone, for when she did, she imagined it, for defensive reasons, to be fraudulent.

This pattern partook of a form of reverse imposture based on a *fear* of being imposturous, which in turn was based on a fragile sense of identity, a constellation described by Greenacre (1958b) in her discussion of the young Fritz Kreisler. Kreisler wrote his own compositions but claimed publicly that he had only edited them. He actually attributed the authorship to others who were older than he and already very famous composers.

This "reverse" imposture, or more accurately, reverse plagiarism, a form of imposture, served Miss B., as Greenacre believed it did the young Kreisler, in warding off the anticipated castration (or abandonment) for oedipal victory. In addition, she connected pleasurable moments in writing with forbidden masturbatory pleasure.

Miss B. feared to expose herself under her own name. The only way she could display her own creative power was to convince herself that someone other than she should be named to receive the title for it. For her own defensive reasons in the unresolved oedipal battle, being publicly acknowledged, even as an adult, as superseding the parental generation, had to be regarded as imposturous.

## PATIENT C.

A less obvious form of imposture is to be found in a male patient, a braggart, a poseur, a claimer of expertise when he is in fact only average in his cultural accomplishments and obviously dilettantish. It is noteworthy that he changed his name, a form of repudiating the hated and dangerous aspects of his early identification with his father. Some "two-timing" of his wife kept him on the razor's edge and chronically excited. The excitement kept him "alive" not only sexually, but in the deepest narcissistic core of his being. Mr. C. seemed to be repeating a period of his childhood and particularly adolescence where any form of forbidden sexuality had been met with unusually severe beatings from his father and had perverse encouragement from his mother.

His subjective sense of identity and his sadomasochistically exciting two-timing were so interconnected that he hid from me his plan for a long-awaited vacation, a move that for him represented a step toward maturity and resolution of a deep-seated oedipal conflict we had been working on. For years, he did not take stock of his financial assets, for even to have assets felt imposturous to him—a decided oedipal triumph, as was the vacation. But to hide his money, as though he had stolen it, like the chronically postponed vacation, kept him on the lifelong tightrope, a state he had great difficulty living without. All of this enhanced his subjective sense of reality. Like Abraham's (1925) patient, he seemed compelled to take revenge on those he saw as depending on him by disappointing them and masochistically submitting to their real or imagined rage and punishment. In the transference, this pattern also took the form of keeping critically important material out of some sessions in order to pretend he is the kind of good man he thinks I want him to be, only to slip, via one or another parapraxis, into looking like a liar, a thief, a fool. When his compulsive attempts to deceive the analyst were identified and analyzed, this intelligent man was compelled to present himself as a "ninny," a charlatan, caught in the act, even or especially if he had done *absolutely nothing wrong*. Like Abraham's patient, "an overpowering repetition compulsion forced him to make himself an outcast over and over again just when he had become everybody's favorite" (p. 300).

On a number of occasions he engaged in a stereotyped routine of self-aborted petty thievery, pilfering a small inexpensive article at a store when the proprietor's back was turned, then stealthily replacing the purloined article just in the nick of time while just barely stifling the impulse to duck, to shield himself from an anticipated blow, and to scream, "I didn't do it!" While this scenario represents in large measure the enactment of a childhood fantasy, it is also intricately woven in with fears and fantasies of imposture: To be in such an elegant store itself was not for the likes of him; his very presence there was a sham. Here is a prime illustration of *feeling* like an impostor.

For Mr. C. being a pretentious poseur reinforces his sense of worth even though those pretensions are generally not validated by others as estimable. His worthiness *is* validated by others in the areas where he is not a poseur but sometimes thinks he is (as in his daily work). When he is honestly self-sufficient, he *feels like* an impostor. In fact, his subjective sense of authenticity increased the more shifting and imitative his identification became, and the more inauthentic and imposturous he felt, the more, by objective standards, he possessed a consolidated, internalized identity. To be a man ("a mensch") threatens him, with its clear oedipal implications. In early life, Mr. C.'s mother was more responsive to the "teacher's pet" aspects of him, the false-sounding recitations of banalities he felt she adored, yet she also found contemptible. He, in turn, cultivated and exaggerated this form of wooing, which most people found obnoxious, which he unconsciously knew. One could not help but be impressed with the quality of self- and other mockery in his ostentatiously self-inflating pretentiousness, especially in his "two-timing." But inevitably this quality would attract a woman—never a man—who would share his mother's perverse, castrative ambitions for him. Such liaisons meshed with his characterological proclivities in a way that reinforced resistances to working through the masochistically and narcissistically tinged oedipal conflicts. In the analytic situation, I was frequently the judge, before whom he had to proclaim his innocence over and over, even when "not guilty." He acted as though I were a "lie detector," especially when he could not determine himself whether or not he was being deceptive.

### DISCUSSION

In all of the case examples I have presented, you will note a fear of seriousness, commitment, taking responsibility for personal action under one's own name—either literally or figuratively. The neurotic component in imposture, a component found in all three patients, along with prestructural pathology of the self, may, I believe, be greatly illuminated by Loewald's (1979) views on latent and unconscious meanings of autonomy and responsibility. He equates developing an authentic sense of identity and experience of oneself as agent— being nonimposturous—with unconsciously replacing the oedipal rival, that is, with parricide. I believe this is a most useful way of understanding the conflicts over imposture. The parricidal fantasy for these patients is especially strong and conflicts about authenticity would be one byproduct. Schafer's (1976) views about disclaimed action are of similar value here. Loewald's view of self-responsibility representing, unconsciously, at once a crime and restitution for a crime embodies a notion of compromise formation which seems particularly apt for the conflicts suffered by those who cannot act under their own name, either literally or in the many derivative ways that constitute imposture in the broader, more ubiquitous sense.

In expanding on the role of illusion in, among other things, defying the limits set by reality on the pleasure principle, I shall turn to a consideration of the functions of reality relations, reality testing, and illusion for impostors and the imposturous.

Mr. A. typifies the analysand who can tolerate the analysis, especially the transference, only if it is experienced as "not real." There is at the same time a fear of being unmasked as "only" illusory. The reliance on and the attempted analysis of omnipotent fantasy to the exclusion of reality testing was a problem for some of my patients who had been, previous to their analyses, in illusion-fostering treatments, with a premium on role playing, or where psychic reality and objective truths are not of paramount importance. These patients found any shifts toward a reality focus to be damaging to the treatment itself. In the previous, pseudoanalytic therapies, the unreal game quality of the role-playing exercises, the experiments, the participation in innovative modalities that sometimes bordered on charlatanism, all served the illusory function of safety and surely must have accommodated the character anomalies of the imposturous, who become threatened when the nonimposturous aspects of the personality are taken too seriously. These modalities did not require of the patients that they call into question their dependence on make-believe to sustain their subjective sense of integration.

A particular transference paradigm makes analysis of the imposturous extremely difficult. The feeling of inauthenticity these patients seek for their cohesive sense of self-identity is antithetical to the very work required in being an analysand. The search for truth, for authenticity, the reality of the transference despite its partial illusory quality, are extraordinarily difficult and often not tolerable for such individuals. Contrary to the aims of analysis, the kind of "as-if" person under consideration has a heightened sense of reality and integration when he or she succeeds in having the imposture believed by others. As Kohut (1971) points out, some patients quite literally seek out psychic structure in the *mirroring* responses of others. When the analyst's mirroring during the initial phases of treatment consolidates the false self, which includes the false *analytic self*, the imposturous analysand behaves even more for the mirror in the inauthentic way he or she has felt reflected. It is then extremely difficult to subject that very mirroring to analysis.

Any consideration of the impostor would be incomplete without some recognition of the importance of the audience to the impostor. It is to the end of enhancing the role of illusion in reality relations that the impostor seeks out the cooperating, colluding audience that may be hoodwinked.

Abraham was aware of the twofold importance of the audience toward whom the impostor consciously or unconsciously directs his performance: its susceptibility to being taken in by imposturousness, and its function in sustaining the impostor's sense of identity. He noted how the impostor-prisoner he studied had always been able to gain the confidence of people, such as prison guards, who would not normally be deceived, only to betray their confidences. The impostor wishes to dupe and to be engaging to everyone in order to gain narcissistic satisfaction from their unending admiration. Then he has to disappoint those who have come to love him in order to take revenge on them. To bring these happy conditions to a speedy end partakes of an overpowering repetition compulsion.

Greenacre (1958a) adds to the repetition compulsion perspective the interpersonal and social significance of a universal wish to be duped by a charmer, hunger to believe in the fraud. The secret of the impostor's appeal to others lies in the universal longing to return to that happy state of omnipotence that adults have to relinquish. Greenacre refers particularly to the role of the audience's confirming reaction in giving the impostor a realistic sense of the "false self" and a heightened subjective sense of integration and reality when he or she succeeds in being believed by others who are taking the place of the idealizing, mirroring mother. The lure of participating vicariously in another's illusions, particularly those of omnipotence that one has renounced oneself, accounts for the "fascinating effect of the narcissistic personality" (Olden, 1941). This effect tends toward the universal, as even those who consciously give up a belief in omnipotence unconsciously have preserved the belief and seek it in others.

There are, naturally, some more susceptible than others to serve as the impostor's audience, and we might grant that certain impostors are sensitive to who those individuals might be. Often the motive is not so much to deceive, but, as I have been emphasizing, to achieve validation for one's sense of identity, as imposturously based as that might be.

So, for the noncriminal impostor-"swindler," swindling of admiration, or narcissistic supplies, is a motive. So is revenge, as in what Finkelstein (1974) points out about his patient Teddy and his imposturous seduction of his audience—that he was identifying with his seductively aggressive mother. An important motive for Teddy, as for Mr. C., was to make fools of his believing audience and thus discharge some of the repressed hostility he felt toward his mother. Mr. C. thus made the representatives of his mother victims of his pathological "lying" or pretentiousness, thereby enjoying castrating the vain, controlling, seductive phallic mother with whom he identified. Here, imposture is seen as overdetermined, a symptom, a compromise formation. Apparently other impostors have had parents who showed the same vicarious satisfactions from their child's role playing, and the same easy acceptance of the child's lying, and the encouragement of imposture, with predictable interpersonal consequences (see also Gottdeiner, 1982).

McDougall (1980) adds the intrapsychic to the interpersonal perspective in her consideration of a particular version of a fantasized audience whom she calls the "anonymous spectator." She believes that such an "other" is a significant influence in the fantasies of those who suffer from perversions. It was essential for the patients she described that this anonymous other watch, but equally important that he be *duped*. In keeping with my observations of individuals with imposturous tendencies, many of whom do indeed suffer from perversions, the patients she described, like my patient, Mr. A., needed the anonymous spectator, a fantasy often projected onto the analyst, to be seen as serious; but the analysis itself must be turned into a game, with all its accomplishments false. In this man, illusions of both infantile omnipotence and incestuous possibilities could be maintained.

I should like to close with a quotation from Erikson (1959), whose famous work on identity includes an important reference to imposture as a severe identity crisis. It also presumes a *motivational* component in the "negative identity" of imposture, namely, a hateful repudiation of the most dangerous and yet the most real identifications with the parents at various critical stages of development over the life cycle. In discussing the case of a young American girl of Middle European descent who convincingly constructed for herself and others an imposturous identity as Scottish, Erikson said:

I went along with the story, implying that it had more inner truth than reality to it. The bit of reality was, as I surmised, the girl's attachment in early childhood to a woman neighbor who had come from the British Isles; the force behind the near-delusional "truth" was the paranoid form of a powerful death wish (latent in all severe identity crises) against her parents. The semi-deliberateness of the delusion was indicated when I finally asked the girl how she managed to marshal all the details of life in Scotland. "Bless you, sir," she said in a pleading Scottish brogue, "I needed a past" (pp. 130–131).

She could have added, "and a present, and a future, too."

## SUMMARY

This paper deals with imposturous tendencies as ubiquitous and heterogeneous. They may enter into neurotic conflict and compromise, and also reflect an ego function disturbance involving multiple, shifting identities and subsequent problems in the subjective sense of reality of the self and objects. Imposture in a person undergoing analysis is, however, not only a function of individual character and psychopathology; it is also a function of certain inevitable requirements of the analytic situation which constitute a "pull" for its emergence. Vulnerable individuals will respond to this pull in revealing ways. Three case summaries illustrate the spectrum of imposturous tendencies.

## REFERENCES

Erikson, E.H. (1959). *Identity and the Life Cycle. Psychology Issues Monograph 1*. New York: International Universities Press.
Fenichel, O. (1939). The economics of pseudologia fantastica In: *The Collected Papers of Otto Fenichel Second Series,* ed. H. Fenichel & D. Rapaport. New York: Norton, 1954 pp. 129–140.
———(1945). *The Psychoanalytic Theory of Neurosis.* New York: Norton.
Finkelstein, L. (1974). The impostor: aspects of his development. *Psychoanalytic Quarterly* 43:85–114.
http://www.pep-web.org/document.php?id=paq.043.0085a
Freud, S. (1921). Group psychology and the analysis of the ego. *S.E.* 18. http://www.pep-web.org/document.php?id=se.018.0000a
Gottdeiner, A. (1982). The impostor: an interpersonal point of view. *Contemporary Psychoanalysis* 18:438–454.
http://www.pep-web.org/document.php?id=cps.018.0438a

Greenacre, P. (1958a). The impostor. In: *Emotional Growth: Psychoanalytic Studies of the Gifted and a Great Variety of Other Individuals,* Vol. 1. New York: International Universities Press, 1971 pp. 93–112.

———(1958b). The relation of the impostor to the artist. In: *Emotional Growth. Psychoanalytic Studies of the Gifted and a Great Variety of Other Individuals,* Vol. 2. New York: International Universities Press, 1971 pp. 533–554. http://www.pep-web.org/document.php?id=psc.013.0521a

Jacobson, E. (1964). *The Self and the Object World.* New York: International Universities Press.

Krohn, A. (1974). Borderline "empathy" and differentiation of object representations: a contribution to the psychology of object relations. *International Journal of Psycho-analysis* 3:142–165.
http://www.pep-web.org/document.php?id=ijp.055.0483a

Kohut, H. (1971). *The Analysis of the Self.* New York: International Universities Press. http://www.pep-web.org/document.php?id=zbk.049.0001a

Loewald, H.W. (1979). The waning of the Oedipus complex, *Journal of the American Psychoanalytic Association* 27:751–755.
http://www.pep-web.org/document.php?id=apa.027.0751a

McDougall, J. (1980). *Plea for a Measure of Abnormality.* New York: International Universities Press.

Nin, A. (1959). *A Spy in the House of Love.* New York: Bantam, 1982

Olden, C. (1941). About the fascinating effect of the narcissistic personality. *American Imago* 2: 347–355.
http://www.pep-web.org/document.php?id=aim.002.0347a

Ross, N. (1967). The "as-if" concept. *Journal of the American Psychoanalytic Association* 15:59–82.
http://www.pep-web.org/document.php?id=apa.015.0059a.

Schafer, R. (1976). *A New Language for Psychoanalysis.* New Haven: Yale University Press.

Thomas, D.M. (1981). *The White Hotel.* New York: Viking.

# Chapter 12: The Plight of the Imposturous Candidate: Learning Amidst the Pressures and Pulls of Power in the Institute

[Gediman, H.K. (1986). The plight of the imposturous candidate: Learning among the pulls and pressures and pulls of power in the institute. *Psychoanalytic Inquiry*, 6: 67–91. Also in Gediman, H.K. and Lieberman, J.S. *The Many Faces of Deceit*. NJ and London: Jason Aronson.]

Psychoanalytic institutes are sometimes more or less "taken in" by candidates who suffer from imposturous tendencies of one degree or other. Supervisors, evaluators, and Progression Committee members may constitute, for the candidate with imposturous tendencies, the "audience" that inadvertently heightens imposturous ego trends. Supervisors may unwittingly reinforce a candidate's "false self" because they are susceptible, as are we all, to identifying unconsciously with the wished-for omnipotence that the imposturous candidate expresses so obviously and ego-syntonically (see Gediman, 1985). What has been identified, often after a long-delayed recognition, as a form of pathological imposture may indeed resemble, phenomenologically, the first steps of the normal process of learning to become a psychoanalyst. In the beginning, we are not surprised if we observe a certain degree of unintegrated role-playing. In addition, the neophyte trainee is encouraged to assume, in a controlled and limited sense, multiple identifications with both patients and supervisors in order to develop empathy and analytic wisdom.

We would hope that in the candidate, the multiple identifications are temporary and goal-related and not indicative of the poorly integrated identity of those suffering from serious imposturous tendencies, but unfortunately such is not always the case. It is particularly not the case when a candidate who *does* suffer from imposturous tendencies comes up against the real power of the institute. The power issue comes into all "tilted" relationships (Greenacre, 1954). And in supervision, we have two tilted relationships, tilted by virtue of the real power invested in the supervisor by both the candidate and the institute. Imposture, in those with significant imposturous tendencies, may be one pathological way of adapting to a real power structure when one's own survival in the institute is dependent on identification with the values, expectations, and roles of the "powers that be." In what follows I attempt to illustrate, at some length, how the distortions of the tilted reality made by an imposturous supervisee often take the form of shifting, mimicking, poorly integrated identifications.

Because a certain degree of role-playing in our candidates is expectable, and functions to serve adaptively to real power, we often miss noticing that it might also suggest a learning or characterological difficulty. When, for example, it persists too long, we should then suspect that we may be dealing with a form of imposture. Such imposturous candidates are often discovered, eventually, and often too belatedly, by supervisors who finally recognize that they have been "hoodwinked." When the supervisors report the difficulty, the candidate may be labeled character-disordered even "psychopathic," and dropped from the institute. Why does it often take so long to recognize such trainees, other than the reasons just offered regarding stages in the learning process? I suggest that perhaps we are too easily "conned" by our "clones." My use of slang is intended to emphasize the importance of the major idea it expresses: we embrace our ideal selves when we think we see them in our students, whose ideal is to be like us by "acting" like us.

And further, I would emphasize that in the ascending triadic systems (patient → analyst → supervisor), (analyst → supervisor → institution) involved in the supervisory situation, there is always the important issue of real power. In the "real" world (Freud's "material" reality) as opposed to the intrapsychic world (psychic reality) there is real power.

Real power *presses* on any candidate insofar as the supervisor evaluates his or her progress, or will have a say about eventual graduation, or even about referrals, promotions, and degree of success as an eventual peer. Howard Shevrin (in Wallerstein, 1981) explains how his "coolness" and exaggerated "objectivity" were open to criticism as modes of analyzing by a supervision study group. According to Shevrin, these modes were due in part to his conviction that the institute expected a cool, objective approach from him, and that his evaluation at the institute and his full-time job depended on it. It was thus only natural for him to emulate his supervisor. Shevrin is quick to point out how these factors of emulation and identification (which are typical of the imposturous) do not relate exclusively to resistance and intrapsychic conflict, but also to institutional role conflict and the theoretical commitments embodied as institutional policy. He goes so far as to conclude that the supervisor-teacher should not have real administrative power and believes that it is unresolved institutional role conflict, based on real social forces, that continues to alienate and infantilize some supervisees.

In my review of Wallerstein's book (Gediman, 1984), I noted how real institutional role conflict (material reality) may be drawn into the orbit of intrapsychic conflict and the transferences and countertransferences (psychic reality) of all three participants in triadic systems:

> This possibility would not preclude that institutionally related role conflicts may not have been operating autonomously (i.e., in and of themselves), relatively unrelated to significant unresolved intrapsychic conflict issues of any of the parties involved. One might then have hard evidence that a decision to be secretive [or imitative] in order to be politically wise may be more or less neurotically motivated at the same time as it is an adaptive decision simply to be politically wise (p. 423).

Because learning to be an analyst and learning to be an analysand lend themselves readily both to *feeling* imposturous and, in some instances, to being imposturous in troublesome ways, it is important to evaluate imposturous tendencies in the context of imitation on the way toward internalization as a normal developmental phase of childhood and of imitation as a normal phase in the learning process on the way toward integrated identifications with analysts.

When the way candidates report to the supervisor seems to be only simply mimicry, reminiscent of childlike role-modeling and patterning of prescribed technique; and when they undergo kaleidoscopic shifts in what is purportedly analytic behavior; and when, in reporting, they enact unreflectively what they believe to be their patient's personality, we do well to suspect character tendencies toward the "as-if" imposturous, above and beyond a normal learning phase. The candidates delude themselves, as it were, with their own impersonations of an idealized imago of the "the analyst." It is particularly the unreflective, imitative enactments, often in an attempt to adapt to perceived real power, that constitute the "pathological parallelisms" par excellence of imposture, phenomena that I include in my illustrative case of the supervisee, Dr. E.

Since imitation or role-playing would normally be a precursor of more consolidated identifications in learning to do analysis, it is only over time and, at that, often very difficult that we can draw the line between what is normal and phase-specific imitative learning, on the one hand, and the role-playing and imitativeness of pathological imposture, on the other. To aid in drawing that fine line, it will be necessary to show that the disturbances in the sense of reality of the imposturous individual are extreme variations of some important but specifically goal-directed requirements of doing and learning to do analysis. For example, trainees *must* make trial and flexible identifications. This requirement is more "dangerous" for some than for others, particularly for those whose fundamental reality sense is disturbed precisely by virtue of multiple, shifting identifications, the very process required in conducting analysis. A therapist *must* empathize with the patient, but if one's point of contact is exclusively either the patient's primitive unconscious, or more superficial peripheral aspects that may be imitated, important failures in empathy will ensue. The very fineness of this line makes it difficult to discern and may delay the detection of serious imposture for a long time, even in the very best of institute settings.

An additional problem is the ubiquity of a spectrum of transitory to stabilized "as-if" states which are to be found among the normal as well as among the characterologically imposturous. Since a consolidated professional identity does not develop until late in the learning process, early detection of imposture is understandably difficult except in blatantly psychopathic cases. One might pose the question this way: Will the supervisor's conveyance or demonstration of the analytic approach, which ideally should parallel or reflect the essence and not the superficial "technology" of the analytic process, lead to deep, consolidated, flexible identifications, or will it lead only to mere shallow imitations? The imposturous candidate is indeed an extreme example of failed identification with the analyst's fundamental way of working. Although it may be rare, a contaminating influence might be discerned in imitations of the training analyst who really could be conducting the candidate's analysis with significant inauthenticity. There are, however, many in-between situations where problems result from various real faulty teaching and learning situations, the consequences of which may not be too easy to distinguish from the characterological problems of the candidate. It is here that the designations made by the COPE Study Group of "dumb spots" (difficulties due to learning problems or inexperience) and "blind spots" (characterological or countertransference difficulties) as related to one another would be well considered.

It has been said that knowledge of the gospel is not sufficient to preach well and honestly. Fred Wolkenfeld (personal communication, 1983) suggested the gospel analogy for understanding an aspect of this important relationship between imitation and reportorial honesty in the learning process. To carry through the analogy of the clergy's use of the self in the transmission of religion and spirituality to the *use of the self* in the psychoanalytic learning situation, knowledge of the "analytic gospel" alone precludes, in part because of its tilt toward the real power pulls, the essential process of doing analysis. This unique requirement of our work has been called by many names: internalizations, identifications, transformations of the self into the cohesive analytic self, or the development of the candidate's potential as an analyzing instrument. A student's attempt to present to a supervisor the gospel truth of his or her sessions with a patient, even though really encouraged by some supervisors, could be fundamentally "dishonest" — as will be seen in the illustrative case of Dr. E.

Another real situation exerting a powerful pull for imposture, and found in all institutes, relates to the candidates' being required to work with several supervisors who work differently from one another. While such differences in ways of working are to be found in even the most homogeneous of training settings, they would be particularly marked in institutes that offer training in more than one theoretical orientation and that encourage "interdisciplinary" crossing back and forth. The shifting multiple vantage points and work-ego identities required to "go with" multiple ways also require adroit, flexible shifting which could potentiate any latent, imposturous tendencies of fluidity and facileness in candidates predisposed in that direction.

Yet another otherwise very valuable, indeed essential, characteristic of the training process that is also conducive to imposture among the vulnerable is to be found in rapport, engagement, and mutual give-and-take between supervisor and candidate. The supervisor's authentic positive input and feedback and validation sustains, heightens, and enhances the subjective sense of integrity and cohesiveness of all supervisees, perhaps even more so in the case of the imposturous than of the nonimposturous. Thus, the requisite positive climate may hold serious masking potential for imposture. Greenacre (1958a, 1958b) noted that the "false" self becomes reflected back, magnified, and strengthened with such mirroring affirmation. So, supervisory situations in which there is good rapport, comfort, and engagement may benefit the self-experience and learning experience of the average-expectable candidate in average-expectable ways, but could have the unfortunate effect of impeding the detection of possible imposturousness for a long time.

Greenacre's (1958b) published thoughts on the connection between the artist and the impostor have alerted us to the reverse phenomenon, that is, *feeling* and *fearing* that we are imposturous when we are not. I think it is common that analysts in training, like the artists to whom Greenacre refers, feel and fear that they are impostors, especially at the beginning of their careers. The fact that various "selves," or more exactly, variations on one "self," are required for analytic work may lead to some of the same fears. That is, the analyst and the artist make changes in self-presentation and self-organization, specific and limited to doing analysis or to creative aesthetic work, respectively. Among the imposturous, these limits do not hold.

## ILLUSTRATIVE CASE MATERIAL[16]

For reasons of accessibility and confidentiality, I am limiting my case illustration to a trainee in psychoanalytic psychotherapy who was not and never has, to my knowledge, become a candidate at a psychoanalytic institute. I subscribe to the idea that there are continuities between the process of psychoanalytic therapy and that of psychoanalysis proper, as well as their supervisees, and so my data should suffice.

The illustrative material will place particular emphasis on the aforementioned disturbances in the sense of reality and how these disturbances differ from average-expectable, phase-acceptable learning processes. I have prepared one reasonably lengthy illustration, Dr. E., to exemplify the problem of hypertrophied and limited empathy and other disturbances in the sense of reality. The material will also include a consideration of imposture as typifying, par excellence, a pathological parallelism: i.e., where problems with multiple, shifting identifications leading to a deficient understanding of the treatment process as reflected in work with the patient is repeated or enacted in parallel fashion in supervision. Such a pathological parallelism, when found in a trainee with the vulnerabilities under scrutiny here must, I believe, be regarded in part as a result of the experience of powerlessness and fragility which an individual with imposturous tendencies would inevitably feel in a training institute.

This kind of enactment is but one form of parallel process, to be discussed in great detail in Chapter 14 of this book is defined (Gediman & Wolkenfeld, 1980; Wolkenfeld, 1984) as a multidirectional representational system in which major psychic events, including complex behavioral patterns, affects, and conflicts, occurring in one dyadic situation — analysis or supervision — are repeated in the other. A nonpathological parallelism, then, could also reflect multiple, shifting identifications, but where they are nonproblematic and remain within the limits of the requirements of doing analytic work. In keeping with my main thesis, then, issues of powerlessness and fragility would not emerge as importantly in these "average-expectable" parallelisms as they do

---

16 The data presented here are not psychoanalytic. That is, they derive from process notes of a supervisory and not a psychoanalytic or psychotherapeutic relationship. Therefore, my references regarding pathology, including those implying fragmented identifications and difficulty in distinguishing self from object and object from object, may not be as reliable as those deriving from the psychoanalytic situation. They should nonetheless serve.

in the pathological parallelisms found among trainees, like Dr. E., who suffer from significant imposturous tendencies.

## SUPERVISEE E.

Although my case material focuses manifestly on illustrating problems with imposture, it would be well to keep in mind, throughout, the corollary issue of power-impact, which is always suggested and always a significant though sometimes latent motivating force underlying Dr. E.'s difficulties in supervision. The supervisor is, after all, not simply a teacher, but an evaluator and a critically determining influence on the student's future, as well. Dr. E. is not representative of the more average-expectable degrees of imposture, but stands as a conglomerate of fairly extreme imposturous tendencies. This tilted weighting should be heuristically valuable for comparison with the average-expectable degree of "as-if-ness" which is inherent in the early stages of the psychoanalytic learning process.

Dr. E. illustrates hypertrophied "empathy-like" responses (see Khron, 1974) in the trainee in psychoanalytic psychotherapy, as well as prototypically imposturous trends related to difficulties in establishing a center of gravity or orientation. Dr. E. was notable as a supervisee compliant to the letter with all that her supervisor asked of her, but she had great difficulty in grasping the spirit of the enterprise. She had originally taken verbatim notes and read them during supervisory sessions. The resulting material had a lifeless, distant, isolated quality. As a corrective and in an attempt to get her to loosen up, I suggested she take minimal process notes in the hope that she could then focus more on engaging with me as supervisor. She followed that suggestion by producing masses of noncohesive material that she "extemporaneously" reported. When I was troubled enough to comment to her about the inauthentic sound of the material presented this way, she revealed that she had still taken six or seven pages of verbatim notes, as lengthy as ever, but since I did not want her to read them in the sessions, she had read them over assiduously in advance of our supervisory session and had been conscientiously repeating them from memory. She revealed this with no apparent insight into the absurdity of her actions. By committing her verbatim notes to memory and then reporting what she remembered, she was acting "as if" she were spontaneous, while in fact she was more stimulus-bound than ever. Whatever characterological problems contributed to this style, an intense anxiety to placate the "powers that be" was also operative.

Yet, despite this "blind" and/or "dumb" spot, she seemed to catch on extraordinarily quickly to the drift of my questions and hunches concerning the patient, and she confirmed all too readily any psychodynamic hunches that she discerned lay behind my questions. She never, however, spontaneously introduced any hunches of her own. The problem that aroused my suspicions was that she started to report as verbatim material something that immediately confirmed my speculative hypothesis, as though it had naturally followed at just that point in the memorized notes of the session at which I had intervened. She appeared to finish my very sentences as soon as I introduced the thought that started them. She acquired a center of gravity, with its excessive attention to my expectations, and thus an excess of misdirected and superficial "empathy," toward what she thought I was asking for. It was as though I represented a doctrine to which she must adhere, unselectively, in order to fulfill her requirement.

I should like to expand here on the shifty way this prototypically imposturous supervisee had of reporting allegedly verbatim material, reminiscent of certain "borderline" or hysterical patients who lapse into "pseudologia fantastica" when they become involved in conveying their experience to another. Dr. E. repeatedly "replayed" vividly a conversation that had taken place between her patient, a man, and a friend of his. It was though she had been where that conversation had taken place and never in the place — her consulting room — where the patient had reported the conversation to her. That is, she and the interaction between herself and her own patient, and her emotional-cognitive responses to him, were simply not present in the material she reported to me. Her point of orientation, or center of gravity, seemed now to be located too "empathically" where the original extra-analytic event took place. She reproduced the latter with such uncannily sounding "accuracy" that I began to suspect it could not be entirely true except in her imagination.

When such a supervisee enacts what a patient was saying about a friend or gives an apparently nearly verbatim account of what a friend told a patient, or what a patient told a friend, *but from the friend's point of view,* there is too much positioning "inside the friend's head." This positioning leaves out entirely what might have been happening in the therapy or analytic session itself with respect to the way the patient was talking, associating, relating, and the way the supervisee as analytic therapist was listening and engaged in interaction with the patient.

Such a supervisee surely appears to be behaving in a psychopathic manner, but is this really so? Like all supervisees, Dr. E. was under real pressure to produce what was expected of her in order to fulfill her training requirements. But unlike all, she might be described as "shifty," not in the more psychopathic sense of being evasive or of producing "fudged" and phony psychotherapeutic data, but as related to nonsolidity and nonrootedness with respect to intrapsychic and interpersonal centers of gravity and boundaries. The way she conveyed no contact with what transpired between her patient and herself was consistent with the manner that her contact with me appeared limited to reading or presenting verbatim notes from memory. When I called the problem to her attention, she said that she was doing the kind of "experiential reporting" she had been taught by former supervisors. Here, too, it sounded to me as though she were imitating what she thought experiential reporting should be without at all understanding its spirit or purpose in the teaching and learning of psychotherapy. The plaguing problem was at least two-fold: *whose* experience was being reported and *what kind* of notes were these where the patient's extra-analytic interactions with significant others were reported with such suspiciously vivid detail?

To check out my hunch, which had become a conviction, that I was dealing with an "as-if" trainee with significant imposturous tendencies, I decided on a new teaching strategy of withholding "mirroring" and feedback. Since the more pathological hypertrophied "empathic" attunement is highly selective in areas relevant to narcissistic gratifications, the fluency of its expression is prone to slippage into arbitrary fluidity once the "other" does not offer enough cues as to how well the supervisee is doing or as to what is "expected." And what is expected may have real consequences for survival in the institute, reinforcing preexisting imposturous tendencies. If supervisory mirroring, or the gleam in the supervisor's eye, is withheld, if the supervisor is "laid back," opaque, refraining from engaging in mutual but potentially "cuing-in" exchanges, the imposturous supervisee may lapse from "as-if" reporting of sessions into communications, the meaning of which are difficult to track; the supervisee could even lapse into extremely disjointed and confused reporting. I decided to remain, to a degree exceedingly greater than would be found in my characteristic supervisory style, more silent, "laid back," nonengaging, opaque, passive.

When I actually remained silent for an entire session, I could hardly make head or tail or the material Dr. E. was reporting. There was nothing that I could empathize with as authentic, that is, as something that one would reasonably expect to transpire between an analytic therapist and patient. Little held together cohesively, consistently, or systematically in the manner of any psychoanalytic reporting or process with which I was familiar, or which would be recognized as such, consensually, by other analysts. It became apparent that her role-playing at what she believed was expected of her became all the more hollow, false, inauthentic, when I no longer provided the scaffolding, structure, schemata, and when I was no longer the colluding audience. When I confronted my supervisee with this difficulty, I sensed bewilderment, stress, a slight degree of muted anger, perhaps. Now there was "trouble in paradise," in contrast to the previous apparent harmony, which looked retrospectively like "sham" interaction and sham engaging rapport. At most, she could sound like a child imitating what she thought she should sound like in the role of an adult analyst delivering an "objective" interpretation. Here is a prime example of the sense of powerlessness among the nontalented — imposturous or otherwise.

But don't we expect role-playing and imitation in the early stages of psychoanalytic education for most of our trainees, including the very talented? It is only when this imitative phase persists long beyond the beginning that we may be dealing with serious pathology and not simply with a normal phase in the learning process. After all, it was not until well into our work that I realized that role-playing seemed to be mostly all that Dr. E. could do. She was not progressing toward a consolidated identity as an analytic therapist, and, unconsciously, she must have sensed her inner powerlessness to do so. Nonetheless, I persisted, without yet realizing that my very persistence was an exercise of real power which only increased her bewilderment and deep anxieties.

Other interesting things began to happen with Dr. E. once I decided, as a "corrective," to be more opaque, and once I had confronted her with her problem in locating a center of gravity in her experiential reporting. We no longer, of course, engaged in the pseudomutuality and "give-and-take" that had felt so rewarding to me for approximately a year. I ceased mirroring her responses, which were informed by a vast but superficial and eclectic knowledge of many points of view to which she had been exposed but where her breadth of knowledge surely exceeded her depth of grasp. As I began to be convinced of the lack of depth in her grasp of the knowledge she was vainly trying to assimilate, I also had an increasingly difficult time in "getting a reading" on her patient. This difficulty was due not only to my increased awareness of her difficulties and my consequent reserve at inadvertently "cuing" her in, but also to her increasingly evident lapses into fragmented, disconnected, now more obviously "inauthentic" reporting. I confronted her with this difficulty, suggesting once again that she stop trying to take or to memorize any detailed process notes, but to come in simply with an outline that she could fill in from memory. I also explicitly told her that I would just listen for a while for I was concerned that our interactions themselves were biasing her mode of reporting.

She then came with no notes at all. She made obvious gestures at searching diligently in the back of her memory for what had happened in the sessions. She engaged in "as-if" reporting, which, without my "cues," sounded to me very incoherent and unfollowable, confirming my hunch about the conditions under which hypertrophied but selective empathy-like responsiveness *fails*. She, too, noticed her increasing incoherence and actually proposed that she was having difficulties in empathizing and therefore in reporting accurately to me because her *patient* was a slippery "as-if" personality and that was a very difficult thing for her to convey accurately in supervisory sessions!

Now, was this student an *impostor*? She did not literally pretend under cover of someone else's name. But she did something very much like that. She pretended under cover of someone else's style and role. She was masquerading herself, psychologically speaking, in the name of a version of psychoanalytic psychotherapist which was not well internalized, but which corresponded to her reading of the expectations and pressures of the training institution.

The question now facing us is, how was this masquerader similar to and how did she differ from *any* student in the beginning phases of learning, phases which should lead to the optimal use of oneself as an analyzing instrument. Even if we accept Deutsch's (1955) view that imposturous tendencies may be found in all human beings, and that the average expectable manifestly differs only in degree from the pathologically imposturous, it is still essential to capture the very nature, the quality of that difference, in order to distinguish the seriously pathological from the psychopathology of everyday life.

First, Dr. E.'s mode of reporting was atypical. Her manner of trying to convey experiential data could be regarded as imposturous, in the artifice of both her straining for phenomenological accuracy and the obvious inauthenticity in her way of producing memorized "process notes." She was also imposturous in her technique. She fancied herself as "making interpretations" whenever she made a verbal statement of any kind to her patient. Asked why she had called a particular intervention an interpretation, she became imposturous at theorizing: "It was an interpretation because it dealt with the unconscious." Now, none of this may look like a gross deviation, for we might expect such loose approximations from any beginner, particularly a very anxious one. But in context she was glib enough to strongly suggest imposture. She knew just enough about experiential reporting; she knew just enough about psychoanalytic theories. The "give-away" was that she knew just enough about *many* theories, some of which were intrinsically incompatible with or contradictory to each other, but whose potentially vexing ambiguities did not seem to raise any question for her as they would for most thoughtful students. She could shift easily from one to another frame of reference, embracing all, and was suspiciously untroubled by theoretical incompatibilities. This propensity for an easy eclecticism embodied more anarchy than flexibility, and it suggested a "miscarrying" of the requisite personal flexibility and multiple viewpoints essential for doing analytic work. She knew just enough about technique, but it did not seem to matter to her if she functioned correctly or incorrectly. And she showed none of the expectable anxiety of a beginner making mistakes. She thought she was doing what she was supposed to do.

Dr. E., then, is not like our more usual nonimposturous beginners for whom distinctions matter and who learn about them either receptively or by actively questioning what they are doing and why, who challenge the supervisor, who don't catch on right away, and who call *themselves* into question. The better integrated neophytes are not so fearful to question, within acceptable limits, the power of authority, and do so by using their own powers of intelligence and discrimination. Rather, Dr. E. unquestioningly accepted everything as though to get on and over with a charade required for completion of training requirements. The pervasiveness of her shiftiness, the blatantly "false" quality of her presentation once I abandoned my encouraging stance in favor of a truly opaque one, revealed a fundamental imposturousness with disturbances in the sense of reality of the self and the world.

I take the liberty at this point of interrupting my case illustration to elaborate two issues. I turn here to the first, that of "what really happened in the analytic hour," which will be subsumed under the topic of "daydreams in common." Although, as I said earlier, my case illustration comes from the supervision of psychoanalytic psychotherapy and not psychoanalysis proper, I am here substituting the terms, analyst, analytic candidate, and analysand, for I believe my conclusions from the case material can be generalized to the supervision of the analytic situation proper.

## DAYDREAMS IN COMMON

"What really happened in the analytic hour" must be reconstructed from more or less ambiguous reports from the analyst or the analyst-in-training (we are talking of the supervisory situation now). The nature of psychic reality and of "material reality" of "objective truth value" and, in particular, of how knowable one person's psychic reality is to another person are central to the problem of imposture. These issues are also central to all teaching and learning of psychoanalysis, but the particular character problems of Dr. E. illustrate the importance of psychic reality in a unique way. The supervisor never really knows what actually transpired, but has "daydreams in common" (Freud, 1907; Arlow, 1969a, b) with the patient and the therapist in a way that holds together according to certain more or less specifiable criteria. Sometimes we can only imagine or fantasize what happens. The built-in aesthetic ambiguity of our work situation lends itself so easily to crossing the line between the imaginative and empathic and the fantastic, and — this is an emphasis I believe to be new — crossing the line into the imposturous. Here we are touching on *psychic reality* which is recognizable and apprehendable, provided that the one who is attempting to convey it has access to it, as the imposturous reporter does not. Dr. E., instead, focused on a particular version of "objective reality" to cover her lack of comprehension of the other, or psychic, reality. However, Dr. E.'s efforts at presenting a so-called phenomenological reality did not even meet the criteria of "material reality" or "objective truth value." That is, her various accounts of her patient's sessions were inconsistent, discontinuous, and over-simplified representations of other people which she could not piece into analytically meaningful patterns. Not only did Dr. E.'s reports not hang together in a psychoanalytically meaningful way; they defied conventional common sense and conventions of coherence. And most important, there was little evidence for their correspondence to anything recognizable that one usually expects to be going on in the analytic situation, mainly because Dr. E.'s process reporting did not contain any graspable account of that situation.

We would expect to detect the presence of material which one expects to hear if an analysis is indeed being conducted, assuming a reasonably well-selected patient: evidence of infantile sexuality and aggression; indications of recognizable defense measures; manifestations of anxiety, shame, guilt, depression; symbolic and other representations of significant body zones and modes; accounts of self-feeling and self-esteem; accounts of separateness and oneness, and a number of other themes. If we never hear these motifs in a sustained, coherent way in the candidate's report, we may safely assume that he or she has not grasped them or picked them up and helped the patient to develop them. And if the candidate still presents process notes as though he or she were unquestionably doing analysis, we must question the authenticity of the work, just as we do when criteria of "objective truth value" are not met. What Dr. E. was doing authentically was the very best that she could, but in a fundamentally powerless way, to conform to what she believed the formally institutionalized power structure expected of her.

I resume the case of Dr. E. by way of a second digression, this time on the relevance of daydreams in common to certain *"pathological parallelisms"* found among the imposturous.

## PATHOLOGICAL PARALLELISMS IN IMPOSTURE[17]

One of the reasons that even a mild degree of imposture in reporting yields pathological parallelisms par excellence is that the requirements of doing analysis and the criteria for imposture, despite their significant and critical *differences*, overlap sufficiently as to encourage the phenomenon to emerge. This follows the line of thinking adopted by Gediman and Wolkenfeld (1980), according to which the structural and dynamic similarities between psychoanalysis (or psychoanalytic psychotherapy) and supervision guarantee the emergence of parallelisms in the supervisory or learning situation. Those similarities, which I now see as relevant to the issue of imposture, center on the requirement of multiple empathic identificatory processes and on the use of the self as an "analyzing instrument."

The disturbances in the sense of reality of the self which are the hallmark signs of imposture all involve some changes in self-organization and self-presentation. And so does being an analyst involve such changes. However, a most important qualification should be underscored in articulating the differences between imposture and learning to be an analyst: The analyst makes changes in self-organization and self-presentation *specific* to the immediate problems of the work and of the analytic situation. The changes in self-organization made by the imposturous supervisee and which lead to the pathological parallelisms are general and not subject to consciously deliberate choice and situational requirements. That empathy, multiple shifting identifications, and multiple "selves" are required for both analytic work and for imposture does not mean that the important differences should be ignored, for they are central to an understanding and possible remediation of the pathological parallelism.

I now return to Dr. E. to show how a pathological parallel process emerged and was handled. I left off my presentation with the significant development when Dr. E. had begun to describe her *patient* in the very terms I would have used to describe *her*, a process I would label a "pathological parallelism." She told me how her patient was one of those very slippery people whose identifications were so shallow and fluid that it was very difficult for her to grasp his experience and report it to me. She explained to me that *his* identifications

---

17 Although parallel process is discussed in detail, explanations of the process are to be found in Chapter 14 of this book.

were very unintegrated, and he must be an "as-if" personality. She confessed that when she was relatively quiet, she had trouble following the drift of what he was saying. Now, for the first time, she began to report about problematic interactions between her and her patient, following my addressing similar problems in the supervisory interaction. She thought the patient's slipperiness must account for *my* expressed difficulty in following the drift of her material when I decided to just listen and not cue her in. All told, she acted like someone powerlessly cornered and flailing at making use of poorly understood notions that I, in her view, was imposing on her. That was her way of surviving. But I did not see that aspect of her difficulties at the time of my work with her, for the issue of imposture was then more manifestly palpable for me than that of power.

Another interesting thing occurred around the time that I was checking out my hunches by refraining from cuing in my supervisee to what I was thinking. Dr. E. reported that her patient had begun to scrutinize her face and her voice for signs of the "correctness" of his own interpretations of his dreams and other material, and for the moral correctness, of certain of his behaviors that he was reporting. She believed that her patient saw her as fluidly shifting her views of him, and that is why, she said, he needed to scrutinize her so carefully. He then, she asserted, began to comply with one after the other of these shifting projected identifications, which he attributed as coming from her.

In this uncanny parallelism, Dr. E.'s description of her patient was suspiciously close to how I perceived her with me. Most important, this reported view of her patient's dynamics *followed* my attempt to convey to her how she was intent on demonstrating to me her version of varied and ever-changing theoretical and technical virtuosity because she expected that I wished to see her do that. The problem was that her attempts to comply resulted in the looseness and fluidity that I have already described. No doubt we both wished to understand: I her work and she her patient. The parallel pressure to know, required for daydreams in common to yield a meaningful discourse in a supervisory context, can also yield the pathological or "derailed" parallelism of the instance described. I say derailed because the supervisee presented her patient as I saw her, the supervisee, but without consciously realizing that she was doing that. It was as though she understood much, unconsciously, but could not, for reasons relevant to the fragmented identity problems of the imposturous, regard herself as the object of what she understood—projecting, instead, onto her patient. The pathological parallelism just described reflects a "projective identification": the supervisee describes the patient in terms that actually describe herself. Such a parallelism constitutes an extreme and particular example of parallel process as defined earlier—the repetition in one dyadic situation, psychotherapy or supervision, of psychic events occurring in the other. It was in observing this parallelism involving projective identification that it occurred to me that the *fluidity of perspective and the multiple viewpoints required in doing analysis and in learning to do it* might provide the situational "pull" for the emergence of the supervisee's "as-if" behavior, shared by or at least projected onto her patient as well.

In a later supervisory session—and this is to illustrate a different but somewhat related point regarding parallelisms—I shared with Dr. E. a speculative hunch that her patient favored the circumventions of ordinary obstacles to his goals and gratifications, and that this proclivity was reflected in his continual use of the "side entrance" metaphor in dreams and fantasies. I conjectured that this metaphor reflected his concerns with his multiple "successful" oedipal circumventions. The patient, for example, was having an affair with his supervisor, a married, somewhat older woman, in his on-the-job training placement. He also believed that when his psychotherapy was terminated he would be able to have a love affair with the therapist. In our next supervisory session, Dr. E. rather glibly reported to me that her patient *told her* how he notices that he uses "side entrance" metaphors to express how he circumvents ordinary obstacles. He said this metaphor reflected how he believed he could have possessed his mother and now believed he could possess the therapist. I asked Dr. E. how she thought her patient's understanding of this dynamic formulation evolved in the treatment situation. I carefully avoided any reference to the fact that the patient's apparent discovery was couched in the very terms that I myself had explicitly offered speculatively in our previous supervisory session. Dr. E. became flustered and, as usual, seemed unable to provide any pertinent sequential data. Then, as though she had empathically caught on to what was on my mind, she reversed what she had presented in her initial version and implied that *she* had interpreted it to *him* in a previous session but she forgot which one, and she had neglected to report that fact to me. You see once more how difficult it was to ascertain this supervisee's center of gravity or whose experience she was reporting. She seemed utterly confused herself and showed no sign of recollecting any actual event in which either she or her patient had "interpreted" what was *my* speculative hunch.

In a much later session, Dr. E. said she found her patient engaged in a "psychological lie." While there may be many reasons for her reporting this, in context it appears as yet another pathological parallelism. Although I have never shared with her my hunches about her artifice in reporting, her account was in keeping with her characteristic empathic-like sensitivity in selected areas, and suggested that she may have divined my suspicions, unconsciously. Specifically, the lie, or actually distortion, to which she referred had to do with her patient's reporting to her that upon completing one phase of his on-the-job training, his supervisor had seduced him sexually, when it seemed in fact to Dr. E. that it was the other way around.

She then went on to describe her patient as having borderline boundary problems. She also wondered how it was possible for a patient with such serious pathology to get A-ratings for job performance and even be offered promotions, and concluded that it must have been due to a joking connection the patient himself had made previously with what he called his many A's for "ambition and adulterous achievement." Dr. E. felt certain that anyone who prevaricated so much must have job-training problems as well.

Here was more evidence of the pathological parallelism. Something I had noted in Dr. E. as a serious characterological problem area and of which she was apparently unaware in herself (a "blind spot") and which also *constituted a learning problem for her* (a "dumb spot") emerged in her report as a parallel difficulty in her patient, the implications of which she only partially understood.

It is precisely this sort of parallelism that constitutes the prototypical example of the kind of parallel impasse requiring a certain kind of supervisory intervention. It is what Gediman and Wolkenfeld (1980) have referred to as the "by-pass." In our recent personal communications, Wolkenfeld (1984) and I have formulated the by-pass as that supervisory intervention whereby the supervisor addresses the problem indirectly, in a way analogous to an analyst offering a "deflected transference" interpretation: it is discussed as a problem for the patient as it is manifest only in extra-analytic situations and not in the here-and-now analytic interaction. The supervisory by-pass, then, avoids the here-and-now supervisory interaction and focuses only on parallel dynamic problems for the patient alone, in the hope of mitigating some "real power" influences.

Yet the emergence of such a parallelism can be read as a sign that the supervisee may know unconsciously that he or she shared the patient's problem and would like the benefit of the supervisor's wisdom. Tact, too, would dictate that remarks regarding, in this instance, imposture, boundary confusion, and identity disturbance be addressed toward the extrasupervisory sphere or to the patient's obvious difficulties. When less obvious or delicate than this supervisee's proclivity toward introjection and projection, or when *more* is really at stake, such as a candidate's suitability to be an analyst, the parallelism phenomenon could be discussed more explicitly. In the case of Dr. E., it was sufficient, at first, to indicate that her difficulties in dealing with patients' problems in this area might be something she would want to discuss in her personal analysis.

With these principles in mind, I asked Dr. E whether her patient truly had engaged in a "lie," suggesting instead that he was genuinely confused as to whether he had been led on by a woman in a position of authority, real power, if you will, or whether he himself was the more seductive one. I suggested that such confusion probably emerged in the transference as well, taking the form of his having a conviction that his therapist was encouraging him to believe in the possibility of a consummated love affair once he was "graduated" upon termination. With respect to her bewilderment about his getting A's and being accepted for advanced career training, I dealt with this additional parallelism also by by-passing any explicit reference to the supervisee's similar concerns (or concerns I imagined she might be having) about my evaluating her work so that she could advance professionally, limiting my remarks to my understanding of the patient only. I reminded her that her patient was working in a very rarefied, esoteric area of specialization, where such boundary slippage not only could go undetected but could be encouraged and rewarded. It was also clear to me from many things she had said that the patient was quite tuned in to issues of innocence and corruptibility in others and that he exercised considerable charm with people for whom these were problems. I assumed that, at least unconsciously, she "heard" my references as being relevant to herself as well.

In our final supervision sessions, a parallelism emerged which I handled not by a "by-pass," or by addressing its significance for the patient alone, but by discussing it directly and explicitly as a parallelism with the supervisee. *Lest we forget the supervisor's very real contribution to parallel process, (see Chapter 14)* it should be noted that at that time I was also mulling over whether *my* "by-pass technique" to circumvent ordinary supervisory obstacles paralleled the patient's "side entrance" metaphor to circumvent oedipal obstacles. The patient had been talking about working for the coming year in a city far enough away to preclude his continuing treatment with Dr. E., for pragmatic reasons having to do with somewhat reduced finances and the commonplace occurrence in his field of frequent geographical relocations. This Dr. E. learned of "*suddenly*," although I had sensed it coming ever since she casually remarked that she had begun to discuss these peripatetic aspects of his work situation. At that time I had asked Dr. E. when she intended to confront her patient with the obvious incompatibility between continuing analytic therapy with her and pursuing his career elsewhere, as well as his wishfully based belief that such a course of action would at last make possible a love affair between himself and his therapist.

It became evident that Dr. E. never made or even considered making such a confrontation. In fact, the patient strove to maintain his illusion of a romance throughout the treatment and never benefited from any proper therapeutic attempts to analyze that fantasy and illusion within the transference. That Dr. E. was concerned, at least unconsciously, that she might have seduced me into believing she could do analysis eventually and have a collegial peer relationship with me is a highly significant related parallelism. It is also noteworthy that she had decided to terminate supervision for pragmatic reasons: her work evaluations were open to question; she was moving to a geographically less accessible area; and she had embarked upon certain costly life changes, all of which curtailed her pursuit of psychotherapy training. So, I identified that parallelism directly and as a parallelism. I pointed out that it seemed of great significance that she, in a manner paralleling her patient's vagueness about terminating treatment, had drifted into a course of action involving likely termination of formal training, supervision, and her personal analysis, and for pragmatic reasons, just like her patient, and at an inopportune time, for she could surely benefit from much more explicit discussion in supervision and other spheres of her training before deciding whether or not she could call herself an analytic therapist. (She was planning to practice privately.)

It was indeed unfortunate that Dr. E.'s own motivations and possible wishes to repudiate them had apparently interfered with the way she conducted the therapy, and they prevented her from dealing with her patient's critical negative transference resistance. I believe that my approach conveyed the fact that I was not seduced by *her* "psychological lie" that she was doing analytic therapy, but I do not know to what extent she registered and assimilated what I had conveyed. I also do not know if there would have been a different outcome had I handled the initial parallelism—her describing her patient as an "as-if" personality caught in a psychological lie—directly and not via the "by-pass operation." Had I talked of the parallelism of the patient's "A" for ambitious but imposturous success in his field, and Dr. E.'s fantasied "A" for analytic therapy, I might have been decidedly correct as to a dynamic interpretation but incorrect with respect to supervisory dosage, timing, and tact. Imposture, like the teaching and learning of psychoanalysis and psychoanalytic psychotherapy, indeed poses difficult problems for therapist or analyst and supervisor alike, particularly in the light of the real power that the supervisor has to influence the future course of the supervisee's life as an analyst or analytic psychotherapist.

## REFERENCES

Arlow, J. (1969a). Unconscious fantasy and disturbances of conscious experience. *Psychoanalytic Quarterly* 38:1–27.
http://www.pep-web.org/document.php?id=paq.038.0001a
———(1969b). Fantasy, memory, and reality testing. *Psychoanalytic Quarterly*
38: 28–51. http://www.pep-web.org/document.php?id=paq.038.0028a
Deutsch, H. (1955). The impostor: Contribution to ego psychology of a type
of psychopath. In: *Neuroses and Character Types*. New York: International
Universities Press, 1965, pp. 319–338.
http://www.pep-web.org/document.php?id=paq.024.0483a
Freud, S. (1907). Creative writers and daydreaming. *Standard Edition* 9. http://
www.pep-web.org/document.php?id=se.009.0000a
Gediman, H.K. (1984). Review of Becoming a Psychoanalyst, ed. R. S.
Wallerstein. In *Review of Psychoanalytic Books*, 2:415–428.
——— (1985). Imposture, inauthenticity, and feeling fraudulent. *Journal of
the American Psychoanalytic Association*, 33: 911–935.
http://www.pep-web.org/document.php?id=apa.033.0911a
——— & Wolkenfeld, F. (1980). The parallelism phenomenon in psychoanalysis and supervision: Its reconsideration as a triadic system. *Psychoanalytic
Quarterly* 49:234–255.
http://www.pep-web.org/document.php?id=paq.049.0234a
Greenacre, P. (1954). The role of transference: Practical considerations in
relation to psychoanalytic therapy. In *Emotional Growth: Psychoanalytic
Studies of the Gifted and a Great Variety of Other Individuals*. New York:
International Universities Press, 1971, pp. 627–640.
http://www.pep-web.org/document.php?id=apa.002.0671a
——— (1958a). The impostor. In *Emotional Growth: Psychoanalytic
Studies of the Gifted and a Great Variety of Other Individuals*. New York:
International Universities Press, 1971, pp. 93–112.
——— (1958b). The relation of the impostor to the artist. In *Emotional
Growth: Psychoanalytic Studies of the Gifted and a Great Variety of Other
Individuals*. New York International Universities Press, 1971, pp. 533–554.
http://www.pep-web.org/document.php?id=psc.013.0521a
Khron, A. (1974). Borderline "empathy" and differentiation of object represen-
tations: A contribution to the psychology of object relations. *International
Journal of Psychoanalytic Psychotherapy* 3:142–165.
Wallerstein, R.S., ed. (1981). *Becoming a Psychoanalyst: A Study of
Psychoanalytic Supervision*. New York: International Universities Press,

pp. 227–268.

Wolkenfeld, F. (1984). The parallel process phenomenon revisited: Some additional thoughts about the supervisory process. Paper delivered at Washington Square Institute, New York City, March 9, 1984.

# PART VI. TREATMENT AND SUPERVISION: INTRAPSYCHIC AND INTERPERSONAL PERSPECTIVES

## AUTHOR'S INTRODUCTION

How we listen is obviously one of the ways that determines how we hear patients' clinical material. One particular anecdote stands out in my mind to illustrate an overt controversy that I believed I reconciled. Let me start with the end of the story and then go back to the beginning. I went to hear Paul Gray present at the New York Psychoanalytic Society in 1997 when he delivered the much-valued Freud lecture. I had met Dr. Gray some years before when he had spoken on a panel on my home turf: New York University's Postdoctoral Program in Psychotherapy and Psychoanalysis. I had also met him at numerous occasions at the American Psychoanalytic Association and in Washington D.C. where I traveled every other weekend to teach and to supervise candidates at what was then called the Washington Program of the New York Freudian Society. During the reception following the Freud Lecture, I approached Dr. Gray and introduced myself. He immediately recognized me and beaming, said, "I love the way your mind works." Although I was at that moment totally overcome and totally clueless, he continued right on. He reminded me that I had been sitting 10 seats in from the aisle in right center during his N.Y.U. presentation when I rose to question a point he had been emphasizing and arguing for. No longer clueless, my memory of that earlier meeting came back in a flash. Dr. Gray had been arguing that "close process attention" was a more valuable way of listening than the more familiar "evenly hovering attention" of free association if one wanted to hear material relevant to the ego's defenses. I said I did not think one listening process should be accorded more value than the other as they were both essential for listening to patients in their entirety. I was unbelievably touched that Paul Gray had remembered who I was, exactly where I sat (!) and what I said on that earlier occasion. I also felt encouraged to move on with my ideas of "both/and" as a replacement for "either/or" thinking, and with my work of building bridges between erstwhile binary-driven points that had been anchoring arguments about psychoanalytic listening in a way that to this day have been troubling me.

In this Part VI on Psychoanalytic Treatment, I have included more papers that I have in any other part of this book. It is the treatment setting, above all, that requires building bridges between diverse clinical-theoretical points of view. My psychoanalytic education was grounded in an open and unambiguous dedication to the idea that psychoanalysis is not a monolithic discipline, but covers a diverse and pluralistic range of approaches, perspectives, and axes. The New York University Program in Psychotherapy and Psychoanalysis was dedicated to that position from its inception, just as I have been from the inception of my formal psychoanalytic training there. When I began training, in 1963, with Postdoc's second class, there were no tracks but there were clearly teaching and supervising psychoanalysts who hailed from different theoretical orientations that emphasized different approaches to theory and the treatment process. The names of these orientations, later to become tracks, changed over time. In the beginning there were two: the "Interpersonal-Humanistic" and the "Freudian." By the time I graduated, in 1968, I was well ensconced in the Freudian track, and when I joined the faculty of the Freudian Track in 1973, a third, "Independent" track was added, and last but not least, the "Relational" track was born. So we finally emerged as a four-track system that remains in place to this day: The Contemporary Freudian, the Interpersonal, the Relational and the Independent tracks. In the beginning, each track zealously guarded its autonomy and independence. Today, we no longer fight to preserve our separate identities, but live together peacefully and collaboratively as we work toward building bridges among us. Two pioneering and gifted leaders sparked and developed the kind of education that nourished "both /and" in favor of "either/or thinking." The first, the Founder and Director of our program in 1961, Bernard N. Kalinkowitz, was replaced, after he died, by Lewis Aron in 1998. Whether one chose predominantly single track or cross-track offerings, the opportunity for cross-fertilization remains central in our current mission of building bridges.

A prime influence of cross-track fertilization within and outside of N.Y.U. occurred in 2006 when I was invited by Jodie Davies, then the editor of *Psychoanalytic Dialogues*, to write on self-disclosure during treatment, (see Chapters 18 and 19, below), a topic that had become very dear to my heart even before that journal saw the light of day

Probably the most widely read paper in Part VI is Chapter 14, the paper on parallel process in supervision and treatment that I coauthored with the late Fred Wolkenfeld. I have already included a case illustrating a pathological parallel process in Chapter 12 on "Imposture." In the year 2011, it was listed by Psychoanalytic Electronic Publishing as one of the most cited papers on its PEP CD ROM. I believe the paper has garnered all the interest that it has because our consideration of the parallelism phenomenon regarded it as embedded in a triadic system of interactions between patient, therapist, supervisor, and the institutional setting in which the supervisory process is occurring. In other words, "it takes a village" of like-minded but independent individuals within organizations to educate a psychoanalyst.

I am proud of all the Chapters appearing in this section. Chapter 16 on the subject of termination of treatment was originally part of a 1993 two-part symposium sponsored by Section I (Psychologist-Psychoanalyst Practitioners) of Division 39 (Psychoanalysis) of the American Psychological Association. The presenters in the first part were Martin Bergmann and Jack Novick; Donald Kaplan was their discussant. Those presenting in the second part were Steven Ellman and Warren Poland; I was their discussant. I must have been very excited to be asked to join such eminent colleagues. Sitting at the very end of the dais in a ballroom of the conference hotel in Washington D.C., my chair had been precariously placed too near the edge, and before you knew it, before anyone had a chance to deliver his talk, my chair toppled right over the edge taking me along with it to the floor. But, as is my wont, I picked myself up and got back in the race, an action that I like to use as a metaphor for my wish to continue writing papers for the rest of my days.

# Chapter 13: The Parallelism Phenomenon in Psychoanalysis and Supervision: Its Reconsideration as a Triadic System[18]

Gediman, H.K. & Wolkenfeld, F. (1980). The Parallelism phenomenon in psychoanalysis and supervision: Its reconsideration as a triadic system. *Psychoanalytic Quar*terly, 49:234-255.

## INTRODUCTION

In psychoanalytic supervision, supervisees manifest toward their supervisors many psychic patterns which parallel processes that are prominent in their interactions with their patients. The reverse influence is also observed: analyst and patient re-enact events of the supervisory situation. An expanded explanation for parallelism is offered which indicates how the structural and dynamic similarities of analysis and supervision link patient, analyst, and supervisor in a complex, multidirectional network that guarantees the emergence of this phenomenon.

Supervisors of psychoanalysis and psychoanalytic psychotherapy have observed a phenomenon in supervision which, despite its regularity, would appear to startle them anew each time they note it. Therapists manifest major psychic events in supervision, including complex behavior patterns, affects, and conflicts, which parallel processes that are prominent in their interactions with their patients in the treatment situation. Furthermore, the therapist does not seem to be aware that he is conveying that impression to the supervisor. The phenomenon of which we speak partakes, in a word, of the "uncanny."[19] A supervisee who so garbles his presentation that his supervisor is rendered

---

18 From the Faculties of the New York University Postdoctoral Program in Psychoanalysis and Psychotherapy, and the Bronx Psychiatric Center of the Albert Einstein College of Medicine. A number of ideas which we have developed in this paper arose in the context of a supervision seminar conducted at Montefiore Hospital by Dr. Francis Baudry and Dr. William I. Grossman, whom we would like to thank for their suggestions for an earlier draft of this paper.

19 The *uncanny* in this context is only one of the ways Freud (1919) used the term, namely, "this factor of involuntary repetition which surrounds what would otherwise be innocent enough with an uncanny atmosphere, and forces upon us the idea of something fateful and inescapable when otherwise we should have spoken only of 'chance'" (p. 237).

helpless to respond intelligently to its content complains bitterly of his patient's exasperating inarticulateness. Or a student analyst asks how to deal with
his patient's insistence on reading his dreams from notes taken immediately
upon awakening in the morning, rather than reporting them from memory,
while the supervisee presses the supervisor to listen to tape-recorded sessions.

Arlow (1963) gives the following account of a psychoanalyst in supervision
with him who was treating a young, male homosexual patient. The therapist
described the patient as ingratiating himself submissively with strong men
whom he admired and whose prowess he wished to grasp in the act of fellatio.
The psychodynamics and the ongoing transference paradigm became clearer
in a dream the patient had, which the therapist reported during a supervisory session. In the dream the patient saw himself lying on the couch, turning
around to face the analyst and then offering him a cigarette. "At this point in
the supervisory session," Arlow writes, "the therapist reached for a pack of
cigarettes, took one for himself, and although he knew very well that I do not
smoke, extended the pack to me and asked, 'Do you want a cigarette?'" (p.
580). The specificity in this example is so marked as to seem bizarre, at least
to those unfamiliar with the parallelism phenomenon. But the very specificity
in Arlow's example, and others which we shall cite, is one of the factors that
have led us to look more closely at the phenomenon, for such specificity occurs so frequently as to make us wonder if it tends toward universality.

A supervisor often discovers these parallelisms when certain of his emotional reactions lead him to realize that his supervisee is engaged unconsciously
with him in a "tension system" which is similar to that occurring in the therapy
situation. For example, a therapist who cannot recognize his patient's hostility
toward him may behave in a similarly hostile manner toward his supervisor.
It is the supervisor's awareness of his feeling attacked that alerts him to the
parallel process phenomenon. This nonproblematic "countertransference"
may be his greatest supervisory asset, for as Searles (1955) recognized some
time ago, the supervisor's emotional responses to his supervisee are highly
informative reflections of the relationship between therapist and patient.

The very words we choose to designate the phenomenon under consideration will bias our accounting for it. We will limit ourselves, therefore, to
"parallel process" or "parallelism" because these terms are most descriptive
and carry least explanatory bias. "Mirroring" and "reflecting," terms found
in the psychoanalytic literature, suggest a unidirectional sort of "domino
theory" whereby something the patient does is automatically mirrored in
something the therapist does in supervision. Our experience compels us to
view the patient-therapist-supervisor interactions as truly triadic: a complex

*multidirectional* network, or system, and not simply a unidirectional process with a set point of origin in the patient. This position is our major thesis to be developed and clinically documented. We shall seek to demonstrate that the specificity and complexity of re-enacted behavior, which together with its frequency of occurrence and, indeed, its inevitability, must be attributed to far more than a reflection process. Most important, we will delineate the overlapping features of psychoanalysis and supervision which constitute the essential conditions for parallelisms.

## CRITICAL REVIEW OF THE LITERATURE

Diverse explanations for parallelism have been offered in recent psychoanalytic literature by (Arlow, 1963; Doehrman, 1976; Ekstein and Wallerstein, 1958; Sachs and Shapiro, 1976, Searles, 1955). Freud's (1914) observation that what is not remembered is repeated through enactment provides the background for most hypotheses offered to account for the phenomenon: "... we may say that the patient does not *remember* anything of what he has forgotten and repressed, but *acts* it out. He reproduces it not as a memory but as an action ..." (p. 150). According to this view, then, when the therapist does not understand the meaning of a patient's enacted communication, he may convey the meaning to his supervisor by a parallel enactment. A special variation and extension of the enactment hypothesis is a view which emphasizes shared identifications of patient and therapist, where the two share unconscious conflicts and anxieties, or may identify with one another in critical conflict-free areas. These identifications are then enacted in supervision.

Searles (1955) views such shared identifications as a "reflection process" whereby the patient, because he cannot yet verbalize a still unconscious conflict, enacts it, and the therapist, in turn, enacts the patient's conflict, *whatever its specific content,* for his supervisor.

Arlow (1963) also was impressed with the importance of the therapist's identification with his patient's conflicts, and his position is presented from the structural point of view: he stresses the potential contribution of all three agencies of the mind to parallel process in the particular identifications which are enacted. Therapist and patient may share fantasy wishes in common (id impulses), anxieties and defenses (ego), and ideals and values (ego ideal and superego).

Ekstein and Wallerstein (1958) have elaborated the role of shared parallel *learning problems* and parallel ways of *seeking help and of helping* in therapy and supervision. The sense of professional identity in the beginning student is particularly dependent upon his ways of seeking help and helping, especially when he discovers that what he reports of his patient's sessions so often parallels problems he, himself, experiences in supervision.

Sachs and Shapiro (1976) are fairly specific about the nature of enacted identifications. Their position holds that the therapist develops unconscious identifications with his patient when *treatment difficulties,* specifically *resistances,* stalemates, and impasses, arise which he cannot resolve. Unable to verbalize these impasses in supervision, he enacts them. Sachs and Shapiro feel that the critical unresolved conflict areas are those related to feelings of inadequacy; they maintain that parallel process phenomena—which in their work were noted in group members of a teaching seminar—emerge primarily in initial treatment phases as "new" patients seek help from "novice" therapists who are just beginning to seek help in supervision. Consequently, they both share painful anxieties about exposing their feelings of inadequacy to others, and so they both enact these narcissistic vulnerabilities.

Our view, which we shall elaborate shortly, also acknowledges the importance of shared narcissistic vulnerabilities. We do not believe, however, that such concerns are limited to novice patients and therapists. Supervisors, too, are potentially vulnerable, and parallel processes may be observed even in advanced treatments reported by experienced, skilled, and well-analyzed analysts who themselves may be excellent supervisors. Observed parallelisms are most frequently *reported* in beginning treatments, supervisions, and case seminars primarily because they are the most common forum for work presentation and for studying the processes. The explanations offered by Sachs and Shapiro are thus necessary but not sufficient, for they are too narrow.

Perhaps the broadest explanation for identificatory enactments is that of oscillating levels of the ego's functioning during the reporting process in both psychoanalysis and supervision. Arlow (1963) speaks of clear-cut shifts in the ways that analytic candidates reported material to their supervisors. These shifts were between objective reporting of data and enacting the experience of the treatment, paralleling the therapist's oscillations between identifying with his patient and observing him, which in turn paralleled the patient's shifts from free association to the use of the observing ego. We would like to add that shifting dominance of ego functions characterizes the supervisor's work in the teaching process as well. Transmitting in action what fails to be reported in words is thus understood as a "regression in the service of the ego" which characterizes both therapy and supervision.

We, too, believe that transient regressions in ego functioning on the part of the therapist are as essential in supervision as they are in psychoanalysis.

The therapist must be able to *empathize* with his patient, and empathy requires a partial suspension of the functions of the observing ego, and a temporary, controlled regression. Only then does the therapist experience what the patient is feeling. These transient regressions, which are critical to empathic understanding of the patient, help the therapist cue in to material which cannot yet be verbalized explicitly when he reports to his supervisor, for he is only preconsciously aware of its meaning. It is as if the therapist were saying to the supervisor, "I cannot tell you in words what the patient is like, but I can *show* you and make you *feel* what the patient is like."

The accounts of parallelism reviewed above, which explain it as an enactment, identification, and reflection, mostly consider it as having a point of origin in the patient and then somehow being transmitted "upward." Although Searles and Ekstein and Wallerstein acknowledge multidirectionality, only Doehrman's (1976) research specifically emphasizes a "reverse mirroring" phenomenon. Doehrman honors the complexity of parallelism by saying that it is often not at all clear which way the mirror is facing; nevertheless, she places greatest emphasis on the impact supervision has on therapy and relatively little on "upward reflection," criticizing Searles, especially for viewing parallel process as having only that one "domino theory" dynamic. In every case she studied, she claimed that therapists behaved with their patients either the same way or the opposite way that they experienced their supervisors' behavior with them, tending to enact or to react against their supervisors' core neurotic problem.

What Doehrman does not deal with are the phenomena of projection and displacement. The therapist's *experience* of the supervisor and its transmission to the patient may not be veridical, but may be based instead on the therapist's transference distortions or on projective identifications, or even on how he experiences himself in relationship to his patient. We shall amplify this point later in some examples which document the difficulties in finding a set point of origin in a complex interactional system. As valuable as the "reverse mirroring" hypothesis is for alerting us to the importance of the supervisor-supervisee interaction, we consider any such unidimensional interaction as but one component of parallelism. In our opinion, the other theories reviewed here are subject to the same criticism. Searles, while apparently aware of the impact of the supervisory relationship on parallel re-enactments in the treatment situation, places greatest emphasis in his theoretical development on "upward reflection." Arlow and Sachs and Shapiro ignore entirely the role of the supervisor in promoting parallelism. And theories which focus on shared conflicts and/or defenses rest the explanation of the complex phenomenon of parallelism on such equally complex and all-encompassing conceptualizations as unresolved neurosis or identification. Unresolved and unresolvable infantile conflicts, especially what Freud (1937) referred to as "latent" conflicts, indeed reside in all of us and are therefore universal. These unresolved sectors of the analyst's and the supervisor's personalities which produce distortions and their sequelae in technique are, of course, implicated in all parallel re-enactments to one degree or another. But it is precisely their all-encompassing nature that renders them not too useful for a comprehensive theory of parallelism.

What is it, after all, that accounts for even experienced psychoanalysts' and sophisticated supervisors' re-enacting in one situation in precise and even bizarre ways behavior experienced in another? To refer to shared identification or to countertransference in a general sense, or to unresolved neurotic concerns, is to render the problem a non-problem. At best such explanations are only partial. At worst, they are circular and beg the question. Evoking such broad conceptualizations is analogous to explaining transference in the analytic situation by reference only to the universal propensity for projection and displacement without recourse to the uniqueness of the analytic setting and its practices and techniques. Our own accounting for parallelism, as we have already stated, requires recognition of the complex interactions among patient, analyst, and supervisor, which bond them in a systemic network, and of the structural and dynamic similarities of psychoanalysis and supervision.

## CLINICAL ILLUSTRATIONS

Consider the following brief vignettes which we offer primarily to demonstrate the difficulty in discovering a set point of origin for the parallelisms illustrated.[20]

---

20 You will note that some of the vignettes include material on how the supervisor makes use in supervision of his awareness of the observed parallelisms. Detailed consideration of the ways that the supervisor may intervene in the interests of *resolving parallel impasses* is beyond the scope of the present paper which aims only to account for the phenomena. Handling parallelisms in supervision constitutes the core of a paper which the authors have in preparation.

It is the very question of *handling* parallelisms in supervision that requires our ability as supervisors to distinguish the *degree* to which unresolved pathology and, therefore, transference-countertransference impasses are implicated. For example, such an impasse may be resolvable only by the therapist's further psychoanalysis, and not in supervision. Or, a particularly dramatic enactment may be handled as Isakower did, according to Malcove (1975), by discussing it directly with the supervisee as a "miscarriage" of the analyzing instrument and encouraging more self-observation in an attempt to understand what led to it.

**CASE I**

A supervisor enjoyed her sessions with a particularly gifted supervisee. The student seemed to have anticipated all issues that crossed the supervisor's mind, had given them serious thought, and had come to similar or identical conclusions as the supervisor with a regularity and congruity which was heartwarming. The supervisor said very little at first, because her supervisee seemed to be doing all the work so well, and this was a source of deep gratification. Soon, however, she experienced a growing sense of unease that there appeared to be not even a minimal degree of tension between her and the supervisee. It was at this point that she noted there appeared to be no resistance on the part of the patient about whom the supervisee was reporting, and this parallel lack of tension alerted her to a previously overlooked, obvious parallelism: the supervisee had described her patient as rare and gifted. In fact, the patient had established a firm working alliance and had demonstrated optimal capacity for self-exploration and reflective awareness. The supervisee was particularly pleased that her patient independently arrived at the very interpretations and understandings that she did.

Aware now of a parallel process, the supervisor learned from the supervisee that her patient had disguised his rage at a previous therapist by saying exactly the things she wanted to hear, thereby "psyching her out." When the supervisor understood that she might be avoiding competitive feelings by being perfectly "in tune" with her supervisee and that such perfect harmony could serve as a resistance or deteriorate into a derailed supervisory situation, the detection of the parallel "smooth impasses" was no longer delayed. It seemed as though neither therapist nor supervisor wished to risk the working alliance. While the harmony was narcissistically gratifying in both processes, therapy and supervision, it prohibited the optimal interpersonal tensions requisite for their continued unfolding.

**CASE 2**

An engagingly attractive supervisee so disarmed her supervisor with her fluent and entertaining reports of therapy sessions with a "charming patient" that the bewitching syntax of her reporting style delayed for an uncommonly long time the supervisor's and supervisee's detection that the charming patient was highly psychopathic and charmingly adept at concluding some very shady business deals.

This account should not be construed as an injunction against introducing charm into the supervisory relationship, but only as an illustration of how the supervisee's charm can illuminate some otherwise hidden meaning of similar characteristics in the patient. It should be noted that once the supervisor pointed out to the supervisee the patient's psychopathy and once he ceased to show obvious delight at the supervisee's entertaining style of reportage, much in the therapeutic and supervisory alliance was risked. The supervisee became more anxious and less engaging, the therapy moved well, although with new struggles which found their parallel in the supervisor-supervisee interaction. The "smooth stalemate" was resolved, and the work proceeded.

## CASE 3

A patient produced minimal "content" in his sessions with a beginning analyst, and his withholding was clearly a derivative of anal-sadistic and retentive impulses. The therapist felt thwarted because he felt that if his patient did not produce, he would have nothing to produce for his supervisor. Unaware of the meaning of his patient's obstinacy, he enacted it in supervision, as if he were saying, "See, I have nothing to report, so how are you going to teach me what I need to know?" The supervisor noted a potential within herself for a feeling of impotent rage which she sensed her supervisee must be enacting and provoking in her. He wanted her to know what it felt like when the one you seek to help appears to block all efforts to do so. How could she do her job when her supervisee was trying to render her as powerless in controlling and conducting her supervision as his patient made him feel about his work of analyzing? Why was the patient doing this? What bonds linked all three, each of whom had such difficulties in producing anything of value in carrying through their respective tasks?

## CASE 4

A supervisee found herself temporarily reporting on one specific patient to two different supervisors because of administrative factors which she partially brought about. In both supervisions she focused primarily on her adolescent patient's anxieties about loyalty conflicts toward her estranged parents. The patient was afraid of "leaking" secrets from one parent to the other, and she feared that confiding in her therapist was tantamount to a betrayal of her mother. The therapist, however, was unaware of the similarities to her own situation, even as she asked the program director to advise her if she might be hurting the feelings of Supervisor A, who was going on sabbatical in two weeks time, if she reported on the case to Supervisor B, the senior of the two. The program director was also contacted by Supervisor A, and he, the program director, became aware of an uncomfortable "middleman" feeling in the whole affair. It was this discomfort in conjunction with his awareness of the trainee's excited involvement with the potentially hurt feelings of her supervisors that finally alerted the program director to the parallel processes being enacted in his department.

This last example is most certainly a dramatic case in point, in which there appear to be "echoes" of a patient's chief complaint reverberating throughout an administrative hierarchy. Or was it the other way around? Perhaps the patient was sensitized to certain unresolved conflicts in her therapist, who in turn was sensitized to certain tensions within the administrative structure of the training institution where she worked. Can we really identify in these examples a set point of origin in the patient or in the therapist or in the supervisor—or in the metasupervisor, for that matter—for the obvious parallelisms? We think not.

From these examples, one may also wonder if a proclivity toward dramatization is critical for parallel process emergence. But just as action or enactment as a modality is as universal as thinking, so dramatization and acting out are reasonably specific variants of these universal modalities. And just as identification and "boundary crossing"(Kernberg, 1977) are universally expectable processes, so projective identification and boundary fusion are their pathological variants. A viable explanation of parallelism, to account for its inevitability, must incorporate an understanding of its full range of manifestations from normal through pathological. Most important, it must account for the intrapsychic representations of multiple interactions among and mutual influences of patient, therapist, and supervisor.[21] All our examples are offered in an attempt to show the specificity and complexity of these phenomena, which, along with their frequency and indeed their inevitability, raise questions about the explanatory power of the hypotheses offered in the literature to date.

## A BROADENED ACCOUNT OF PARALLELISM

It is our belief that the structural and dynamic similarities of psychoanalysis and supervision link patient, analyst, and supervisor in a highly complex

---

21 We acknowledge the contribution to parallel process of the supervisee's analyst (and the supervisor's analyst), but have not included a detailed consideration of that influence because, as supervisors, we cannot have direct access to all the relevant data.

Building Bridges

representational system of interaction, which not only fosters parallelism but provides the *conditions* for the inevitability of multidirectional re-enactments. By structure, we refer to those implicit and explicit rules governing the two situations and the consensually defined role expectations of each member of the triad. The structural similarities of all psychoanalysis and supervisory settings include such factors as time allotments, fees, and contracts for services; degree of choice in selection of patient, therapist, and supervisor; institutional and training requirements, and so forth. We do not wish to belabor the obvious fact that psychoanalysis and supervision *differ* in many crucial ways. We wish only to emphasize that the many ways in which they are similar lay the groundwork for a viable explanation of parallel process.

The structural features of each situation guarantee highly charged dynamic tensions which require empathic identifications on the part of all three members of the triad for their resolution. It is these shared dynamics pursuant to and congruent with the structural similarities that provide the "emotional soil" for parallelism.

The major structural and dynamic similarities are by no means mutually exclusive; that is, they overlap one with the other in a variety of ways. But for expository purposes we would summarize them as follows:

1. Both psychoanalysis and supervision are *helping processes.*
2. Both psychoanalysis and supervision require involvement of the *self.*
3. Both psychoanalysis and supervision rely heavily for effectiveness on *multiple identificatory processes.*

We have already indicated other similarities and will add more in the ensuing discussion, but we believe them to be derivatives of the three listed above.

**THE HELPING PROCESS**

Structurally speaking, the feature that is probably most important for understanding parallelism is that supervision and psychoanalysis are both helping processes. The very position of needing help places one in a subordinate role for which the parent-child relationship serves as the universal prototype. The conflict between the life-long craving for authoritative guidance, to which Freud (1910) referred, and the need to forge one's own identity applies to both the patient in relation to the analyst and the analyst in relation to the supervisor. What is less publicized, and infrequently documented, is the supervisor's craving to be an authoritative guide, as it were; seeing the supervisee as a potential extension of himself conflicts with his central supervisory objective of facilitating the student's innate, autonomous growth potential as a

278

psychoanalyst. Thus tensions and anxieties relating to the giving and seeking of help, as well as conflicts between the need for change and the wish to cling to the familiar, are inevitable in all creative learning situations, including psychoanalysis and supervision, and will be experienced by both student and supervisor.

The structural features of supervision, analogous to the formal aspects of psychoanalysis, therefore predicate that powerful emotions will be mobilized. Feelings of admiration for the supervisor and a desire to emulate are generated readily, along with feelings of envy, fear, and even hostility. Nor should we ignore the real power a supervisor has over his students, for he is not only teacher but also evaluator.

For teaching and learning to progress, the supervisor must acknowledge and contend with these emotionally charged issues which might include his own competitive feelings toward his supervisee and anxieties about the inevitability of the supervisee's eventually becoming his peer.

It should be clear from the above that attitudes about giving and receiving help, shared by patient, therapist, and supervisor alike, will contain elements deriving from any psychosexual or developmental stage, which will trigger drive derivatives, fantasies, and anxieties typical for these phases. For example, oral conflicts about taking in what is fed and about feeding may be activated in the learning situation; anal conflicts might emerge if teaching and learning are imbued with impulses to control the "helpless" one or *to submit* to the idealized parental image; phallic concerns and castration anxiety may be aroused if the roles of giving and receiving help provoke oedipal and/or exhibitionistic fantasies, and so on. These fantasies, whatever their nature, are universal and represent a potential which may be activated in any patient, therapist, or supervisor. Whatever the nature of these specific conflicts, however, they are facilitated in these settings—therapy and supervision—by the shared structural and dynamic features of the helping-learning situation.

## INVOLVEMENT OF THE SELF

Supervision and psychoanalysis differ structurally from most other learning and therapeutic situations in that exposure of the self is an integral and absolute *requirement* for progress to occur. Therefore, these processes inevitably foster concerns with self-esteem regulation and the preservation of the integrity of the work ego. The scope of exposure of the self for the therapist in supervision is far more narrow than that of the patient in treatment, but it is not necessarily less profound.

Ekstein and Wallerstein (1958) correctly point out that the requirement of exposing oneself in order to learn is at the core of the resistance to learning, and Gitelson (1949) notes that one of the difficulties in supervisory teaching relates to the student's narcissistic need to keep his image of himself intact. The point we wish to stress is that one's self participates in all learning situations, but the *self as an instrument in the process* is unique to certain psychotherapies, particularly psychoanalysis.

The supervisor also shares some of these concerns. He is more or less preoccupied with his teaching reputation as it is displayed to the student body of his particular community. He may also be a colleague of his supervisee's analyst and conceivably could be more or less concerned with the image of himself that his student may convey to his analyst. DeBell (1963) was aware of the potential dangers in misusing the supervisory position for narcissistic purposes and summarized them in his comprehensive review of psychoanalytic supervision.

As we see it, all three members of the triad are in a position of narcissistic vulnerability, although to markedly different degrees. If the authoritative transmission of technical skill, or of theoretical formulations, or even of insights into the patient therapist interaction were all that was necessary, then exposure of the self and narcissistic vulnerability would not be central issues. But supervision is a dynamic process which has as its ideal objective the development of the novice therapist into what Isakower (1957) has called an "analyzing instrument." In striving toward this objective, the supervisor must recognize, above all, that imitation and compliance on the part of the student analyst are only initial phases in learning and are potential defenses against further, more meaningful change. He must thus contend with the temptation of molding the therapist, in his, the supervisor's, own image, a potential but lamentable source of narcissistic gratification. The supervisor's work ego depends on his ability to handle effectively a variety of resistances and on fostering a helping-learning atmosphere in supervision. Only then may the therapist promote the same in the therapeutic situation. The work egos, then, of both therapist and supervisor are dependent on the establishment and maintenance of a good working alliance in therapy and supervision, respectively. Fleming and Benedek (1966) have referred to the *learning alliance* in supervision as essentially parallel to the therapeutic alliance: the acceptance of a mutually shared educational goal involving expectations of giving and receiving help and initiating a bond of trust without which the work cannot proceed. Any rupture in either the working alliance or the supervisory alliance is a potential threat to self-esteem.

Consider the supervisee who announced that he had serious countertransference difficulties and was anxious about coming for supervision because he knew he was not supposed to have such feelings. It was as if he were deliberately misunderstanding the supervisory alliance, particularly his supervisor's view on the informational value of countertransference phenomena. The supervisor, in turn, who goes beyond utilizing the informational value of countertransference by offering genetic-dynamic interpretations is distorting the supervisory alliance.

Since much of the work in the first year of therapy is precisely the establishment and maintenance of the working alliance and since most supervision is sought early in the supervisee's training career, his narcissistic investment in his work is greatly magnified. As Sachs and Shapiro (1976) state, parallelisms are seen frequently in setting up and maintaining a treatment situation, the area of greatest potential threat to the work ego, because, if the therapeutic process cannot get off to a proper start, nothing in the way of teaching and learning can continue in supervision. Perhaps such distortions in the supervisory alliance explain a most common parallelism, frequently overlooked as a parallelism: that of the therapist canceling supervision when his patient has canceled sessions. The plea that "supervision won't be necessary this week because my patient didn't show" is often but a rationalization for the repetition, despite its compelling congruence with "reality." And the supervisor's agreement with the cancellation is probably a collusion with that resistance.

## MULTIPLE IDENTIFICATORY PROCESSES

It is clear that the essential mechanism of parallelism is identification. It is the purpose of this section of our paper to demonstrate how all three principals of the triad—patient, analyst, and supervisor alike—are involved in multiple identificatory processes because a variety of identifications are *required* for the unfolding of the therapy and of the supervision.

It is the patient's identification with the analyst's analytic approach that constitutes the essence of the working alliance. And it is this identification that sustains the relationship despite the emotional turmoils and intense negative transference reactions. Similarly, the achievement of a truly collaborative effort in supervision, which has as its goal more than the teaching and learning of theory and technique, is dependent on the establishment of a supervisory alliance. It is through identification with the supervisor's analytic attitude that conflicts and anxieties surrounding self-exposure in this "tilted emotional relationship," to borrow Greenacre's (1954) phrase, can be overcome. Progression from imitative to autonomous and creative learning, correction of the student-analyst's distortions of professional ego ideals, and enhancement of his empathic capabilities are dependent on the development of a supervisory alliance.

Arlow (1963) has likened the optimally effective supervisory process to an aesthetic experience, in that it discourages mechanistic, word-for-word reporting of the patient-therapist interaction. Indeed, as supervising psychoanalysts we recognize that the therapist's report has been edited unconsciously and that through empathic identification the therapist has absorbed more than he can readily verbalize. Freud, in *Creative Writers and Daydreaming* (1907), was well aware of the unique situation of the analytic patient as reporter. He implied there that the patient's reports provide an opportunity for patient and analyst to share fantasies, as the analyst can never have direct access to all aspects of the patient's experience. We would agree that the analyst frequently can only imagine or fantasize what the patient's actual experience is and that, similarly, the supervisor frequently can only fantasize what actually transpired between patient and therapist. But in the more aesthetically ambiguous settings to which we refer, all three—patient, analyst and supervisor—rely heavily on imagination, fantasy, and cognitive-affective apprehension, generally, to fill in the knowledge gap, to do justice to the ambiguity and, through empathic identification, to grasp the "experiential identities" (Kohut, 1966). These "daydreams" in common and experiential identities might be viewed as transitional phenomena which are "self-created" to some extent by all three participants and which bond them together. In order for the supervisor to apprehend directly and to fill in the gaps of both analyst's and patient's experience, he must have the capacity for fluctuations in level of ego functioning. Transient regression in ego functioning, or oscillation between observing and experiencing on the part of the supervisor, are as central to the supervisory process as are the fluctuations implied in "evenly hovering attention" to the analytic process.[22]

Perhaps this mutuality of shared experiences sheds some light on another

---

22 While this paper was in preparation, our attention was called to another paper, now in press (Balter, Lothane, and Spencer, 1980), which elaborates certain intrapsychic and interpersonal processes characterizing Isakower's concept of the analyzing instrument. The authors abstract their position as follows: "The analyzing instrument has two constituents: a voluntary and controlled, situation specific and goal-specific regressed state of mind in the analysand and a near-identical one in the analyst. These parts function together through a mutually evocative, communicative transaction leading to the elucidation of the analysand's unconscious fantasy-memory constellations." This operational definition, referable to a dyad, reflects the same basic position we have taken and have extended to a triadic representational system which includes the supervisor's controlled regressions or shifting dominance of ego functions.

frequently observed phenomenon, namely, that beyond the supervisor's motivation for the student analyst to do well, a secondary identification with the patient is frequently formed with the concomitant unconscious investment in the patient's also doing well. The principal point, however, is that parallel re-enactments, neurotic or otherwise, occur because identifications and empathy on the part of all three members of the triad are *required* for the unfolding of the analysis and of the supervision. Boundary fusion, to take a pathological example, occurs because boundary crossing (Kernberg, 1977) is required. It is no surprise, therefore, that with their sensitivity to personality nuances, in the context of a helping process, and with transient identifications with both therapist and patient, supervisors so often slip and say, "the *patient* said ..." when they are referring to the analytic candidate who is their supervisee.

The supervisee is the critical intermediary in the triadic system. However, in marked contrast to other authors we believe that his centrality to parallelism is more apparent than real, since we need only place the supervisor in a similar relationship to a metasupervisor, such as in a continuous case supervision seminar, and he then becomes the apparent central person. In one such study group, consisting of senior supervisors and supervising psychoanalysts, parallel re-enactments emerged relentlessly. With maximal exposure of one's supervisory skills and in a setting which is structurally defined as a helping process it could hardly be otherwise. The members of the group decided to study the supervisory process and particularly the parallel process phenomenon in depth, but most preferred the vignette form of presentation to the ongoing continuous supervision case. It would, they felt, at least preserve the confidentiality of the trainees about whom they were reporting, for they were, after all, their junior colleagues and potential peers. It soon became apparent, however, that the confidentiality issue was one of many "red herrings" onto which the supervisors displaced considerable anxiety about self-exposure. This group (and others we know of) was disbanded by the members, largely because some of them were reluctant to present their work.

We would urge the formation of more such groups, for a supervision seminar with a continuous case presentation format is obviously the best setting for studying the supervision process. It is also the best arena for testing the hypotheses deriving from our position that parallel process is a complex triadic system. For only in this setting can the contributions of all three participants be scrutinized—and by those who are most experienced and best trained to understand them. It is ironic that those most schooled in understanding the unconscious should shy away from one of its fascinating manifestations, as when residues of their own unconscious processes are exposed through parallelisms. It is as if we as supervisors continued to believe that supervision is governed exclusively by conscious rational processes, even while acknowledging the omnipresence of unconscious phenomena. This paradox accounts for the experience of the uncanny when supervisors are confronted by a parallel re-enactment. For this signifies the unexpected emergence of the unconscious—its disregard for time, place, and seniority.

## SUMMARY

We have attempted to demonstrate that parallel process phenomena derive from a complex triadic system to which all three participants in the supervisory situation—patient, analyst, and supervisor—contribute. Multiple identificatory processes are required for the unfolding of psychoanalysis and of supervision, which together with the overlapping structural and dynamic similarities of the two situations, establish the conditions for multidirectional parallel re-enactments. Both patient and analyst share a need *for* help; both analyst and supervisor share a need *to* help; and all three share a concern with self-esteem issues.

## REFERENCES

Arlow, J.A. (1963). The supervisory situation. *Journal of the American Psychoanalytic Association* 11: 576–594.

Balter, L. Lothane, Z.; & Spencer, J.H. (1980). On the analyzing instrument. *Psychoanalytic Quarterly* 49:474-504.

De Bell, D.E. (1963). A critical digest of the literature on psychoanalytic supervision. *Journal of the American Psychoanalytic Association* 11:546–575. http://www.pep-web.org/document.php?id=apa.011.0546a

Doehrman, M.J.G. (1976). Parallel processes in supervision and psychotherapy *Bulletin of the Menninger Clinic* 40:3–104.

Ekstein, R. And Wallerstein, R.S. (1958). *The Teaching and Learning of Psychotherapy.* New York: Basic Books, Inc.

Fleming, J. & Benedek, T.F. (1966). *Psychoanalytic Supervision: A Method of Clinical Teaching.* New York: Grune & Stratton, Inc.

Freud, S. (1907). Creative Writers and Daydreaming *Standard Edition* IX pp. 143–153. http://www.pep-web.org/document.php?id=se.009.0115a

———(1910). The Future Prospects of Psycho-Analytic Therapy. *Standard Edition* 11:41–151. http://www.pep-web.org/document.php?id=se.009.0141a

———— (1914). Remembering, Repeating and Working-Through (Further Recommendations on the Technique of Psycho-Analysis II). *Standard Edition* 12:147–156.
http://www.pep-web.org/document.php?id=se.012.0145a

———— (1919). The "Uncanny." Standard Edition 17:219–252.
http://www.pep-web.org/document.php?id=se.017.0217a

———— (1937). Analysis Terminable and Interminable. Standard *Edition* 23:216–253. http://www.pep-web.org/document.php?id=se.023.0209a

Gitelson, M. (1949). *Concerning the Problem of Countertransference. Discussion of Papers* by T. F. Benedek and E. Weiss at Chicago Psychoanalytic Society. Unpublished.

Greenacre, P. (1954). The role of transference: Practical Considerations in relation to psychoanalytic therapy. In: *Emotional Growth: Psychoanalytic Studies of the Gifted and a Great Variety of Other Individuals,* Vol. 2. New York: International Universities Press, 1971, pp. 627–640.
http://www.pep-web.org/document.php?id=apa.002.0671a

Isakower, O. (1957). Report to curriculum committee. New York *Psychoanalytic Institute Mimeographed.*

Kernberg, O.F. (1977). Boundaries and structure in love relations *Journal of the American Psychoanalytic Association* 25:81–114.
http://www.pep-web.org/document.php?id=apa.025.0081a

Kohut, H. (1966). Forms and transformations of narcissism. *Journal of the American Psychoanalytic Association* 14:243–272.
http://www.pep-web.org/document.php?id=apa.014.0243a

Malcove, L. (1975). The analytic situation: Toward a view of the supervisory experience. *Journal of the Philadelphia Association for Psychoanalysis* 2:1–14. http://www.pep-web.org/document.php?id=cps.011.0001a

Sachs, D.M. And Shapiro, S.H. (1976). On parallel processes in therapy and teaching. *Psychoanalytic Quarterly* 45:394–415.
http://www.pep-web.org/document.php?id=paq.045.0394a

Searles, H.F. (1955). The informational value of the supervisor's emotional experiences. *Psychiatry* 18:135–146.

## Chapter 14: Discussion of Two Articles: "Criteria for Termination" by Steven J. Ellman and "On Long Analyses" by Warren S. Poland

Gediman, H.K. (1997). Discussion of two articles: "Criteria for termination." By Steven J. Ellman and "On Long Analyses" by Warren S. Poland. *Psychoanalytic Psychology* 14:211-220.(1997).

The two speakers who have preceded me in today's symposium approach the question, "How long is too long?" from two different but equally valid angles. Dr. Ellman (1994) thoughtfully reviews and critiques theory-based outcome criteria for achieving specific analytic goals that indicate when an analysis is complete and ready to be terminated. He also proposes his own interesting process-related criteria based on extensive clinical case material. Dr. Poland (this issue) is not concerned here with theories and outcomes, but presents a case and engages us in a delightful personal and philosophical discourse on time, including various influences on the time it takes to complete an analysis. His discourse on the relativity of time as a function of a particular analyst with a particular patient at a particular temporal juncture has more to do with the variations of character, style, and personal tempo than with the more specific outcome and process goals of treatment that Ellman chooses as his focus.

I turn first to Dr. Poland's article (this issue), to read you some remarks he made in the cover letter he wrote to me accompanying his timely submitted manuscript, remarks that I read as a cautionary tale and that inspired my critique of some of his ideas. He wrote: "Generally, I am a hopeless rewriter, one who has to avoid my own published articles lest I try still to refine sentences to improve them. Most likely I will make no more changes in this manuscript before the presentation, and any changes I cannot resist will be only those of polishing, not conceptual alterations." And, as you heard him say in a case illustration, his patient felt that he had gained and accomplished all he wanted, and he also believed that were the analysis to proceed any longer, it was merely because his analyst was caught up with his own perfectionism. So, it is natural for me to conjecture, and I trust Dr. Poland will tolerate my exercising of the analytic prerogative, or at the very least my flight of fancy, that his comments to me in his cover letter might at least in part have been influenced by thoughts of the termination process. Could Dr. Poland, at some level, have wanted to communicate to me that his wish to present a well-polished article stood as a metaphor, wherein polishing and refining stand for the final workmanship of an analysis? What conscientious and dedicated analyst hasn't worked long, perhaps longer than necessary, in her or his pursuit of refinements and improvements of the work of analysis? The pursuit of the better and the best is common among analysts and analysands alike. Freud (1937), in "Analysis Terminable and Interminable," said, "The better is always the enemy of the good" (p. 231). However, although they may be guided by the metaphor of polishing and refining, good analysts also know the value of restraint, which mitigates against overzealous polishing of a gem past its best fine buff and sparkle, and draw the line that prevents rubbing down to the point that contaminates our art and skill. I was interested to learn, as I reached a later portion of his article, that Dr. Poland had terminated the case he used for his illustration at the very time he sat down to write it up. And, judging from his prompt delivery to me of the manuscript, he knows and respects how long it takes some of us to analyze, to write articles, and to prepare discussions.

I turn now to elaborate on some of Dr. Ellman's observations. His primary realm of discourse is the timing of termination in accordance with outcome criteria. He reviews the ways in which outcome and termination relate to theories, whether of pathogenesis, therapeutic action, or cure. He questions such beliefs as those espoused by Freud (1937) at times, and also by Brenner (1982) that *the* curative element of analysis derives solely from the benefits of insights derived from interpretation. The termination phase, according to this line of reasoning, is the culmination of years of interpretive work with a patient who forms a good working alliance early on and free-associates readily all along. But we know that others working analytically with difficult patients have discovered that the ability to form a working alliance and to free-associate, analyzability criteria regarded by classicists as appropriate for beginning an analysis, are among the cardinal signs of the capacity to terminate. Ellman adds and elaborates his own criterion of "analytic trust" and the way the analysand responds to interpretive efforts as critical determinants of the termination process. He also proposes a broader view than Brenner (1994) and Novick (1993) of the self-analytic function as a criterion for successful and mutual terminations. As you have heard more than once this morning, good alliances, good hours, and good moments are few, but, like analytic trust, increase with the progress of an analysis.

This ironic psychoanalytic fact suggests that although active application of insights acquired via interpretation undoubtedly is a proper termination criterion for some patients, interpretation alone, even by a good enough analyst, does not inevitably lead to cure. Ellman rightly questions the older view that the patient who has a negative therapeutic reaction to correct interpretations by the analyst is not analyzable. Well then, Freud, Brenner, and (I would add) Arlow might say, the patient who does not meet this criterion of applying insights acquired from interpretation is not analyzable, and should we persist in our interpretive efforts, the analysis would by definition be a "nonanalysis," and on that account would be too long. However, many patients once and still considered unanalyzable by some, would be considered analyzable by analysts who define the therapeutic action of psychoanalysis as something more than simply insights gained from interpretation. When the therapeutic action is believed to be dependent on additional factors, such as dealing with a basic fault, as providing a holding environment at certain times, as creating a new therapeutic object relationship—the familiar factors—then analyses are going to be longer, not shorter, and criteria for cure will be different than Arlow's, Brenner's, and Freud's.

In his most recent work, Brenner (1994) deconstructed the structural model, implying specific criteria for termination, and therefore, how long is too long. His new poststructuralist model hinges on the idea that conflict, because it is ubiquitous, is not resolvable. In the arguably bygone old days, when analysts recognized specific agencies or structures of the mind—namely id, ego, and superego—conflict resolution was the criterion for termination. And this criterion was met according to Freud's dictum, "Where id was, there ego shall be." Adherents of the structural theory presumably had no difficulty determining this transposition of structure and function. The length of an analysis depended on the analyst's discerning when the goal was met. Now, if as Brenner (1994) maintained, conflict is indeed ubiquitous and therefore not resolvable, we would be dealing by definition with an interminable process, should we wait for it to be resolved. It is now simply a matter, he says, of determining whether the conflict and compromise formations are normal or pathological. His criterion of normality is the cost to the individual of the way the particular balance of the components of conflict and compromise formation play out during the course of an analysis. Analyses can be assumed to have lasted just long enough when the analyst makes a good, discerning judgment as to when that time is reached in which the benefits outweigh the costs of inevitable conflict and compromise. But how does one know when a normal compromise formation replaces a pathological one? According to Brenner (1993):

> If a compromise formation allows for an adequate amount of pleasurable gratification of drive derivatives, if it does not arouse too much

unpleasure, if it does not entail too much inhibition of function as a result of defense, and if it does not involve too much by way of self injury and suffering as punishment for moral transgressions, it qualifies as normal. If not, a compromise formation deserves to be called patho- logical. No simpler or more precise distinction is possible at present between normality and pathology in mental life. (p. 21)

If Brenner and his followers use this criterion of normality of compromise formation as a criterion for termination, we could imagine them concluding that analyses proceeding beyond the point when this criterion is met are too long. But it is the individual analyst in collaboration with the analysand who must judge when that criterion is met and, as Poland reminds us, some indi- vidual analysts, in anticipation of termination, do fall prey to such conditions that surface at that time: perfectionism, fear of separation, neurotic guilt, or excess zeal to protect the patient. I remind you of some of the deeper mean- ings of termination that Donald Kaplan (1993) reviewed in the 1993 Section I Symposium on that topic: the common associations to death, geographical separation, and hostility, meanings that impart, by definition, a negative color- ing to the unconscious significance of separation during the termination phase of a psychoanalysis. The phase itself then raises new issues for analysis that prolong its duration. Fearsome separations and countertransferential zeal in the analyst call into question the one simple criterion of normal compromise formations in the analysand. By considering these and other realities, we have entered the realm of personal factors and their variations among analysts. That is the realm that Dr. Poland inhabits in his presentation to us.

Poland says that even when Freud found interpretation and insight to be effective as curative factors, he was not content to let it rest at that. Among the factors that make an analysis last longer than the time it takes to gain insights into conflicts are, as Ellman notes: (a) the turning of insight into ef- fective and lasting action, (b) doing the work of mourning—the final working through of a separation from the analyst as an object representative of drive derivatives from all levels of development, and (c) the development of mutual trust. However, it may take years of a termination phase to *convert* insight *into action* because of many factors, among which I would number the ad- hesiveness of the libido that Freud recognized, a strong "constitutional" dose of passivity, and the range of idiosyncratic unconscious meanings of insight and interpretation to certain patients. For example, as Kohut (1971) and others have noted, certain patients with narcissistic personality disorders experience interpretations as a humiliation, or as the analyst's intent to devalue. An analysis approaches the termination phase for such patients when they no longer feel humiliated by interpretations, and can, at last, accept interpretations as interpretations. It is then and only then that patients can make use of their previously inhibited ability to conduct the analysis to some extent by themselves—one of Ellman's criteria for termination. Kleinians report how interpretations may stimulate the patients' envy of the analyst's interpretive skills. They also report how fantasies about putting the analyst's interpretation to active use feel, to the patient in the paranoid-schizoid position, like robbing the analyst of "Good Breast" contents. For Bion (1959), interpretations invite attacks on linking, or on the very functions of meaning and of imparting insight. Other variants of the "negative therapeutic reaction" to interpretations have been noted by analysts of all persuasions.

As for the time it takes to complete the work of mourning, which includes analyzing the denial of the contemplated loss, I am thinking of a patient who needed a long period of analytic work to progress from one level of understanding of this problem to another, presumably deeper level. At Level 1, she refused to put insight into action for herself, for fear that if she got better, the analysis would end and she would lose me. At Level 2, like many a prototypical Kleinian patient, she elaborated on a fantasy to which she adhered despite all my attempts at properly dosed empathic interpretations. She stubbornly persisted in a belief that if she accepted and used on her own what she had learned from me—that is, if she internalized me as a good object—she would be taking away from me my analytic skill, which she idealized, insisting that only one of us, never both, can have it. To be ready to terminate was tantamount to robbing me to fill herself, leaving me empty, ready to be trashed as garbage. She would not only feel guilty about what she did to me, but could not tolerate the image of herself as ready to dispense with a person who is no longer of any use to her. Only men, she thought, used women in this exploitative way; only men displayed no constancy, loyalty, or fidelity. Women did not do that to other women. This fantasy opened up a whole range of formerly latent conflicts to be analyzed, including those involved with penis envy and envy of men as well as of the "Good Breast." However, her inability to let go of the fantasy in favor of active application of insight was an example of adhesion of the libido that Freud (1937) recognized, in his main article on termination, as one of the obstacles to a shorter, successful analysis. In this instance, her adhesion to me as the only one of us two who could do interpretive work preceded a period during which she could also use me transitionally, without, in Ellman's words, the illusion of the analysis and the analyst being lost. She accomplished this during my vacations by reading books on psychoanalytic subjects, including one that I wrote. Her activities did indeed constitute a "transitional space" and heralded in the termination phase that, in her case, was a long one.

Some other theory based outcome criteria that inform Dr. Ellman's speculations on how long is too long are to be found in Arlow's (1986) work on relating pathogenesis to psychoanalytic therapy. He reviewed a number of theories differing in what is considered the pathogen to be eliminated. For the purpose of my discussion, I presume that Arlow would agree that if the pathogen is no longer present, then a continued analysis is too long an analysis. By simplifying the relation of pathogen to outcome, Arlow tilts at an array of what I believe to be straw men, but which, I am afraid, Arlow regards as unreasonable forces to be reckoned with. Here are some examples of Arlow's (1986) tongue-in-cheek reasoning that, I shudder to think, might be seized as termination criteria by certain managed-care peer review boards whose members believe that any analysis is too long. If the pathogen were dammed-up undischarged sexual tensions, then successfully completed abreaction and catharsis of these tensions would be a sign that the analysis was long enough. If the pathogen were early split-object representations, a manipulative strategy of showing the patient how the parent, or analyst, can be both bad and good, and yet at the same time one whole person, meets the treatment goal, and any more analysis is too long. If the pathogen is a failure of developmentally necessary mirroring by unempathic mothering, the "corrective emotional experience" of the analyst's empathy should reach the outcome that defines long enough analysis. But if the outcome that both Arlow (1986) and Brenner (1994) desire is met, that is, the replacement, by interpretation and insight, of a pathological by a normal compromise formation, who has the final say on what is long enough and what is too long?

Other analytic theorists see more complexity in the therapeutic action and in termination criteria. Bird (1972) argued that too much rapport at the expense of interpretation, particularly of negative transference, leads to overly long analyses. Modell (1976), despite being a most renowned proponent of the therapeutic action of the holding environment, recognized its limitations when he said:

> Interpretation leads to the dissolution of magical fantasies associated with the holding environment in a manner analogous to the dissolution of the transference neurosis. If these fantasies associated with the holding environment are not sufficiently analyzed, there is a danger, in the narcissistic character disorder, that the analytic process itself may

become a transitional object and the patient would then be addicted to an interminable analysis. (p. 305)

Other aspects of treatment that can continue for a frightfully long time, and that occupy Dr. Ellman's attention, are the repetition of old patterns and interactions. Those enactments, if unanalyzed, would certainly prolong an analysis. Even their proper interpretation could account for a longer analysis than usually occurs in those so-called classical cases where repetitions and enactments are not analyzed because they were presumed, wrongly, to be unanalyzable.

I hope I have given you some sense of the pitfalls of a simplistic approach to theory and outcome criteria, the worst of which would be to declare the patient unanalyzable if the patient, after a long enough time, does not meet certain questionable criteria for termination. This approach seems to work only if we specify criteria for what the expected outcome of an analysis should be. Then we have some basis to determine what is too long. But matters can never be that simple, for even when we specify as neatly as possible our therapeutic goals of analysis, some subjective factors will always enter into our judgment of whether or not that criterion is met, and, therefore, in the decision as to when it is time to stop.

I would like to turn back now to some more philosophical and depth psychological considerations of lengths of analyses. Nothing could contrast more with Arlow's spoofs than Poland's treatise on goals, time, and change. Dr. Poland says we need not apologize for the length of an analysis, respecting the patient's right to stop when he feels better as well as respecting his wish to continue on toward more insight and mastery (1994, p. 81). But things do not always work so smoothly and out of the realm of conflict and passionate feelings in the transference, Peanuts' dragonfly friend with his twenty-four hour lifespan prompting "If only I knew at 9 a.m. what I know now," echoes the poetic and proverbial Robert Burns lament, "Of all the sad words of tongue and pen, the saddest are these 'it might have been.'" What analyst has not, in the termination phases of a treatment, been berated with some variation of, "Why didn't you say that to me ten years ago?" Such Monday morning quarterbacking implies vicissitudes of envy and gratitude. The reproach also reflects the temptation to blame someone, something, reality's limits, perhaps, for the sense, often at the end of the hardest work, of lost and wasted time and effort on the parts of both analyst and analysand. Specific variations of this reproach, in longish analyses by today's standards, might be: "Why did you ever let me join that corporate law firm; marry that demanding woman; have more children than I possibly could afford to bring up properly?" In his discourse on time, Poland notes how time is wondrously relative. A minute is too long for some things and a lifetime too short for others. Long, he says, means different things to different people, depending on their phase of life and how that phase interacts with a sense of urgency, or on whether they are characteristically impulsive or characteristically laid back. As for the now defunct practice of injunctions against making important life decisions while an analysis was ongoing, the saying goes, "Those were the days when analyses were short and marriages were long." And, we might add, when positions with tenure were more common than massive layoffs, and when we rarely heard the now frequent complaint of the "biological time clock" running out.

In this same vein, I have a few remarks on Dr. Ellman's critique of Freud's ideas of making latent content manifest so that it can be analyzed. Contrary to what Freud, in his day found, namely that certain patients' life circumstances did not stimulate sufficiently certain latent issues during treatment, we often find today the reverse. Life circumstances are more complex, certainly more complex than Ferenczi's allegedly happy marriage and successful secure career. Life seems less stable, and more ever-changing, therefore stimulating an apparently limitless number of latent conflicts to rise to the surface during treatment. Greater longevity brings out more conflicts, too, making for longer analyses than Freud thought would be necessary even if he forced the latent conflicts to surface. But Ellman asks us to consider that the analysis generates a life of its own through the unfolding of the transference, which is not always restricted by the circumstances of the patient's life at the time of the analysis (Ellman, 1994 p. 104). I would think, as Freud at times other than in "Analysis Terminable and Interminable" did, that indeed the transference takes on a life of its own, related not only to more complex real present events but also to displacements from the past. In addition, we find in the transference projections of repudiated aspects of the analysand, projections that surely generate for the transference-countertransference matrix a life of its own. This analytic life space may be relatively independent of any specific current life circumstances, such as illness, loss of fortune, divorce, abandonment, establishing new and difficult relationships, hostile takeovers disrupting a lifetime successful career, and hosts of other personal and professional trauma and narcissistic wounds. No matter what the present brings, analyses contain various meaningful measures of repetition of past object relationships.

We know we have come a long way when instead of giving injunctions about rushing into things before the analysis is over, or even before sufficiently analyzing intrapsychic conflicts around life decisions, we analyze common and terrible existential anxieties. We address unconscious meanings of fears of taking the wrong turn in the road; of the absolute reality of how every choice to move in a specific direction limits our possibilities of moving in others; of doubts and uncertainties about which of two or more forks in the road will lead to the desired goal. The assault on patients' omnipotent fantasies by reality-imposed time limits, and by the realities of the analyst's limited omniscience, are better analyzed than responded to by injunction, or worse yet, by the directive "proactive" therapist, such as one working for a managed care organization, telling a patient which life path leads to a shorter, more cost-efficiently conducted treatment.

Poland's rhetorical question, "Can there be any among us who wishes our analysis had been longer?" and his reference to Donald Kaplan's witty complaint about his analyst's tickets for loitering, remind me of other such wishes for longer analyses. A patient complained that both of her two analyses were aborted for the same reason: Her first analyst thought the benefits from the real relationship of the patient's upcoming marriage would be a suitable substitute for continuing the analysis. The marriage turned out to be a not entirely happy one and was terminated by divorce. The patient, many years later, entered a second analysis, hoping to avoid the same sort of inauspicious premature ending. She spent much of the reanalysis expressing the anger she felt toward her first analyst for keeping the analysis too short for the wrong reasons. However, her second analyst offered a similar rationale for terminating, suggesting that should the analysis last too much longer, it might interfere with a more important pending real relationship. Was the patient enacting something with both analysts that led to a repetition of what she thought were two too-short analyses, paralleling two too-short relationships with men? Could both analysts have been influenced, it seems mistakenly, by similar convictions of when too long was too long? In any event, that patient did wish that each of her analyses had been longer, but it is not clear whether those possibly conflictual wishes were analyzed or analyzable. How often have I heard patients say something like, "This is an elitist treatment"; "I am indulging myself"; or "My husband thinks I am indulging myself"; or the wish-fear expressed as "Who wouldn't want to come seven days a week forever to talk about myself and hear you talk about me." And how often have we heard certain reaction formations to this wish for analysis interminable: "I feel too guilty coming here when others can't afford even a clinic," or "Whenever I feel less pain, I think of all the others who have not had the good fortune to do this kind of work, so I'd better not progress any further for fear of jinxing my good luck;" or, the clincher, "It's OK for Woody Allen but not for me." All of this is analyzable material, reflecting unconscious fantasy and conflict.

I also like Dr. Poland's analogy about the proper dosage of medicine, when he wonders how much is enough and enough for whom. A patient likened her analysis to taking homeopathic doses of medicine for whatever ails her, claiming, that when she had taken enough of the remedy, it worked on its own, and she did not have to do anything. She believed the homeopathic remedy metaphor stood well for her analysis, and I wondered, as might Dr. Ellman, if she were beginning to trust fully the analyst and the results of treatment, and to take control of the analytic process more fully, That is, I wondered if she had in mind that she could terminate once she took over the analyst's function by conducting her own self analysis, the way analysts in training do. It turned out that she had no such process in mind, but simply did not want to deal with her compliance anxieties of being too influenced by external agents, like homeopathic medicines and her analyst. Because she was not autonomous enough from either her own drives or from environmental influences, it could hardly be concluded that enough was enough yet for her. But, as Dr. Poland said of the value of closure in the closing portion of his presentation, "Some things can be accomplished and realized alone that cannot be accomplished with someone else" (p.21). The judgment call has got to be made by one, the other, or both. Length and depth do tend to get confused whether we are speaking of doses or of analyses.

Some patients need to trash analyses when they do not yield the mythical state of cure. Because, as Dr. Poland says, the average expectable analyst is not an exploitative knave, we need not be defensive or apologetic when lengthy procedures are called for, and we need not be moralistically taken in by the patient's complaint that long and costly treatment is an indulgence. Finally, we should not succumb to the implied threat of knavery when managed care organizations—what Poland recognizes as the "tiger at the gate"—accuse us of offering exploitative, (because lengthy), medically valueless treatment, when we aim to help our patients grow to be less vulnerable to the psychic pains for which they sought relief by consenting to long, arduous, and courageous work.

## REFERENCES

Arlow, J.A. (1986). The relation of theories of pathogenesis to psychoanalytic therapy. In A.D. Richards & M. Willick, (Eds.) *Psychoanalysis: The science of mental conflict. Essays in honor of Charles Brenner* (pp. 49–63), Hillsdale, NJ: The Analytic Press.

Bion, W.R. (1959). Attacks on linking. *International Journal of Psycho-Analysis*

40:308–315.

Bird, B. (1972). Notes on transference: Universal phenomenon and hardest part of analysis. *Journal of the American Psychoanalytic Association* 20:267–301

Brenner, C. (1982). *The Mind in Conflict*. New York: International Universities Press.

—— (1994). The mind as conflict and compromise formation. *Journal of Clinical Psychoanalysis* 3:473–488.

Ellman, S. (1994, April). To continue or not to continue: Benefits and draw-backs. In O. Kerner (Chair), How long is too long?: Further thoughts on termination. Section I Symposium conducted at the 14th Division 39 spring meeting, Washington, DC.

Freud, S. (1937). Analysis terminable and interminable. *Standard Edition* 23:209–253.

Kaplan, D. (1993). Discussion of J. Novick's paper, "Termination-conceivable and inconceivable" and Martin Bergmann's paper, "Why termination has become the Achilles's heel of psychoanalysis." In O. Kerner (Chair), *Go the Distance: Thoughts on termination*. Section I Symposium conducted at the 13th Division 39 spring meeting, New York.

Kohut, H. (1971) *The Analysis of the Self*. New York: International Universities Press.

Modell, A.H. (1976). "The holding environment" and the therapeutic action of psychoanalysis. *Journal of the American Psychoanalytic Association* 24:285–307.

Novick, J. (1993, April). Termination-conceivable and inconceivable. In O. Kerner (Chair), *Go the Distance: Thoughts on Termination*. Section I Symposium conducted at the 13th Division 39 spring meeting, New York.

# Chapter 15: The Therapeutic Action in the Real, Transferential, and Therapeutic Object Relationship

[Gediman, H.K. (1998). The therapeutic action in the real, transferential, and therapeutic object relationship. In: C.S. Ellman et al, Eds. *The Modern Freudians: Contemporary Psychoanalytic Technique.* Northvale, New Jersey: Jason Aronson.]

There is a basic assumption that the dichotomy of transference and real is arbitrary, false, misleading, and fundamentally out of synch with Freudian psychoanalysis today. That false dichotomy assumes that the therapeutic action of psychoanalytic treatment is based solely on the technique of interpretation of intrapsychic conflict. However, our present understanding of the therapeutic action of psychoanalysis has evolved significantly into a more broadly based, multiperspectival approach to the psychoanalytic treatment of a widening scope of patients.

I once had occasion to consult with a woman whose analysis was stalemated. The analyst, apparently concerned with the degree of his patient's pathology, had decided it was important to be very "real." The patient feared she was not being analyzed. Being real meant to him doing something extra-analytic or nonanalytic. He revealed such personal information as the kind of car he drove, the names of his children, and his favorite restaurants and vacation spots. I suggested to the patient that her analyst's self-disclosure seemed to have made her worry that her analyst thought she was a fragile patient and that she needed a real relationship with him because he believed she could not withstand the rigors of analytic work. By rigors, I had in mind the three cardinal hallmarks: neutrality, abstinence, and anonymity. I later had occasion to speak with the analyst who agreed that this was indeed his rationale. Was the analyst's choice of the contents of his self-disclosure, which by definition always involves some modification of the principle of anonymity as we once understood it, a travesty of what is meant as a "real relationship"? I think so. That slippage in an understanding of the real relationship was not unique to him and led me to organize this chapter around a central question: How do we maintain the analytic attitude with its usual safeguards of neutrality, abstinence, and anonymity, and also honor the modifications that have evolved with those steady refinements and progression of our understanding of the way the mind works and in our analytic technique that characterize Freudian psychoanalysis today?

When we speak of the real relationship and the therapeutic action from the point of view of contemporary Freudian psychoanalysis, obviously we are not advocating telling the patient what kind of car we drive, where we take our vacations, whether or not we are married, or how many children we have. The value of the concept of the real relationship does not center on feeding a patient herring, as Freud (1909) did to the "Rat Man." It is not typified by letting a patient use the telephone in an emergency. It is not limited to such emergency actions as that of an analyst lending a patient money to get her car out of a parking garage on the day the patient was mugged. These are all real occurrences; however, they are extra-analytic. Events such as these have the potential for real repercussions on how the analysis will progress, because they are responded to by the analysand as meaningful events that stimulate conscious and unconscious fantasies, conflicts, and other psychic events, in-cluding real emotionally charged interaction patterns with the analyst that are often highly analyzable. When we speak of the real relationship, what we all, I expect, are limiting ourselves to is a real relationship that is part and parcel of and often indistinguishable from the therapeutic relationship, that impacts significantly on the transference, and that is a crucial part of the therapeutic action of psychoanalysis. Loewald (1960) and then Grunes (1984) pioneered the evolving historical context from which this basic position derives. To highlight the essence of the position, I shall present some clinical material and then discuss four main technical areas that touch on new ways of looking at neutrality, abstinence, and anonymity. These are the areas of technique, self-disclosures by the analyst, intersubjectivity, and interaction.

## PROCESS FROM SELECTED SESSIONS

I have chosen two different series of sessions with one analysand, Ms. D., oc-curring over the course of several weeks, to illustrate how a "real" event, not intrinsic to the analytic process, led to repercussions and to other "real" events that subsequently became intrinsic to the process. These latter events involved interactions that centered on the transference-countertransference, became part and parcel of the therapeutic relationship, and contributed significantly to the quality of the object relationship with my patient and to the therapeutic action of the analysis that I was conducting. These accounts of process are consistent with the major point made by Grunes (1984): "Analyst and patient are not pausing for a detour into a real relationship and then getting back to the serious business of analytic treatment. They are ipso facto in a special illusional and real relationship which is part of the very process of analysis itself" (p. 136).

## FIRST SERIES OF SESSIONS

In the vignettes to follow, there was indeed a "real" component to the interaction, that is, real in the sense that it wasn't what usually happens, and was determined by extra-analytic conditions—the weather and my buzzer system. Just to mention these factors renders them minute and pedestrian, hardly approaching the real factors in the relationship that have seemed to others to be so significant. However, these events had repercussions leading to interactions within the analysis that were far more important and touched directly on the therapeutic action with this patient. Shortly after Ms. D.'s return from a ten-day vacation, a real incident served to highlight the real and how it may be employed therapeutically. It also highlighted how the therapeutic has very real aspects. There is something intrinsic to the therapeutic process that is very real and alive and it is this very realness in the therapeutic interaction that is indispensable to the therapeutic action of psychoanalysis. Loewald (1960) and Grunes (1984) thought that in what constitutes the therapeutic action, the analyst does very little that is real outside of what the analyst normally does in conducting an analysis. Both distinguished their positions, as I would distinguish mine, from those who employ an extra-analytic corrective emotional experience as a new real experience in an effort to effect new change. The idea of a real relationship that transcends the therapeutic is not a useful way of looking at therapeutic action. My view is also in line with Strachey's (1934) ideas on the therapeutic action and the mutative interpretation: the interpretations that produce real change are those that are directed to something that is "hot" and "real" in the ongoing transference. The two incidents I am about to review qualify as real and alive not simply because they were spurred on by extra-analytic realities, but because they were affectively hot in the transference. The first was the patient's phone call to me at my home, not my office, on the evening before her first scheduled post vacation appointment in which she said she would be unable to make the appointment because a blizzard forced her plane to land in another city. She called me at home again the next evening, still delayed in the distant city, to tell me she would call as soon as she got back to schedule an extra appointment if I had the time.

The first session after the vacation was a regularly scheduled working session when the "real" did not enter in. I am using the word *real* in quotation marks to illustrate, once again, how I think the distinction between real and therapeutic is arbitrary, misleading, and confusing. The second meeting after her vacation was a double session (easy to do on a snowbound day) and the first of two specially scheduled make-up sessions. That double session had ended with her saying "I'll see you tomorrow morning" (a regularly scheduled session) and I said, "Yes, at 9:00, I'm sorry, 8:15," to which she responded, "Tomorrow's is at 8:15, Friday's extra one is at 9:00." I had arrived at my office for the third session after the vacation break, the second specially scheduled makeup session, just before 7:45. At 8:15 I had not yet heard the buzz on the handset of my intercom system. In that sense, the session was characterized by a "real" incident. Ms. D. was almost never late and usually considerably early, so I was concerned that the snow conditions were making navigating through the city quite difficult. Yet this patient certainly would have left plenty of extra time. At 8:33 the buzzer on the handset rang, she announced herself, and I buzzed her in. She stormed into the room, looking at me wrathfully, and said, "Where were you when I buzzed at 7:50? And I buzzed you again at 8:10." I told her that I was right here in my chair. "You couldn't have come in the building or I would have seen you. I was on the sofa in the lobby the whole time." She was clearly confused, but I was not. I had noticed from time to time that my buzzer did not always ring loudly. Sometimes I only heard a barely audible "ping," and I was meaning to have the system checked out. I felt bad that I had been postponing that chore, and told her that sometimes it was hard to hear the buzzer, and I had noticed that that was particularly true if the button outside the door was pressed too lightly and didn't make the proper connection. Undaunted, and undoubtedly defensive, I then suggested to her that if she ever buzzes and does not get an answer, she should press the bell on the door that is not connected to the buzzer system. I make this suggestion to all patients, because sometimes, when they come early and ring, I am not in my consulting room but somewhere else in the suite—the kitchen, the bathroom, or my office partner's consulting room. She reminded me later that I had suggested that to her, too. I apologized to her for the inconvenience.

During this session, less than twenty minutes in length, the patient at first did not know what to do. "Is this a session or not?" She then got off the couch and stomped toward the door as though to leave and I said, "Sit down, please." Her anger, clearly directed at me, soon turned back around upon herself. "I'm so stupid. I should have pushed the doorbell harder." Then, "As I was sitting out in your lobby, I had the thought that something must have happened to you, but today is my birthday and I felt abandoned. I felt that way, even though I know it was absurd. And now that the situation is clear, I still am so furious. It doesn't make any sense but that's how I feel." I made use of this material in the usual way, interpreting how old feelings can surface in these conditions even though rationally they do not appear justified. It is important to note that I claimed full responsibility for the buzzer problem. The system was not perfect. She contrasted her reaction to that of being stranded in the faraway city for three days, saying that she was calm and untroubled by that act of fate, knowing it was not anyone's fault and nothing bad would come of the delay. I pointed out how it was important for her to blame someone, and even though I claimed responsibility, she had to maintain that it was her fault. I was aware that I had not yet touched on her longing to be with me while she was on vacation, when she returned, and now, waiting for me. The closest I could get was to refer to the possibility that she may have had the idea that I had not been thinking of her at just the time when she was most eager to see me, and so she then turned her longing into fury, and then the fury at me was turned around into anger at herself for making a mistake, for not being perfect. "That's how it always was. When my mother turned away from me, I had to find out what I was doing wrong to get her back. I actually thought you got the time mixed up, that you thought today was at nine and tomorrow at 8:15." I said: "And then you had to be the little girl taking charge of things, knowing more and better than the mother who makes mistakes." In this and other ways, the aborted session turned something in the extra-analytic "real" relationship to something analytically real in the transference and in the therapeutic interaction. In a calculated violation of the rule of abstinence, I offered to extend the next session to make up for the time we had missed today—another "real" action on my part with implications for the real therapeutic object relationship.

During the next of this series of sessions, she told of a string of mishaps—events at her office that she was not there to take charge of as she usually would; more plane delays, and so on. She told me the reason she did not call my office, but called me instead at home the night she knew she was stranded was because she did not know if I checked my office answering machine from home, and did not even know if one could do so. I told her it was clear that she wanted to make contact with me, but feared that I might not care enough to check on her whereabouts by calling my machine. She was focusing instead on her failing to be as conscientious as she felt she should be, mainly because she believed and presumably wished, unconsciously, that she had intruded on me. She was also afraid of intruding on my patients if she had called the office. I noted how she always got angry when there were telephone-ringing intrusions on her sessions. So there were the more obvious themes of reproaching herself and me, which really seemed to be covering up her desire to make contact after a frustrating and lonely separation.

As for the real, the therapeutic, and the transference relationship, real analytic events were set off by her analytically meaningful call to me at my home. There was also the extra-analytically real issue of my door buzzer. Either there was a mechanical failure, and/or she did not press hard enough. She got a real, nonanonymous response from me about my concern about my patients, for I assured her I checked my machine for messages regularly on weekends. This was said for the purpose of calling her attention to how untrustful she was of anyone except herself to take care of her properly. I had also offered her extra time, which she accepted. I had scheduled an extra appointment, and apologized for the buzzer problem.

I told a little anecdote to her, of how her response to coming home reminded me of how little children when separated from their mothers due to trips or illness, long to be with mother and eagerly await the reunion. But as soon as they are reunited, instead of being happy they turn angry and reproach mother. I told her that that was what I thought was being repeated when she was so angry with me that I was not there on time after her return. She said, "So, I'm really having a reaction to my mother and not to you." She was clearly ambivalent about the possibility that I might attribute her unplanned affective responsivity simply to displaced transference. She made clear her discomfort that I might be inauthenticating her response, distancing it from the aliveness in the here-and-now transference or from the real relationship that included all the volatile, stormy, and intimate events that had really transpired between her and me. Those real events that had occurred outside the expected therapeutic frame, that started by chance with the blizzard, and that then spiraled into all sorts of unusual unpredictable ramifications and real responses to me and from me in the real and transferential analytic relationship, had set a brand-new tone in the treatment, centering on a set of interactions that were clearly analyzable. Ms. D. searched for a phrase to characterize this new relationship precisely. She settled on "real, but not quite real, perhaps artificial," or "only transference." This sounds a lot like Winnicott's (1951) transitional space—the transference being real and not real at the same time. This patient was troubled if she did not know all the "rules" of treatment. The rules helped her feel in control of things by offering her guidelines about how to be on good behavior and how to do what she was supposed to do in this process. She was an angry perfectionistic child in gleeful combat with her maternal counterpart. Anxiety and rage emerged when real events that transcended the expectable structure of the analytic situation—the fundamental rule, the neutrality, abstinence, and anonymity that define the analytic situation—took her by surprise. The new and unpredicted tone in our relationship lent a sense of authentic urgency, providing the analytic "hot spots" that define the optimal setting for interpretations of the interface of the real and the transferential in the therapeutic object relationship. I cared to listen, I accommodated her, I reassured her—all real. But I also calmly interpreted her projection of her perfectionism and need for nonintrusion onto me. The therapeutic action indeed included the interface of the real with the transference. It is not a matter of one or the other.

Before going on to the second series of sessions, it would be helpful to review the way Grunes (1984) fleshes out aspects of that interface as one theoretical context for understanding the treatment I am reporting. There has been, outside of contemporary Freudian analysis, too arbitrary a distinction made between the real relationship, the transference, and the therapeutic object relationship. Grunes bases his argument on the problematic nature of the continuing, excessive dichotomy in the psychoanalytic literature between the transference and the actuality of the treatment relationship. Particularly among the more regressed, or as we now like to say, "widening-scope" patients, there is a "relationship demand factor in the treatment which cannot be met by interpretation alone" (p. 123). I would extend this idea to neurotic patients as well. They also require a therapeutic object relationship, perhaps with different emphases than Grunes has advocated for the more disturbed. Grunes uses the term *therapeutic object relationship* interchangeably with such terms as *analyst-patient relationship* and *therapeutic interaction.* He characterizes it as a situation of primal intimacy between patient and analyst that contains both an illusional or transference and a real aspect. The intimacy involves a special type of empathic permeability of boundaries between analyst and patient. "One very early form of the primal transference would involve the pleasure . . . of self-definition through feeling focused upon by mother and focusing upon her focusing upon him" (p. 138). That relationship, which is a parent-child analogue, is the matrix of change in which interpretation and analysis of transference occur. Most important, the relationship between the transference and the actualities of the analyst's own real presence through his or her empathy, interactions, and even certain disclosures—this combined real and transference relation—is organically related to psychoanalytic treatment in the first place and does not constitute a parameter to be analyzed (see Eissler 1953). Grunes's (1984) and Loewald's (1960) focus on interactions and notions of reciprocal, symbolic-creative communication, and Renik's (1995) recent advocacy of disclosing to the patient his way of thinking insofar as it is relevant to the joint venture of analytic work, are all congruent with the hallmark of Freudian psychoanalysis today: in the way we interact and in what we disclose, the patient is always at the center.

## SECOND SERIES OF SESSIONS

Within days of returning from *my* vacation in Mexico and a break of nearly two weeks, an additional incident occurred that heightened the feelings that had emerged during *her* vacation when she became stranded and sorely needed to contact me. I apparently had some viral condition, jet lag, Mexican sleeping sickness, call it whatever, which led to sporadic fatigue and sleepiness for about two weeks. One morning, I actually dozed off during my first session of the day, which was the session that preceded Ms. D.'s. This was the first time I had ever had the experience of falling asleep, or at least of entering this particular, and highly atypical for me, altered state of consciousness during a session. The patient I was with, not Ms. D., noticed something wrong, remarked that I looked unsteady on my feet and somewhat faint, and said she felt reluctant to talk about her own troubling matters when I looked to be so clearly under the weather. I remember struggling very hard to stay awake during this session, but all my willpower and determination would not allow me to do that. To my great surprise, I was brought back with a jolt when I heard my first patient of the day say, "I think I should leave now." We had actually run over by 10 minutes. Perhaps I should have canceled my next session, the one with Ms. D. But since I had not as yet fully realized the extent of my indisposition, I proceeded on with my work, assuming, falsely, as it turned out, that my usual alertness and energy level would be restored in short order.

Ms. D. was in the waiting room, and when I went to meet her, she looked extremely troubled. She lay down on the couch and said, "When I was in the waiting room and you didn't come out on time I thought you died." She had thought of calling my son whose name she knew from her prior researches into my real life, but did not have his address. She had also forgotten the address of my office, so she thought it would be useless to call 911 for help. She had thus remained paralyzed to do anything about saving me, like calling the police or someone who knew how to do CPR. She had the idea that I was dying of a heart attack as her mother had a few years ago. Mother was then exactly the same age as she knew me to be, having looked up my birth date in a library archive earlier in the treatment. In response to my inquiry, she said she had not thought to have my doorman call 911. She simply thought I had died and she could do nothing about it. To my surprise and dismay, I was still in the grip of this strange fatigue and dozed off for brief moments periodically during this session.

During my next session with Ms. D., when I truly had regained most of my normal energy level, she said she had worried quite a bit on the day of the previous session when I was late to meet her and when she thought I might have died. My hair had not look combed, and I looked disheveled and out of character, as her mother did on the morning she had her heart attack and died. On that morning, just shortly before Ms. D. started treatment with me, she heard strange sounds emerging from her parents' bedroom that frightened her, but neither she nor her father did anything about it, such as calling 911. She now believes that the sounds were the death rattle, but at the time had mistaken them for sexual moans and therefore did not enter the room to check on her mother's condition and possibly save her life. She had been angry at her father for not calling the police. She was angry at herself for not learning CPR. Any of these moves might have been able to save her mother, a selfless person who did very little to take care of herself. Ms. D. told me *I'd* better go see a doctor right away. I said, "You seemed paralyzed to do anything then, just as you felt paralyzed to do anything to save me when you thought I might be either dead or dying."

In a deliberate discarding of the ideal of anonymity, I decided to tell the patient that I had originally had jet lag and then developed fatigue, which my doctor told me sounded like a viral infection, caught from recirculated air in the jet plane, and that the symptoms should let up entirely within another week. I also told her I felt well enough to work right now. As I rethink the incident at this present time, it would have been best if I had also told her that in retrospect, I realized it might have been better if I had canceled our session on the day I had dozed off with my first patient and let her know that I needed to check out my condition with a physician immediately.[23] Like Renik (1995), I believe that the question is not *whether* to disclose, but how to *manage* the unavoidable condition of constant disclosure. I shared that bit of reality about my medical diagnosis with her because it seemed cruel, heartless, and untherapeutic or antitherapeutic or simply tone deaf to deal at that moment only with the fantasies in the transference. The analytic "hot spot" of my dozing off, a critical or pivotal moment in the analysis, eventually would provide ample opportunity for mutative interpretation. As it turned out, my action, or enactment, if you will, was in tune with her thinking: she did not want to talk about her strong feelings for me as simply a replica of those experienced in

---

23 I am grateful to Dr. Irving Steingart for his help on this issue.

connection with her mother's death because then I would brush them off as transference. I said, "You want to be sure that I also understand that you care personally about me—that there was something alive and present going on in your concern for me that was not just a repetition of your ambivalent feelings at the time of your mother's death." That turned out to be a very helpful intervention, but the patient still could not get the sexualized "death rattle" sounds in her mother's bedroom out of her ears during our session. If only she had paid more attention, she would have brought mother to the hospital and saved her life. But it wasn't right to barge into her mother's bedroom while father was there when she heard sounds that she did not heed or do anything about at the time, becoming similarly paralyzed then as now when she thought it wasn't right to barge into my office or even knock on the door with another patient in there. Doing the right thing became more important than saving the life of selfless people like her mother, or me. I was selfless because I showed up to help her when I was sick. This selflessness is also typical of the patient's own self-representation, in which she often disregards her own well-being by sacrificing autonomy in doing what is right for herself in the interests of doing the right thing for an "other." Needless to say, there is a big reaction formation element in this pattern, for her own self-interests are often put first, as they were in her failing to take action in "rescuing" me when she thought I might be dying.

Shortly thereafter, she had pains in her abdomen, for which she refused to see a physician for fear he would think she was being hypochondriacal. "I'm actually envisioning a fast and painful death from cancer." Suicidal thoughts frequently masked ambivalent and murderous feelings. She had a dream, remembering only the fragment, "You died in your chair." It was the anniversary of her mother's death. I said, "There's a connection between wanting to rejoin the dead and your thoughts about your mother's death and mine." There was a real person in Ms. D.'s life, G., offering possibilities for real contact, but with me she could remain in the safe world of fantasized transference objects. The night before the dream of my dying in my chair, she had read, for the second time, Freud's (1915) paper, "Observations on Transference-Love." Her profession is as far removed from psychoanalysis as any could be. She thought she could maintain her self-sufficiency by reading about transference, a sort of enactment, rather than asking me directly about what I meant when I said that thoughts of joining her mother through death at just the time when the possibility for a real and lasting relationship were opening up for her and were connected with thoughts about me—some longing to be with me if I had died. What was going on with G., a colleague, and now with me since the day of my indisposition, had become all too real and bewildering. I said, "You have been trying desperately through reading the dead Freud's words on transference love to avoid the real live aspects of your relationships with G. and with me."

Was my telling her of my jet lag and fatigue gratuitous? I do not think so. She was relieved to hear I was basically fine. But that didn't stop her from fantasizing about my death. From her point of view, I turned out to be fallible, imperfect, falling asleep during a session—contemptible enough to justify her suicidal fantasies. My disclosure was irrelevant from that point of view, for this issue would have come up in any event. But my disclosure in this instance, and in the instance of telling her I check my machine to keep my patients as a focus of my attention during a weather emergency, did matter from the point of view of restoring authenticity and aliveness to our relationship as a backdrop for the analysis of the transference. Without that authentic counterpoint, she could more easily experience the analysis as make-believe. Rendering the treatment gamelike could convert it into a perpetual analysis at the expense of growth, development, and meaningful analysis of the transference. The transference would have been forced out of that optimal transitional space between play or fantasy and of reality. In this instance, it could take on a malignant character and derail the treatment. Aliveness in the real relationship as a backdrop for authentic transference analysis often requires us to drop temporarily the analysis of repetitions and of unconscious fantasies, particularly those based on projections in the transference. We might say, for example, when a patient distorts the meaning of what we do, "That was not my intention." That sort of disclosure brings in a note of authenticity to the analysis that makes it more than the sterile game it too easily can become. One often hears from patients about to slam the door on treatment, "Don't play mind-fucking games with me." In the less neurotic and more "widening-scope" patients, such disclosures may prevent a regressive transference from disrupting and ruining the process.

## COMMENTARY

The classic adherence to the analytic ideals of neutrality, abstinence, and anonymity, have, in Freudian psychoanalysis today, been abandoned in their original and rigid forms in favor of the evolved contemporary technique that I shall now discuss under four main rubrics: (1) the therapeutic action consists of more than the simple technique of interpretation leading to conflict resolution via interpretations; (2) disclosure in a departure from the ideal of anonymity is inevitable; (3) intersubjectivity, in a Freudian frame, implies a degree of asymmetricality that keeps the patient at the center and does not diminish the authority of the analyst; (4) interaction between patient and analyst is crucial to the therapeutic action.

## TECHNIQUE: BEYOND NEUTRALITY, ABSTINENCE, AND ANONYMITY

Arlow and Brenner (1990) have made the point repeatedly in their recent work that the psychoanalytic process itself consists only of technique, and the technique consists exclusively of imparting insight via the interpretation of conflict and compromise formation. This particular and limited technique, they say, constitutes the therapeutic action of psychoanalysis. Their view is oversimplified, because in fact the technique and the therapeutic action encompass more than the interpretation of conflict—and the unconscious processes that inevitably enter in—by consistently applied technique in a standard analytic situation. There have always been analysts who regard the psychoanalytic process as something other than, or in addition to, or as transcending that technique. Technique, in the view being critiqued, is limited to the dynamic interactions of the patient's conflicts and the analyst's technical interventions. What I wish to emphasize is that interpretations of conflict within the transference matrix are not worth their salt unless they refer to real experiences within the here-and-now relationship. The psychoanalytic process and its therapeutic action are far more than synonymous with changes brought about simply, as Arlow and Brenner would have it, by consistently applied technique in a standard analytic situation, and by the analyst's interpretations, alone. It is not that the standard technique has changed, or that the analyst does anything radically different. It is just that more, and more complex, things happen than analysts working simply out of older traditions have acknowledged.

In a panel presented at the Columbia Association for Psychoanalytic Medicine (1996), "Change Within the Analyst," the participants, Jacobs, Kernberg, and Renik, agreed that what makes analysis work goes beyond uniform application of standard technique. They addressed the issue of changes in our basic attitudes toward the once sanctified values of neutrality, abstinence, and anonymity. Kernberg rightly maintained that technical neutrality no longer refers to the analyst being simply a blank screen or a reflecting mirror of the patient's projections. Neutrality is not disgruntled indifference but is an objective, concerned stance about the patient's problems, requiring a position equidistant between the contradictory forces operating in the patient's mind. Renik (1996), even more recently, speaks of the "perils of neutrality" as including not just the fallacy of the analyst as blank screen, but also the undesirability of remaining equidistant between contradictory forces. There indeed has been a tradition among many Freudian analysts of opposing the patient's harsh superego by vigorously disagreeing with the patient's irrational self-criticisms. The Columbia panel understood correctly that interpretations may, in and of themselves, be gratifying, and in that regard, they rightly called into question the analytic ideal of abstinence. Loewald (1960), Stone, (1954), and others have always thought that gratifications for both parties in the dyad were inherent in the standard method. Furthermore, many have discovered that there are also gratifications in the new analytic object relationship. Chused (1996), in her work on abstinence and the therapeutic action, argues for maintaining the idea, not the ideal, of abstinence. She expands on the traditional notion, and sees abstinence as a means of providing a special, new context in which the patient gains informative experiences about how he or she needs to make new objects into old ones. In other words, abstinence, so conceived, provides conditions for the patient to learn about transference. Analysts are no longer timid about gratifying the patient by interpretation and by real interactions intrinsic to the process—interactions that are not simply a mutually indulgent pink tea, but ones that encourage the advancement of the process and promote growth in the patient. And since disclosure of aspects of the analyst's personality is inevitable to one degree or another, modifications in our ideal of anonymity are required. As originally conceptualized and applied, the stances of abstinence, anonymity, and neutrality could and often did become stereotypical and dehumanizing, and not necessarily the basic constituents of the analytic attitude and the therapeutic action. Any rigid adherence to these stances could actually squelch the possibilities for alive, real, authentic, interactive, relational work, deadening its contents in keeping with certain revered but outmoded traditions of the past. There seemed to be an interesting consensus among the Columbia panelists that when we place exclusive emphasis on these values in their original context only, without regard to the subtleties of our impact on our patients, we are identifying with the rigidities of our analytic ancestors, sometimes in the extreme, as with the aggressor. The participants believed, as do I, that it would be best at this juncture in the history of our profession not to get bogged down in our introductory teaching with the technical aspects of neutrality, abstinence, and anonymity, in their historically antiquated contexts, but to start candidates' education with where we stand today in regard to our evolved technique. Curricula should then move back to the historical origin of the concepts, and then move back on forward to our present rationales for modifying them, from the less to the more real, authentic, and engaged.

## DISCLOSURE

Where do Freudian analysts today stand on the issue of disclosure? Renik's (1995) view that the analyst disclose his or her own reality in order to increase the self-awareness of the other person is a wise guideline to follow. He articulates and communicates everything that in his view will help the patient understand where the analyst thinks he or she is coming from and trying to go with the patient: "I propose that it is useful for the analyst consistently to try to make sure that his or her analytic activity is understood as fully as possible by the patient. . . . An analyst should aim for comprehensibility, not inscrutability. I am not advocating imposing one's thinking upon a patient, but I am suggesting that one's thinking should be made available" (p. 482). It is difficult to dispute the view that total and complete anonymity is a myth that encourages idealization of the analyst and distorts technical neutrality, for even the analyst's way of formulating interpretations give clues about his or her personality. Technical neutrality is eminently compatible with a full exploration of the patient's realistic and unrealistic perceptions of the analyst. Our acts of disclosing do not purport to enhance our exhibitionism, or narcissism, or masochism, but only to benefit the patient. In Freudian analysis today, the principle of disclosure does not serve to enhance some extra-analytic real relationship, although the patient often fantasizes that it does, and those fantasies must be taken up and analyzed. This approach to disclosure is a relevant aspect of the real relationship for contemporary Freudian psychoanalysis: in the way we interact, and in what we disclose, the patient is always at the center.

## INTERSUBJECTIVITY

What is critical to the Freudian position on intersubjectivity, as contrasted with my understanding of the relational view, is a more asymmetric view of transference and countertransference influences. Freudians attribute a greater degree of authority to the analyst than to the patient. This topic is center stage now, as in Brenner's (1996) paper spearheading an issue in the *Psychoanalytic Quarterly* devoted to the topic. The paper was presented originally at a meeting of the New York Psychoanalytic Society, at which Steven Mitchell was the discussant. Mitchell argued against Brenner's defense of the position that we should attribute greater authority to the analyst than to the patient. Brenner's position, he said, ignored the relational school's assumption of intersubjectivity in which neither of the two parties, analyst or analysand, has a better hold on *the* truth. If that is the position of the relational school, then it is entirely constructionistic, and ignores the interminglings of objective and psychic realities. Those espousing an extreme symmetrical view of intersubjectivity would dispense entirely with the concepts of technical neutrality, anonymity, and abstinence, rather than modifying them in accordance with contemporary developments in our understanding of technique.

In his critique of the relational position on intersubjectivity, Kernberg (1996) points out the dangers of too much symmetry in transference and countertransference analysis: "An analyst's excessive concern with the effects of authority on the patient—with the patient's 'vulnerability' to any viewpoint different from the patient's own—may bring about a masochistic submission to the patient's pathology and a loss of the psychoanalytic perspective, rather than the analytic resolution of the origins of this vulnerability as a defense" (pp. 147-148). Since there should not and cannot be, if the analyst is well analyzed and well trained, a constant symmetry of countertransference and transference, too much communication of the analyst's values and reality colludes with a vulnerable side and prevents analysis of the patient. Although the realities of the transference and the therapeutic and the real relationship do get explored, they are not disclosed indiscriminately.

## INTERACTION

The most mutative thing that happens in the psychoanalytic process, and that is on a par with the interpretation of conflict, relates to the significant and inevitable interactions between patient and analyst that ultimately lead to structural change and personal development. By structural change, Loewald (1960), who was ahead of his time in grasping the importance of therapeutic interactions, meant aspects of ego development, which he assumed are resumed in the therapeutic process in psychoanalysis. This ego development is contingent on the relationship with a new object—the analyst—that, in turn, derives from the earliest mother-child dyad. But he did not suggest any new modifications in technique. He simply argued for a different way of understanding the role of interactions and object relations, which he wished to integrate into the Freudian mainstream, long before others had the foresight to do, as central to therapeutic change—to the therapeutic action.

I now skip three decades to address one of the newest and most creative contributions to this area, that suggested by Wilson and Weinstein (1996). They borrow the concept of the zone of proximal development (ZPD) from Vygotsky (1978) to refer to important interactions in the optimal interpersonal context of psychoanalysis that is outside of but works in tandem with the transference. Mutual influences between analyst and analysand are inevitable, and interactions are inevitable and desirable, and must be recognized for what they, as real relationships, contribute to the therapeutic action of psychoanalysis. Consider, for example, Grunes (1984), who zeroed in on a specific quality of desirable mutuality in his characterization of the therapeutic object relationship as a mutually interpenetrative emotional force field of empathic permeability and primal intimacy between analyst and patient.

The precursors of the ZPD concept are the unobjectionable positive transference, the therapeutic alliance, and the holding environment. The ZPD construct "supersedes the false dichotomization of the real relationship and the transference" (Wilson and Weinstein 1996, p. 173), and provides for a multileveled view of transference and the interactive role of the analyst. It builds on Bird's (1972) notion that later transference is built on powerful dyadic interactions, similar to but not necessarily identical to earliest object relations. ZPD is a present-day extension of Loewald's germinal ideas that the analyst not only interprets transference distortions but conveys a new reality that the analysand internalizes, because it explicates how mutative interpretations are internalized.

The ZPD is particularly important in sustaining the buffeting of transference. The analyst strives to be inside the ZPD but outside of the transference of the analytic work, and not to be the oft-caricatured blank screen of personal indifference. The ZPD involves ordinary discourse for the purpose of clarification of meanings in the context of real related interactions, and is often more important than transference analysis, especially in early volatile stretches that need to be tempered by meaningful analytic dialogue, when it is particularly important to sustain the therapeutic action. Perhaps we could usefully regard my remarks to Ms. D. about my viral condition as a timely positioning of discourse within the ZPD.

While we are accustomed to thinking of volatile stretches of work with the widening scope patient, I have learned that we encounter them in all patients, because all patients at one time or another require some version of a therapeutic object relationship to guarantee the therapeutic action of good technical interpretations of intrapsychic conflict inside and outside of the transference. Real dialogue—not a deliberately manipulated corrective emotional experience, not giving up analytic authority while being seduced into accepting that transference and countertransference have symmetrical status—provides the interactive context that brings to life the latent potential of the intrapsychic. The new object relationship is real and grows from real interactions that are part and parcel of the transference and its interpretation. Ergo, transference promotes rather than opposes a real relationship. That is how Freudian analysts think today about the transference and the real relationship. What is different in Freudian psychoanalysis today, from the way it was and from other approaches, is not an essentially new technique. One need only consult Fenichel's (1941) magnificent small volume on technique for an appreciation of the enduring legacies that still inform the bread-and-butter part of our daily work. What is different is an essentially new appreciation that has evolved over the years of the realness of transference-countertransference and other interactions that promote new growth and development in a new relationship with the analyst and with significant others. This argument, so basic to contemporary Freudian psychoanalysis, is predicated on the idea that the analyst as simply a reflecting mirror in the reactivation of the infantile neurosis in the crystallization and resolution of the transference is an outmoded notion. Even when the analyst does function abstinently and as a neutral mirror, that very functioning creates certain interactions and inspires fantasies that must be analyzed, and prompts new integrative and, as Chused (1996) notes, informative experiences that constitute a new object relationship. Loewald (1960) said that by the very act of analyzing transference distortions, the analyst becomes available to the patient as a truly new object, but not by providing a corrective emotional experience. The newness consists of the patient's rediscovery of early paths of object relations. This rediscovery then leads to new ways of relating to objects and of being oneself. Here is the crux: infantile and contemporary object may be united into one. Any real relationship also involves a transfer of past and present unconscious images onto present-day objects. This context for real dialogue in tandem with the transference, while the analyst maintains authority in a nonsymmetrical basic real relationship, is the hallmark of Freudian psychoanalysis today.

## REFERENCES

Arlow, J.A., and Brenner, C. (1990). The psychoanalytic process. *Psychoanalytic Quarterly* 59:678-692.

Bird, B. (1972). Notes on transference: universal phenomenon and hardest part of analysis. *Journal of the American Psychoanalytic Association* 20:267-301.

Brenner, C. (1996). The nature of knowledge and the limits of authority. *Psychoanalytic Quarterly* 65:21-31.

Chused, J.F. (1996). Abstinence and informative experience. *Journal of the American Psychoanalytic Association* 44:1047-1071.

Eissler, K (1953). The effect of the structure of the ego on psychoanalytic technique. *Journal of the American Psychoanalytic Association* 1:104-143.

Fenichel, O. (1941). *The Problems of Psychoanalytic Technique.* New York: Psychoanalytic Quarterly.

Freud, S. (1909). Notes upon a case of obsessional neurosis. *Standard Edition* 10:153-318.

——— (1915). Observations on Transference Love. *Standard Edition* 12:157-171.

Grunes, M. (1984). The therapeutic object relationship. *Psychoanalytic Review* 71:123-143.

Kernberg, O. (1996). The analyst's authority in the psychoanalytic situation. *Psychoanalytic Quarterly* 55:137-157.

Loewald, H. (1960). On the therapeutic action of psychoanalysis. *International Journal of Psycho-Analysis* 41:16-33.

Panel (1996). *Change within the Analyst.* Participants: Theodore Jacobs, Otto Kernberg, and Owen Renik. Presented at the meeting of the Association for Psychoanalytic Medicine, New York, March.

Renik, O. (1995). The ideal of the anonymous analyst and the problem of self-disclosure. *Psychoanalytic Quarterly* 54:466-495.

——— (1996). The perils of neutrality. *Psychoanalytic Quarterly* 65:495-517.

Stone, L. (1954). The widening scope of indications for psychoanalysis. *Journal of the American Psychoanalytic Association* 2:567-594.

Strachey, J. (1934). The nature of the therapeutic action of psycho-analysis. *International Journal of Psycho-Analysis* 15:127-159.

Wilson, A., and Weinstein, L. (1996). The transference and the zone of proximal development. *Journal of the American Psychoanalytic Association* 44:167-200.

Winnicott, D.W. (1951). Transitional objects and transitional phenomena. In *Collected Papers: Through Paediatrics to Psycho-analysis,* pp. 229-242. New York: Basic Books, 1958.

Vygotsky, L. (1978). *Mind in Society. The Development of the Higher Psychological Processes.* Cambridge, MA: Harvard University Press.

# Chapter 16: Facilitating Analysis with Implicit and Explicit Self-disclosures

[Gediman, H.K. (2006). Facilitating Analysis With Implicit and Explicit Self-Disclosures. *Psychoanalytic Dialogues*. 16:42-262. An earlier version of this article was presented at the Section One, Division of Psychoanalysis of the American Psychological Association Meeting in Kansas City, October 12, 2002. A shortened version was presented on January 6, 2000, in New York City at the New York University Postdoctoral Program in Psychotherapy and Psychoanalysis Colloquium.]

## FACILITATING ANALYSIS WITH IMPLICIT AND EXPLICIT SELF-DISCLOSURES

I propose to get beyond the false stereotypes that have divided contemporary Freudian and relational psychoanalysts with regard to self-disclosure. Understanding self-disclosures made by analysts of all persuasions in the course of their everyday work requires a relational and intersubjective perspective, but not a paradigm shift. Disclosures of everyday analytic work are based on a two-person relationship in which two subjectivities are devoted to the "one-person psychology" of the patient. Three extensive clinical illustrations compare and contrast inevitable self-disclosures that are part and parcel of psychoanalytic treatment with those that are more explicit, conscious, and deliberate and serve a specific aim of treatment. Disclosures and interactions, as understood within this framework, are intended to demonstrate mutuality but not necessarily symmetry and equality of authority in the analytic relationship. The analyst's self-disclosures, although undoubtedly informed by countertransferences and other very personal reactions, are meant to facilitate and deepen a process in which the patient's psychic life is at the center.

## INTRODUCTION

The recent debate over whether analysts should or should not disclose aspects of their own psychic lives to their patients has moved, dialectically, from dichotomous, absolutistic, stereotyped positions to a place where analysts of varying persuasions appear to be entering a more harmonious realm of discourse. I am convinced that both relationalists and today's Freudians aim to disclose what is therapeutically valuable in the intersubjective-relational matrix that is now just about universally acknowledged as part and parcel of critical analytic interactions, particularly those relevant to understanding transference-countertransference. Although analysts guided primarily by one orientation might tend toward disclosing more frequently, and those guided by the other less frequently, both disclose within the boundaries of preserving an analytic stance that would include neutrality in its method-ological and not stereotypically behavioral sense. As Meissner (2002) said, self-disclosure and neutrality are not incompatible, but "neutrality provides for discerning whether self-disclosure is therapeutically indicated and ad-vantageous" (p. 830). Nonetheless, the debate originated when certain "new view" (see Eagle, Wolitzky, and Wakefield, 2001; Eagle, 2003) relational analysts (Renik, 1996; Stolorow and Atwood, 1997) challenged the mythic stereotype of traditional analysts as rigidly withholding blank screens in their unflagging adherence to values of neutrality, abstinence and anonymity in the analyst' patient dyad. Traditional analysts (Abend, 1995; Meissner, 2002; Boesky, 2003) countered by challenging the new view as another mythic stereotype in which the analytic process is exclusively subjective and co-constructed in a symmetrical analyst-patient dyad and in which the analyst has virtually no more authority than the patient when it comes to discerning analytic truths.

Some relational analysts were criticized for regarding the dyad as exag-geratedly fluid, at times consisting of what were essentially two patients, each analyzing the other. I aim to counteract both of these stereotypes by way of three case summaries that illustrate the difference between inevitable implicit self-disclosure, what Meissner (2002) called *self-revelation,* or what I refer to in this article as "the disclosures of everyday analysis," and selective explicit conscious and deliberate self-disclosure.

I believe that once these two types of self-disclosure have been distin-guished, we will notice a diminution in the tendency to be polarized in our thinking on the topic. Self-disclosure has been regarded as inevitably not neutral and correlated with relational psychoanalysis; in contrast, prohibi-tions against self-disclosure have been characterized as inevitably neutral and correlated correspondingly with traditional or Freudian psychoanalysis. I contend that this once heuristically valuable but now false dichotomy was based on an erroneous set of assumptions about analytic neutrality that have recently been questioned and largely abandoned by both relational and con-temporary Freudian psychoanalysts. That is, analysts from most schools no longer regard neutrality as mere technical concrete behavior of "blank screen" withdrawal and minimal interaction to safeguard against revealing aspects of one's personal psyche (Meissner, 2002). Analysts of all persuasions have been engaged in reevaluating such "neutrality" as a set of guiding therapeutic principles. These guiding principles assume no intrinsic incompatibility between neutrality, anonymity, and abstinence, on one hand, and use of the self as an analyzing instrument (Freud, 1912; Isakower, 1992) on the other hand. Both approaches are fundamental to the advancement of psychoanalytic process and are in the interest of the patient's progress in treatment. I agree with Meissner (2002) when he stated, "As long as neutrality is cast in behavioral terms related to an authoritarian and totally abstinent stance, we are forced into a false dichotomy between openness and disclosure versus detachment and withdrawal" (p. 854).

The distinctions between technique and methodology recently emphasized by Boesky (2003) have also informed my ideas. Boesky, somewhat wryly, characterized technique as something the analyst sometimes does when he or she does not understand what is going on and has become embroiled in an enactment with the patient. Once this distinction between technique, which can often be mindless rote behavior, and methodology as guiding underlying principles is clear, arguments based on behavioral caricatures should decrease. The stereotypes of relationalists who disclose willy-nilly their thoughts, dreams, personal lives, and feelings, and Freudians who remain neutral via blank screen unremittingly icy reserve and withdrawal will lessen and be relegated to the atavistic stockpile of strawman attributions that we hope will disappear.

Although Renik (1995, 1996) said that neutrality, abstinence, and anonymity are unrealizable ideals, and as such are therefore dispensable, I like to think he would now refer to these benchmarks as literal behavioral technical precepts and not as guiding principles. In that sense he was right when he said that self-disclosure is inevitable, no matter how desirable or undesirable analysts may once have thought it to be. Rather than unrealizable, these analytic ideals are, I believe, best thought of "as a mental perspective on ongoing clinical experience in which all aspects of the interaction are processed and evaluated [with respect to what is] facilitative of both the analytic process and the therapeutic benefit of the patient" (Meissner, 2002, p. 830).

*Polarized distinctions have also been made between objectivity* and subjectivity in psychoanalysis (Smith, 1999; Eagle et al., 2001). Although unquestionably intersubjective, the analyst's personal judgments about the patient are not irreducibly or exclusively subjective; they also are relatively objective, in that they are informed, as Eagle (2003) noted, by material presented by the patient, knowledge of the literature, training, and past experience. Eagle stated, "It is one thing to reject the claims of infallible access to the truth about the patient's mind and another thing to reject altogether the possibility that one can reliably infer certain truths about the patient's mind" (p. 417). Renik (1993, 1998a, b) in contrast, proposed that the nature of psychoanalytic treatment is exclusively and irreducibly subjective, as neither analysts nor patients have an unquestionable pipeline to the truth. Self-disclosures, then, help in negotiating a mutually arrived at understanding of differing subjective perspectives on the patient's mental life. These false dichotomies and polarizations of objective versus subjective, like neutrality versus self-disclosure, may also have been useful historically to underscore the excesses and rigidities of certain traditional analysts and the excesses and fluidities of some early relational-intersubjective analysts. Today, however, they serve only to foster pseudo arguments that do not advance our mutual interests. I believe that we can promote and facilitate productive dialogue between different schools once we recognize self-disclosure as a useful form of interactive intervention subject to a set of guiding principles that contribute to the patient's benefit and the analytic process.

The case material from the analyses of the three patients I present, along with considerable commentary relating to the controversial issues I just summarized, illustrates varieties of self-disclosure that should be very familiar to contemporary Freudian, interpersonal, and relational analysts. The first case of self-disclosure is representative of the mostly implicit and inevitable self-revelations of everyday psychoanalytic life. The second case revolves around an explicit and deliberate use of disclosure at termination of treatment. The third involves those explicit, conscious, and deliberate disclosures of certain realities in the analyst's life when the analyst suffers a real illness that impacts in highly significant real ways on the psychoanalytic treatment. In these illustrations I aim to show that we are dealing with *new perspectives* on what analysts do but did not always know that they did, *not with a new paradigm* to replace valuable and now much more easily realizable aspects of an older one. Relational analysts, by virtue of their particular emphasis, have raised the consciousness of many other analysts of whatever persuasion to recognize the importance of interactional intersubjectivity. Contemporary Freudians have revived their interest in the importance of the analyst's emotional reactions for understanding their patients' psyches. The analyst's use of the self as an analyzing instrument has taken on importance in new and renewed theoretical and clinical contexts.

## THE IMPLICIT DISCLOSURES OF EVERYDAY ANALYSIS

Analysts of all persuasions make disclosures in the course of their everyday work. Such everyday self-disclosures have often been referred to as inevitable self-revelations as opposed to deliberate and consciously intended self-disclosure (Abend, 1995; Meissner, 2002). *I "disclose" up to a point the thinking and feeling that goes into my interpretations.* I disclose to you, my readership or audience, my thinking, introspection, parallel associations, resonance, ego activity, close process monitoring, thoughts, and feelings occurring to me during evenly hovering attention to show how I think about what I will eventually convey to my patient that is useful for him in an analytic experience. I do not disclose in quite the same way to my patient as I do to you, but I do disclose. My disclosure, although consistent with Mitchell's (1988, 1997) groundbreaking position, is not radically different from the ego psychoanalytically based method of sharing with my patient the way that my mind works psychoanalytically (see Gray, 1994; Busch, 1995, 1996). My disclosure does not require a new analytic paradigm. Intersubjectivity, construction, and co-construction of interpretive meanings interest me as ongoing processes in a dyad that is more "asymmetrical" than "symmetrical"; that is, despite core joint constructions, the analyst is assumed to be more authoritative than the patient. As inevitable as self-disclosure is, I should like to emphasize that mutuality, as opposed to symmetry in the dyad, is critical and that many analytical truths are not simply constructed but tend toward a degree of objectivity that is discernible in a collaborative, interactive, relational matrix that nonetheless keeps the patient at the center of concern.

*The self-disclosures of everyday analysis do not require a new technical, interpersonal, relational, inter subjective paradigm of technique. All analysts self-disclose.* Taken to its radical extreme, the position advocating a paradigm shift holds that because analyst and patient each base judgments solely on his or her own subjective experience, neither has a greater claim on analytic authority or truth than the other. The everyday nonradical disclosure of which I speak is an extension of the traditional way that analysts have always been informed by their very real, largely subjective, but also to some degree "objective," reactions to their patients. These disclosures preserve that asymmetrical dyadic configuration in which the patient's subjective intrapsychic world and interpersonal experiences are at the center of both participants' concerns. The disclosures of everyday analytic life are then based on a two-person intersubjective relationship in which two subjectivities aim only to explicate the "one-person" psychology of the patient. As Eagle (2003) said,

… even when I am trying to understand my own psychic reality, it is in the service of better understanding you. I am making a personal judgment about what is going on in you. Furthermore, although it is a personal judgment, it may be warranted by the evidence and one that on the basis of the evidence, others might reach. Therefore, it might be objective in this sense too. (pp. 421–422).

This two-person patient-centered focus differs from both the caricature of the icily remote blank screen traditional and the caricature of the symmetrical equalitarian relational positions regarding disclosure. The analyst's disclosure is based, optimally, on measured, discerning judgments about the patient that at the same time are informed by his or her subjective and objective emotional responses to the patient channeled into therapeutically essential introspection, empathy, and associative resonance. Such sequelae of emotional attunement are used asymmetrically by contemporary Freudians, self psychologists, Kleinians, interpersonal, and relational analysts who all optimally utilize self-disclosure so that the psychology of one person, the patient, is always at the center of the two-person dyadic working team despite recognition of important mutual influences on the analytic process. The analyst's inevitable subjectivity as well as objective viewpoints and judgments are but means to this end. The case I present next illustrates how picking up on aspects of the interaction or transference is inevitably self-revealing for *any analyst of any school*.

### PATIENT I. IMPLICIT SELF-DISCLOSURE IN THE SELF-REVELATIONS IN EVERYDAY PSYCHOANALYTIC INTERPRETATIONS

A 74-year-old man returned for psychoanalytic treatment quite decisively retired from his secure and high-level position and spent the next few years procrastinating about any serious creative work in his life and his analysis. The patient believed that his procrastination expressed mainly sadism and hostility, but this character trait struck me as also unmistakably autoerotic and masturbatory. He busied himself with the kind of scutwork projects that automatically regenerate themselves, epitomized by clearing a desk that was a repository for daily accumulations of mail and memos. He kept busy, trying to keep up with small but endlessly demanding tasks yet at the same time took advantage of every opportunity to procrastinate in the big things like writing his will and wrapping up some of his writing stuck at the data-collecting stage, a paralysis that painfully inhibited his moving on to integrate and synthesize any final drafts that could show his potentially fine skills to public advantage.

Chapter 16: Facilitating Analysis with Implicit and Explicit Self-disclosures

I seek here to illustrate and explore the limits of self-disclosure as a vehicle for my everyday analytic formulations and interpretations of his conflicted transferences in both his total life and analytic situations. I rely heavily on my empathic sense, or definitive subjective emotional responses and cognitive convictions, that the patient is unequivocally involved with me in an eroticized transference with clearly autoerotic and self-pleasuring tones, particularly in his ceaseless musings and tortured ruminations about the meaning of his procrastinations. I *feel strongly* that he is autoerotically procrastinating in the transference by trying to analyze ad infinitum his tendencies to procrastinate. My strong feelings inform the interpretations, which include the self-revelations that I refer to here as the inevitable self-disclosures of everyday analytic life.

I had noticed for a long time that the patient, who does not wear a watch, did not cease in his anal-erotically colored ruminations toward the end of the hour but went on and on as if there were no end to the session, so I always had to interrupt him to say it was time to stop for today. I asked him if it had ever occurred to him that it might make me uncomfortable to constantly interrupt his eroticized reverie with a reminder that time was up. He was aware of this pattern, wanted to analyze it, and although he would usually respond, "I guess it is time to go," he never ceased trying to provoke me to "call time" by setting the conditions for me to interrupt him in the middle of an endless sentence. Some might consider my consistent (and persistent) interruptions to end the session as an enactment or counter enactment, but then how else would one usually respond to such a patently enacted controlling maneuver at the end of a session? Sometime in the 4th year of the return treatment, I interpreted to him via a self-revealing disclosure that it seemed to me, based on *my sense* of his inner drivenness, body language, and predictable repetitiveness, that he was procrastinating with me just as he had in other situations. In essence, my sense, my feeling, my subjective reactions, which I do not believe were countertransferential, informed my interpretation. There is little new in this idea itself that emotional "vibes" inform interpretations. What is new is the growing and explicit recognition that we have always self-disclosed in our everyday psychoanalytic encounters.

I told my patient that the most prominent feature of his ceaseless musings and tortured ruminations about the meaning of his procrastinations felt to me to be his determination to seek out the autoerotic gratification of going on unimpeded by me, almost as though he were in a self-pleasuring trance that he wanted to perpetuate forever in my presence. *I told him that I strongly felt the autoerotic impact of his procrastination as he spoke and wondered if he were in touch with those feelings himself.* Thus, I directed him via my disclosure of the kind that I believe both relational and contemporary Freudian analysts have emphasized toward his own self-reflection. The patient acknowledged some motivation to make the sessions last forever and to be with me forever, just as he had become aware of trying to make other things last forever as a way of warding off, in fantasy, his death.

The patient had been diagnosed with and treated for cancer, which he believed he had battled successfully. Nonetheless, his procrastination helped him avoid his certain knowledge that his death was inevitable. This newly contextualized meaning of his symptom of procrastination reflected anxieties relative to his current position in his life cycle. However, he had been repeating variations of this pattern his whole life, and this tendency toward eroticized procrastination was deeply embedded in his obsessional, anal character structure. I fully expected that my transference-"disclosure" interpretation, stating that I strongly felt the autoerotic impact of his procrastination, would help to traverse an impasse and would soften the anal-erotic character trait in which his autoerotic procrastinations sought refuge. Note that my disclosure included no biographical information and nothing of my idiosyncratic life history, which would have had no value for him at all save some dubiously useful prurient excitement. My self-disclosure of my personal reactions to his autoerotic libidinal expressions was based on a rationale akin to Jacobs's (1999) advocating that such noncountertransferential self-disclosures might help the patient to have a real impact not only on the analyst but also on others in his life outside the treatment situation.

My self-revelation was met consistently with new resistances to giving up a profoundly important sense of pleasure that came from musing about pragmatic planning. That gratification, reinforced hugely by the adhesiveness of the libido, prompted him more than ever to talk about his "procrastination impulse" in a procrastinating manner. "Procrastination is social behavior directed aggressively towards myself and others." I disclose that I hear in this more of the autoerotic gratification than he appears to hear. "You mean I get pleasure?" (That is what I suggested last session, and I still feel it palpably here in the room.) My intervention revealed an aspect of my personal reaction, quite short of some more conscious and deliberate form of self-disclosure. Hoffman (1983) and Renik (1999) both held that *because self-disclosure is inevitable, it is not so deviant from ordinary practice to be explicit to the patient about one's own experience of sensing how the patient might be feeling.* Although Hoffman and Renik never proposed abandoning considered and measured judgment about what should be disclosed beyond what is inevitable, they clearly were also reacting to the stereotype of the classical analysts who presumably adhered to the ideal of neutrality as the analyst's presentation of a cold, withdrawn, and expressionless blank screen. To counter this stereotypic neutrality, certain relational analysts rallied behind the idea that because this form of legitimate self-disclosure was inevitable it was technically required. Hoffman's and then Renik's position led logically to the extreme conclusion that patients sometimes analyze their therapist's experience and therapists sometimes become their patient's patient. One hopes that this caricature of relational analysis has become as outmoded as the caricature of the traditional analyst's icy nonresponsiveness.

The patient continues, "You hear me better than I hear myself." (I guess there are times when I do hear you somewhat differently from the way you hear yourself.) Thus, I addressed my own subjectivity and his, as well as our different viewpoints, aspects of the treatment methodology that have always been at least tacit if not always acknowledged as significant features of a classical approach to interpretive work. "Thank goodness for that." He knows he is here for analysis and respects the authority of the analyst, accepting at some level of awareness that we are simply two separate but equal subjectivities requiring a mutual yet asymmetrical exchange of self-disclosures. One is tempted to think of him as a good old-fashioned analysand who works well under the conditions of a good old-fashioned analysis. "Pleasure," he says, "is putting things off by asserting myself. I do what I feel like doing. That's self-indulgent." (That is how you come across when you get stuck in the pleasures of the past and the dilemmas of the present. I think it is true what you say about your procrastination involving anger against others, but it also strikes me as autoerotic self-indulgence. You get stuck procrastinating, you get stuck talking to me about the meaning of your procrastination, you get fixated, like it is too comfortable to try to get out of that stance.) I am proposing that when I say, "it also strikes me ..." I am engaging in that ubiquitous form of self-disclosure, referred to here as *implicit self-revelation,* which is and always has been involved in the interpretations of everyday analysis, so much so that as tautological as it sounds it merits emphasis for the conceptual distinctions I am illustrating.

Although I have disclosed my reaction, I emphasize that I am being neutral by maintaining a position equidistant from id, ego, superego, and reality. That idea of neutrality does not correspond in any way to the caricature of the blank screen, withdrawn analyst playing his or her cards close to the chest but instead, in Renik's (1999) terms, coming across more forthrightly, more "face up." I present my "sense" or "feel" of the instinctual reality to me of his self-indulgence as a psychoanalytic fact that he and I agree upon and not as a judgment that he fails to engage his superego functions to contain his response to autoerotic pleasure. My disclosures express the spirit of a contemporary psychoanalytic methodology, Freudian, relational, interpersonal, or otherwise, respectful of *neutrality* in its fundamental but not caricatured behavioral sense. At the same time, my disclosures are now informed by a *relational intersubjective stance* that earlier classical analysts most usually had employed but rarely considered explicitly as a major aspect of their interpretive work. To repeat: The patient would prefer to stress the sadism and hostility behind his procrastination, but because I subjectively and strongly experience this characterological trait as an autoerotic indulgence, I have "disclosed" via my transference interpretation our sense of our different subjectivities. In that way, our respective subjective perspectives open up the potential for both of us to grasp multiple meanings in a conflictual context. At this juncture, I judged that interpretations should proceed in the direction of his using aggression to defend against and resist awareness of pleasurable anal eroticism.

I reemphasize here my ideas on one-person and two-person psychologies of free associations, empathy, introspection, intersubjectivity, and disclosure. My evenly hovering parallel associations and resonance, introspection, and empathic immersion in the patient's experience prompt me to disclose feelings and other responses that relate exclusively to my patient, especially when such revelations are essential to advance the analytic process. My job as analyst is to interpret the meanings to the patient of the inevitable asymmetrical aspects of the dyad, because I am confident in the utility of my subjective reactions and I expect my authority on unconscious process, and so forth, to be at least a step beyond that of the patient's, and my patient shares my expectation.

When I disclose to him that I *feel* as though he is luxuriating, I am exemplifying what I mean as a quintessential disclosure of everyday analytic life. I disclose my feeling, my subjectivity, *but it is not about me, it is about him*. Therefore, my disclosure is compatible with classical interpretive technique as well as that of present-day relational theorists. He picks up with the insight of the good analysand once again. His further associations appear to confirm the value of my "everyday analysis" form of disclosure that contained my interpretation.

He begins the next session with a report about a dream he has had about a protégé trainee of his who is being admired by his father in a way his father never admired him. He at first presents his father's indifference to his own accomplishments simply as manifestly accurate historical data, replete with obsessional details about the dream elements, and with no real associations. I assume he is once again simply procrastinating and autoerotically self-indulgent, but lo and behold, I am happily mistaken. Asked to associate, he thinks of Felix Mendelssohn being a genius, of Mendelssohn's grandfather being a genius and an accomplished man, and of Mendelssohn's father as simply the man in the middle, a nobody. (When you give up the defense and pleasure of procrastinating via repetitive details, you come up with a brilliant creative solution to the meaning of the dream: You wish to be the distinguished grandfather and grandson, not the middling father.) In actuality, his father was and his son is more extraordinarily distinguished and better known in their respective fields than he is in his line of work. In the analysis, then, he has moved forward, able now to let go of obsessively holding on to and repeating details that had served as a compromise helping him to defend against the grandiosity of his wish to be like one of the great Mendelssohns while helping him to obtain gratifications of an addictive, compulsive, perverse nature. He asks, "What kind of bird holds on and never lets go even if it keeps him from singing?" I refrain from disclosing my instant association: "It's a Kaka bird." I reasoned to myself that such a disclosure would be more my idiosyncratic association touching on his important anally retentive colored fantasy and would probably not be mutatively interpretive at that moment because of my countertransferentially based desire to exhibit my virtuosic talents at access to primary process language. Although some might have regarded my exhibitionistic urge as contributing to a co-constructed interpretation, my considered judgment is generally to bite my tongue when I suspect a primarily countertransferential motivation for a self-revelation, ever hopeful that I would come up soon enough with a formulation that keeps the patient's psyche and not mine at the center.

It is a major truism that all analysts "disclose" something about themselves simply by virtue of being analysts and doing what analysts ordinarily do. Some, in fact, disclose more, and with different rationales than others. Analysts identified with the relational school may often disclose for reasons differing considerably from those of an analyst identified as a contemporary Freudian because they believe more in the relationship of disclosure to co-constructions. Nonetheless, even the contemporary Freudian believes that self-disclosures are inevitable, often important, and always intersubjective relational phenomena.

## EXPLICIT, CONSCIOUS, AND DELIBERATE SELF-DISCLOSURE

I introduce two new clinical examples to try to tease out the differences between conscious and deliberate self-disclosures and the "disclosures of everyday life," keeping in mind the critical question of whether these different types of self-disclosures require a theoretical paradigm shift. Significant issues around deliberate self-disclosure arose in connection with the emphasis that relational analysts (Greenberg and Mitchell, 1983; Hoffman, 1983; Stolorow, Brandchaft, and Atwood, 1987; Mitchell, 1988, 1993, 1997; Stolorow and Atwood, 1992, 1997; Davies, 1994; Orange and Stolorow, 1998) placed on co-constructed and co-created intersubjective aspects of the analytic process. Relational analysts have tended to claim that these aspects require self-disclosures across the spectrum of all patients and situations. Recently, such concerns have increasingly entered the domain of contemporary Freudian psychoanalytic thought, partly in response to the relational school's arguments but mainly to emphasize that analysts of all schools recognize the importance of subjective and interactive factors in traditional and contemporary treatment processes. A significant number of contemporary Freudian analysts, however, would not agree that all psychoanalytic understanding is co-constructed. I discuss two treatment situations, one involving explicit self-disclosures during the termination phase of a long-term analysis coming to its natural end and another involving explicit disclosures during the termination phase of an analysis in which the patient died from and the analyst survived a serious malignant cancer.

**PATIENT 2. SELF-DISCLOSURES DURING THE TERMINATION PHASE**

I turn to illustrative material from a second patient who was ready to terminate a long analysis. Termination has traditionally been the time when analysts "disclose" something more than usual about themselves to their patients, often rationalized as preparation for the real separation and the real possibilities of encountering the analyst in certain professional and/or social situations. These possibilities certainly materialize frequently for candidates terminating with analysts working in their same institutes, and they also come up in one degree or another for any patient terminating treatment.

I present this material to illustrate how an analyst sometimes relates, consciously and deliberately, anecdotes about people she knows personally to engage a patient's readiness to hear and respond affectively to important interpretations that otherwise might be ineffective. Such explicit self-disclosure needs to be woven into the fabric of the analysis to maximize the likelihood that the personal aspects of the analyst's disclosures end up not in the forefront of the patient's mind but as the background context for enhanced understanding of herself. At the end of a 13-year analysis, a 50-year-old female patient beset with manifest separation anxieties was finally able to enter the termination phase and to actually terminate treatment. She rose to the top of her profession, with huge administrative and personnel responsibilities for the well-being of others, but after a traumatic divorce, she never again developed interest in marriage or any seriously committed intimate personal relationship. In fact, she took pride in not being "saddled down" like other women. As an infant, it is likely that she had a very insecure attachment to two parents who rarely responded to her with any optimal degree of attunement. She constantly envisioned the time she would never see and enter through my office door again once she terminated. As soon as she entered treatment, her primary conscious wish was to establish a life-saving attachment to me as a substitute object for her inevitably-to-be-lost mother. In her mind, the analysis was to serve that purpose, and most of our work consisted in analyzing the various functions that this amazingly effective and high-functioning woman's fantasy of receiving "perpetual care" from me served for her.

During the course of treatment, it became clear that in addition to these early insecure attachments, the patient also had developed a strong need for power, which she discovered at age 3 when her mother succumbed to her phobic reaction to going to school. The little girl successfully intimidated her mother to allow her to drop out of nursery school and to remain home with the housekeeper during the years that other children from her milieu were attending preschool. As a very young girl she became aware of an elated sense of power and control over others whenever she stubbornly refused to move, or stubbornly, persistently, and perseveratively held on to ideas that even she considered to be very absurd and ridiculous. She thereby ridiculed unconsciously those who tried to correct her irrationality, including the analyst when she attempted to interpret this dynamic. "It's just like that," she said, "I cling to your couch the way I clung to the back of our couch at home and worried the daylights out of everyone by making them see how phobic I was."

My first conscious and deliberate explicit disclosure took place about 2 weeks prior to the termination date set by the patient and mutually agreed upon by both of us. In the midst of some stubborn refusal she was making to "move" from the favorite sticky spot of the moment, I reasoned to myself that I could risk telling her a personal anecdote in the interest of loosening up her last bastion of resistance to separation and to facilitate the actual termination experience for her. I told her she reminded me of a little girl of 2 years 9 months with whom I had spent time that weekend and who discovered her powers in a museum. Instead of happily going along, as she had all morning, from one dinosaur to another mastodon, she suddenly stopped still as she became entranced with the rubber grips on the stairs inside of the museum and attended to them with amazingly focused fascination. I told my patient that when I asked the little girl what she was thinking, she asked about the grips: "What are they?" "What are they for?" "What are they made of? "Who put them there?" "Why did they do that?" and on and on. My next bold step of self-disclosure was to describe how *her father and I* explained the way the grips and treads worked and that the little girl stopped and stalled for a full 10 minutes, pondering what she had been told, apparently mesmerized by the grips and by her power, tiny as she was, to stop her *father and grandmother* from moving on and taking her to a nice restaurant for lunch. She just didn't want us to make her leave. In this narrative, then, I consciously and deliberately disclosed that the little girl was my granddaughter. Furthermore, I am absolutely certain that this self-disclosure was not remotely similar to anything I usually do in my self-revelations of everyday analytic life. These are generally limited to disclosing my thoughts and feelings to the patient so that he can understand how my mind as an analyst works in an effort to encourage him to self-reflect similarly. In contrast, my anecdotal self-disclosure had a different purpose based on a reasonably countertransference-free judgment call that would facilitate the last phase of analysis and the patient's progress toward ending.

I was struck by the contrast as well as the similarities between my patient's extremely excited phobic reaction of childhood when she stubbornly clung to her couch and refused to leave home for school and the excitement of the other little girl, my granddaughter, when she discovered that she could sit to her heart's content on the stoop at the outside of the museum and restrict the mobility of her father and grandmother, who wanted to get on to the business and pleasure of going off to lunch with her. There was also the obvious connection between the little girl's refusal to leave the museum and my patient's reluctance to leave me as the analysis drew mighty close to termination. When I disclosed this personal anecdotal information as a parable for the patient's major life motifs and struggles, she was touched in some profound way, most unusual for her, and began, most uncharacteristically, to cry. "I know that feeling, there is nothing more exhilarating in the world than feeling so little and yet so powerful." I thought that she was finally in touch significantly with the fact that her lifelong separation anxiety symptom had not only caused her great psychic pain but also afforded her great pleasure: That is, the symptom of separation anxiety, though reinforced by early insecure attachments, had come to serve as a true compromise formation.

Continuing to disclose, I pointed out the difference between her experience of her own detached and intimidated father and my observations, as neutral as

I believed they could be (!), of this little girl's father, who did not capitulate to her "power-plays" but who exasperatingly yet lovingly swooped her up and carried her piggyback to the restaurant. I said to my patient that the child was then even more exhilarated than she was in her isolated and stubbornly defiant act of discovering her powers via her inspection of the rubber grips inside and by the momentary success of her sit-down strike on the outside museum steps. My intention was to remind my adult patient that the pleasures of being swept up into the arms of a loving "oedipal" man could exceed those of receiving perpetual care from a "preoedipal" maternal person. The patient was both touched and bothered by my disclosure. She mourned her lack of an affectively responsive father, yet she was ambivalently pleased at discerning correctly that I probably would never have offered this personal anecdotal material except as part of the termination weaning' separation procedure. I had convinced myself that this self-disclosure was the best way, paradoxically, to bring the patient's concerns to the center in a way that would be therapeutically effective, even as it risked provoking the patient's envy of this other little girl's relationship with her father and of my relationship with my son and granddaughter. But such are the trade-offs in such adamantly resistant cases.

She had wanted for years to hear something, anything, about my private life—where I lived, the social gatherings she believed I hosted, and particularly who was in my family. Principles of neutrality, abstinence, and anonymity generally had guided my decisions not to disclose this information, because to do so would not have fostered and probably would have impeded the progress of her analysis. Now that I had judged self-disclosure as useful and had acted on my judgment, she was gratified, yet she had very ambivalent feelings about knowing some facts of my family life. I present her reaction as a cautionary tale to those advocating disclosure as a deliberate technical device simply to facilitate the "realness" of the termination stage. My rationale was based not on being real for the sake of being real, in which there are aspects of the realities of stopping work that transcend aspects of the therapeutic alliance as such, but on my conviction that the termination stage can promote and increase the therapeutic alliance up to the end.

My decision to disclose such personal information was influenced by multiple factors, including the fact that this session followed by one week an incident when something startlingly real broke the traditional analytic frame we had both observed so conscientiously during the course of this long analysis. Because my cleaning lady had inadvertently locked the door to my consulting room, I had decided to conduct just that one session in the small kitchen of my office suite while waiting for the locksmith to arrive to reinstate the normal analytic frame. During this time, the patient had something of a claustropho-bic reaction to sitting face-to-face and being so close to me in such a small enclosure. She re-experienced some similar awkward and traumatic moments she had felt as a child, when she was enclosed in small places, like the car, with her father, when neither of them seemed to know what to do except to fall self-consciously silent and drift apart emotionally.

This event is relevant to my self-disclosure because the loosening up of the literal frame "primed" me to loosen up my usual strictures on disclosures in-volving my personal life experiences. In addition, as it happened, the events culminating in breaking the frame of the structured analytic situation turned into one of those so-called extraordinary transformational moments as its unex-pectedness promoted my ability to access material within myself. I was able to use the unexpected to disclose in a way that would advance the therapy in what might otherwise have been some potential transferential and countertransferen-tial gratifications of sharing information about my family with my patient who was not too much longer going to be my patient. Such accidental and serendipi-tous occasions often provide an opportunity for inadvertent self-revelations, but in this instance it clearly inspired me toward that self-restraint that bought me time to formulate and carry into action after due deliberation between sessions, an explicit and conscious self-disclosure that was in the patient's interest, not mine. It was no coincidence that these events closely followed 9/11 when there also were many frame bendings and shared realities. I frequently called my patient or she called me to reassure me she was all right, as she was responsible, professionally, for helping out with major sequelae at Ground Zero and I often did not know where and how she was from one day to the next.

During our final session I thought of much that I could have disclosed but I chose not to. I could have disclosed where I was going on vacation or what my favorite restaurant was—aspects of my life about which she had often voiced curiosity—but what would these disclosures have to do with the crippling compromise formation that had dictated the course of the patient's life and analysis? Such disclosures reflect only on the analyst's real life and are not compatible with maintaining a neutral analytic stance that fosters the alliance at every step of treatment including the very last. The patient began talking of internalizing me all along and of her plans to do that in the months to come by holding imaginary conversations with me during the aftermath of the actual separation. It was interesting that she also recalled having such internal conversations with her mother. In fact, after she had come to terms with her mother's death 2 years previously, she had initiated many pleasant internal conversations with her. As her analyst, with my evenly hovering attentions and parallel private associations, I recalled to myself in that final session, but did not disclose to my patient, the dream I had had the preceding night about my own mother and father, who are in fact deceased. I was wondering if I should tell my parents that I was planning to leave two jobs, which in the dream I had been engaged in presently, to concentrate my efforts on my increasingly demanding private practice. The two jobs were research positions, one at a hospital and one at a university where I was not being paid much and was just being kept on even though no one had very much for me to do. In the dream, they were just token jobs, although they could impress others as prestigious. I felt compelled to tell my parents and ran back to tell them again and again that I decided not to leave the hospital or give up my professorship. I did not want to displease them by cutting back on any efforts that had brought them, vicariously, so much pride and narcissistic gratification.

As I sat thinking during this session with my patient, I realized that my dream represented an actual psychological experience of my own that paralleled something that the patient was telling me she had experienced. We were both engaged in bringing back the lost object via internalized representations to deal more effectively with separations, endings, leavings, and ultimately death. I was obviously ambivalent about my patient leaving, and even though I thought she would not have much analytic work left to do at this time, *I opted not to disclose to the patient this countertransferential dream and my associations to it*. Even in the last session, I did not want to position the treatment as though we were now in that often caricatured relationship of two patients, one analyzing the other, but as two people who have worked distinctly all along as analyst and analysand. As interesting as my countertransferential reactions might have been to my patient, and as exciting a relatively symmetrical dyadic relational experience they may have provided as some sort of termination gift I fantasized presenting to her, such self-disclosure would have added nothing therapeutically valuable. Rather, it would have intruded not just on the alliance but also on the state of the patient's well-being and on our mutual attunement relative to the impending "final" separation of that hour.

My understanding of my undisclosed countertransferential reactions did inform my analytic strategy importantly. So I immediately went to my computer after the patient left and wrote down my parallel associations, not just to discharge my need to express what I had noticed but abstained from disclosing but in the interest of neutrality, sensitivity, empathy, and attunement. I believe I facilitated the relational intersubjective aspects of the end of the termination phase by adhering to principled if not concretely behavioral analytic neutrality. My approach is in contrast to the position that because behavioral anonymity is an impossible goal, one cannot observe neutrality in its fundamental if not concrete behavioral sense. I believe that a strategy encompassing fundamental methodological neutrality would keep the patient's interests more central than a symmetrical exchange of our respective individual psychic realities would. That latter approach could risk the hazards of abandoning the analytic attitude at the last minute by casting the analyst's unconscious wishes into the limelight at the expense of keeping central the patient's efforts at termination and their critical importance to her optimal intrapsychic and interpersonal balance.

## PATIENT 3. ILLNESS AND IMPENDING DEATH IN THE ANALYST

The explicit, conscious, and deliberate self-disclosures made by analysts regarding their illnesses or impending deaths almost always, when in keeping with methodological if not behavioral principles of neutrality, center on those realities in the analyst's life that might seriously affect the treatment (see Abend, 1982; Dewald, 1982; Lasky, 1990a, b; Meissner, 1996; Pizer, 1997). Direct, factual disclosures at such times, however, may and should be in keeping with analytic principles that foster the development of the treatment as much as possible, especially when both participants in the dyad share a real concern with the analyst's well-being. "Even severe illness does not escape the governing perspective of neutrality" (Meissner, 2000, p. 895). However, we should not forget that even in unusually extreme circumstances too much "real" extrinsic relatedness as opposed to the average' expectable intrinsic relatedness of the real "therapeutic object relationship" (Loewald, 1960; Grunes,1984, 1998) does risk the therapeutic alliance.

Edwards[24] (2002) presented the details of a termination phase of a treatment she conducted in which her patient was dying from metastatic cancer at a time when she herself had survived three cancer surgeries. For reasons that seem to me to be completely in synch with a good rationale for conscious and deliberate self-disclosure, Edwards disclosed, in response to her patient's direct questions, the fact of her own cancer to her dying patient. There were times she did not look or feel all that well, and I believe that to not be forthcoming in her disclosures abut her situation would have been a violation of the analytic attitude and merely representative of stereotypical behaviors of a caricature of analytic neutrality. She brought

---

24 As of this writing, Nancy Edwards has died. I am grateful for her having given me permission, earlier, to present portions from her fine and courageous work.

her patient up to date on her own medical condition but without going into details. Her disclosure of the realties of her life relevant to the treatment process not only deepened and facilitated that process, it was also the only humane thing to do. She reported and analyzed dreams she had about her patient and herself, but she restricted her disclosures of her own death anxieties to her own analyst, to whom she had returned for treatment, and to her psychoanalytic audience, sparing her dying patient the burden of that self-awareness.

I support Edwards's position that one must bend the strictures of the analytic frame where the work commanded. As much as I admire and support what this courageous and sensitive analyst did with her patient, and as much as I agree that her approach represents a specific relational perspective, I question her designation of her self-disclosure as a mutually processed co-construction. Her modification of behavioral neutrality simply dealt with important realities of her illness and her patient's, enabling the emergence of new transference-countertransference and other interactional configurations. I do not believe that a relational, intersubjective, and even at times a mutually co-constructed perspective represents a paradigmatic shift. I disagree with her when she concludes that because her disclosures were tailored to this particular dyad her approach is to be considered uniquely relational, intersubjective, and co-constructed. As Eagle (2003) stated, interactional and relational aspects of the analytic dyad do not rule out the fact that there are also independent, stable properties of the mind that are not co-constructed. In this instance, Edwards's relational *perspective* and strategy constituted an important part of good analytic work, but her disclosures did not comprise a uniquely relational psychoanalytic methodological *paradigm*. Quite the contrary, flexible perspectivism is compatible with good analytic work of all theoretical persuasions. Flexible shifting from one good analytic perspective to another must always be tailored uniquely to the dual subjectivities of any given particular analyst-analysand dyad.

## CONCLUSION

In the major arguments I made in this article, I claimed that the implicit self-revelations of everyday analysis and the explicit conscious and deliberate self-disclosures are both part of the analytic frame and certainly do not constitute a new paradigm of analysis called "relational/intersubjective," or such. Although self-disclosures certainly reflect the subjectivity of both participants, they relate primarily to what is objectively discernible in the psychic life of the patient. It is important that all psychoanalysts today acknowledge that *relational, subjective, and intersubjective perspectives are domains that are shared, along with intrapsychic, interpersonal, and objective perspectives by all good analysts, and all those multiple perspectives inform the reasons and ways that analysts disclose what they disclose.*

The kinds of interactions that Edwards had with her patient, as well as the kinds that I aimed to have with my patients, were indeed subjectively influenced interactions of two human beings. However, it is a mistake to say that they define a new relational/intersubjective paradigm. In the cases that I presented, including Edwards's dying patient, the patient, and discernible, interpretable aspects of the patients' psychic life, were at the center. The work was the dyadic work of two interacting persons, each with her or his own psychology, but was not for those reasons symmetrically "co-constructed," even though each party in the dyad grasped the other's individual subjectivity in such attunements. Even though the means toward promoting the analytic process was in many instances more or less interpersonal, interactive, subjective, and relational, the focus in all the disclosures was on the one-person psychology of the patient with the end goal of promoting the patient's advancement in treatment. The analyst's subjectivity reflected the analytic value of the analyst as analyzing instrument in fostering mutual engagement directed toward understanding the mind and psyche of the patient. I hope I have reached my goal of demonstrating that many of the issues that have engaged relational and contemporary Freudian analysts in debate have been based on stereotypes and caricatures of both subjectivity and neutrality. However useful these dichotomous views may have been heuristically in sharpening the differences between various approaches to psychoanalytic technique, methodology, and theory, it is no longer too important to sharpen differences. We have reached the point where we have clarified the diverse phenomena and guiding principles of self-disclosure; we now need to see if we can produce a coherent unificatory position in treatment and methodology.

## REFERENCES

Abend, S. (1982). Serious illness in the analyst: Countertransference considerations. *Journal of the American Psychoanalytic Association* 30:365–375.
——— (1995). Discussion of Jay Greenberg's paper on self-disclosure. *Contemporary Psychoanalysis* 31: 207–211.
http://www.pep-web.org/document.php?id=cps.031.0207a

Boesky, D. (2003). *Psychoanalytic controversies and clinical evidence: A model of clinical disputes*. Paper presented at the New York Psychoanalytic Society, October, New York.
http://www.pep-web.org/document.php?id=paq.071.0445a

Busch, F. (1995). *The Ego at the Center of Clinical Technique* (chap. 1). Northvale, NJ: Aronson.

——— (1996). The ego and its significance in analytic interventions. *Journal of the American Psychoanalytic Association* 44: 1073–1099.
http://www.pep-web.org/document.php?id=apa.044.1073a

Davies, J.M. (1994). Love in the afternoon: A relational reconsideration of desire and dread in the countertransference. *Psychoanalytic Dialogues* 4: 153–170. http://www.pep-web.org/document.php?id=pd.004.0153a

Dewald, P.A. (1982). Serious illness in the analyst: Transference and reality responses. *Journal of the American Psychoanalytic Association* 30: 347–363. http://www.pep-web.org/document.php?id=apa.030.0347a

Eagle, M.N. (2003). The postmodern turn in psychoanalysis: A critique. *Psychoanalytic Psychology* 20: 411–424.
http://www.pep-web.org/document.php?id=ppsy.020.0411a

———Wolitzky, D.L. & Wakefield, J.C. (2001). The analyst's knowledge and autonomy: A critique of the "New View" in psychoanalysis. *Journal of the American Psychoanalytic Association* 49: 453–488.
http://www.pep-web.org/document.php?id=apa.049.0457a

Edwards, N. (2002). The ailing analyst and the dying patient: A relational perspective. Paper presented at the Second Joint International Conference, Deaths and endings, finality, transformations, new beginnings. Trinity College, August, Dublin, Ireland.
http://www.pep-web.org/document.php?id=pd.014.0313a

——— (2004). The ailing analyst and the dying patient: A relational perspective. *Psychoanalytic Dialogues* 14:313–335.
http://www.pep-web.org/document.php?id=pd.014.0313a

Freud, S. (1912). The dynamics of transference. *S.E.*, 12:97–108. 1961.
http://www.pep-web.org/document.php?id=se.012.0097a

Gray, P. (1994). *The Ego and the Analysis of Defense* (chap. 1 & 2). Northvale, NJ: Aronson.

Greenberg, J. & Mitchell, S. (1983). *Object Relations in Psychoanalytic Theory*. Cambridge, MA: Harvard University Press.
http://www.pep-web.org/document.php?id=cps.049.0011a

Grunes, M. (1984). The therapeutic object relationship. *Psychoanalytic Review* 71: 123–143. http://www.pep-web.org/document.php?id=psar.071.0123a

———— (1998). The therapeutic object relationship—II. In: *The Modern Freudians: Contemporary Psychoanalytic Technique*, eds. C. S. Ellman & S. Grand. Northvale, NJ: Aronson, pp. 129–140.
http://www.pep-web.org/document.php?id=psar.071.0123a

Hoffman, I.Z. (1983). The patient as interpreter of the analyst's experience. *Contemporary Psychoanalysis* 19: 389–422.
http://www.pep-web.org/document.php?id=cps.019.0389a

Isakower, O. (1992). The analyzing instrument in the conduct of the analytic process. *Journal of Clinical Psychoanalysis* 1:181–194, 1957.
http://www.pep-web.org/document.php?id=jcp.001.0181a

Jacobs, T. (1999). On the question of self-disclosure by the analyst: Error or advance in technique? *Psychoanalytic Quarterly* 68:159–183.
http://www.pep-web.org/document.php?id=paq.068.0159a

Lasky, R. (1990a). Catastrophic illness in the analyst and the analyst's emotional reactions to it. *International Journal of Psycho-Analysis* 71:455–473.
http://www.pep-web.org/document.php?id=ijp.071.0455a

———— (1990b). Keeping the analysis intact when the analyst has suffered a catastrophic illness. In: *Illness and the Analyst*, eds. H. Schwartz & A. Silver. New York: International Universities Press, pp. 177–198.
http://www.pep-web.org/document.php?id=ijp.073.0127a

Loewald, H. (1960). On the therapeutic action of psycho-analysis. *International Journal of Psycho-Analysis* 41:16–33.
http://www.pep-web.org/document.php?id=ijp.041.0016a

Meissner, W.W. (1996). *The Therapeutic Alliance*. New Haven, CT: Yale University Press. http://www.pep-web.org/document.php?id=pi.016.0039a

———— (2002). The problem of self-disclosure in psychoanalysis. *Journal of the American Psychoanalytic Association* 50:827–867.
http://www.pep-web.org/document.php?id=apa.050.0827a

Mitchell, S.A. (1988). The intrapsychic and the interpersonal: Different theories, different domains, or historical artifacts? *Psychoanalytic Inquiry* 8:472–496. http://www.pep-web.org/document.php?id=pi.008.0472a

———— (1993). *Hope and Dread in Psychoanalysis*. New York: Basic Books.

———— (1997). *Influence and Autonomy in Psychoanalysis*. Hillsdale, NJ: The Analytic Press. Orange, D. M. & Stolorow, R.D. (1998). Self-disclosure from the perspective of intersubjectivity theory. *Psychoanalytic Inquiry* 18:530–537. http://www.pep-web.org/document.php?id=pi.018.0530a

Pizer, B. (1997). When the analyst is ill: Dimensions of self-disclosure. *Psychoanalytic Quarterly* 66:450–469.
http://www.pep-web.org/document.php?id=paq.066.0450a

Renik, O. (1993). Analytic interaction: Conceptualizing technique in the light of the analyst's irreducible subjectivity. *Psychoanalytic Quarterly* 62:553–571. http://www.pep-web.org/document.php?id=paq.062.0553a

——— (1995). The ideal of the anonymous analyst and the problem of self-disclosure. *Psychoanalytic Quarterly* 64:466–495. http://www.pep-web.org/document.php?id=paq.064.0466a

——— (1996). The perils of neutrality. *Psychoanalytic Quarterly* 65:495–517. http://www.pep-web.org/document.php?id=paq.065.0495a

——— (1998a). The analyst's subjectivity and the analyst's objectivity. *International Journal of Psycho-Analysis* 79:487–498. http://www.pep-web.org/document.php?id=ijp.079.0487a

——— (1998b). *Knowledge and Authority in the Psychoanalytic Relationship.* Northvale, NJ: Aronson.

——— (1999). Playing one's cards face up in analysis: An approach to the problem of self-disclosure. *Psychoanalytic Quarterly* 68:521–539. http://www.pep-web.org/document.php?id=paq.068.0521a

Smith, H.F. (1999). Subjectivity and objectivity in analytic listening. *Journal of the American Psychoanalytic Association* 47:465–484. http://www.pep-web.org/document.php?id=apa.047.0465a

Stolorow, R.D. & Atwood, G.E. (1992). *Contexts of Being: The Intersubjective Foundations of Psychological Life.* Hillsdale, NJ: The Analytic Press.

——— (1997). Deconstructing the myth of the neutral analyst: An alternative from intersubjective systems theory. *Psychoanalytic Quarterly* 66:431–449. http://www.pep-web.org/document.php?id=paq.066.0431a

———Brandchaft, B. & Atwood, G. (1987). *Psychoanalytic Treatment: An Intersubjective Approach.* Hillsdale, NJ: The Analytic Press. http://www.pep-web.org/document.php?id=ijp.072.0363a

[Gediman, H.K. (2006) Reply to commentaries by Chris Bonovitz, Stephen
Hartman, and Joyce Slochower. *Psychoanalytic Dialogues*, 16:305-316.]

## REPLY TO COMMENTARIES

Responding to these three commentaries is hardly a neutral task. I have decided to begin with the one that is most negative toward me and my work,
Stephen Hartman's, and then to proceed on to one that is far more constructive, Christopher Bonovitz's. My last reply is addressed to Joyce Slochower's
commentary, because hers is most in keeping with a major aim of my paper:
it provides space for respectfully building bridges between and among multiple psychoanalytic perspectives. When appropriate, I refer back to my earlier
responses as I move on to the last.

In all three replies, I use the term *Relational,* with a capital R, to refer to
Relational Theory or the Relational School of psychoanalysis. I use the term
*relational,* with a lowercase r, to refer to a relational perspective or point of
view that may be held by various analysts from various schools, including
many contemporary Freudians whose work is informed by this perspective. I
aim to explicate these differences gradually and contextually as I move along.

## REPLY TO STEPHEN HARTMAN

Hartman's basic assumption, which underlies his fundamentally negative and
often disrespectful criticism of my ideas, is that there is not room for coexistence between or shifting back and forth or for building bridges between
and among psychoanalytic paradigms. He believes that Relational theory has
already replaced the traditional models simply because it has, and that is that.
I have spent the last 35 years of my life advocating for pluralism, diversity,
multiple models, and other forms of multiplicity, in an attempt to reconcile
and work with the best that all psychoanalytic schools have to offer.

Hartman rejects both a multimodel approach and, by implication, "working in hybrid paradigms." This latter approach was advocated by Adrienne
Harris, a Relational psychoanalyst, in her respectful 2005 discussion of my
2005 paper "Premodern, Modern, and Postmodern Perspectives on Sex and

341

Gender Mixes." To characterize her own work, Harris (2005) stated, "I, like many others, work for the most part in hybrid paradigms." She went on, "There are a number of recent commentaries on this situation ... urging us to tolerate the multiplicity of theoretical positions, the mixed models we are all deploying" (p. 1083).

Hartman, holding consistently to his position of privileging Relational psychoanalysis as the only viable paradigm in psychoanalysis today, believes that Mitchell hedged on the question of whether Relational psychoanalysis constituted a new paradigm and that he waffled on the usefulness of coexisting competing models. The relative merits of a single paradigm approach as opposed to a multiple models or even a multiple perspectival approach is very much alive today and is being debated as a subject of much controversy. It was the topic of a lively panel at the most recent meeting of the American Psychoanalytic Association (New York, January 2006), at which the single paradigm of conflict and compromise was advocated by Sander Abend and the multimodel approach by Fred Pine, who had the welcome support of the vast majority of the audience.

Hartman, who presents himself clearly in his commentary as an opponent of multiplicity, puts me in the position of rebutting some strong statements he marshals against me in support of his advocacy of one single Relational-Subjective-Constructionist paradigm. Some examples: "Gediman suffers Burke's fate: to have championed a no longer viable regime" (p. 274). "Perhaps chivalry is gone, despite Gediman's noble effort, and *it is time, once and for all, to give the old paradigm the boot* [italics added]" (p. 291). The way Gediman sees it, according to Gediman, is that Hartman contradicts his own position that paradigms shifts and a postmodern perspective are not choices, but "they just are" (p. 275). That is, he contradicts his own allegedly postmodern position by advocating what postmodernists decry above all: the adherence to a single monolithic paradigm that dispenses with the multiplicity and opening up of diverse perspectives that I, as well as even more committed postmodern analysts, advocate as central to the advancement of ideas in today's complex and ever-changing world. He has, as Shakespeare wrote in *Hamlet,* hoisted himself upon his own petard. The bomb he intended to direct at me backfired and blew up on his own person. I should like to see Hartman work himself out of his inherently self-contradictory bind and strengthen the potential merit of the position he advocates so passionately.

Despite his admittedly negative overall assessment of my ideas, he does, in all fairness, find a way to be positive, but only minimally, as far as I am concerned. He says that I argue some points wisely and persuasively and that my "instrument" is thoughtfully honed. Having gotten the amenities out of the way, he proceeds to set me up as having said and done things in my psychoanalytic treatments that I have never said and done, and then he launches his destructive attacks by knocking down one by one these straw men that he alone has created. There is no going back, he says, to a privileged one-person point of view, a position I have never taken or even remotely hinted at in my article.

Things deteriorate as he moves along. He says that I consign the patient's anal-erotic life to procrastination. Because there is nothing in my case write-up remotely consistent with his line of interpretation of my work, I can only conclude that he is projecting into my illustrative material his own ideas. He says flat out that I have an urge to overtake my patient. I must remind Hartman that I am not writing about homoerotic life but about self-disclosures in relation to one particular patient's anal pleasures that are often accompanied by sadism and aggression, anxieties, defenses, and resistances to help analyze the character trait of procrastination. He uses the terms *defense* and *resistance* pejoratively when he says that "anal pleasure has been consigned to bad behavior (a.k.a. resistance)" (p. 284). I have never used the terms *defense* and *resistance* pejoratively, but I believe that they refer to ubiquitous psychoanalytic facts in all individuals. I also do not consign anal erotism and the aggressive components that sometimes accompany it exclusively to psychopathology. Psychopathology is found neither in the mere presence of psychosexual and aggressive content in the patient's anal-erotic wishes and fantasies nor in the fact of defense against pleasure. It is to be found only when these mental processes result in a high-cost compromise to the patient's well-being. Excessive rigidity and interference with uninhibited functioning in love and work determine psychopathology in an otherwise ubiquitous compromise formation.

I should like to refresh Hartman's memory on the meaning of procrastination as a character trait. Consensus has always been, as far as I know, that procrastination is often a defense against anal-erotic pleasure. Simultaneously, procrastination fosters that very same pleasure by allowing disguised anal-erotic gratification without conscious awareness of its psychosexual implications. Furthermore, there is nothing that casts aspersions on gay men's longing for sexual submission in a theory that acknowledges anal-erotic pleasures and anxieties that might be expressed in procrastinations. Such feelings are experienced, or potentially experienced, by all individuals, including homosexual, heterosexual, bisexual, and transgendered boys and girls, men and women. Hartman is simply mistaken when he claims that Freudian discourse equates anal pleasure, even when experienced by gay men, as perversion. Freud was very explicit in his Three Essays that sexual "inversion," his term for homosexuality, was not perversion, and Freud's position is reflected in the views of Freudian analysts today.

Hartman is right in suspecting that my patient gleans how I feel about his procrastinations. My patient knows at some level that I see him as a Kaka bird, and he responds to his own preconscious knowledge of my preconscious thoughts. He knows this because I inevitably disclose my strongest hunches even when I do not put them into words. That very knowledge primes him to elaborate on our joint knowledge of him and my feelings about him. Thus he expands on our implicit and covert understanding of the Kaka bird narrative. He knows that he because he is very much in touch with his crystallized character trait of procrastination, and he also knows it because of what comes through to him of my theoretical paradigms and personal leanings in our co-constructed understandings of the meanings of his fantasies. But Hartman is wrong is stating that my theory was uttered. However, I have no doubt that my theories of psychosexuality inform what I hear in my state of evenly hovering attention to his ways of expressing himself, just as they will have an inevitable impact on how the patient understands how I understand him. The subtleties of the ideas that inform me then prime the patient to extend and expand his own personal narrative, or to get tracked onto these ideas. This kind of interactive effect is not limited to Freudian discourse, however, but applies to any paradigm utilized in any clinical psychoanalytic encounter. We know that Kohutian patients produce narratives, say, of self-cohesion. And patients of Kleinian analysts get tracked onto narratives of destroying the good breast. The more paradigms we have at our disposal, the more varied will be the patient's narratives, because our evenly hovering attention is receptive to picking up on more clinically relevant themes than when we were limited to only one paradigm.

Hartman's critique is replete with pretentious language, verging, at the very least, as in his title, on the "clangy" verbal punning, which is not funny. He indulges in obscure metaphors such as "a blip in the Matrix" (p. 288), which he explicates with even more esoteric metaphors and private references like "the downtown crowd" (p. 290) without so much as a clue as to what and to whom these phrases refer. Perhaps others of his generation know what he means, but those of us who are not so steeped in pop culture are sure to feel left out. He attacks my use of the term *compromise formation* as a commitment to the structural model alone, which it is not. He would do well to read Brenner's (1994) elegant deconstruction of the structural model, which he did in order to rid it of entities. Hartman might then get a crack at understanding more of what I mean by his straw man arguments. My support of Brenner here does not extend to his use of a single paradigm, conflict and compromise, any more than I support Hartman on using a single-model paradigm, but only to his relegation of reified entities to an atavistic stockpile.

I remind Hartman of the myriad analysts who have devoted their works and their lives to revising, modifying, and replacing outdated and wrong aspects of a cherished theory in order to open up the possibilities for multiple models, diversity, hybrid paradigms, and flexible shifting among the best that one school of thought has to offer other schools of thought. It is he, not we, who forecloses by booting out paradigms rather than striving for good composites, if not common ground. It is still possible to respect some of the older views and have respect for the newer paradigms as well. It comes as no surprise that within the throwing out of the baby with the bathwater context of Hartman's nihilistic views of contemporary Freudian analysis that he does not manifest the scholarship to cite even one single article from among those who have embraced what he would like to boot out of our psychoanalytic universe. His erasures of psychoanalytic history are, to my mind, no more than psychoanalytic genocide.

## REPLY TO CHRISTOPHER BONOVITZ

Christopher Bonovitz, from his very first paragraph on, sets a tone that I read with pleasure as an understanding and appreciation of precisely what I am attempting to do: to use self-disclosure as a means of finding points of intersection among varying points of view. He rightly understands that the groups I refer to are not homogeneous or monolithic, and thereby he conveys his openness to finding points of agreement as well as disagreement with my ideas in a way that opens up possibilities for fruitful dialogue. He is probably right in saying that I underestimate the extent to which Relational theory makes self-disclosure something different from what I am describing. Nonetheless, with the possible exception of minor nuanced differences, I wholeheartedly endorse the centrality he attributes to the two points he feels characterize a relational perspective. It goes without saying that his use of the word *perspective* rather than *paradigm* distinguishes him in my mind from Hartman and predisposes me to take his ideas most seriously, in contrast to the rather dismissive way I have just responded to Hartman's commentary.

It was most helpful for me to be reminded that Relational analysts are interested in the interactional matrix, in uncertainties and ambiguities, and in the mutual influence and impact of the patient's and analyst's psychologies on the interaction. Contemporary Freudian analysts, by and large, share these interests, for we have learned much from the relational emphasis. Bonovitz certainly knows that Freudian analysts are also interested in other matters as well, such as intrapsychic conflict and fantasy, and how these aspects of the way the mind works play out in interpersonal and relational domains. I also agree with his second point: We are disclosing unintentionally all the time in a variety of ways we are largely unaware of. I thank him for reminding me that even in the implicit disclosures of every day analysis, of which I speak, that we are disclosing something about our selves *unbeknownst to ourselves*. Unconscious processes of one sort or another are, of course, endemic to the work of all psychoanalysts. So in addition to my disclosure to my first patient in which I seem to be aware and measured about what I was disclosing, I was, of course, also disclosing in ways that were not so clear to me at the time.

I could not agree more with Bonovitz's addition to my explanations: the indisputable importance of disclosure and its *aftermath*, or what I sometimes refer to as *repercussions* or *sequelae,* often very surprising ones, that were not predictable at the time of the self-disclosure of my feelings about his autoerotic procrastinations. And as to my timing, I hope he would join with me in getting me off the hook by acknowledging that I was selecting only limited clinical data as illustrative of my major argument—those points relevant to distinctions between implicit and explicit disclosure—and that I was not presenting a complete case history of my treatment strategies with this particular patient in all their complexities. Despite my rationale for selecting material for illustrative purposes, I would also, of course, find it incumbent upon myself to wonder whether and/or to what extent I might unknowingly have been procrastinating in offering my interpretation in what seemed to Bonovitz to be a belated and untimely way. In the interest of timing, tact, and my sense of what the patient could process at that moment, I decided not to disclose my private association. Just to update the reader, I did offer my "Kaka bird" interpretation at a later date, after much more groundwork had been done to enhance the likelihood that the patient and I had consolidated our understandings of his procrastinations. At that later date, he was far more able to access his heretofore unconscious fantasies and anxieties about relating to me in a more humanized, less mechanized manner, which had been a repetition of his identifications and interactions with his "robotic" mother.

I trust that Bonovitz, unlike Hartman, meant that the analyst's authority *might* foreclose on the possibility of listening optimally. Hartman, unlike Bonovitz, made an undocumented allegation that my recourse to my authoritative knowledge *did* prevent me from listening properly. In looking back, I do not believe that foreclosure occurred in my case. Even though the analyst may be closed off to grasping the full impact and implication of her disclosure to the patient in the moment she is making it, I hope she is open to listening to ramifications she had never considered consciously before. That new knowledge is then included in a productive dialogue with her patient as ambiguities morph into the clarity of mutual understandings. It goes without saying that the analyst's postdisclosure consciousness of herself expands along with her ever-increasing understanding of the patient's understanding. A judicious use of authority in informing both implicit and explicit self-disclosure is not a tool to reduce openness and receptivity to multiple possibilities and multiple meanings of what is going on in the patient's mind, and in the countless patient-analyst interactions that inhabit the minds of both patient and analyst. I do believe that one can and must respect one's authority while respecting the moment-to-moment ambiguity, uncertainty, and variability that any interpretation may unleash, despite relative consistency and constancy underlying knowable trends. My focus was on an aspect of the process that was central to my interest and did not exclude other important sequelae of interpretation and disclosure. It is important to realize that the images induced in the reader by psychoanalytic writing about process cannot be isomorphic or veridical with that process in vivo.

In Bonovitz's commentary on my second case—the woman with whom I had shared anecdotal material about my granddaughter—I agree with him that no disclosure can be completely "countertransference-free," but only relatively so. I might very well have overstated my case in writing it up. And the patient had indeed, all along, been privy to other self-disclosures that sometimes the analyst had and sometimes had not been aware of, either before or mostly after the fact. He notes, correctly, that there were reasons other than termination that prompted me, such my impending loss of a patient I had come to care for deeply, and even love. In this case, Bonovitz was "right on the money" in characterizing my timing of my self-disclosure as relating to my intense feelings about termination. Very little has been written on the analyst's feelings of love, loss, and mourning during termination. One notable exception is the article by Bergmann (1997). However, these issues are very much in the picture for many nonreporting and non-self-disclosing analysts.

I thank him for his accurate summations of what I intended to accomplish in this second vignette and for his sensitive proposal of the "locksmith" metaphor to stand for my internal negotiations with myself for opting on what to lock or unlock for my patient to see. I am in full agreement with him that we personally reveal much more about ourselves when we find ourselves in situations for which we are completely unprepared than when we disclose something that has been neatly formulated beforehand. These surprise situations are the very stuff of critically important "transformational moments" that I referred to in passing in this paper but discussed at greater length in my contribution (Gediman, 1998) on the therapeutic action of psychoanalysis. I thank him as well for his appreciation of my capacity to make judgments, an appreciation that contrasts so starkly with Hartman's negativity in assuming that my supposedly outdated theory powerfully limits my disclosures to foreclosures.

I do take issue with Bonovitz's belief that I am more wedded to my rationales and theoretically based principles than to my instincts and "feel" for the situation. I believe, rather, that as analysts, our instincts and feelings are always informed by some secondary process theory and rationale, and vice versa, even when these forces are operating below the level of consciousness. Once again, it is not an *either/or* matter but one inclusive of the rational *and* the intuitive. I trust Bonovitz can see that he risks perpetuating a stereotype of contemporary Freudians as more theory bound and Relational analysts as more experience-near in his otherwise well thought out and respectful appreciation of my mission to counter stereotyping of different schools of thought when it comes to self-disclosures.

Mainly, I thank Christopher Bonovitz for his intelligent emphasis on the after-the-fact repercussions of self-disclosure and for enlightening me about certain relational positions with which I was not as familiar as I have come to be thanks to this dialogue. It now appears more evident than ever that analysts of all schools do not read enough of the works of analysts of other schools to be truly informed about certain state-of-the-art trends that are, inevitably, grasped initially more at the parochial than at the wider level. Like Hartman, Bonovitz's references do not include any articles by contemporary Freudian authors. I hope the aim of cross-fertilization, which includes whom we read and whom we cite, will come closer to realization as a result of dialogues such as these.

## REPLY TO JOYCE SLOCHOWER

Joyce Slochower's commentary is, as far as I am concerned, a strong and close to ideal response to my paper. Of all three of the discussants, she unquestionably is best at understanding and articulating the position and arguments I have presented. I feel immediately at ease when she makes it clear from the beginning that "moving beyond psychoanalytic stereotypes, Gediman aims at building bridges rather than caricatures by underscoring what we share" (p. 264). Her acknowledgment of the perils of casting aspersions on alternate theories places her several millennia away from that paradigm booter Stephen Hartman. She appreciates how the Freudian stance has moved toward self-disclosure and that my discussion has brought me closer to the Relational position. Slochower respectfully understands and appreciates the gist of my position and directs her remarks in an orderly and persuasive fashion to what she sees as the convergences and divergences between her Relational position and my contemporary Freudian position. She aims to focus on convergences and divergences with an eye to explication, not denigration, to deepen our mutual understanding rather than divide us further. She succeeds, and one can only admire the forthright stance and spirit of her inquiry.

At the outset, let me state that I do not regard the divergences she perceives between us as divergent as I think she does, and I explicate this assertion as I move forward in this reply. From the start, Slochower disagrees with my contention that Relational theory does not require a paradigm shift away from the Freudian model. At this juncture in my understanding of Relational theory, I might very well agree with her, but only once we make the distinction between a Relational *theory* and a relational *perspective*. I do not think a relational perspective requires a paradigm shift, because perspectival shifts allow for hybrid paradigms and multiple models for understanding clinical psychoanalytic data, clinical process, and theory. Most important, I realize now that I was not as clear in my own mind as to what I meant by a "paradigm shift" when I originally wrote this paper as I am now. I am objecting only to the idea that we are ready for a total paradigm shift away from one model and toward another that replaces it completely. I do not object to the idea, but in fact advocate it strongly, that it is time for paradigm shifts back and forth among multiple models in ways that make sense in the actual psychoanalytic clinical encounter. This is a totally psychological notion that does not seem to have roots in such philosophical ideas as those put forth by Kuhn (1963).

I also challenge the extent of her second point of divergence, that the Freudians interpret and disclose with more certainty than Relational analysts who require a stronger commitment to uncertainty than do their Freudian colleagues. She does make a strong case for her position, but her actual reasoning would indicate to me that she would acknowledge that contemporary Freudians must and do leave room for uncertainty. They are really, for the most part, not that arrogant a bunch, at least those of my acquaintance in the present time. If I come across as strongly certain as Slochower says I do, I should like to correct that impression. I am not that immodest as I apparently came through as being. The basic difference that emerges for me regarding certainty and authoritative knowledge is that Relational theorists are more prone than contemporary Freudians to downplay the importance of objectivity and/or material reality, whereas within the relational *perspective*, analysts of any persuasion can accept the some times paradoxical coexistence of objectivity and subjectivity. I do agree with Slochower's fundamental position that the "relational ideal concerns the analyst's capacity to enter into an asymmetrical treatment relationship and to tolerate the uncertainty generated therein" (p. 270). I do not believe she would take issue with my adding that the relational ideal also concerns the patient's capacity to tolerate that uncertainty, a tolerance that is a function of the basic trust that develops as the analytic process progresses.

Slochower is not quite correct that I use my subjectivity to inform myself of the patient's experience *rather* than about the dyad's relational dynamic and its historical antecedents, although I see how I may have given that impression by emphasizing the former at the expense of the latter in the way I wrote up my material. It is clearly incumbent on any analyst to understand what is being repeated and with whom, originally, in the interactional context of the analysis. I meant to convey simply that I keep the patient's history, and relational and other experiences, at the center, and I suspect she does the same thing, as she acknowledges the asymmetrical relationship between patient and analyst.

Our biggest divergence, over the relative importance of certainty and objectivity, yields only to the narrow gap that she implies, although I think it most important that she has worked so assiduously to sharpen areas of difference. However, I could not agree more with her position that the analyst's emotional response to a patient cannot represent a veridical readout of the patient's experience. Like Freud (1907, 1937), I believe we construct as much as reconstruct the patient's present as well as past: We are dealing with what Freud called "daydreams in common" (Freud, 1907; see also Gediman and Wolkenfeld, 1980) whenever we speculate on anything about the way our patients' minds work, especially on their imagery of experiences that they are reporting, and we are representing mentally in our mind in an attempt to achieve some reasonable correspondence, but never with absolute veridicality. I would regard the relational concepts of mutuality and co-construction as a present-day and creatively developed variant of Freud's seminal contribution. On the subject of objectivity, I respond most positively to her belief that my position echoes Winnicott's belief that objective responses can be separated from the analyst's subjective countertransference. I stand corrected if I gave the impression that I do not regard my subjectivity as partially unknowable.

Because I am not omniscient, I see our views on the subject of uncertainty as less divergent that she does, because I agree with her totally that I cannot ever apprehend totally all the personal intents and other reasons I have for any disclosure I implicitly or explicitly make.

I also agree basically with her position on analytic authority. Although I might not have been using the term *dyadically co-constructed* to characterize the patient's need for some basic trust in my authority, Slochower explicates her use of the term so well as to open up the possibility for my using it in the future. I am most grateful to have learned from her something I did not know before, and I thoroughly agree with her support of the need for patient and analyst to establish a shared illusion of therapeutic potency.

When Slochower notes that the therapeutic action of psychoanalysis involves the patient and therapist as playing out old relational patterns while creating something new between them, she appears to me to be right on Loewald's (1960) territory of a new therapeutic object relationship. Although she does not cite Loewald, she does cite a good number of contemporary Freudians as well as Relational source material in her references—one sign, perhaps, of a range of reasons that she and I share more common ground than my other two discussants and I do.

When I read Slochower on and between the lines, I conclude that neither of us is reductionistic. Psyche cannot be reduced to mere intrapsychic conflict and compromise any more than it can be reduced to what transpires within the relational matrix. Both and more domains coexist. As I explicated in my reply to Bonovitz, I try as best as I can to follow through on the unexpected impact and sequelae of my self-disclosures and all other interventions. Like Bonovitz, Slochower points out that I do myself an injustice in implying structural entities—id, ego, superego—from which I maintain equidistance in the interest of neutrality. In my defense, I can say only that the metaphors of our psychoanalytic theoretical past influence our present language in ways that are often infelicitous. So I agree with her, as I mentioned in my reply to Hartman, and I think Brenner (1994) now also would agree and insist that it is not possible to demarcate discrete psychic areas. It is better to revise the lexicon than boot out the paradigm.

Despite our divergent positions on objectivity, I think new objectivities emerge following self-disclosures. Despite our harboring some different views, Slochower acknowledges, as do I, the many clinical bridges between our positions. Here's to a future of strengthening bridges while respecting the differences that she has so beautifully delineated in this dialogue. I hope that contemporary Freudians would want to incorporate tolerance of uncertainty more explicitly into the precepts that guide their theoretical and clinical corpus. Correspondingly, I would hope that Relational theorists would move toward more exploration of unconscious fantasy. I apologize for implying that Relational theory *merely* makes explicit what is implicit in Freudian theory. I think it sometimes does that, but I do not want anybody to lose track of my major and fundamental respect for the ways that aspects of the relational point of view, the relational perspective, and Relational theory have added to and are being incorporated into contemporary Freudian points of view. I thank Joyce Slochower, as she thanks me, in her very words, "for opening the door to theoretical mutuality and, I hope, continued theoretical dialogue" (p. 272).

## REFERENCES

Bergmann, M.S. (1997). Termination. *Psychoanalytic Psychology* 14:163–174.
Brenner, C. (1994). The mind as conflict and compromise formation. *Journal of Clinical. Psychoanalysis* 3:473–488.
http://www.pep-web.org/document.php?id=jcp.003.0473a
Freud, S. (1907). Creative writers and daydreaming. *S.E.* 9:143–153.
——— (1937). Constructions in analysis. *S.E.* 23:257–269. London: Hogarth Press, 1961. http://www.pep-web.org/document.php?id=se.023.0255a
Gediman, H.K. (1998). The therapeutic action in the real, transferential, and therapeutic object relationship. In: *The Modern Freudians: Contemporary Psychoanalytic Technique*, ed. C. Ellman & S. Grand. Northvale, NJ: Aronson, pp. 141–160.
——— (2005). Premodern, modern, and postmodern perspectives on sex and gender mixes. *Journal of the American Psychoanalytic Association* 53:1059–1078. http://www.pep-web.org/document.php?id=apa.053.1059a
——— Wolkenfeld, F. (1980). The parallelism phenomenon in psychoanalysis and supervision: It's reconsideration as a triadic system. *Psychoanalytic Quarterly* 49:234–255.
http://www.pep-web.org/document.php?id=paq.049.0234a
Harris, A. (2005). Gender in linear and nonlinear history. *Journal of the American Psychoanalytic Association* 53:1079–1095.
http://www.pep-web.org/document.php?id=apa.053.1079a
Kuhn, T. (1962) *The Structure of Scientific Revolutions*, Chicago; University of Chicago Press.
Loewald, H. (1960). On the therapeutic action of psychoanalysis. *International Journal of Psycho-Analysis* 41:16–33.
http://www.pep-web.org/document.php?id=ijp.041.0016a

# EPILOGUE

## AUTHOR'S INTRODUCTION

My Epilogue, Chapter 18, emerges from two distinct but related experiences. One was my many years of teaching a course entitled "Psychoanalytic Theory after Freud" at the New York Freudian Society, later to become known as The Contemporary Freudian Society, especially in their Washington D.C. Program, of which I was a co-founder. In later years, the course topic was changed to "Cutting Edge Controversies in Psychoanalysis." The second was my opportunity to work with a group of very senior analysts who had made major contributions to psychoanalysis that had been assembled and led by Harold P. Blum, M.D. in response to a grant offered by The Psychoanalytic Research and Development Fund. The fruits of this group's work were published together in 2011 in Special Issue 5 of *The Psychoanalytic Review*, edited by Harold P. Blum and entitled: *Diversity, Controversy and Innovation in Contemporary Psychoanalysis*. Among the other members of the Study Group who were main contributors to this issue were Harold P. Blum, Otto Kernberg, and Martin Bergmann.

In Blum's words:

"The trenchant issues of diversity and theoretical pluralism stimulated the formation of a study and research group under the independent auspices of the Psychoanalytic Research and Development Fund. The group, with members from different backgrounds, institutes, analytic interests, and experience, deliberated monthly for two years. It was a great privilege to organize and participate in our meetings, which were intriguing, stimulating, edifying, and, on the whole, very rewarding for all. What follows in this special issue are original papers by members of the group, representing their individual ideas and response to our divergent and convergent, freewheeling discourse and debate. The group members were Drs. Harold Blum, Chair; Martin Bergmann, Helen Gediman, Samuel Herschkowitz, Carl Jacobs, Helene Keable, Otto Kernberg, Peter Neubauer, Robert Penzer, and Joseph Reppen. Three members of the group, Drs. Peter Neubauer (deceased), Robert Penzer, and Joseph Reppen, to whom we are greatly indebted, were regrettably unable to contribute to this special issue of the *Psychoanalytic Review*."

My contribution follows as Epilogue to *Building Bridges* because it is the best summary of my way of thinking during the many years I have spent dedicated to my profession.

# Chapter 18: Cutting Edge Controversies: True Contradictions and False Dichotomies

[Gediman, H.K. (2011) Cutting edge controversies: True and false dichotomies. *Psychoanalytic Review*, 98:613-632.]

Diverse and often contentious polarities raise dilemmas in psychoanalytic controversy today. Shall we be thinking in either/or or both/and terms? Are binaries or polarities inherent in dichotomous points of view true or false? Will multiplicities of outlook replace binaries? I personally think we are in a better position than ever to mine the riches of our expanding knowledge base because increasingly no important school is a monolithic or homogeneous representative of a particular view, and we now have myriad opportunities to dialogue with representatives of other positions. Now well past the millennium, we are bursting forward eagerly to dispel rigidities of old dogmas and to integrate old and newly articulated polarities that are on the cutting edge of psychoanalysis and that are providing so much of today's excitement and intellectual fervor. No longer are we as uniperspectival as we once were, no longer are we as dependent on one theoretical foundation as we used to be, no longer are we as internally coherent and cohesive in our beliefs as we once thought we were. Diversity, contradiction, and controversy require multiple perspectives, but they do not necessarily require a unitary theory. Despite the fact that analysts hailing from different traditions are still engaged in turf wars in which we hurl stereotypes and caricatures at each other, we do share common theoretical and clinical ground. Nonetheless, we also hold legitimate differences in viewpoints in which we are beset by contradictions all along the line. I will delineate from among the many controversial polarities ones that seem to be major although hardly all-inclusive, summarize arguments from different and opposing points of view, and offer my opinions on whether or not certain apparent contradictions are reconcilable.

In my 1999 address to the graduates of the New York Freudian Society I said,

> "... this seems to be a time like no other, and I think it augurs even better times, because increasingly, the proponents of one set of ideas listen to and learn from the proponents of another apparently controversial set. In fact, despite the claim that analysts hailing from different traditions

do share common theoretical and clinical ground, we are beset by contradictions all along the line" (Gediman, 1999).

In 1999 I emphasized the polarities, binaries, or dimensions of objectivity and subjectivity, intersubjectivity and authority, intrapsychic and interpersonal points of view, interpreting in the genetic past and interpreting in
the here and now present, narrative truth and scientific truth, consolidation
and expansion, unificatory theories and pluralistic ones. Since then, more
and more has poured into the psychoanalytic soup as more diverse ways of
looking at theory and technique have entered cutting edge psychoanalytic
controversy. From soup to nuts, the feast goes on as the cooking, hopefully,
gets more and more refined. In these days of pluralism, diversity, overdetermination, multiple function, complementarity, and multiperspectival views,
it is commonplace to hear the merits of one approach being offered along
with the merits of its opposite, contradictory view. The fact of the matter is,
conflict and controversy, and outright contradiction, at least in the manifest
content of arguments, are commonplace and ubiquitous and are even to be
found in the way our language expresses our ideas. Contradictions coexist
for many reasons, prominent among which is the fact that hardly any theory
is monolithic or lays claim to unique areas of interest. Insistent pleas for
coexisistence of inconsistent and contradictory explanations persist side by
side with equally insistent pleas for replacing one psychoanalytic paradigm
with another that appears less inconsistent. By now it should be clear that
like Leo Rangell (2000), I look at most current psychoanalytic controversies
not in either/or but in both/and terms.

I stand true to my 1999 convictions that we are grappling with an unsurpassed
proliferation of ideas within psychoanalysis. In my 2010 address to the New
York Freudian Society graduates (Gediman, 2010), I was taken not only by diversity and multiple paradoxes, but also by the outright contradictions between
one dearly and clearly held position and another. I used, as my springboard, the
inevitable and ubiquitous contradictions permeating our language. Freud, in his
1910 gem, "The Antithetical Meaning of Primal Words" said:

> The way in which dreams treat the category of contraries and contradic-
> tories is highly remarkable. It is simply disregarded. "No"seems not to
> exist so far as dreams are concerned. They show a particular preference
> for combining contraries into a unity or for representing them as one
> and the same thing (p. 214).

Quoting Abel's 1884 work, Freud concluded:

In view of these and many similar cases of antithetical meaning ... it is beyond doubt that in one language at least there was a large number of words that denoted at once a thing and its opposite. However astonishing it may be, we are faced with the fact and have to reckon with it (p. 215).

Developing my own spin on the linguistic foundation for contradiction and controversy, I drew special attention to some well-worn proverbs and aphorisms in which linguistic contradictions spring up with apparently endless variations. I noted parallelisms between pairs of proverbs that contain contrary wisdom and pairs of psychoanalytic propositions that similarly appear to contain contradictory messages and directions of thought. Each compelling saying can be paired with another one that conveys just the opposite meaning. For example, I paired "Don't count your chickens before they hatch" with "A bird in the hand is worth two in the bush." Another, "Look before you leap" was paired with its apparent opposite, "He who hesitates is lost." And how about "Haste makes waste" and "A stitch in time saves nine." These pairs can be taken as metaphoric parallels for the opposite psychoanalytic therapeutic strategies of seizing the moment and/or waiting. Clearly, I was looking for parallels between the structure of language in time-tested sayings and the structures of apparently different listening modes that inform dosing, timing, and tact in when we intervene sooner and when later, or when we say as little as we can and when we say as much as we are able.

Freud's (1905) Complemental Series, that is, his schema for accounting for the relative and reciprocal influences of heredity and environment, constitution and innate and acquired traits and experience, provides the historical background for my way of thinking. Freud's principle provides the fundamental and most reliable precedent for looking at apparent polarities as potentially complementary and integratable, and not as binaries. Most binaries, upon examination and clinical testing, are often bound to turn out as false.

I now turn to some controversies that I have selected from a vast array of many more polarities in psychoanalytic theory and in principles of psychoanalytic treatment. There are many ways of slicing the pie in the myriad ways of stating dichotomies and polarities. My categorization is preliminary, by no means exhaustive or exclusive, and can be modified to be more inclusive or more compact and condensed.

## DIVERSITY AND CONTROVERSIES RELATING
## PRIMARILY TO PSYCHOANALYTIC THEORY

### I "OBJECTIVE" REALITY AND PSYCHIC REALITY: INFLUENCES
### OF INTRAPSYCHIC AND INTERPERSONAL FORCES

*A. The Actual Neuroses and the Psychoneuroses.* Some analysts have accorded
no importance at all to the phenomena of actual neuroses and have abandoned
Freud's (1926) early ideas on the topic altogether. They have replaced the
paradigm completely with intrapsychic and early developmental influences
of fantasy on the psychoneuroses. However, I (Gediman, 1984, 1991) and others, including Freud (1914), have maintained that actual, "objectively real" or
"materially real" sexual and aggressive tensions, among others, are as important as ever in the etiology of neuroses, character pathology, and personality
disorders. Such "real" factors do not rule out the importance of unconscious
fantasy as a prime motivational factor in personality development. As ever,
we respect the influence of psychic reality and intrapsychic conflict between
and among various sectors of the personality. The coexistence of both phenomena, actual tension build-up and psychic reality, is consistent with the fact
that Freud's (1926) second anxiety theory, which holds that anxiety motivates
defenses, never replaced his first, which holds that defensive activity, particularly hysterical repression, causes anxiety. The two paradigms coexist. One
has never fully replaced the other. (See Rangell, 1968; Gediman, 1984.)

*B. Reality and Fantasy in Trauma.* Complemental approaches to the relative influences of reality and fantasy on the genesis and effects of psychic
trauma are preferable to an either/or approach (Gediman, 1991). Seduction
trauma, as well as cumulative developmental and maturity-onset trauma,
such as posttraumatic stress disorder, produce serious interpersonal noxious
sequelae, but so too do the ways that their meaning is elaborated in fantasy.
All of the diverse processes subsumed in this polarity bear importantly on
subsequent psychological outcomes. I believe we can and always do make use
of complemental intrapsychic and interpersonal perspectives on fantasy and
reality, and seduction trauma is a test case par excellence.

Freud did replace his belief in an "exclusive traumatic pathogenesis" (Blum,
1986). That is, he abandoned the seduction theory qua theory—that an individual's seduction as a child caused neurosis, particularly hysteria—but he
never relinquished his belief that seduction usually leads to the accumulation
of unbearable tensions and persistent noxious intra- and interpersonal sequelae
(Freud, 1896). That is, his convictions about the noxious effect of dammed up

libidinal, aggressive, and other tensions persisted along with his belief in the importance of conscious and/or unconscious fantasies as crucial underpinnings for psychic development. Despite Janet Malcolm's (1984) locking horns with her "bête noir," Jeffrey Masson (1984), over the idea that all patients treated in accordance with the flawed and defunct seduction theory should be recalled, like the old Ford Pinto, what is truly called for today is an interperspectival approach that permits new ways of looking at the relative contributions of each of many diverse factors, separately and together, to etiology and pathogenesis. Complemental approaches to the relative influences of reality and fantasy, as well as interpersonal and intrapsychic factors, on genesis and effects of psychic trauma are preferable to any polarizing presumptions of a binary.

*C. Conflict and Deficit Models of Etiology and Psychogenesis.* Once considered mutually exclusive models, both paradigms, the drive-defense model and the early-life deficit model proposed by Kohut (1971) and the Self-psychologists, may now be considered as useful approaches to understanding the development of the personality in its normal and pathological variants (see Gediman, 1989). They are complemental approaches to etiology and pathogenesis of the psychoneuroses and of narcissistic disorders. The early failures in maternal empathy that Kohut once regarded as critical to deficit pathogenesis might well predispose patients to later difficulties in conflict resolution. Similarly, excessive conflict leads to experiences of dissolution of the self. Both Self-psychologists and conflict psychologists have endorsed using methods of empathy, attunement, and introspection along with the method of free association. Where they still differ theoretically is in the area of two distinct developmental lines, one leading to the narcissistic pathology of "Tragic Man" and the other to the psychoneuroses of "Guilty Man." This idea that different developmental pathways underlie different trajectories of psychogenesis has never been appropriated by mainstream psychoanalysis. Conflict, once generally thought of exclusively in terms of psychic reality, and deficit, once thought of exclusively as constitutional—environmental and self- and object-relational realities can be combined in a unificatory point of view. A once raging controversy appears to have morphed silently into a prime example of reasonably peaceful coexistence, if not perfect unification.

## II THE POSTMODERN TURN AND THE CLASSICAL-RELATIONAL DIVIDE

*A. Drive Theory and Object Relations Theory.* Never truly an either/or binary, drive and object have always been intimately related. Whether the only connection is simply that a drive always has an object, or whether the connections are multiple and more complex and deal with other important interactional—relational components, the notion of drive or object is a truly false dichotomy. Caricaturing and stereotyping each other's positions on drive and object is commonly engaged in between contemporary Freudians, who tend to underplay the role that Relational analysts attribute to sex and aggression, and to Relational School analysts, who wrongly accuse Freudians of adhering to a "pure" drive sans object theory. Such warring controversies are counterproductive to our ideal aims of honoring diversity as well as similarities in approaches to theoretical and clinical material. Attributing momentary primacy to drives, just as attributing momentary primacy to object relations, need not assume dichotomous either/or thinking but reflects only the relative emphasis or primacy of interest placed on one or the other pole, an emphasis that may vary from situation to situation. Aspects of internalization, Kernberg's (1970, 2006) contributions on positive and negative affective valences that accompany self and object representations, and research findings on the early internalization of representations of self and object in interaction are all central to the dissolution of this polarity.

  *B. Essentialism and Co-creation of Psychoanalytic Narratives.* Different epistemologies are at the center of controversies between the modern "enlightenment" or "essentialist" view and the postmodern turn (see Eagle, 2003; Eagle, Wolitzky, & Wakefield, 2001). The latter has often been called the New View, which centers on constructionism and deconstructionism of psychoanalytic meanings and on the interactional—relational turn in psychoanalysis. That is, the modern, scientific, enlightenment view honors "objective truth," in a real world of essential truth, and objectively verifiable facts, whereas the postmodern new view is basically an interpretive discipline that exclusively pursues "narrative truth" and socially based co-creation of meaning, especially between analyst and patient.

  The two views are often pitted against one another and imply an either/or false binary. Controversies between the two views center on to what extent psychoanalysis is a discipline to be included in the natural sciences, and have evolved into a marriage between postmodernism and the interactional—relational turn in psychoanalysis. The postmodern, hermeneutic outlook on interpersonal and intrapsychic reality maintains at its core social constructionism and deconstructionism, relativism and postmodernism, and intersubjectivity. The enlightenment view purports to pursue truth and objectivity, while the postmodern vision involves the pursuit of solidarity in the social construction of meaning. The postmodern era has ushered in extreme adherence to the philosophical position that rules out the possibility of discovering absolute truths about the mind and the way it works. In the postmodern way of thinking, the mind is interpretively constructed, and any understanding of the patient's psychic reality should be independent of a particular school of interpretive reconstructions and constructions. Adherents of constructionism believe that assumptions of constancy about how the mind works stack the deck in favor of one biased theory or another. They believe that co-created analytic interactions rather than stable a priori knowable personality configurations organize the patient's mind. Postmodernism has entered into a congenial marriage to the relational turn in psychoanalysis because both are guided by ideologies that embrace the philosophical position that rules out the possibility that absolute organizational principles configure the human mind. The postmodern view holds that the patient's mind is interpretively co-created by conjoint analyst—patient interventions. In contrast, the enlightenment view holds that stable personality configurations organize the patient's mind.

Do we agree with Eagle et al. (2001) that there is no inherent contradiction between experiences being irreducibly subjective as well as objective? Do we believe these epistemological contradictions are as real as any that inevitably and inexorably constitute the human condition, and that contradictory epistemological strategies in tandem are good-enough ways of looking at the dilemma? Those who have addressed these questions are concerned with the corollary issues of whether research in psychoanalysis should be evidence-based or should concentrate exclusively on the case-study method. Despite passionate partisanship (see Hoffman, 2009; Shedler, 2004; Shedler & Westen, 2007) in one or the other of these two dominant philosophical positions of our time, I believe the jury is still out on which will reign, and to what extent contradictions and controversies will prove consensually resolvable. Let us now turn to one outstanding arena that delves deeply into this dilemma.

*C. Core Gender and Sociopolitically Constructed Gender Markers.* The older and the considerably different contemporary theories of gender development and identity constitute a prime example of diversity of positions in the theoretical differences that can be clearly arrayed along the classical/relational divide (Bassin, 1996, 1999; Gediman, 2005). It is not unusual to hear that both sex and gender constitute false binaries and that each in fact involves multiplicities (Harris, 2005a, 2005b). Psychoanalysts from the "Relational" (with a capital "R") School, and those contemporary mainstream analysts like myself who adhere to a "relational" (with a lowercase "r") along with other perspectives have been known to discard many male and female gender markers which they contend produce false binaries in the way we think. Active—passive is the case in point (Gediman, 2005). Analysts from the Relational School (Butler, 1990; Harris, 2005a, 2005b; Mitchell, 1996) have argued for sex and gender multiplicities that would, they say, loosen the stranglehold that they believe "essentialism," or the old theories of essential factors found in nature have placed upon our traditional understanding of men and women, male and female, masculine and feminine, heterosexual and homosexual as well as all other pairs of opposites that constitute old and, they say, outdated ways of thinking about sex and gender. Some (Rivera, 1989) even go so far as to designate multiple personalities as a norm replacing cohesive self-identities that would of course include sex and gender.

Along with Ethel Person (2005), I would say that for the majority of people, self-identification as female or male plays a major role in shaping the pathways of sex and gender, pathways that are sometimes, and for some more than others, more "decisive" and sometimes show more plasticity. To completely jettison the idea of an "essential," innate, or biological component in sexual object choice and gendered self-identification may not be as easy as some postmodernists think, even though we certainly should not rule out social construction and cultural and sociopolitical contributions to notions of the body that coexist with more essentially universal aspects in these identifications. As Adrienne Harris (2005b) notes, not only does the body cook the mind, but the mind also cooks the body. The psyche-soma is indeed always with us as an exemplary reconciliatory model in all mind-body connections in addition to those relating to sex and gender.

*D. Drive Theory and Attachment Theory.* Current research (Silverman, 1991, 2002) on real early attachment patterns and how they are "mentalized" can be worked into more traditional views of sexual and aggressive drive development in relation to both self-representations, object representations, and especially to representations of the interactions between self and object in sexually and aggressively charged contexts. The fact that infants attach to parents and vice versa, and adults attach to each other to satisfy needs both for safety and security as well as for pleasure, provides a firm foundation for dispelling attachment needs versus pleasure needs as a false binary.

## DIVERSITY AND CONTROVERSIES RELATING PRIMARILY TO PSYCHOANALYTIC TREATMENT

### III EVENLY HOVERING ATTENTION AND FREE ASSOCIATION ALONG WITH "CLOSE PROCESS MONITORING" IN DEFENSE AND RESISTANCE ANALYSIS

*A. Psychoanalytic Listening: Interpreting Defense and Resistance and Interpreting Unconscious Contents.* This binary achieved prominence initially in the famous 1941–1945 Melanie Klein—Anna Freud controversies (see King & Steiner, 1991). Then, as now, certain "ego psychologists" (Busch, 1995, 1999; Gray, 1982, 1994) have advocated interpreting—a questionable characterization of the interventions offered—only overt, manifest markers of defense and resistance, such as long pauses in associative flow, and have assumed that unconscious contents and drive derivatives related to defense and resistance aspects would spontaneously emerge. This singular emphasis on resistance analysis is closely related to Strachey's (1934) earlier position that only superego interpretations related to the transference are mutative. In one specific contemporary debate on listening, those who identify themselves as contemporary ego psychologists, such as Busch and Gray, argue that listening with focused attention or close process monitoring of shifts in manifest content should replace evenly hovering attention, which was originally thought to be the analyst's mental activity that works in tandem with the patient's free associations.

Certain depth-oriented Kleinians, such as Joseph (1978) and Segal and Britton (1981) stand in binary opposition to both the more limited ego psychologists and the more encompassing contemporary Freudians. They tend to interpret mainly unconscious drive-related contents to the relative exclusion of defense, resistance, and even complete conflict analysis. An integrative approach to these diverse technical emphases would require a simultaneous weighting of and attention to both the resistance or warded-off threatening unconscious drive-related material *and* the unconscious, often conflictual, defensive functioning that protects the individual against their emergence. Take as exemplary of binary thinking some contemporary views on listening and interaction and enactment. Those of us who are "chronologically compromised" are sure to remember the halcyon days when a young analyst was told that *the* way of listening to the patient's free associations was with the complementary stance of evenly hovering attention (Freud, 1900, 1912). That was *the* way to assure that a particular mode of listening was the one and only way to pick up primary-process thinking as well as unconscious fantasies that were derivatives of unconscious instinctual drives. Our evenly hovering attention in the listening process was our analyzing instrument (Isakower, 1992) and the one and only way to enable and guarantee that our unconscious would be attuned to the patient's unconscious. This was the received information and wisdom of the time (mine goes back to the 1960s), and there was little or no question about other ways of looking at the heart of the psychoanalytic treatment process.

At this present time, in contrast, the buzz words are every bit as likely to be "interaction" or "enactment" in the analytic relationship as it used to be "associative listening." The analyzing instrument is said now to work bi-directionally: The patient's attunement to the analyst's unconscious is often considered on a par with the analyst's attunement to the patient's (see Chused, Ellman, Renik, & Rothstein, 1999; Hoffman, 1983, 1996). "Transference-countertransference," increasingly presented as one word, is often "induced" interactively and occurs significantly often in both the genetic then and there and the present here and now. These days, when we attend local, national, and international meetings, and when we pick up even the most traditionally based psychoanalytic journals, we are sure to hear and read about interaction and enactment in their many forms. We are bombarded by endless debates on whether psychoanalysis is a one-person psychology, a two-person psycholo-gy, or a two-person psychology with one database, that is, the psychic life of the patient. Additionally, there are analytic "thirds" and "analytic "fourth"s and even more multiples" (Ogden, 1994). We are steeped in new and broad-ened ideas about "transference-countertransference," in the then and there and the here and now. We hear about intersubjectivity, dialogue, engagement, disclosure, and the analyst as blank screen or mirror and the analyst as real new therapeutic object. Remember, now, that from examples of ubiquitous multiplicity and contradiction in the language of aphorisms and proverbs, we hear "Silence is golden," and, don't forget, "A squeaky wheel gets the grease."

Whatever our theoretical predilections about unidirectional or bidirection-al listening, nobody doubts any more the informational value of the analyst's emotional experiences vis-à-vis the patient—a giant step toward the integra-tion of once highly diverse views.

*B. Listening "to" and Listening "for."* Theories that guide the way we lis-ten to the material in our treatment sessions may be either experience-near—consistent with the once-named Clinical Theory, or experience-distant—con-sistent with the once-named Metapsychological Theory (Freud, 1899; G. S. Klein, 1959) often discussed in just those binary terms. There are undeniable advantages to openness in listening and being receptive to diverse aspects of material brought up in the psychoanalytic situation just as there are unde-niable advantages to respecting the inevitable influence of one's theoretical conviction on what material one hears and in which contexts. What Rangell (1982) has called "transference to theory" may arguably privilege "listening for"— that is, being vigilant to pick up on what one expects—over "listening to" whatever may be there. Analysts practicing in today's climate of theo-retical diversity might do well to guard against the fallacies inherent in that privileged "listening for" as well as in that counterpart of unbounded and unguided "listening to." To repeat my caveat, one never listens exclusively to or exclusively for. Our theorizing informs our listening, and what we listen to helps build our theorizing to ever more refined and usable signposts.

## IV INTERPRETATION OF HERE AND NOW TRANSFERENCE AND INTERPRETATIONS OF EARLY GENETIC MATERIAL

A. *Relational Matters and Early Genetic Forerunners.* "Displacement" transference and "projection" transference are two ways of looking at convergent and divergent classical and relational perspectives.

Displacement refers to old transferences to original objects that are experienced with new objects in the here and now. Displacement transferences span classical and relational perspectives. By displacement transference we also mean that the patient's current experiences of the analyst, which may include what have been traditionally considered as "distortions," contain and sustain early images of significant others that are based primarily on repetitions of experiences from his or her past, and which are superimposed on the person of the analyst with minimal regard for his or her here and now "realness" that might or might not correspond to those earlier images. By projection transference, we mean that the patient is projecting a repudiated, often ego-alien and unconscious aspect of himself or herself, for example, sadistic superego demandingness, onto the person of the analyst who may be seen, in this instance, as far more critical than he or she actually is. Both forms of transference, then, include distortions and misperceptions of the analyst that are based either on old displaced repetitive images or on current projective interpretations of the analyst. Transference-countertransference that involves interactional-intersubjective factors includes the aforementioned induced countertransference, projective identifications, role responsiveness (Sandler, 1976), and so forth. These are the underpinnings of Relational (capital "R") psychoanalysis, as well as relational (small "r") aspects of more contemporary Freudian mainstream treatment approaches.

B. *Enactment in the Transference—Countertransference and Repetitions of Early Object Relationships.* Recently I attended a meeting at which the Relational presenter relentlessly provoked her oppositional contemporary Freudian discussant to be relentlessly critical of her position on the subject under review. Each of the two then became increasingly hostile, defensive, and righteous about the rightness of her own position or about the absurdly wrong "badness" of the other's. One audience member parodied certain new Relational Theory paradigms yet simultaneously adhered to traditional classical and contemporary outlooks when she sized up the scene we were looking at and listening to by saying "We were just witness to the mutual co-creation of a sadomasochistic enactment. In any event, it was a 'perfect storm.'" The point I wish to make derives from Loewald's (1960) major contribution, whether plain old sadomasochism or New View co-creation determined the quality of the interaction: that is, the very work of analysis, as well as discussions between analysts of what analysis is all about, itself provides a new, shared experience, a new object relationship between patient and analyst, or between colleagues. In that sense, something that is new, and that is not necessarily a calculated correctional emotional experience (Alexander & French, 1946) and that is not simply a dyadic interaction repeated from the past transpires between two people. Such a new relationship optimally will promote new growth; in that sense, a new object relationship (see Grunes, 1984) is co-created. We understand now what is going on in all psychoanalytic therapeutic interactions much more relationally than we once did, whether the new relationship repeats a mutual enactment of a past archaic maladaptive interaction or whether a healthy new object relationship is being co-created. New View, or postmodern, and Relational theorists have correctly insisted that the analytic encounter is a two-person situation in which the participants inevitably interact, emit cues, and influence each other. Why then, should there not be enactments that are also inevitable? The television series *In Treatment* (Garcia, 2008–2009), for example, is replete with enactments in which the treating therapist appears to deviate substantially from the classical analytic triad of the ideal positions of neutrality, anonymity, and abstinence. A crucial question that emerges from our newly forming diverse perspective is to what extent do the patient-analyst interactions that we now are much more primed to see than we used to be require a new theory of the mind, and to what extent do they represent significant additions to, subtractions from, and modifications of older points of view?

## V NEUTRALITY AND SELF-DISCLOSURE

A. *Implicit and Explicit Self-Disclosures.* Neutrality and self-disclosure were once thought to be antithetical treatment strategies, but actually any intervention involves a self-disclosure on the part of the analyst, in that it reveals what he or she chooses as the most important issue to address (see Gediman, 2006; Jacobs, 1999; Renik, 1996, 1999). Such ubiquitous self-disclosures differ in important ways from those that are conscious and deliberate and may violate the *ideal* of neutrality as once understood, but they do not necessarily violate fundamental neutrality in the long run. Self-disclosures that have a higher weighting in their entirety of countertransference than others are indeed distinguishable, but not always easily, from those that are less subject to countertransferential influences. The less countertransferentially loaded disclosures may serve not only to demystify but also to advance the treatment. That is, they let the patient in, collaboratively, on the way analysis works, and on how the analyst is thinking about the patient with the aim of helping the patient to take over the self-analytic function. Today's rationale for such self-disclosure contrasts with those of the days when self-disclosure was always thought to be a counterenactment of the analyst that violated that triad crucial to the analytic attitude: neutrality, anonymity, and abstinence. Now we respect these principles as ideals that provide flexible guidelines and not as absolute rigid rules. Because we make the constituents of the old traditional triumvirate transparent to our patients, it is easier to reconcile the coexistence of neutrality with self-disclosure, and with enactments. As ever, we must distinguish those instances in which the analyst's self-disclosure closes off opportunities to deepen explorations and other aspects of treatment from those in which it opens up these very critical opportunities. Self-disclosure at its best levels the analytic playing field, which though remaining "asymmetrical" is nonetheless at the same time collaborative.

## COMMON GROUND, PLURALISM, AND DIVERSITY

Finally, we need to decide whether or not we ultimately would gain from consolidating a unifying, coherent theoretical structure to integrate the undeniably diverse points of view that dominate contemporary psychoanalysis and eventually subsume them in one and only one unitary theory. This latter has been proposed by Rangell (2000, 2004) in his work on *Total Composite Theory* and in the less unificatory but still multimodel view proposed by Fred Pine (1988) in his work on the "four psychologies" of drive, ego, object, and self points of view. Unificatory psychoanalytic theories aim to unite diverse and sometimes intrinsically incompatible and flagrantly contradictory ideas between and within points of view. Theoretical incompatibilities are not unique to psychoanalysis but are actually found as well in physics. Intrinsically contradictory theories of quantum mechanics and of relativity coexist, but physicists are now developing "string theory" or the overarching "Theory of Everything" ("TOE") in an attempt to work with intrinsically incompatible theoretical frameworks.

The ideas of one psychoanalysis or many, or of common ground in diverse theories, were originally suggested by Wallerstein (1988, 1990), and have been revisited in the context of controversy and diversity in its present form. Subtleties and nuances generate present-day thinking on controversy and contradiction. We have reached a point where we also must distinguish the separate implications of pluralism and diversity. Pluralism does not require a unificatory theory. Diversity may or may not. The serious studies of convergences and divergences of one point of view from another have clearly replaced inexorable either/or thinking, There is no doubt that embracing the omnipresence of diversity and building bridges between those who have various slants on what they all regard as psychoanalysis have replaced extruding dissidents whose ideas seem incompatible with our body of knowledge. I believe it is possible to build bridges between diverse aspects of theory with or without a consensually agreed upon unified theory. Wallerstein's original question as to whether we have one psychoanalysis or many, or if there is indeed common ground in diverse theories, opened up myriad considerations of controversy and diversity. Pluralism, on the other hand, would seem to involve fragmentation rather than integration of the diverse ideas that underpin our theory of practice, whether or not that integration requires a unificatory theory such as Rangell (2000, 2004) proposes, that involves simply accretion, adding, subtracting, and modifying. Diversity stays with us whether or not we opt for integration and unification as opposed to multiple models or pluralism.

Accordingly, our notions about paradigm shifts must change. We do not replace an old paradigm with a new one, the famous strategy proposed by Kuhn (1962). Paradigm replacements would be analogous to throwing out an old regime or model to make room for the new. Paradigm shifts, on the other hand, involve shifting back and forth, in timely ways, between various old and new perspectives, which we often do before we have committed to the idea of whether or not diverse paradigms simply coexist or are ultimately integratable. That is, one perspective embodied in a particular paradigm may be more useful for us at one moment than at another, just as for some situations one paradigm is more useful while in others an alternative is more useful. Timely applications of various paradigms help make sense of clinical data, whether or not the diverse multiple paradigms are integratable or are to remain theoretically incompatible. Such judicious moving back and forth between multiple perspectives will not foreclose on any final disposition toward either pluralism or unification. A paradigm shift would no longer mean that we throw out the old model and replace it with a new, but that we shift, in timely ways, from one to another without getting uptight that we could be abandoning Freud in favor of the early Mitchell and Greenberg. Timely shifts mean only that we attend to both old and new, not exactly alike, but at least proportionally at any given moment. As you mull over the ambiguity and contradiction inherent in the way we are thinking in our current struggles, you will see that ambiguity, conflict, contradiction, and controversy are with us forever in the field we have all chosen to pursue.

So the idea is to stay with conundrum and paradox, as Freud did in his "Antithetical Meaning of Primal Words." If we do that, we should rest assured of the common ground held by psychoanalysts of all persuasions: defense and resistance, the unconscious, the centrality of the relationship and of transference—countertransference analysis. That legacy remains as a steady backdrop for us all to embrace conundrum, paradox, and ambiguity. And so we come back full circle to appreciating contradictions in language itself, the ambiguities in meaning of primal words and the pairing of proverbs referred to earlier. Most important, we may appreciate those ubiquitous contradictions as beacons to guide us in assessing the true and false binaries in cutting edge controversies.

### REFERENCES

Abel, K. (1884). Uber den Gegensinn der Urwole, *Leipzig*, 154:155–161.

Alexander, F., French, T.M. (1946). The principle of corrective emotional experience. In *Psychoanalytic Therapy, Principles and Application*. New York: Ronald Press.

Bassin, D. (1996). Beyond the he and she: Toward the reconciliation of masculinity and femininity in the postoedipal female mind. *Journal of the American Psychoanalytic Association* 44 (Suppl.):157–190.
http://www.pep-web.org/document.php?id=apa.044s.0157a

Bassin, D. ed. (1999). *Female sexuality: Contemporary engagements*. Northvale, N.J.: Aronson.

Blum, H. (1986). The concept of the reconstruction of trauma. In A. Rothstein, ed., *The reconstruction of trauma* (pp. 7–27). New York: International Universities Press.
http://www.pep-web.org/document.php?id=zbk.080.0007a

Busch, F. (1995). *The ego at the center of clinical technique*. Northvale, N.J.: Aronson.

———. (1999). *Rethinking clinical technique*. Northvale, N.J.: Aronson.
Butler, J.

——— (1990). *Gender Trouble: Feminism and the Subversion of Identity*. New York: Routledge.

Chused, J.F., Ellman, S.J., Renik, O., & Rothstein, A. (1999). Four aspects of

the enactment concept: Definitions, therapeutic effects, dangers, history. *Journal of Clinical Psychoanalysis* 8:9–61.
http://www.pep-web.org/document.php?id=jcp.008.0009a

Eagle, M.N. (2003). The postmodern turn in psychoanalysis: A critique. *Psychoanalytic Psychology* 20:411–424. http://www.pep-web.org/document.php?id=ppsy.020.0411a

——— Wolitzky, D. L., & Wakefield, J. C. (2001). The analyst's knowledge and autonomy: A critique of the "New View" in psychoanalysis. *Journal of the American Psychoanalytic Association* 49:453–488.
http://www.pep-web.org/document.php?id=apa.049.0457a

Freud, S. (1896). Further remarks on the neuro-psychoses of defence. *S.E.* 3:159–185. http://www.pep-web.org/document.php?id=se.003.0157a

——— (1900). The interpretation of dreams. *S.E.* 4,5:1–626.

——— (1905). Three essays on the theory of sexuality. *S.E.* 7:125–246.
http://www.pep-web.org/document.php?id=se.007.0123a

——— (1910). The antithetical meaning of primal words. *S.E.* 11:153–162.
http://www.pep-web.org/document.php?id=se.011.0153a

———. (1912). Recommendations to physicians practicing psychoanalysis. *S.E.* 12:109–120. http://www.pep-web.org/document.php?id=se.012.0109a

——— (1914). On the history of the psychoanalytic movement. *S.E.* 14:1–66.
http://www.pep-web.org/document.php?id=se.014.0001a

——— (1926). Inhibitions, symptoms and anxiety. *S.E.* 20:77–175.
http://www.pep-web.org/document.php?id=se.020.0075a

——— (1954). *The origins of psychoanalysis. Letters to Wilhelm Fliess, drafts and notes 1887–1902,* transl.(E. Mosbacher & J. Strachey. New York: Basic, 1899. http://www.pep-web.org/document.php?id=zbk.051.0244a

Garcia, R. (Producer). (2008–2009). In treatment. [Cable television series]. HBO.

Gediman, H.K. (1984). Actual neurosis and psychoneurosis *International Journal of Psycho-Analysis* 65:191–202.
http://www.pep-web.org/document.php?id=ijp.065.0191a

——— (1989). Conflict and deficit models of psychopathology: A unificatory point of view. In D. W. Detrick & S. Detrick, eds., *Self psychology.* Hillsdale, N.J.: Analytic Press.

——— (1991). Seduction trauma: Complemental intrapsychic and interpersonal perspectives on fantasy and reality. *Psychoanalytic Psychology* 8:381–401. http://www.pep-web.org/document.php?id=ppsy.008.0381a

——— (1999). Thoughts for the millennium on diversity, controversy, integration and dialectic. Invited faculty address to the 1999 graduates, The

New York Freudian Society Graduation Ceremony, New York City.

————— (2005). Premodern, modern, and postmodern perspectives on sex and gender mixes. *Journal of the American Psychoanalytic Association* 53:1059–1078. http://www.pep-web.org/document.php?id=apa.053.1059a

————— (2006). Facilitating analysis with implicit and explicit self- disclosures. *Psychoanalytic Dialogues* 16:241–262. http://www.pep-web.org/document.php?id=pd.016.0241a

————— (May, 2010). Invited faculty address to the 2010 graduates, The New York Freudian Society Graduation Ceremony, New York City.

Gray, P. (1982). "Developmental lag" in the evolution of technique for psychoanalysis. *Journal of the American Psychoanalytic Association* 30:621–655. http://www.pep-web.org/document.php?id=apa.030.0621a

————— (1994). *The ego and analysis of defense.* Northvale, N.J.: Aronson.

Grunes, M. (1984). The therapeutic object relationship. *Psychoanalytic Review* 71:123–144. http://www.pep-web.org/document.php?id=psar.071.0123a

Harris, A.H. (2005a). *Gender as soft assembly.* Hillsdale, N.J.: Analytic Press. http://www.pep-web.org/document.php?id=sgs.001.0223a

————— (2005b). Gender in linear and nonlinear history. *Journal of the American Psychoanalytic Association* 53:1079–1095. http://www.pep-web.org/document.php?id=apa.053.1079a

Hoffman, I.Z. (1983). The patient as interpreter of the analyst's experience. *Contemporary Psychoanalysis* 19:389–422. http://www.pep-web.org/document.php?id=cps.019.0389a

————— (1996). The intimate and ironic authority of the psychoanalyst's presence. *Psychoanalytic Quarterly* 65:102–136. http://www.pep-web.org/document.php?id=paq.065.0102a

————— (2009). Doublethinking our way to "scientific" legitimacy. *Journal of the American Psychoanalytic Association* 57:1043–1069. http://www.pep-web.org/document.php?id=apa.057.1043a

Isakower, O. (1992). Chapter five: The analyzing instrument. *Journal of Clinical Psychoanalysis,* 2:181–208. http://www.pep-web.org/document.php?id=jcp.001.0200a

Jacobs, T. (1999). On the question of self-disclosure by the analyst: Error or advance in technique? *Psychoanalytic Quarterly* 68:159–183. http://www.pep-web.org/document.php?id=paq.068.0159a

Joseph, B. (1978). Different types of anxiety and their handling in the analytic situation. *International Journal of Psycho-Analysis* 59:223–227. http://www.pep-web.org/document.php?id=ijp.059.0223a

Kernberg, O.F. (1970). A psychoanalytic classification of character pathology.

*Journal of the American Psychoanalytic Association* 18:800–822.
http://www.pep-web.org/document.php?id=apa.018.0800a

———— (2006). Identity: Recent findings and clinical implications. *Psychoanalytic Quarterly* 75:969–1003.
http://www.pep-web.org/document.php?id=paq.075.0969a

King, P., & Steiner, R. (1991). *The Freud-Klein Controversies 1941–45*. London: Tavistock/Routledge.
http://www.pep-web.org/document.php?id=nlp.011.0001a

Klein, G.S. (1959). Consciousness in psychoanalytic theory: Some implications for current research in perception. *Journal of the American Psychoanalytic Association* 7:5–34.
http://www.pep-web.org/document.php?id=apa.007.0005a

Kohut, H. (1971). *The Analysis of the Self*. New York: International Universities Press. http://www.pep-web.org/document.php?id=zbk.049.0001a

Kuhn, T. (1962). *The structure of scientific revolutions*. Chicago: University of Chicago Press.

Loewald, H.W. (1960). On the therapeutic action of psycho-analysis. *International Journal of Psycho-Analysis* 41:16–33.
http://www.pep-web.org/document.php?id=ijp.041.0016a

Malcolm, J. (1984). *In the Freud archives*. New York: Knopf.

Masson, J.M. (1984). *The Assault on Truth: Freud's Suppression of the Seduction Theory*. New York: Farrar, Straus, & Giroux.

Mitchell, S.A. (1996). Gender and sexual orientation in the age of postmodernism. *Gender and Psychoanalysis*, 1:45–73.
http://www.pep-web.org/document.php?id=gap.001.0045a

Ogden, T.H. (1994). The analytic third: Working with intersubjective clinical facts. *International Journal of Psycho-Analysis* 75:3–19.
http://www.pep-web.org/document.php?id=ijp.075.0003a

Person, E.S. (2005). A new look at core gender and gender role identity in women. *Journal of the American Psychoanalytic Association* 53:1045–1058.
http://www.pep-web.org/document.php?id=apa.053.1045a

Pine, F. (1988). The four psychologies of psychoanalysis and their place in clinical work. *Journal of the American Psychoanalytic Association* 36:571–596. http://www.pep-web.org/document.php?id=apa.036.0571a

Rangell, L. (1968). A further attempt to resolve the "problem of anxiety." *Journal of the American Psychoanalytic Association* 16:371–404.
http://www.pep-web.org/document.php?id=apa.016.0371a

———— (1982). Transference to theory. *Annual of Psychoanalysis*, 10:29–56.
http://www.pep-web.org/document.php?id=aop.010.0029a

———— (2000). Psychoanalysis at the millennium. *Psychoanalytic Psychology*, 17:451–466. http://www.pep-web.org/document.php?id=ppsy.017.0451a

———— (2004). *My Life in Theory*. New York: Other Press.

Renik, O. (1996). The perils of neutrality. *Psychoanalytic Quarterly* 65:495–517. http://www.pep-web.org/document.php?id=paq.065.0495a

———— (1999). Playing one's cards face up in analysis: An approach to the problem of self-disclosure. *Psychoanalytic Quarterly* 68:521–553. http://www.pep-web.org/document.php?id=paq.068.0521a

Rivera, M. (1989). Linking the psychological and the social: Feminism, post-structuralism, and multiple personality. *Dissociation* 2:24–31.

Sandler, J. (1976). Countertransference and role-responsiveness. *International Review of Psycho-Analysis* 3:43–47. http://www.pep-web.org/document.php?id=irp.003.0043a

Segal, H., & Britton, R. (1981). Interpretation and primitive psychic processes: A Kleinian view. *Psychoanalytic Inquiry*, 1:267–277. http://www.pep-web.org/document.php?id=pi.001.0267a

Shedler, J. (2004). Clinical and observational psychoanalytic research: Roots of a controversy. *Journal of the American Psychoanalytic Association* 52:610–618. http://www.pep-web.org/document.php?id=apa.052.0610a

———— Westen, D. (2007). The Shedler-Westen Assessment Procedure (SWAP): Making personality diagnosis clinically meaningful. *Journal of Personality Assessment* 89(1):41–55.

Silverman, D.K. (1991). Attachment patterns and Freudian theory: An integrative proposal. *Psychoanalytic Psychology*, 8:169–193. http://www.pep-web.org/document.php?id=ppsy.008.0169a

———— (2002). Sexuality and attachment: A passionate relationship or a marriage of convenience. *Psychoanalytic Quarterly* 70:325–355. http://www.pep-web.org/document.php?id=paq.070.0325a

Strachey, J. (1934). The nature of the therapeutic action of psychoanalysis. *International Journal of Psycho-Analysis* 50:277–292. http://www.pep-web.org/document.php?id=ijp.050.0275a

Wallerstein, R.S. (1988). One psychoanalysis or many? *International Journal of Psycho-Analysis* 69:5–21. http://www.pep-web.org/document.php?id=ijp.069.0005a

———— (1990). Psychoanalysis: The common ground *International Journal of Psycho-Analysis* 71:3–20. http://www.pep-web.org/document.php?id=ijp.071.0003a

www.ingramcontent.com/pod-product-compliance
Lightning Source LLC
Chambersburg PA
CBHW060306030426
42336CB00011B/955